60p

MANAGING ALLERGY

Managing
Allergy

EDITED BY

A CUSTOVIC, TAE PLATTS-MILLS

CLINICAL PUBLISHING

OXFORD

CLINICAL PUBLISHING
an imprint of Atlas Medical Publishing Ltd

Oxford Centre for Innovation
Mill Street, Oxford OX2 0JX, UK
Tel: +44 1865 811116
Fax: +44 1865 251550
Web: www.clinicalpublishing.co.uk

Distributed in USA and Canada by:
Clinical Publishing
30 Amberwood Parkway
Ashland, OH 44805, USA

Tel: 800-247-6553 (toll free within US and Canada)
Fax: 419-281-6883
Email: order@bookmasters.com

Distributed in the UK and the Rest of the World by:
Marston Book Services Ltd
PO Box 269
Abingdon
Oxon OX14 4YN UK

Tel: +44 1235 465500
Fax: +44 1235 465555
e mail: trade.orders@marston.co.uk

© Atlas Medical Publishing Ltd 2009

First published 2009

A catalogue record for this book is available from the British Library

ISBN-13   978 1 84692 025 7
ISBN-ebook 978 1 84692 593 1

The publisher makes no representation, express or implied, that the dosages
in this book are correct. Readers must therefore always check the product
information and clinical procedures with the most up–to date published
product information and data sheets provided by the manufacturers and the
most recent codes of conduct and safety regulations. The authors and the
publisher do not accept any liability for any errors in the text or for the misuse
or misapplication of material in this work

Project manager: Gavin Smith, GPS Publishing Solutions, Herts, UK
Design by Pete Russell, Faringdon, Oxon, UK
Typeset by Mizpah Publishing Services Private Limited, Chennai, India
Printed by Marston Book Services Ltd, UK

Contents

Editors and contributors

Editors

ADNAN CUSTOVIC, *DM, MD, PhD, FRCP*
Professor of Allergy, University of Manchester, Manchester, UK

THOMAS A. E. PLATTS-MILLS, *MD, PhD*
Professor of Medicine and Microbiology, Department of Medicine, University of Virginia, Charlottesville, Virginia, USA

Contributors

STAFFAN AHLSTEDT, *PhD, FAAAAI*
Professor; Senior Scientific Advisor, Center for Allergy Research, National Institute of Environmental Medicine, Karolinska Institute, Stockholm; Phadia AB, Uppsala, Sweden

MICHAEL R. ARDERN-JONES, *BSc, MBBS, MRCP, Dphil*
Consultant Dermatologist / Senior Lecturer in Dermatology, Inflammation Infection and Repair Division, Dermatopharmacology, School of Medicine, Southampton General Hospital, University of Southampton, Southampton, UK

BINITA BHOWMICK, *MRCP*
University Hospital of South Manchester, Manchester, UK

LARRY BORISH, *MD*
Professor of Medicine, Asthma and Allergic Diseases Center, Carter Immunology Center, University of Virginia Health System, Charlottesville, Virginia, USA

MARTIN K. CHURCH, *MPharm, PhD, DSc, FAAAAI*
Emeritus Professor of Immunopharmacology, School of Medicine, University of Southampton, Southampton General Hospital, Southampton, UK

PAUL CULLINAN, *MD, FRCP, FFOM*
Consultant Respiratory Physician, Department of Occupational and Environmental Medicine, Royal Brompton Hospital, London, UK

JEFFREY A. CULP, *MD*
Fellow Physician, Division of Asthma, Allergy and Immunology, Department of Medicine, University of Virginia Health System, Charlottesville, Virginia, USA

ADNAN CUSTOVIC, *DM, MD, PhD, FRCP*
Professor of Allergy, University of Manchester, Manchester, UK

PASCAL DEMOLY, *MD, PhD*
Professor, Exploration des Allergies et INSERM U657, Maladies Respiratoires, Hôpital Arnaud de Villeneuve, University Hospital of Montpellier, Montpellier, France

DAVID W. DENNING, *MB, BS, FRCP, FRCPath, DCH*
Professor of Medicine and Medical Mycology, Honorary Consultant Physician, School of Translational Medicine, The University of Manchester, University Hospital of South Manchester, Manchester, UK

ELIZABETH A. ERWIN, *MD*
Assistant Professor, Asthma and Allergic Diseases Center, University of Virginia, Charlottesville, Virginia, USA

PAMELA W. EWAN, *MA, MBBS, FRCP, FRCPath*
Allergy Department, Addenbrooke's Hospital, Cambridge University Hospitals NHS Foundation Trust, Cambridge, UK

ANTHONY J. FREW, *MA, MD, FRCP*
Professor of Allergy and Respiratory Medicine, Department of Respiratory Medicine, Brighton and Sussex Medical School, Brighton, UK

PETER S. FRIEDMANN, *MD, FRCP, FMedSci*
Emeritus Professor of Dermatology, Dermatopharmacology Unit, Southampton General Hospital, Southampton, UK

LEN FROMER, *MD, FAAFP*
Assistant Clinical Professor, Department of Family Medicine, UCLA School of Medicine, Los Angeles, California, USA

ALEXANDER KAPP, *MD, PhD*
Consultant Dermatologist and Allergologist; Professor and Chairman, Department of Dermatology and Allergology, Hannover Medical School, Hannover, Germany

JENNIFER M. MALONEY, *MD*
Allergist and Immunologist, Department of Pediatrics, Division of Allergy and Immunology, Mount Sinai School of Medicine, New York, USA

THOMAS A. E. PLATTS-MILLS, *MD, PhD*
Professor of Medicine and Microbiology, Department of Medicine, University of Virginia, Charlottesville, Virginia, USA

HUGH A. SAMPSON, *MD*
Allergist and Immunologist, Department of Pediatrics, Division of Allergy and Immunology, Mount Sinai School of Medicine, New York, USA

GLENIS K. SCADDING, *MA, MD, FRCP*
Consultant Allergist/Rhinologist, Royal National Throat, Nose and Ear Hospital, London, UK

ANGELA SIMPSON, *BA, MD, MRCP*
Senior Lecturer in Respiratory Medicine, University of Manchester, Manchester, UK

DAVE SINGH, *MRCP, MD*
University Hospital of South Manchester, Manchester, UK

LARS SÖDERSTRÖM, *MSc*
Director, Scientific Affairs, Biometrics, Scientific and Medical Research, Phadia AB Uppsala Sweden

JOHN W. STEINKE, *PhD*
Assistant Professor, Asthma and Allergic Diseases Center, Beirne Carter Center for Immunology Research, Department of Medicine, University of Virginia Health System, Charlottesville, Virginia, USA

BETTINA WEDI, *MD, PhD*
Consultant Dermatologist and Allergologist; Professor, Department of Dermatology and Allergology, Hannover Medical School, Hannover, Germany

JUDITH A. WOODFOLK, *MBChB, PhD*
Associate Professor of Medicine, Asthma and Allergy Disease Center, University of Virginia Health System, Charlottesville, Virginia, USA

PART I

Diagnosis

1

IgE antibody tests in diagnosing allergy

STAFFAN AHLSTEDT, LEN FROMER, LARS SODERSTROM

KEY POINTS

1. Without firm diagnosis, conditions with allergic aetiology are difficult to distinguish from conditions with different aetiology.

2. Sensitization and presence of IgE antibodies is not a dichotomous, 'yes/no' but rather a quantitative phenomenon that needs to be interpreted in the context of the case history.

3. The presence of risk factors increases the risk of allergy as a contributing factor to symptoms, and this is multiplied by the presence of IgE antibodies and exposure to the allergens.

4. Exposure to different allergens in the sensitized individual works in concert. This can be emphasized even more by immunological cross-reactivity between different allergen components.

5. The sum of IgE antibodies quantitatively demonstrate:
   a. the risk of current allergy and
   b. risk of reaction and exacerbation,
   c. aggravating the effect by confounding factors as well as
   d. the allergy evolving over time.

6. Decreasing IgE antibody levels can demonstrate development of tolerance and outgrowth of the allergy.

Introduction

Diagnostic testing is used to provide evidence for an allergic as distinct from a non-allergic aetiology, to establish the degree of atopy, and to identify the offending allergen/s. Since allergic diseases generally present as a multitude of symptoms and signs and since they tend to evolve over time, the conditions are often difficult to differentiate from similar clinical conditions that are non-allergic in origin. Thus, as many as 60–70% of conditions commonly suspected as allergic may have a different aetiology |1|. For example, respiratory symptoms that resemble allergy presenting seasonally or perennially, may actually be due to infections, vasomotor reflexes, anatomical conditions |2|, or chronic obstructive pulmonary disease. Furthermore reactions elicited by foods may give identical signs regardless of being of allergic or non-allergic nature i.e. lactase or diamino oxidase insufficiency |3,4|. To date there are no prospective studies that have specifically aimed to differentiate between allergic and non-allergic reactions in the respiratory tract on the basis of clinical symptoms, signs, and physical examination. Attempts have been made to distinguish between different aetiologies for food reactions, especially those of the anaphylactic type |5|. This chapter presents information regarding how case history and physical examination provide a certain level of diagnostic information and how this level can be elevated and improved upon when combined with accurate and objective diagnostic tests. In reaching the diagnosis the time and costs for diagnostic procedures need to be considered in the context of patient management and utilization of the resources of the healthcare system. This also relates to the formulated goals of the healthcare system as characterized by safety, effectiveness, timeliness, patient focus, cost and efficiency |6|.

Definitions

It is essential to define the terms used when discussing allergic disease. The definitions of several key terms are given in Box 1.1 (from |7|).

Box 1.1

- **Total and specific IgE:** total IgE (tIgE) means the total amount of the immunoglobulin IgE present in blood, irrespective of what these IgE molecules may bind to; specific IgE means specific IgE (sIgE) antibodies binding to particular and identifiable allergens.

- **Sensitization** means that sIgE antibodies have been formed due to previous allergen exposure, as evidenced by blood or skin tests.

- **Atopy** is the propensity to produce specific IgE (sIgE) antibodies upon exposure to common allergens in the environment.

- **An allergic reaction** is an immunologically-determined clinical reaction to an identified substance or allergen. **IgE-mediated allergy** means that the immunological mechanism is related to sIgE.

- **Clinical sensitivity and specificity: sensitivity** is defined as the ability of a test to identify patients with the condition; **specificity** defines the ability of the test to correctly exclude those who do not have the condition.

What to accomplish by setting the diagnosis

There are well-documented genetic–environmental interactions between sensitization and the development of disease as well as other contributing factors in the expression of the disease. For example, 40% of young children with atopic dermatitis have been shown to develop asthma later in life |8|. In such a context, to be able to provide the best care for the patient, the diagnostic information should

Box 1.2 Goals to be accomplished with a diagnostic work-up.

Diagnosis
    Distinguish allergy vs non-allergy
    Identify allergen(s) which may be involved
Risk patient prediction
    Confounding factors
        Virus infection
        Exposure to environmental factors
        Other allergies e.g. food, drug
Disease course prediction
    Transient vs persistent disease
    One symptom followed by other symptoms: Allergy March
    Sensitization as a prognostic parameter to predict upcoming allergic disease
        Early vs late
        Mono vs multi
    Natural course of allergic disease: food allergy and wheeze/asthma
Treatment prediction
    Responsiveness to pharmacotherapy
    Avoidance strategies:
        inhalants
        food diets
        combinations between avoidance and pharmacotherapy to lower the medication burden
Outcome of specific immunotherapy

also include prognostic information for evaluation of the disease process and possibly also prediction of the outcome of treatment. Examples of accomplishments with any diagnostic work-up should cover the aspects listed in Box 1.2.

Establishing an allergy diagnosis

Considering the difficulties in distinguishing between allergic symptoms and those symptoms that are non-allergic in origin (or both), and to accomplish the diagnostic goals, as a first step any practising physician needs to consider several important questions:

1. Is allergy contributing to the presence of symptoms (e.g. wheeze, rhinitis, eczema)?
2. Is allergy contributing to the severity and frequency of the symptoms?
3. Will the symptoms become continuous or persistent or resolve?

Information about the family history of allergic disease and the individual's own possible other allergic diseases may help in this decision-making process. Particular and pertinent questions to ask the patient and evaluate in the environmental context would include:

1. Do your symptoms get worse when in contact with dust and during cleaning the house, or when you're in contact with cats, dogs, pollens, or in environments with mould?
2. Are symptoms worse during any particular time of the year? Have you had symptoms during the last 12 months?
3. Are your problems associated with your eyes, nose, lungs, stomach or skin?
4. Have you had hay fever? Have you been tested for allergy before and were the tests positive; and has a doctor already diagnosed you with rhinitis or asthma?
5. Do other substances like tobacco smoke, or odours from flowers and perfume, increase your problems?
6. Does anybody in your family suffer from asthma, hay fever or eczema?

In addition to those questions, more recent publications suggest that information regarding obesity, physical inactivity and time spent indoors may add to the precision of the diagnosis |9,10|. The importance of a thorough case history can be illustrated from several epidemiological studies. They have addressed some of the questions and related them to an increased risk if the factor is present, usually expressed as odds ratio (OR). The OR represents a measure of whether the probability of a certain event or disease is the same (OR = 1) or different (OR higher or lower than 1) for individuals from two different populations. Box 1.3 gives some examples of approximate risk as published in the literature if a certain factor is present.

Box 1.3 Risk factors found in several studies on children. Odds ratios approximated from the literature |11–15|.

In relation to persistent wheeze

Male gender?	OR = 2
Did the child wheeze before 3 years of age?	OR = 3
Does mother have asthma?	OR = 4
Does any parent have asthma?	OR = 3
Did mother smoke during pregnancy?	OR = 2
Was there eczema before 2 years of age?	OR = 2

In relation to persistent eczema

Is there a parental allergy?	
This is atopic eczema	OR = 2
Will this eczema stay and get worse until school age?	
Frequent scratching	OR = 6
More than 2 allergic family members	OR = 2
Having early wheeze	OR = 2

Thus, asking simple questions can raise suspicions as to what the aetiology of the symptoms may be. However, although contributing to the diagnosis, case history and physical examination are on their own not sufficient to diagnose the presence and extent of allergy. This is especially true in patients with rhinitis, asthma and/or atopic dermatitis, and stinging insect anaphylaxis. Such cases require confirmation of the presence of a sIgE-mediated aetiology |16,17|.

Information on the IgE system

The level of total IgE (tIgE) is a function of the genetic control of IgE production and the synthesis of specific IgE antibodies (sIgE). Total IgE levels can be elevated in a number of non-allergic conditions such as parasite infestation, ataxia telangiectasia, etc. In atopic dermatitis, tIgE levels have some—albeit weak—relation to the severity of atopy. They are also to some extent associated with the severity of allergy in asthma/rhinitis. However, the tIgE values in normal and atopic individuals vary with age and selection of the reference population |18|. Thus, there is a considerable overlap between non-atopic and atopic patients, and also between the different allergic diseases, making the interpretation of the total IgE levels in an individual patient of uncertain value. Further, the tIgE levels do not reveal much information regarding the progress of allergic disease. tIgE is not a good marker for screening to identify atopic individuals, although high tIgE levels suggest the need for further investigation. In contrast, sIgE are specifically produced following exposure of a susceptible individual to an allergen. sIgE levels reflect exposure to the offending allergen/s and more importantly the clinical reactivity of a given patient. Allergen-specific IgE molecules are present on mast cells in the skin and other organs as well as in blood. They bind to these cells in these tissues and can thereby initiate a clinical reaction upon subsequent allergen exposure. Thus, the presence, quantity, and specificity of sIgE can be regarded as a risk factor for clinical allergy in the respiratory tract, skin, and gastrointestinal tract, upon exposure to the allergen.

The diagnostic performance of a test for specific IgE antibodies—i.e. its ability to detect an allergic aetiology—is usually expressed as its clinical sensitivity and specificity using an arbitrarily chosen cut-off value as compared to the actual diagnosis. Good sensitivity and specificity results for IgE antibody tests compared both with doctor's diagnosis and with skin prick testing (SPT) have been documented for a variety of allergens using different methodologies |19|. However, in this context it is important to realize that there is an uncertainty in the determination of sIgE antibodies with SPT as well as in the doctor's conclusion |20|. Data for the best documented system include clinical and serological information for thousands of patients in more than 3 000 peer-reviewed publications. For this system, values above 90% sensitivity, specificity, and positive predictive value have been demonstrated |21|. Similar documentation for other systems is less clear but they frequently compare their analytical performance with ImmunoCAP |22–24|.

There is a considerable documentation that information on the presence of sIgE antibodies from a well-established assay system adds significantly to the precision of the diagnostic work-up. In more general terms, for a variety of reasons, studies have shown that when clinicians use only the history and physical examination, the accuracy of their diagnoses rarely exceeds 50% |20|. Box 1.4 gives some examples from the literature of approximate increase of risk if a specific factor is present in conjunction with sIgE antibodies.

Box 1.4 Risk factors to consider in the diagnosis of a child with symptoms of wheezing |11–15|.	Signs at 2 years of age	IgE antibodies also at 7 years of age
Does mother have asthma?	OR = 4	OR = 16
Was there eczema before 2 years of age?	OR = 2	OR = 10
Was there eczema and sensitization before 2 years of age?	OR = 7	
Was there sIgE to inhalants before 2 years of age?	OR = 3	OR = 10
to foods and inhalants?	OR = 9	
Diagnosis of a child with eczema		
Is there a parental allergy?		
Risk for atopic eczema	OR = 2	
Are there sIgE antibodies?		
Risk for severe atopic eczema	OR = 3	
Having sIgE antibodies before 12 months of age is worse than at 24 months of age		
Will eczema stay and get worse until school age?		
Presence of sIgE antibodies		
To food	OR = 3	
Wheat	OR = 7	
Soy	OR = 5	
Inhalant	OR = 2	
Any	OR = 3	

Dose–response relationship between exposure to allergens and formation of sIgE

It is important to emphasize that development of allergy and formation of sIgE is a cumulative process. Therefore, it should not be regarded as an 'all or nothing' phenomenon. Instead, all individuals (even if they are sensitized) have a certain level of tolerance to exposure to offending substances. However, when such exposure to the offending substance is increased, symptoms may become evident. In this context, it is also important to understand that several allergens may have components with similar structures, i.e. they are cross-reactive and they can induce sIgE antibodies and elicit clinical reactions. As a consequence, the individual allergen load may be higher than that which appears immediately obvious. Thus, birch, alder and hazel contain similar structures, as do different grasses. Furthermore, pollen allergy may manifest as a clinical reaction to certain vegetables due to structural similarity of some of the molecules of the food compared with the pollen |25–27|. The risk of such clinical reactions to food has been estimated and is indicated in Box 1.5 |28|.

Box 1.5 Estimated risks of clinical reaction to cross-reacting allergens if allergy is present to one allergen as verified by double-blind placebo-controlled food challenge |28|.

If allergic to	Risk of reaction also to	Estimated risk
Pollen	Fruits/vegetables	55%
birch, ragweed	apple, peach, honeydew	
A legume	Other legumes	37%
like peanut	peas, lentils, beans	
A grain	Other grains	20%
wheat	barley, rye	
Peach	Other Rosaceae	55%
	apple, plum, cherry, pear	
A tree nut	Other tree nuts	37%
walnut	brazil, cashew, hazelnut	
Melon	Other fruits	92%
	watermelon, banana, avocado	
A shellfish	Other shellfish	75%
shrimp	crab, lobster	
Cow's milk	Beef	10%
	hamburger	
Latex	Fruits	35%
	kiwi, banana, avocado	

There is a close link between allergy to birch, alder and hazel pollen, and oral allergy to hazelnut, apple, pear, stone fruits, tomato and almond. Similarly, mugwort exhibits cross-reactivity with celery, carrot and certain spices. More information has demonstrated a relationship between grasses and legumes while grass pollen has also been associated with reactions to tomato and peas, including peanut and wheat, and also melon, watermelon and orange, whereas ragweed is associated with melon and banana. There are also well-documented common structures between arthropods like mite and shellfish, and between latex, banana, kiwi and avocado. In such cases, the different allergens can work in concert adding to the relative amount of similar structures presented to the individual, which can increase production of sIgE levels reactive to the allergen in question. For further information on cross-reactivity the reader is referred to |25–28|.

In a multi-sensitized individual, the sum of the individual sIgE antibody levels and the consequences of multiple allergen exposures may be functionally additive or synergistic in activating the inflammatory processes leading to symptoms |29|. In addition, the extent of exposure to a given allergen may be an important factor in producing symptoms. When it is practical, avoiding allergen exposure for sensitive individuals is a useful tool in the management of the patient. It has been shown that children with dust mite allergy who have symptoms at sea level where dust mite exposure is high improve clinically by moving to higher altitudes where dust mites are not present |30|. In contrast, there has been a recent debate as to whether very high exposure to an allergen can actually decrease clinical reactivity and permit development of tolerance in the patient and induce protection of the allergic subject |31,32|. In fact, heavy exposure to allergen, particularly from pets (such as cats and dogs), may preferentially drive other immune responses rather than sIgE formation, and therefore result in less allergy |32,33|. This emphasizes the need to understand both the qualitative and quantitative extent of relevant exposures in the investigation of the patient.

Using sIgE results for risk assessment in patients with allergy

A higher level of exposure to allergens generally results in corresponding sensitization and formation of specific IgE antibodies to those allergens. Consequently, by utilizing a quantitative approach to the IgE antibody results, rather than a dichotomous 'yes/no' approach, recent studies suggest that for the individual patient, even higher precision can be achieved. This was first demonstrated in food allergy by Sampson and his colleagues |34,35|. In those studies, a higher sIgE antibody value implies that the subject has a substantial risk of reacting with symptoms upon exposure and the patient can be diagnosed without further measures. In contrast, a lower, albeit 'positive', value may not be completely predictive of whether or not the subject will exhibit a clinical reaction upon exposure. In these cases a referral to an allergist for a challenge procedure should be considered. A still lower value implies a rather low probability that the subject will react upon exposure. Consequently, the food may not be considered as a likely problem for symptoms (Fig. 1.1). Despite this, in cases with a convincing history despite a low sIgE value, further investigation may be necessary. Factors to consider are that the levels depend on age and that different food allergens vary in their potency and show different values for when a clinical reaction is likely to occur |36–39| (Fig. 1.1). Thus, it is necessary for the physician to get a feeling for the probability related to the allergy in question. For this reason, for patients with food allergy it may be appropriate to consider referral to an allergist. In this context it must be emphasized that other reactions to food like gliadin in coeliac disease, lactose in lactase deficiency, histamine in histamine-containing foods also need to be considered in relation to the case history and these are not associated with IgE antibody results.

For inhalant allergy, implementing sIgE antibody testing may increase the accuracy of the diagnosis and the management of the patient to a considerable extent. In particular, with this knowledge, a number of uncertain and equivocal cases can be given a firm diagnosis |40,41|.

Quantitative sIgE antibody patterns and symptom induction similar to those described for food allergy have been revealed for a variety of allergens, providing information on the extent to which allergy contributes to the expression of symptoms

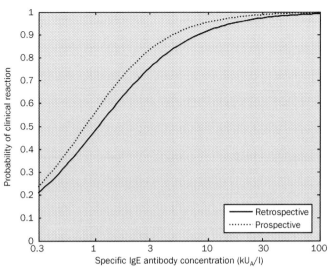

Fig. 1.1 Probability curves for whether a patient will have a reaction when ingesting hen's egg in relation to the levels of sIgE antibodies. With permission from the American Academy of Allergy, Asthma and Immunology |34,35|.

|20,33,42|. Since most allergic individuals exhibiting symptoms have sIgE to several allergens and rarely only to one, quantitative sIgE evaluation may reveal the relative importance of the different offending allergens. Thus, reports from a prospective birth cohort study demonstrate that a single positive sIgE test was seldom on its own associated with clinical allergic disease. In contrast, in that study, when there were four or more positive sIgE tests out of a total of 14 common allergens, or a sum of the individual sIgE antibody levels above $34 kU_A/l$ to these allergens, there was a 75% likelihood of identifying those individuals with allergic disease |43|. In practical terms, this implies that to obtain an adequate diagnosis, allergy tests should be performed to the most common allergens evident in the patient's environment, and that quantitative information should be gained and evaluated both for individual allergens and summated (see below and Fig. 1.2).

Recent information also demonstrates that the sum of sIgE antibody levels against the most common inhalant allergens in the environment of the individual can answer whether allergy contributes to the clinical expression of wheeze in preschool children (Box 1.6) |33|. In fact, with increasing levels of sIgE antibodies, the risk of having current or persistent wheeze and impaired lung function in children increases. As an example, $10 kU_A/l$ of sIgE to the allergens of cat, dog and mite summed, corresponds to a three-fold increase in the risk of symptomatic wheeze compared to those without such sIgE, and $30 kU_A/l$ a four-fold increase in risk (Fig. 1.2). In contrast, tIgE does not provide such information. Using quantitative sIgE results in such a way needs well-standardized methods. Evaluation of the size of the skin prick test weal may also give similar information provided that the testing and interpretation is carefully standardized. Such standardization and evaluation of the procedure has to be done in each clinical setting and may be difficult in clinical routine practice. In practical terms, the available information implies that patients with allergic asthma should be investigated by measuring their

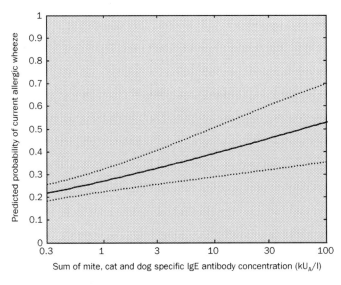

Fig. 1.2 Probability that a reaction of wheeze in a 5-year-old child is of allergic nature in relation to sIgE antibodies to mite, cat and dog. The 95% percentile is given. With permission from the American Academy of Allergy, Asthma and Immunology |33|.

sIgE antibody levels to the most prominent allergens in their environment. Such measures will allow the optimization of pharmacotherapy along with attempts to decrease the allergen exposure. On the contrary, a low or negative sIgE antibody level indicates the need to consider an alternative 'non-allergy' treatment.

Box 1.6 Diagnosis of a child with symptoms of wheezing |33|.

Is this related to an allergic reaction?
    10 kU$_A$/l* corresponds to **30%** probability of allergy relation
    100 kU$_A$/l* corresponds to **60%** probability of allergy relation

Will the present wheeze develop into persistent wheeze during next years to come?
    10 kU$_A$/l* corresponds to **50%** probability of development into persistent wheeze
    30 kU$_A$/l* corresponds to **90%** probability of development into persistent wheeze
    * sum of sIgE values for mite, cat and dog

Since asthma exacerbations are well known with viral infections, much focus has been placed on the role of viral infections and the susceptibility of asthmatic subjects to such infections. Recent information points to extensive synergistic effects of virus infections and allergic inflammation both in children and adults |9,44–45|. Furthermore, in a recent study it was reported that not only was being sensitized a risk factor but that the risk increased with increasing specific IgE levels |44|. Further similar analysis of results in schoolchildren showed that the sum of mite, cat and dog specific IgE was associated with an increased risk of hospital admission with an asthma exacerbation. Thus, a sum of 10 kU$_A$/l sIgE increased the risk almost 2.5 times and a sum of 30 kU$_A$/l increased the risk three-fold. This

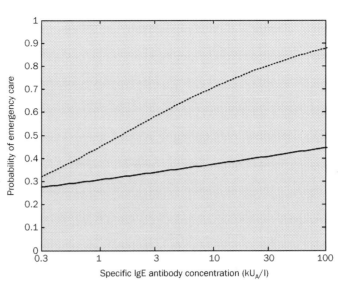

Fig. 1.3 The probability that a patient with asthma will need emergency care in relation to only sIgE antibodies and exposure to allergens (solid line) and virus infection together with sIgE antibodies and exposure to allergens (dotted line). With permission from the General Practice Airways Group |7,44|.

corresponds to a 30–40% probability of being admitted to hospital due to an asthma exacerbation (Fig. 1.3, solid line) |7,44|. Elevated sIgE levels and exposure to allergens in conjunction with a virus infection appear to strongly increase the probability of hospitalization among childhood asthmatics over and above that of the sIgE alone. In such cases, a sum of as little as 3 kU$_A$/l of sIgE may correspond to a 60% probability, and a sum of 30 kU$_A$/l as greater than a 80% probability, of hospital admission (Fig. 1.3, dotted line) |7,44|. This information points to the importance of optimized allergy management of patients at risk and measures undertaken to both decrease allergen exposure in relation to the sIgE levels and include prescription of increased anti-inflammatory therapies particularly during periods of time when other contributing factors like virus infections are likely.

To use quantitative IgE information in a clinical setting, a system for highly precise, reproducible, and accurate determination of the IgE antibody levels is essential |46|. It has to be emphasized that this approach is not generally applicable and has been well documented with one testing modality (ImmunoCAP) after very careful standardization |46|. Data from the system that has been used for developing quantitative probability models attributing the risk of clinical disease cannot be generalized. Since the IgE results obtained using other test systems may differ significantly |22,23|, prescribing clinicians and testing laboratories need to be aware of possible differences in the results from different systems |24|. Similar results may be obtained using carefully performed skin prick tests with high quality extracts and precise assessment of the weal size. However, this is unlikely to be applicable to a general clinical setting, where skin tests are performed on a routine basis by different operators using a range of different allergen extracts which may not be standardized |33,47|.

The natural course of allergy development (Allergy March)

In many or most allergic children, their symptoms evolve along a particular path (Allergy March). Symptoms of eczema and wheeze as well as sensitization and IgE antibody formation to first food and later inhalant allergens may occur early during this path. These symptoms can evolve from mild eczema and wheeze into severe conditions. However, on the contrary about half of the children lose their symptoms when growing older. Although early wheeze is frequently triggered by virus infection, it may also have an allergic component. It has been noted that two out of five children are sensitized and have sIgE antibodies to inhalants but only 25–30% of those develop asthma |14,15,48|. Of asthmatics in general about two out of three asthmatics are sensitized and have sIgE antibodies to inhalant allergens. Furthermore, those having higher sIgE antibody levels have a higher likelihood of allergic wheeze and asthma developing over time |14,15,48|.

A major concern for many patients is to know whether their disease will persist or resolve. In a young child with wheeze there are several options available for improving the accuracy of the diagnosis—the clinical history with information on family history, family smoking habits and other environmental exposures, all adding a certain level of risk of the diagnosis (see Box 4). Some results have shown that the persistence of wheeze at age 5 years can be predicted using the sIgE antibody levels at age 3 years |33|. For example, 10 kU_A/l of sIgE in the presence of a positive family history gives a probability of current wheeze of about 90%, corresponding to a 30-fold risk. The same 10 kU_A/l of sIgE, even with a negative family history, gives a probability of current wheeze of 65%, corresponding to an eight-fold increased risk (Fig. 1.2). When evaluating sIgE to allergens in this context, sIgE to food must not be neglected even if the symptom is asthma |49–50|. Together with the patient's case history, such information would allow the physician to reveal the likelihood of allergy and exposure to a specific allergen as being the driver of symptoms and disease. Furthermore, this would allow the physician to adopt the appropriate therapy accordingly, since it is not likely that a patient with very low sIgE level to relevant allergens would benefit from allergen-specific treatment and corticosteroids.

In situations when the allergy is expected to disappear or is already fading away, sIgE antibody determinations may also be useful |51|. Declining levels of sIgE antibodies can be taken as a marker of decreased allergen exposure, or of emerging allergen tolerance. This has been well documented in children with food allergy, where a high (>30 kU_A/l) level of sIgE is seen to slowly decrease (over more than 12 months) which indicates that tolerance may not be evolving, whereas a moderate to low value (approx 10 kU_A/l), decreasing by more than 75% in 12 months, is highly predictive of evolving tolerance |51|. Again such information is not revealed by tIgE.

Conclusion

In allergy, clinicians frequently follow a 'trial and error' process, by progressing directly from patients presenting signs and symptoms to pharmacotherapy. Empirical management may result in inadequately controlled symptoms and repeat office visits, as well as unnecessary referrals and drug use. The addition of sIgE antibody results improves the accuracy of diagnosis. The goal by using a sIgE antibody test is to change the probability that a patient has a certain diagnosis from the one without using such a test. Thus, allergy testing should be considered as an adjunct to the clinical history and physical examination similar to other diseases such as hypercholesterolaemia and diabetes. In these situations all information from case history, physical examination and diagnostic test results is evaluated together to guide optimal therapeutic decision-making. However, in some patients despite an intermediate or high probability of allergy, as assessed by history and physical examination, the sIgE antibody results may prove to be negative. In such cases, extensive analysis of the case history and empirical drug therapy is warranted with further testing for those who do not respond adequately |16,17,52|.

It must also be pointed out that allergic diseases are variable and can change over time from a sensitized situation without any obvious symptoms, to symptoms that may change from eczema to wheeze to rhinitis, the so-called Allergy March, and sometimes even escape to a symptom-free state.

Generally, all individuals with severe and/or persistent/or recurrent symptoms like those typically ensuing from allergic reactions should be examined for an allergic condition and tested for which allergens may be the cause of those symptoms |53|. Furthermore, the age of the individual, the family history as well as the character of the symptoms, including whether they are diurnal and/or occur during certain periods of the year |53|, need to be evaluated during the diagnostic process and should be taken into account when evaluating the specific IgE antibody levels.

References

1. Kurukulaaratchy RJ, Matthews S, Arshad SH. Defining childhood atopic phenotypes to investigate the association of atopic sensitization with allergic disease. *Allergy* 2005; **60**(10): 1280–6.

2. Quillen DM, Feller DB. Diagnosing rhinitis: allergic vs. nonallergic. *Am Fam Physician* 2006; **73**(9): 1583–90.

3. Ahlstedt S. Mediators in Allergy Diagnosis. *ACI International* 1998; **10**(2): 37–44.

4. Jarisch R, Wantke F. Wine and headache. *Int Arch Allergy Immunol* 1996; **110**(1): 7–12.

5. Shreffler WG, Beyer K, Chu TH, *et al*. Microarray immunoassay: Association of clinical history, in vitro IgE function, and heterogeneity of allergenic peanut epitopes. *J Allergy Clin Immunol* 2004; **113**(4): 776–82.

6. Committee on Quality of Health Care in America, I.o.M., *Crossing the Quality Chasm: A New Health System for the 21st Century.*

Washington DC. Committee on Quality of Health Care in America, Institute of Medicine, 2001.

7. Ahlstedt S, Murray CS. *In vitro* diagnosis of allergy: How to interpret IgE antibody results in clinical practice. *Prim Care Respir J* 2006; **15**(4): 228–36.

8. Kulig M, Bergmann R, Tacke U, *et al.* Long-lasting sensitization to food during the first two years precedes allergic airway disease. The MAS Study Group, Germany. *Pediatr Allergy Immunol* 1998; **9**(2): 61–7.

9. Platts-Mills TA, Erwin E, Heymann P, Woodfolk J. Is the hygiene hypothesis still a viable explanation for the increased prevalence of asthma? *Allergy* 2005; **60**(Suppl 79): 25–31.

10. Luder E, Ehrlich RI, Lou WY, *et al.* Body mass index and the risk of asthma in adults. *Respir Med* 2004; **98**(1): 29–37.

11. Martinez FD, Wright AL, Taussig LM, *et al.* Asthma and wheezing in the first six years of life. *N Engl J Med* 1995; **332**(3): 133–8.

12. Gustafsson D, Sjöberg O, Foucard T. Development of allergies and asthma in infants and young children with atopic dermatitis – a prospective follow-up to 7 years of age. *Allergy* 2000; **55**(3): 240–5.

13. Gustafsson D, Sjöberg O, Foucard T. Sensitization to food and airborne allergens in children with atopic dermatitis followed up to 7 years of age. *Pediatr Allergy Immunol* 2003; **14**: 448–52.

14. Illi S, von Mutius E, Lau S, *et al.* The natural course of atopic dermatitis from birth to age 7 years and the association with asthma. *J Allergy Clin Immunol* 2004; **113**(5): 925–31.

15. Illi S, von Mutius E, Lau S, *et al.* The pattern of atopic sensitization is associated with the development of asthma in childhood. *J Allergy Clin Immunol* 2001; **108**(5): 709–14.

16. Wood RA. The diagnosis of allergy: why is it so difficult? [comment]. *Ann Allergy Asthma Immunol* 2003; **91**(1): 1–2.

17. Biermann CW, Pearlman DS. *Allergy, Asthma and Immunology from Infancy to Childhood*, 3rd edition. WB Saunders, Philadelphia, 1995.

18. Nickel R, Illi S, Lau S, *et al.* Variability of total serum immunoglobulin E levels from birth to the age of 10 years. A prospective evaluation in a large birth cohort (German Multicenter Allergy Study). *Clin Exp Allergy* 2005; **35**(5): 619–23.

19. Yunginger JW, Ahlstedt S, Eggleston PA, *et al.* Quantitative IgE antibody assays in allergic diseases. *J Allergy Clin Immunol* 2000; **105**(6 Pt 1): 1077–84.

20. Williams PB, Ahlstedt S, Barnes JH, *et al.* Are our impressions of allergy test performances correct? [see comment]. *Ann Allergy Asthma Immunol* 2003; **91**(1): 26–33.

21. Poon AW, Goodman CS, Rubin RJ. *In vitro* and skin testing for allergy: comparable clinical utility and costs. *Am J Manag Care* 1998; **4**(7): 969–85.

22. Williams PB, Barnes JH, Szeinbach SL, Sullivan TJ. Analytic precision and accuracy of commercial immunoassays for specific IgE: establishing a standard. *J Allergy Clin Immunol* 2000; **105**(6 Pt 1): 1221–30.

23. Szeinbach SL, Barnes JH, Sullivan TJ, Williams PB. Precision and accuracy of commercial laboratories' ability to classify positive and/or negative allergen-specific IgE results. *Ann Allergy Asthma Immunol* 2001; **86**(4): 373–81.

24. Hamilton RG. Responsibility for quality IgE antibody results rests ultimately with the referring physician. *Ann Allergy Asthma Immunol* 2001; **86**(4): 353–4.

25. Jenkins JA, Griffiths-Jones S, Shewry PR, *et al.* Structural relatedness of plant food allergens with specific reference to cross-reactive allergens: an in silico analysis. *J Allergy Clin Immunol* 2005; **115**(1): 163–70.

26. Weber RW. Patterns of pollen cross-allergenicity. *J Allergy Clin Immunol* 2003; **112**: 229–39.

27. Asero R. Plant food allergies: a suggested approach to allergen-resolved diagnosis in the clinical practice by identifying easily available sensitization markers. *Int Arch Allergy Immunol* 2005; **138**(1): 1–11.

28. Sicherer SH. Clinical implications of cross-reactive food allergens. *J Allergy Clin Immunol* 2001; **108**(6): 881–90.

29. Nopp A, Johansson SGO, Ankerst J, *et al.* Basophil allergen threshold sensitivity: a useful approach to anti-IgE treatment efficacy evaluation. *Allergy* 2006; **61**(3): 298–302.

30. Boner AL, Peroni DG, Piacentini GL, Venge P. Influence of allergen avoidance at high altitude on serum markers of eosinophil activation in children with allergic asthma. *Clin Exp Allergy* 1993; **23**(12): 1021–6.

31. Hesselmar B, Aberg N, Aberg B, *et al.* Does early exposure to cat or dog protect against later allergy development? *Clin Exp Allergy* 1999; **29**(5): 611–17.

32. Platts-Mills T, Vaughan J, Squillace S. Sensitisation, asthma, and a modified Th2 response in children exposed to cat allergen: a population-based cross-sectional study. *Lancet* 2001; **357**(9258): 752–6.

33. Simpson A, Soderstrom L, Ahlstedt S, *et al.* IgE antibody quantification and the probability of wheeze in preschool children. *J Allergy Clin Immunol* 2005; **116**(4): 744–9.

34. Sampson HA, Ho DG. Relationship between food-specific IgE concentrations and the risk of positive food challenges in children and adolescents. *J Allergy Clin Immunol* 1997; **100**(4): 444–51.

35. Sampson HA. Utility of food-specific IgE concentrations in predicting symptomatic food allergy. *J Allergy Clin Immunol* 2001; **107**(5): 891–6.

36. Boyano-Martínez T, García-Ara C, Díaz-Pena JM, *et al.* Validity of specific IgE antibodies in children with egg allergy. *Clin Exp Allergy* 2001; **31**(9): 1464–9.

37. García-Ara C, Boyano-Martínez T, Díaz-Pena JM, *et al.* Specific IgE levels in the diagnosis of immediate hypersensitivity to cows' milk protein in the infant. *J Allergy Clin Immunol* 2001; **107**(1): 185–90.

38. Roberts G, Lack G. Diagnosing peanut allergy with skin prick and specific IgE testing. *J Allergy Clin Immunol* 2005; **115**(6): 1291–6.

39. Eigenmann PA. Are specific immunoglobulin E titres reliable for prediction of food allergy? *Clin Exp Allergy* 2005; **35**(3): 247–9.

40. Crobach MJ, Hermans J, Kaptein AA, *et al.* The diagnosis of allergic rhinitis: how to combine the medical history with the results of radioallergosorbent tests and skin prick tests. *Scand J Prim Health Care* 1998; **16**(1): 30–6.

41. Duran-Tauleria E, Guedan MJ, Peterson CJ. The utility of specific immunoglobulin E measurements in primary care. *Allergy* 2004; **78**: 35–41.

42. Soderstrom L, Kober A, Ahlstedt S, *et al.* A further evaluation of the clinical use of specific IgE antibody testing in allergic diseases. *Allergy* 2003; **58**(9): 921–8.

43. Wickman M, Lilja G, Soderstrom L, *et al.* Quantitative analysis of IgE antibodies to food and inhalant allergens in 4-year-old children reflects their likelihood of allergic disease [erratum appears in *Allergy* 2005; **60**(11): 1458. Note: van HageHamsten, M (corrected to van Hage-Hamsten, M)]. *Allergy* 2005; **60**(5): 650–7.

44. Murray CS, Poletti G, Kebadze T, *et al.* Study of modifiable risk factors for asthma exacerbations: virus infection and allergen exposure increase the risk of asthma hospital admissions in children. *Thorax* 2006; **61**(5): 376–82.

45. Green RM, Custovic A, Sanderson G, *et al.* Synergism between allergens and viruses and risk of hospital admission with asthma: case-control study [erratum appears in *Br Med J* 2002; May 11; **324**(7346): 1131]. *Br Med J* 2002; **324**(7340): 763.

46. Ahlstedt S. Understanding the usefulness of specific IgE blood tests in allergy. *Clin Exp Allergy* 2002; **32**(1): 11–16.

47. Portnoy J. Diagnostic testing for allergies. *Ann Allergy Asthma Immunol* 2006; **96**(1): 3–4.

48. Illi S, von Mutius E, Lau S, *et al.* Perennial allergen sensitisation early in life and chronic asthma in children: a birth cohort study. *Lancet* 2006; **368**(9537): 763–70.

49. Roberts G, Patel N, Levi-Schaffer F, *et al.* Food allergy as a risk factor for life-threatening asthma in childhood: A case-controlled study. *J Allergy Clin Immunol* 2003; **112**(1): 168–74.

50. Wang J, Visness CM, Sampson HA. Food allergen sensitization in inner-city children with asthma. *J Allergy Clin Immunol* 2005; **115**(5): 1076–80.

51. Shek LP, Soderstrom L, Ahlstedt S, *et al.* Determination of food specific IgE levels over time can predict the development of tolerance in cow's milk and hen's egg allergy. *J Allergy Clin Immunol* 2004; **114**(2): 387–91.

52. Gendo K, Larson EB. Evidence-based diagnostic strategies for evaluating suspected allergic rhinitis. *Ann Intern Med* 2004; **140**: 278–89.

53. Host A, Andrae SH, Charkin S, *et al.* Allergy testing in children: why, who, when and how? *Allergy* 2003; **58**(7): 559–69.

PART II

Allergic airway disease

Asthma treatment: introduction and background

ELIZABETH ERWIN, THOMAS PLATTS-MILLS

KEY POINTS

1. The increase in asthma has been so great that treatment should reflect or respond to the causes of the increase.

2. A large proportion of patients with mild, moderate or severe asthma are sensitized to one or more of the common inhalant allergens.
- Identification of this sensitization by skin tests or *in vitro* assays is important for education as well as treatment.
- Specific treatment with allergen avoidance or immunotherapy is recommended in the new asthma guidelines.
- Both the prevalence of sensitization and the titre of IgE antibodies to dust mite and cockroach allergen reflect indoor exposure.

3. Distinguishing different causes of severe asthma such as allergic bronchopulmonary aspergillosis (ABPA), aspirin triad, vocal cord dysfunction (VCD) or brittle asthma due to allergen exposure requires specific investigation.

Introduction

In modern western society a large proportion of the population are allergic as judged by skin tests or *in vitro* assays. The primary route of exposure is by inhalation of particles through the nose or mouth while the commonest sources of allergenic proteins are pollens or mould spores outdoors and the major indoor allergens. Most decisions about the treatment of allergic disease are dependent on understanding the extent to which allergen exposure contributes to the diseases. These questions are relevant to rhinitis, atopic dermatitis (AD) and anaphylaxis, however nowhere has the question been more critical than in understanding the relevance of allergen-specific treatment in the management of asthma [1–3].

For allergens that have a strict season or a specific location, causality may be obvious. Thus the seasonal 'epidemic' of asthma in Northern California coincides with the season for rye grass pollination and the patients are predominantly allergic to allergens derived from rye grass pollen |4|. Equally, most patients who develop asthma while working as a baker are found to be allergic to one of the ingredients of flour and improve when they stop working in this environment |5|. The causal relationship may also be clear for some patients who are allergic to cat allergens and develop symptoms of asthma within minutes or hours of entering a house with an animal. By contrast, the majority of patients who become allergic to allergens such as dust mites, cockroaches or *Alternaria* spp. are not aware of any temporal relationship between exposure and their lung symptoms |6|. This creates real problems in management both because the relationship of a given exposure to disease is difficult to establish, but also because it may be difficult to convince the patients about the need to control exposure.

On a world basis the single most common and probably the most important source of non-seasonal allergens is the dust mite |7–9|. Thus, it is not surprising that much of the argument about causality has related to this allergen. This is true both for arguments about the role of allergen-specific treatment and for understanding the relevance of allergen exposure to the increased prevalence and severity of asthma. Detailed discussion of allergen avoidance and immunotherapy are included in Chapters 13 and 14. In this chapter we will address:

- Evidence about the role of allergens in asthma.
- The relevance of understanding possible causes of the increase in asthma.
- The reasons why it is essential to define sensitivity.
- The identification of allergic factors in severe asthma.

Time course of the increase in allergic disease and asthma

In the UK, allergic disease was first recognized as a problem in 1873 by Charles Blackley, who focused on hay fever |10|. By 1910 hay fever was sufficiently well recognized that:

- The island of Heligoland in the North Sea was advertised as a colony for hay fever sufferers; and
- Noon introduced immunotherapy as a method of moderating the toxic effects of seasonal pollen |11|.

Evidence about the high prevalence of hay fever came from New York in 1935 and 1946, from Bill Frankland's clinic numbers in the 1950s, and epidemiology in Michigan in 1955 |12–15|. All these studies precede evidence about the increase in asthma that was first reported in studies in Birmingham schoolchildren in 1968 compared to 1958 |16|. Since then evidence about asthma prevalence has come from many different countries and many different types of study. However, most important there has been an increase in symptomatic wheezing |17,18|, in the numbers of children on treatment or hospitalized for asthma |19,20|. Our own evidence on African-American children in Charleston, South Carolina showed a 20-fold increase in asthma admissions over the period 1960 to 1995 |21|.

Although the evidence for the increase is clear and the time course has been consistent in many different countries, the scale of the increase has been very different. Two reviews ten years apart illustrate the differences in prevalence of wheezing between countries such as Greece, Spain, Albania and Scandinavia (1–6%) on the one hand, and New Zealand, Australia, UK and Japan (~20%) on the other |17,18|. Indeed in many ways the differences between countries are more impressive than the increase over time. Thus, there are two questions:

- Why has asthma increased?
- Why is the prevalence (and severity) so much higher in some countries?

The hygiene hypothesis in its current form is correctly credited to David Strachan; however, the idea was suggested earlier |22|. In fact, Charles Blackley, writing in 1873, pointed out that hay fever was uncommon among individuals working on a farm |10|. Many authors have used the hygiene hypothesis as an explanation for the increase in asthma |23|. This idea is related conceptually to the protective effect of close contact with farm animals |24|. However, the primary observation that Strachan built on was the lower prevalence of rhinitis among children with older siblings, which has not proved consistent. Most recently a study from Denmark reported the opposite finding that children with older siblings were more likely to have been infected at age 1 month and that these children had an *increased* prevalence of eosinophilia, elevated immunoglobulin (Ig)E and wheezing at age 5 years |25|. More troubling for the hypothesis is the fact that the major changes in hygiene in the USA occurred prior to 1920, i.e. long before the increase in asthma started. Taking New York (or London) as a model, shoes were universal (~1900), the streets were cleaned (1900–1920), water supplies were chlorinated (1920) and both helminth infections and malaria had been eradicated prior to 1920. The disease that increased following these changes was hay fever, which was epidemic by 1950. Thus it is possible, and indeed likely, that some elements of hygiene were necessary for the rise of *allergic disease* but that even with these changes asthma did not significantly increase until after 1960.

The question can then be rephrased to ask what changes since 1960 could have influenced the prevalence, persistence and severity of asthma |26|. The list is not short and includes:

1. Changes in houses in the UK, Australia and New Zealand that could have improved the environment for dust mites |1,7|.
2. Progressive increase in the number of hours that children (and adults) spend watching television or computer screens |27|, resulting in:
   - Increasing obesity in children |28|;
   - Decreased physical activity and prolonging periods with inadequate expansion of the lungs |29|;
   - Decreased sunlight with resulting decrease in Vitamin D |30|.

3. Introduction and widespread use of broad-spectrum antibiotics; with consequent changes in gut flora |31|.
4. Introduction and widespread use of inhalers to deliver adrenergic agonists: with clear evidence of harmful effects from isoprenaline (1967), fenoterol (1978), salmeterol (2005) and formoterol (2006) |32|.

At this point it is clear that no simple answer can be given to explain the increase in asthma. Indeed it is likely that a sequence of different events is involved |26|. However, what is relevant here is that this raises real questions both about proposals to decrease the prevalence of the disease and also about the optimal management of symptomatic asthma.

Epidemiological evidence on the role of allergens in the development of asthma

In cross-sectional studies allergen sensitization is consistently associated with asthma. Results have come from population-based studies in schoolchildren and case–control studies |16,33–36|. These studies have addressed both wheezing in a community and also acute asthma in an emergency department or hospital. In addition to evidence about the role of sensitization, these studies have provided evidence about the role of allergen exposure and viral infections |34,35,37,38|. Some conclusions are clear but they are age related. Under age 3 years the evidence from studies on acute asthma or bronchiolitis provides very strong evidence for the role of viral infections. By contrast, it is not clear that allergic sensitization is relevant to acute asthma under three years. After age 3 years and increasingly up through young adults allergen sensitization is very strongly associated with asthma |39|.

Prospective studies have greater power to establish causality, however they often lack power in relation to acute episodes and they take time! The first study to enrol children before birth and include measurements of allergen exposure was carried out in Poole, Dorset between 1979 and 1990 |9|. That study reported many findings that have been confirmed in subsequent larger studies. In particular the full association between sensitization and asthma was not apparent until age 10 years. Perhaps equally significant, those children who had wheezing episodes before age 5 years but did not have symptoms or bronchial hyper-reactivity (BHR) at age 10 years were no more allergic than the children who never reported wheezing |9|.

The pattern of early non-allergic or viral-induced wheezing which generally remits, and persistent (often later onset) asthma related predominantly to indoor allergens has been clear in each of the long-term studies |40–43|. This was particularly obvious with the MASS study from Berlin where a report in 2001 suggested that allergen exposure was not an important factor in asthma at age 5 years |40|. Evaluation of the same cohort at age 10 showed a highly significant effect of both sensitization and allergen exposure |41|. Similarly, in the Tucson birth cohort, the investigators had difficultly seeing an association between sensitization and wheezing at age 5 whereas at age 10 years the relevance of sensitization to *Alternaria* spp. was clear |43,44|.

Although there are major differences in the relevant allergens in different cohorts, in general, indoor or perennial allergens have been found to be more significant than pollens. This was spelt out in several early studies and it was particularly clear in the Dunedin study. In that cohort Sears carried out multivariate analysis on the relevance of allergen sensitization at age 11 years |42|. The results showed that dust mite, cat and *Aspergillus* sensitization were strongly associated with asthma. By contrast, although 30% of the children were skin sensitive to grass pollen, this sensitization was not significantly associated with asthma.

Over the last ten years *in vitro* assays for IgE antibodies have developed so that the quantification is consistently in absolute units |45,46|. Using CAP assays on sera from New Zealand, it is clear both that the titre of IgE antibodies to mite allergen can be very high and also that IgE antibodies to this specific allergen can make a major contribution to total serum IgE |47,48|. By contrast, IgE antibodies to cat or dog allergens are lower in titre and in general do not represent a significant part of total serum IgE. Our own data suggest that IgE antibody responses to mouse allergens are also lower titre than mite, cockroach or pollen responses |49|.

The implication of the results is that those allergens that induce high titre IgE antibodies will also increase total IgE. Given the strong correlation between total IgE and asthma we would argue that those allergens that play the biggest role in asthma are typically those that increase total IgE.

The cat paradox

Björkstén and his colleagues first reported that children raised in a house with a cat were *less* likely to become sensitized to cat allergens |50|. This finding was such a profound reversal of our traditional thinking/teaching that many investigators fought against the idea with an almost religious zeal |51|. However, the data have developed with results from many different cohorts, and in countries with very different exposure levels. Our own results on middle schoolchildren in the USA showed a significant *decrease* in prevalence of sensitization among those who were living with exposure over 8µg Fel d 1/g |52|. We added the finding that many of the children raised with high exposure had made an immune response including IgG and IgG_4 antibodies to Fel d 1 without becoming sensitized. We used the term 'modified Th2 response' to describe this form of tolerance because expression of the IgG_4 isotype is dependent on interleukin (IL)-4 |52,53|. Since then we have shown that subjects who have IgG_4 antibodies without IgE antibodies:

1. Have circulating T cells that respond *in vitro* to produce IL-10 |54|.
2. Are not at increased risk of wheezing compared to children who have made no antibody response to cat allergens |36|.
3. Do not have increased levels of total serum IgE |48,55|.

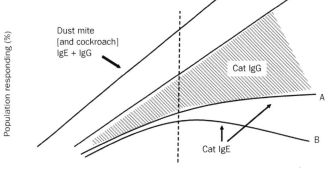

Population responding (%)

Dust mite [and cockroach] IgE + IgG

Cat IgG

Cat IgE

A

B

Airborne allergen exposure µg/day

Fig. 2.1 Contrast between exposure to dust mite or cat allergens and the relevant immune responses

The dashed line indicates the approximate value of 20 µg Fel d 1/g floor dust or the presence of a cat.

Several elements of the studies on cat exposure have influenced interpretation of the results. In some studies the effect appears to require more than one animal and is non-specific. For example, Ownby and colleagues found that a cat and a dog in the home was associated with decreased sensitization to allergens in general |56|. By contrast, a study initiated by Julian Crane in New Zealand found that a cat in the house *was* associated with decreased sensitization to cat but had no effect on the IgE antibody response to dust mite |47|.

Overall there are several conclusions that are consistent (Fig. 2.1) |57|. The presence of a cat in the house does not increase the prevalence of sensitization to cat allergens and the maximum titres of IgE antibodies to cat are lower than the maximum titres to dust mite, cockroach or pollen. The reasons for the different responses to cat allergens are not simple. Exposure to the cat allergen Fel d 1 occurs in all homes and schools and rises to very high levels in homes with a cat. However, high titre IgE antibodies is unusual with either high or moderate exposure. Presumably, cat (and dog) allergens are not very effective in stimulating responses at low dose possibly because of the limited evolutionary distance (~65 million years) between mammals and primates. At high doses these antigens are likely to stimulate the production of mature germinal centres where production of IgG and IgG_4 B cells is increased but where IgE responses are generally switched off (Fig. 2.2) |58|. Whether IgG_4 antibodies play a protective role remains controversial, however a recent report has provided extensive evidence about the structure of IgG_4 and the biological role of this isotype |59|.

In the early analysis of the MASS study from Berlin it looked as though increasing cat exposure led to increased sensitization |40|. However, the average levels of Fel d I in houses in Germany were lower than in the USA, UK or New Zealand. When the minority of children with truly high exposure were analysed separately it was clear that a significant proportion of these children had become 'tolerant' |60|. An important aspect of the 'paradox' is that those children living in a house with a cat who do become sensitized have a high risk of developing symptoms.

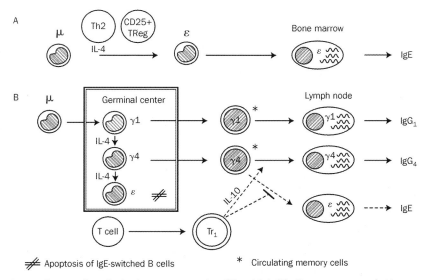

Fig. 2.2 Isotype diversity in the response to low (A) or high (B) allergen exposure (with permission from |52|).

Thus, the primary effects of high exposure to cats are a decreased prevalence of sensitization rather than decreased symptoms among allergic children.

Severe asthma in adults

Asthma has traditionally been classified either by severity or as allergic (extrinsic) or non-allergic (intrinsic) |61,62|. Intrinsic asthma as defined by Rackemann was characterized as late onset, severe, non-allergic and eosinophilic. However, he also included the observation that these patients didn't get better simply because they were admitted to hospital. In adults, severe disease has several special forms, which present a challenge for treatment. The obvious examples are ABPA (see Chapter 3), chronic sinus disease with nasal polyps and aspirin sensitivity (see Chapter 5) and vocal cord dysfunction (Table 2.1) |63,64|. The correct management of these cases is distinct and in many cases the published guidelines on asthma treatment do not address the issues well. We would include other forms of asthma that can be severe:

1. Dermatophyte infection and associated sensitivity.
2. Special forms of upper airway dysfunction.
3. *Form fruste* ABPA or allergic bronchopulmonary mycosis (ABPM) i.e. cases where there is evidence for colonization of the lungs with fungi but without the full syndrome of ABPA. Finally, in any discussion of severe asthma in adults we should include patients who are both allergic and heavily exposed to relevant allergens in their home |65|. Some of these cases present as persistent severe

Table 2.1 Evaluation of severe or moderate-severe asthma in adults

History/physical examination
- History of seasonality or exacerbation in relation to exposures such as work, cat or dog
- Voice changes; sensitivity to chemicals or perfume; rapid changes in symptoms—consider VCD
- Productive cough and colour of sputum; brown, orange, grey or black sputum suggests fungal involvement
- Physical examination for nasal polyps; evidence of fungal or yeast colonization in nails, skin or throat; skin exam for atopic dermatitis

Evidence of inflammation
- Eosinophilia ≥300 eosinophils/cubic mm
- Exhaled NO ≥20 ppb
- Sinus CT showing extensive disease (score ≥12)

Evidence for inhalant or other allergen sensitization
- Symptoms
- Skin tests
- Serum assays for total IgE and specific IgE antibodies

Productive cough
- Sputum colour, and culture for fungi
- Bronchoscopy; BAL culture
- Lung CT

(or brittle) asthma and the response to a complete change in environment can be dramatic |8,66|.

The classical definition of intrinsic asthma implied that these cases were idiopathic |61|. However it is not easy to classify patients using a simple intrinsic/extrinsic division. Cases that really fit the model proposed by Rackemann are not common and indeed may not have increased over the period when other forms of asthma have increased dramatically. Some cases of sinus disease with polyps present the full syndrome of intrinsic disease and can become severe rapidly. In addition, some cases with fungal infection present as 'intrinsic' disease and can become severe |67,68|. By contrast, ABPA is more often a complication of long-standing allergic asthma. Vocal cord dysfunction in its pure form presents a very different phenotype with normal peripheral blood eosinophil counts (i.e. <200 eosinophils/mm³), low exhaled nitric oxide (NO), negative sinus computed tomography (CT) and no evidence of sensitization to inhaled allergens. A guide to evaluating and treating these cases is presented in Tables 2.1 and 2.2.

Relevance to management of asthma

Given the scale of the increase in asthma over the last 50 years, it could be argued that treatment is unlikely to be successful unless it addresses/reverses the changes

Table 2.2

Subgroups of severe asthma in adults	Specific treatment
A. High exposure to allergen in an allergic subject; with or without *Rhinovirus* infection	Allergic avoidance ± allergen Immunotherapy
B. *Chronic hyperplastic sinusitis*	
i. With aspirin sensitivity	Aspirin desensitization
ii. Without aspirin sensitivity	
C. *Fungal colonization*	
i. Allergic bronchopulmonary apergillosis (ABPA)	Oral antifungal treatment; itraconazole, voreconazole.
Other species *Curvularia, Candida* etc.	
Form fruste ABPM, i.e. fungus or *Candida* in the lungs without the full syndrome	
ii. Dermatophytosis with associated sensitization to fungal allergens.	Topical and oral antifungal treatment; fluconazole
D. Upper airway or vocal cord dysfunction	Local treatment including nebulized Cromolyn, or lidocaine, speech therapy, Botox injections to vocal cords, etc

that have caused the increase. However, there is no general consensus about the causes of the increase. Furthermore, logical approaches to treatment are easier to propose for some causes than others. Reducing allergen exposure, increasing exposure to endotoxin in early childhood, or increasing physical activity of children are easy in concept but difficult in practice. When we come to other possible *causes* of the increase it may be almost impossible to make changes. If prolonged periods of sitting watching video or computer screens are harmful to the lungs |27,29,69,70|, it may be very difficult to change this practice. Equally, if the widespread use of adrenergic agonists is an important *cause* of increased severity it would require compelling trial evidence to persuade patients not to use relief inhalers.

Regardless of the specific causes of the increase in asthma, allergen exposure is an important element both for sensitization and in ongoing inflammation of the lungs. Thus, decreasing allergen exposure should be an important part of the treatment. However, as pointed out by Dr Custovic in Chapter 14, there are real questions about the effectiveness of allergen avoidance in routine treatment. We do not agree with all his conclusions, primarily because we are much less impressed with the studies that enrol large numbers of patients using an avoidance protocol that is not consistently effective |71,72|. However, we are biased because we know that studies in which patients are moved into a low antigen environment have been consistently effective |8,66,73|. Thus, patients moved to a hospital room or a sanatorium with low allergen levels experience a dramatic improvement in symptoms, lung function and bronchial reactivity |8,73,74|. The problem with interpreting those studies is that in most cases the patients also had a progressive *reduction* in the use of beta-adrenergic inhalers *and* a marked increase in physical activity.

Conclusions

It is now 20 years since it was generally accepted that asthma is characterized by widespread inflammation of the bronchi. This finding led inevitably to a focus on anti-inflammatory agents in treatment. Not surprisingly, the main agents in use for control of the disease are drugs that are widely anti-inflammatory (i.e. steroids) or that block specific parts of the inflammatory process, such as theophylline (adenosine antagonist) or the leukotriene antagonists. This understanding has encouraged extensive experimental studies both in man and mice aimed at understanding the inflammatory process in the lungs. All these experiments assume that the inflammation is caused by inhalation of foreign proteins into the lungs of a specifically sensitized individual. In keeping with this the only known method of inducing bronchial hyper-reactivity in man is bronchial provocation with allergen in a specifically allergic patient. Similarly, the best established non-pharmacological approach to decreasing BHR is to decrease allergen exposure either in a hospital room, in a sanatorium or at home |3,8,66,73,74|. In keeping with this, the new National Heart, Lung and Blood Institute (NHLBI) guidelines for asthma management recognize a primary role for allergen-avoidance as well as allergen-specific immunotherapy (IT) |62|.

Defining the sensitivity of patients can be achieved by skin tests or *in vitro* assays. The *in vitro* assays are accurate, highly repeatable and can give results in the same units that are used for total IgE |45,46|. On the other hand, skin tests are rapid, and make it possible to react to the results and carry out further tests during the same visit. Perhaps more importantly, reviewing the results of skin tests can be an effective method of educating patients about the role of allergens in their disease. The investigation of some forms of sensitivity is best carried out with skin tests. The most obvious example is fungal sensitivity where intradermal skin tests may be necessary and the *in vitro* results are not as sensitive.

The commonest sensitivity in chronic asthma is to one of the major perennial allergens such as dust mite, cat, dog, cockroach or *Alternaria* spp. The importance of each of these allergens can vary dramatically from community to community even within one country. In the USA there are areas or cities where each of the above mentioned allergens is dominant |34–36,75,76|. Apart from emphasizing the importance of defining sensitivity, the results strongly support the argument that these exposures are causally related to asthma. However, in addition, there is good evidence that exposure to some allergens, particularly dust mite or cockroach, is at least partially responsible for the high prevalence of asthma in the UK, New Zealand, Australia, Taiwan, Japan, and the American inner cities |17,18,48|. Defining sensitivity or the risk of sensitivity is also an important part of investigating cases of asthma that do not respond to routine treatment (Tables 2.1 and 2.2).

The range of treatment approaches for moderate persistent or severe asthma demands careful investigation. Thus, the decision to carry out aspirin desensitization; to use antifungal treatment; to introduce Anti-IgE; or to focus on treatment of the upper airway requires careful investigation well beyond what is necessary for managing mild cases. It is also worth keeping in mind that occasional cases reflect foreign bodies, benign tumours of the lung, helminth parasitization, fungal infection away from the lungs or the effects of diet. Thus, it is important to re-investigate cases if they do not respond to treatment.

Finally, we need to remember that the true cause or causes of the increase in asthma remain poorly defined. When it seemed likely that changes in homes were responsible for the increase in the UK, the implications were obvious. However this is not a convincing explanation for the pattern of increase that has occurred in most parts of the developed world. If the increase has been driven by changes in lifestyle or antibiotic use, it may be impossible to reverse these changes. However, we need to remain aware that there may be other approaches to treatment that could not only help us to manage patients, but could also help to reverse the current high prevalence.

References

1. Dust mite allergens and asthma – a worldwide problem international workshop report. *J Allergy Clin Immunol* 1989; **83**(2 Pt 1): 416–27.

2. Platts-Mills TA. Allergen avoidance in the treatment of asthma and rhinitis. *N Eng J Med* 2003; **349**: 207–8.

3. Platts-Mills TA, Vaughan JW, Carter MC, Woodfolk JA. The role of intervention in established allergy: avoidance of indoor allergens in the treatment of chronic allergic disease. *J Allergy Clin Immunol* 2000; **106**(5): 787–804.

4. Pollart SM, Reid MJ, Fling JA, *et al.* Epidemiology of emergency room asthma in northern California: association with IgE antibody to ryegrass pollen. *J Allergy Clin Immunol* 1988; **82**(2): 224–30.

5. Malo JL, Yeung MC. Occupational Asthma. *Middleton's Allergy Principles & Practice.* 2003; **73**(2): 1333–71.

6. Platts-Mills TA, Chapman MD, Pollart S, *et al.* Specific allergens evoking immune reactions in the lung: relationship to asthma. *Eur Respir J* 1991; **13**(Suppl): 68s–77s.

7. Platts-Mills TA, Vervloet D, Thomas WR, *et al.* Indoor allergens and asthma: report of the Third International Workshop. *J Allergy Clin Immunol* 1997; **100**(6 Pt 1): S2–24.

8. Platts-Mills TA, Tovey ER, Mitchell EB, *et al.* Reduction of bronchial hyperactivity during prolonged allergen avoidance. *Lancet* 1982; **2**(8300): 675–8.

9. Sporik R, Holgate ST, Platts-Mills TA, Cogswell JJ. Exposure to house-dust mite allergen (Der p I) and the development of asthma in childhood. A prospective study. *N Engl J Med* 1990; **323**(8): 502–7.

10. Blackley CH. *Experimental Researches on Hay Fever.* Dawson's of Pall Mall, London, 1959.

11. Noon L. Prophylactic inoculation for hay fever. *Lancet* 1911: 1572–3.

12. Ratner S. Prevalence of hay fever in New York city 1935–1950. Allergic disease in New York 10–13%.

13. Walzer M, Siegel BB. The effectiveness of the ragweed eradication campaigns in New York City; a 9-year study; 1946–1954, *J Allergy* 1956; **27**(2): 113–26.

14. Brown HM. Would oral desensitization for peanut allergy be safer than avoidance? *Ann Allergy Asthma Immunol* 2007; **98**(2): 203.

15. Broder I, Barlow PP, Horton RJ. The epidemiology of asthma and hay fever in a total community, Tecumseh, Michigan, Il. The relationship between asthma and hay fever. *J Allergy* 1962; **33**: 524–31.

16. Smith JM, Disney ME, Williams JD, Goels ZA. Clinical significance of skin reactions to mite extracts in children with asthma. *Br Med J* 1969; **2**(5659): 723–6.

17. Beasley R, Crane J, Lai CK, Pearce N. Prevalence and etiology of asthma. *J Allergy Clin Immunol* 2000; **105**(2 Pt 2):S466–72.

18. Eder W, Ege MJ, von Mutius E. The asthma epidemic. *N Engl J Med* 2006; **355**(21): 2226–35.

19. Beasley R, Pearce N, Crane J. International trends in asthma mortality. *Ciba Found Symp* 1997; **206**: 140–50.

20. Woolcock AJ, Peat JK. Evidence for the increase in asthma worldwide. *Ciba Found Symp* 1997; **206**: 122–34.

21. Crater DD, Heise S, Perzanowski M, *et al.* Asthma hospitalization trends in Charleston, South Carolina, 1956 to 1997: twenty-fold increase among black children during a 30-year period. *Pediatrics* 2001; **108**(6): E97.

22. Strachan DP. Family size, infection and atopy: the first decade of the 'hygiene hypothesis'. *Thorax* 2000; **55**(Suppl 1): S2–S10.

23. Matricardi PM, Rosmini F, Panetta V, *et al.* Hay fever and asthma in relation to markers of infection in the United States. *J Allergy Clin Immunol* 2002; **110**(3): 381–7.

24. Braun-Fahrländer C, Riedler J, Herz U, *et al.*; Allergy and Endotoxin Study Team. Environmental exposure to endotoxin and its relation to asthma in school-age children. *N Engl J Med* 2002; **347**(12): 869–77.

25. Bisgaard H, Hermansen MN, Buchvald F, *et al.* Childhood asthma after bacterial colonization of the airway in neonates. *N Engl J Med* 2007; **357**(15): 1487–95.

26. Platts-Mills TA. Asthma severity and prevalence: an ongoing interaction between exposure, hygiene, and lifestyle. *PLoS Med* 2005; **2**(2): e24.

27. Platts-Mills TA, Sporik RB, Chapman MD, Heymann PW. The role of domestic allergens. *Ciba Found Symp* 1997; **206**: 173–85.

28. Kim S, Camargo CA Jr. Sex-race differences in the relationship between obesity and asthma: the behavioral risk factor surveillance system, 2000. *Ann Epidemiol* 2003; **13**(10): 666–73.

29. Fredberg JJ, Inouye DS, Mijailovich SM, Butler JP. Perturbed equilibrium of myosin binding in airway smooth muscle and its implications in bronchospasm. *Am J Respir Crit Care Med* 1999; **159**(3): 959–67.

30. Litonjua AA, Weiss ST. Is vitamin D deficiency to blame for the asthma epidemic? *J Allergy Clin Immunol* 2007; **120**(5): 1031–5.

31. Björkstén B. Effects of intestinal microflora and the environment on the development of asthma and allergy. *Springer Semin Immunopathol* 2004; **25**(3–4): 257–70.

32. Pearce N, Crane J, Burgess C, Beasley R. Beta-agonist use and death from asthma. *JAMA* 1994; **271**(11): 822–3.

33. Miyamoto T, Oshima S, Ishizaki T, Sato SH. Allergenic identity between the common floor mite (Dermatophagoides farinae Hughes, 1961) and house dust as a causative antigen in bronchial asthma. *J Allergy* 1968; **42**(1): 14–28.

34. Squillace SP, Sporik RB, Rakes G, *et al.* Sensitization to dust mites as a dominant risk factor for asthma among adolescents living in central Virginia. Multiple regression analysis of a population-based study. *Am J Respir Crit Care Med* 1997; **156**(6): 1760–4.

35. Gelber LE, Seltzer LH, Bouzoukis JK, *et al.* Sensitization and exposure to indoor allergens as risk factors for asthma among patients presenting to hospital. *Am Rev Respir Dis* 1993; **147**(3): 573–8.

36. Perzanowski MS, Rönmark E, Platts-Mills TA, Lundbäck B. Effect of cat and dog ownership on sensitization and development of asthma among preteenage children. *Am J Respir Crit Care Med* 2002; **166**(5): 696–702.

37. Rakes GP, Arruda E, Ingram JM, *et al.* Rhinovirus and respiratory syncytial virus in wheezing children requiring emergency care. IgE and eosinophil analyses. *Am J Respir Crit Care Med* 1999; **159**(3): 785–90.

38. Murray CS, Poletti G, Kebadze T, *et al.* Study of modifiable risk factors for asthma

exacerbations: virus infection and allergen exposure increase the risk of asthma hospital admissions in children. *Thorax* 2006; **61**(5): 376–82.

39. Heymann PW, Carper HT, Murphy DD, *et al.* Viral infections in relation to age, atopy, and season of admission among children hospitalized for wheezing. *J Allergy Clin Immunol* 2004; **114**(2): 239–47.

40. Lau S, Illi S, Sommerfeld C, *et al.* Early exposure to house-dust mite and cat allergens and development of childhood asthma: a cohort study. Multicentre Allergy Study Group. *Lancet* 2000; **356**(9239): 1392–7.

41. Illi S, von Mutius E, Lau S, *et al.* Multicentre Allergy Study (MAS) group. *Lancet* 2006; **368**(9537): 763–70.

42. Sears MR, Herbison GP, Holdaway MD, *et al.* The relative risks of sensitivity to grass pollen, house dust mite and cat dander in the development of childhood asthma. *Clin Exp Allergy* 1989; **19**(4): 419–24.

43. Martinez FD, Wright AL, Taussig LM, *et al.* Asthma and wheezing in the first six years of life. The Group Health Medical Associates. *N Engl J Med* 1995; **332**(3): 133–8.

44. Halonen M, Stern DA, Wright AL, *et al.* Alternaria as a major allergen for asthma in children raised in a desert environment. *Am J Respir Crit Care Med* 1997; **155**(4): 1356–61.

45. Erwin EA, Custis NJ, Satinover SM, *et al.* Quantitative measurement of IgE antibodies to purified allergens using streptavidin linked to a high-capacity solid phase. *J Allergy Clin Immunol* 2005; **115**(5): 1029–35.

46. Simpson A, Soderstrom L, Ahlstedt S, *et al.* IgE antibody quantification and the probability of wheeze in preschool children. *J Allergy Clin Immunol* 2005; **116**(4): 744–9.

47. Erwin EA, Wickens K, Custis NJ, *et al.* Cat and dust mite sensitivity and tolerance in relation to wheezing among children raised with high exposure to both allergens. *J Allergy Clin Immunol* 2005; **115**(1): 74–9.

48. Erwin EA, Rönmark E, Wickens K, *et al.* Contribution of dust mite and cat specific IgE

to total IgE: relevance to asthma prevalence. *J Allergy Clin Immunol* 2007; **119**(2): 359–65.

49. Platts-Mills TA, Satinover SM, Naccara L, *et al.* Prevalence and titre of IgE antibodies to mouse allergens. *J Allergy Clin Immunol* 2007; **120**(5): 1058–64.

50. Hesselmar B, Aberg N, Aberg B, *et al.* Does early exposure to cat or dog protect against later allergy development. *Clin Exp Allergy* 1999; **29**(5): 611–17.

51. Apter AJ. Early exposure to allergen: is this the cat's meow, or are we barking up the wrong tree? *J Allergy Clin Immunol* 2003; **111**(5): 935–46.

52. Platts-Mills TA, Vaughan J, Squillace S, *et al.* Sensitization, asthma and a modified Th2 response in children exposed to cat allergen: a population-based cross-sectional study. *Lancet* 2001; **357**(9258): 752–6.

53. Jeal H, Draper A, Harris J, *et al.* Modified Th2 responses at high-dose exposures to allergen: using an occupational model. *Am J Respir Crit Care Med* 2006; **174**(1): 21–5.

54. Reefer AJ, Carneiro RM, Custis NJ, *et al.* A role for IL-10-medicated HLA-DR7-restricted T cell-dependent events in development of the modified Th2 response to cat allergen. *J Immunol* 2004; **172**(5): 2763–72.

55. Perzanowski M, Rönmark E, Lündback B, *et al.* Does the antibody response to cat allergen influence allergic responses to birch pollen or dog allergens. 2008 (submitted for publication).

56. Ownby DR, Johnson CC, Peterson EL. Exposure to dogs and cats in the first year of life and risk of allergic sensitization at 6 to 7 years of age. *JAMA* 2002; **288**(8): 963–72.

57. Platts-Mills TA, Perzanowski M, Woodfolk JA, Lundbäck B. Relevance of early or current pet ownership to prevalence of allergic disease. *Clin Exp Allergy* 2002; **32**(3): 335–8.

58. Aalberse RC, Platts-Mills TA. How do we avoid developing allergy: modifications of the TH2 response from a B-cell perspective. *J Allergy Clin Immunol* 2004; **113**(5): 983–6.

59. van der Neut Kolfschoten M, Schuurman J, Losen M, *et al.* Anti-inflammatory activity of human IgG4 antibodies by dynamic Fab arm exchange. *Science* 2007; **317**(5844): 1554–7.

60. Lau S, Illi S, Platts-Mills TA, *et al.*; Multicentre Allergy Study Group. Longitudinal study on the relationship between cat allergen and endotoxin exposure, sensitization, cat-specific IgG and development of asthma in childhood—report of the German Multicentre Allergy Study (MAS 90). *Allergy* 2005; **60**(6): 766–73.

61. Rackemann FM, Burrage WS, Irwin JW. Intrinsic asthma. *Postgrad Med* 1950; **8**(2): 134–40.

62. National Asthma Education and Prevention Program Expert Panel Report. Guidelines for the diagnosis and management of asthma. National Institutes of Health, Bethesda, MD, 2007.

63. Wood RP 2nd, Milgrom H. Vocal cord dysfunction. *J Allergy Clin Immunol* 1996; **98**(3): 481–5.

64. Peters EJ, Hatley TK, Crater SE, *et al.* Sinus computed tomography scan and markers of inflammation in vocal cord dysfunction and asthma. *Ann Allergy Asthma Immunol* 2003; **90**(3): 316–22.

65. Tunnicliffe WS, Fletcher TJ, Hammond K, *et al.* Sensitivity and exposure to indoor allergens in adults with differing asthma severity. *Eur Respir J* 1999; **13**(3): 654–9.

66. Kerrebijn KF. Endogenous factors in childhood CNSLD: methodological aspects in population studies. In: Orie NGM, van der Lende R (eds). *Bronchitis III.*, C. C. Thomas, Springfield, IL, 1970, pp 38–48.

67. Ward GW Jr, Karlsson G, Rose G, Platts-Mills TA. Trichophyton asthma: sensitization of bronchi and upper airways to dermatophyte antigen. *Lancet* 1989; **1**(8643): 859–62.

68. Ward GW Jr, Woodfolk JA, Hayden ML, *et al.* Treatment of late-onset asthma with fluconazole. *J Allergy Clin Immunol* 1999; **104**(3 Pt 1): 541–6.

69. Firrincieli V, Keller A, Ehrensberger R, *et al.* Decreased physical activity among Head Start children with a history of wheezing: use of an accelerometer to measure activity. *Pediatr Pulmonol* 2005; **40**(1): 57–63.

70. Hark WT, Thompson WM, McLaughlin TE, *et al.* Spontaneous sigh rates during sedentary activity: watching television *vs.* reading. *Ann Allergy Asthma Immunol* 2005; **94**(2): 247–50.

71. Woodcock A, Forster L, Matthews E, *et al.*; Medical Research Council General Practice Research Framework. Control of exposure to mite allergen and allergen-impermeable bed covers for adults with asthma. *N Engl J Med* 2003; **349**(3): 225–36.

72. Terreehorst I, Hak E, Oosting AJ, *et al.* Evaluation of impermeable covers for bedding in patients with allergic rhinitis. *N Engl J Med* 2003; **349**(3): 237–46.

73. Peroni DG, Piacentini GL, Costella S, *et al.* Mite avoidance can reduce air trapping and airway inflammation in allergic asthmatic children. *Clin Exp Allergy* 2002; **32**(6): 850–5.

74. Ehnert B, Lau-Schadendorf S, Weber A, *et al.* Reducing domestic exposure to dust mite allergen reduces bronchial hyperreactivity in sensitive children with asthma. *J Allergy Clin Immunol* 1992; **90**(1): 135–8.

75. Sporik R, Ingram JM, Price W, *et al.* Association of asthma with serum IgE and skin test reactivity to allergens among children living at high altitude. Tickling the dragon's breath. *Am J Respir Crit Care Med* 1995; **151**(5): 1388–92.

76. Rosenstreich DL, Eggleston P, Kattan M, *et al.* The role of cockroach allergy and exposure to cockroach allergen in causing morbidity among inner-city children with asthma. *N Engl J Med* 1997; **336**(19): 1356–63.

3

Fungus (or mould) allergic pulmonary disease

DAVID DENNING

KEY POINTS

1. Fungi are ubiquitous and are inhaled daily. Sensitization is common in atopy and associated with severe asthma, allergic bronchopulmonary mycosis and allergic fungal sinusitis.

2. Allergic bronchopulmonary aspergillosis is associated with many genetic traits and responds to antifungal therapy with itraconazole in asthmatics.

3. Severe asthma with fungal sensitization is associated with numerous fungi, and asthma control and quality of life is improved by antifungal therapy.

4. Several occupational diseases have been associated with fungal exposure including 'Cheese workers lung', 'Suberosis' and 'Mushroom workers lung'.

Introduction

One of the facts of life is exposure to fungi, via the respiratory tract, gut and skin. Exposure is high level to airborne fungi, with some seasonal geographical and local environmental variations. Airborne fungal spore levels may be up to 1000 times higher than pollen levels. A culture-based survey of lung tissue from patients dying suddenly or undergoing elective surgery showed that >75% of patients harbour fungi in their lungs, most commonly *Aspergillus* spp. |1|. Most gut exposure is to commensal fungi, such as *Candida albicans*, but any fungi found on fruit or vegetables, also pass through the gastrointestinal (GI) tract. Perhaps what is remarkable is how little disease these organisms do cause, probably a reflection on genetic characteristics of the host and the relative scarcity of allergenic proteins, especially on spores or conidia. This chapter explores the relationship between fungi and man, from the perspective of allergy and sensitization, and lower respiratory tract disease. It ignores invasive, saprophytic and chronic infections with fungi, principally caused by *Aspergillus* spp.

The nose is a filter for airborne fungi, and what is culturable from the anterior nares is a good indication of local exposure. An extremely large number of fungi can be cultured from the nose, and it is possible that all are allergenic |2|. However, some fungi are particularly common, including *Aspergillus fumigatus* and other species, *Alternaria* spp., *Cladosporium* spp., *Penicillium* spp. and others. While *Alternaria* spp., *Cladosporium* spp., *Penicillium* spp. are rare invasive pathogens, *A. fumigatus* causes multiple diseases in humans including acute and subacute invasive aspergillosis, aspergilloma of the lung and maxillary sinus, and chronic pulmonary aspergillosis |3|. Invasive aspergillosis occurs primarily in patients who are immunosuppressed with functional T-cell or phagocytic defects or neutropenia |4|. In contrast, allergic fungal disease affects those with atopy, who are probably genetically predisposed, although this point requires additional confirmation. There are several different disease phenotypes associated with fungal allergy, and the principal ones are listed in Table 3.1. Delineation of the different phenotypes of fungal allergy of the nose requires additional work, and is not covered in this chapter.

Table 3.1   Respiratory tract allergy associated with fungi
Lung
Allergic bronchopulmonary aspergillosis
Severe asthma with fungal sensitization
Thunderstorm asthma
Occupational asthma, working with fungi
Extrinsic allergic alveolitis
Sinuses
Allergic *Aspergillus* sinusitis
Eosinophilic fungal rhinosinusitis

Fungi implicated

Table 3.2 shows the common fungi implicated in fungal allergy. This list is far from exhaustive, and relates to those fungi which have been tested, and does not exclude the possibility of other fungi being implicated in the future. Most allergic fungi described are Ascomycetes, rather than Basidiomycetes, possibly because of the difficulties of preparing pure and reproducible extracts from field fungi, which are difficult to cultivate *in vitro*. While some fungi are undoubtedly particularly common causes of fungal allergy, the current methodology for determining sensitivity and allergy is crude and limited by availability of certain fungal reagents. For example, immunoglobulin (Ig)E RAST tests are available for

Table 3.2 Fungi probably important in respiratory tract allergy
Aspergillus fumigatus (and other aspergilli)
Alternaria alternata
Cladosporium herbarum (and possibly other species)
Penicillium spp. (probably multiple)
Trichophyton interdigitale (mentagrophytes)
Aureobasidium pullulans
Candida albicans
Malassezia furfur (Pityrosporum orbiculare)
Rhodatorula rubra
Epicoccum nigrum
Botrytis cinerea
Helminthosporium halodes

numerous fungi, including *Acremonium kilense, Alternaria alternata, A. fumigatus* (and other *Aspergilli*), *Aureobasidium pullulans, Botrytis cinerea, C. albicans, Chaetomium globosum, Cladosporium herbarum, Curvularia lunata, Epicoccum purpurascens, Fusarium proliferatum, Helminthosporium halodes, Malassezia furfur (Pityrosporum orbiculare), Mucor racemosus, Penicillium chrysogenum* and *glabrum, Phoma betae, Rhizopus nigricans, Stemphylium herbarum, Trichophyton interdigitale (mentagrophytes)* (and other species), *Trichosporon pullulans* and *Ulocladium chartarum.* Most of the same fungi are prepared as skin tests, but there are some differences. For example, different *Aspergillus* species, *Exserohilum rostratum*, different species of *Fusarium, Neurospora sitophila, Serpula lacrymans* and *Sporothrix schenkii* are all available as skin tests. It has been demonstrated that there is a considerable mismatch between skin prick test (SPT) and serum IgE RAST qualitative results.

There are significant seasonal fluctuations in airborne fungi counts in outside air. For example, in south Wales, maximal levels of *Cladosporium* spp. are seen in July, *A. alternata* and hyaline basidiospores in August, uredospores in September and coloured basidiospores in October with similar results elsewhere in northern Europe. The fungi encountered indoors differ to an extent from those encountered external to the house.

Allergens

Most allergens are eukaryotic proteins from plant, fungal, animal and mite sources. Certain cross-reactive allergens are well characterized having both conserved function and sequence homology (i.e. enolase, thioredoxin, or cyclophylin) [5]. Others are conserved across the fungal kingdom (i.e. some proteases or glucanases), or are conserved in the fungal and plant kingdom (i.e. flavodoxin). Some allergens are specific to individual species or genera (i.e. Alt a1 in *A. alternata* and Asp f1 in *A. fumigatus*). About half of all known allergens are common to most eukaryotes implying that potential cross-reactive allergens are ubiquitous and plentiful in our environment, especially in vegetables, fruit and both edible and environmental fungi and fungal products (bread, alcoholic drinks, sauces etc). However, most proteins found in eukaryotes are not allergens. In *A. fumigatus*, for example, the recently determined genomic sequence showed that there are only ~67 allergenic proteins out of an estimated 9900 gene products [6]. The intrinsic characteristic of an allergen is not known, and only a few crystal structures of allergens have been published and epitope mapped. As with non-fungal allergens such as Der p1, Fel d1, many fungal allergens are proteases, suggesting a direct role in causing tissue damage which could be important in inciting and perpetuating an allergic response [7].

Allergic bronchopulmonary aspergillosis (ABPA)

ABPA is characterized by several clinical and immunological responses to *A. fumigatus* antigens, which colonize the bronchial tree of genetically predisposed patients [8]. *A. fumigatus* grows saprophytically in the bronchial lumen resulting in persistent bronchial inflammation typically leading to proximal bronchiectasis. Rarely, other fungi may induce a syndrome similar to ABPA known as allergic bronchopulmonary mycosis.

Epidemiology

ABPA occurs primarily in adults with asthma and cystic fibrosis, although it is described occasionally in those without either condition. The frequency of ABPA is not known but is estimated to be ~1% of the adult asthmatic population referred to hospital and ~12% of the adult cystic fibrosis population [9,10]. It has a worldwide distribution, with no well-described locales with very high or low frequencies.

Clinical presentation

Most patients with ABPA present with worsening asthma or pulmonary function in cystic fibrosis, typically with wheeze. A common clinical feature is major coughing bouts relieved by coughing up a thick plug of mucus. Sometimes these plugs resemble the interior of the airways and may be described as spaghetti-like, slug-like or so large they cause choking. They are usually pale grey, yellow, orange or brown but are usually thick and may be hard. Once coughed up, some patients then describe additional thin mucus, which may be green. Some patients do not describe coughing up plugs at all, but may present with consolidation or atelectasis on chest radiograph or computed tomography (CT) scan, which may be relieved by suction of thick material on bronchoscopy.

Other less common presentations include fatigue, with almost no pulmonary features, culture of *A. fumigatus* from respiratory secretions, chronic persistent asthma, unresponsive to maximal medical therapy, and positive *A. fumigatus* precipitin or RAST test. A fixed patch of erythema may be present when the disease is active. Many patients present with the features of bronchiectasis, ABPA only being uncovered by serology. Many patients also have chronic sinusitis, often with nasal polyps, a condition known as the sinobronchial allergic mycosis (SAM) syndrome.

Diagnosis

The cardinal diagnostic features of ABPA include an elevated total serum IgE, together with evidence of *Aspergillus* sensitization as evidenced by positive *Aspergillus* precipitating IgG antibody, *Aspergillus* specific RAST or SPT, culture of *A. fumigatus* from respiratory secretions and peripheral eosinophilia (before starting systemic corticosteroids) (Table 3.3). Common features include problematic asthma or cystic fibrosis, central bronchiectasis and evidence of episodes of pulmonary obstruction or pneumonia on chest X-ray.

Table 3.3 Criteria for the diagnosis of ABPA and SAFS compared

Criterion	ABPA	SAFS
Asthma?	Usually	Always
Cystic fibrosis?	In some cases	No (not studied)
Mucus plugs	Often	No
Eosinophilia	Usually	Often
Aspergillus fumigatus sputum culture positive	Usually	Rare
Total serum IgE	Always >500, usually >1000 IU/l	<1000 IU/l
A. fumigatus precipitins (IgG) detectable	Usually	Sometimes
A. fumigatus RAST test or SPT positive	Almost always	Common
C. herbarum RAST or SPT positive	Occasional	Common
C. albicans RAST or SPT positive	Occasional	Common
A. alternata RAST or SPT positive	Occasional	Common
P. chrysogenum RAST or SPT positive	Occasional	Common
Trichophyton spp. RAST or SPT positive	Occasional	Common

Pathogenesis and genetics

ABPA develops as a result of an aberrant Th2-type response to *A. fumigatus* [9]. It is marked by remarkable sensitization to certain allergens of *A. fumigatus*. Development of allergy to *A. fumigatus* depends on the mode and frequency of exposure and typically occurs in combination with other aeroallergens. In susceptible atopic individuals fungal spores and hyphal fragments lead to the production of specific IgE. Exposure to allergens of *A. fumigatus* triggers an IgE and/or eosinophil-mediated allergic inflammatory response in the bronchi.

Various human leukocyte antigen (HLA) Class II genotypes confer either susceptibility of protection from ABPA, including DQ2 being protective. Several single nucleotide gene polymorphisms confer increased risk including being a cystic fibrosis carrier, higher interleukin (IL)-10, IL-13, IL-15 and IL-4 activity (via an alteration in IL-4 receptors), low tumour necrosis factor alpha (TNFα) production and a defect in surfactant A2 function but not mannose binding protein activity [11,12].

Treatment and outcome

Exacerbations of ABPA are best treated with a course of oral steroids such as 10 days of 40 mg prednisolone or prednisone. Aside from treating asthma itself, it is now absolutely clear that many patients derive benefit from itraconazole treatment (200 mg twice daily initially) [13,14]. Therapeutic drug monitoring is advised for itraconazole to optimize exposure to itraconazole, which may require switching between capsules and oral solution, and sometimes raising or lowering the dose. Productive patients appear to benefit most, perhaps because there is a reduction in mucus production with the reduction in immune stimulation. There may be an apparent deterioration in the first week or two of therapy, as large amounts of mucus are coughed up, with subsequent improvement. The duration of itraconazole therapy is not clear, but should not be less than 6 months, in those who tolerate it, and may be extended safely, with benefit, for years.

Some patients have such thick tenacious mucus plugs that therapeutic bronchoscopy may be required. Physiotherapy is also of value. In patients with persistent symptoms, despite itraconazole therapy, nebulized hypertonic saline (5 ml 7% NaCl once or twice daily after challenge to ensure they don't get significant bronchospasm) may be of value.

In cystic fibrosis patients the impact of antifungal therapy is generally less marked [9]. Absorption of itraconazole is highly variable from one patient to another, and often itraconazole oral solution is better. Sufficient serum concentrations do not predict adequate sputum concentrations. If the response is poor, usage of an alternative agent such as voriconazole may be appropriate. Voriconazole also has variable kinetics and it is wise to monitor concentrations to ensure adequate exposure, at least in blood.

Bronchiectasis is a common sequel of ABPA. Sometimes patients do better with long-term macrolide treatment (i.e. azithromycin), if they are highly symptomatic, but this should not be used lightly, and should be started with 'cleaned out airways' after alternative antibiotics to prevent immediate acquisition of organisms with macrolide resistance.

Some patients with ABPA develop chronic cavitary pulmonary aspergillosis [15]. These patients should be managed with long-term antifungal therapy. Others get pulmonary fibrosis, but the precise frequency and cause of this complication is not clear.

Severe asthma with fungal sensitisation

Asthma is common affecting ~7% of the US population (~17.5 m) and a proportional number in the UK (~5 m). Most asthma patients have sufficient respiratory symptoms to limit their activities and are dissatisfied with their lifestyles, indicating that they feel that their disease is not treated very effectively. Probably about 20% of asthmatics suffer from severe asthma, and roughly 50% of these patients are at the very severe end of the spectrum, utilizing about 70% of the total resource expended on asthma. Worldwide, it is estimated that ~100 000 people die of asthma annually, especially in high-risk inner city populations. Many of the worst affected are also sensitized to fungi |16,17|, and so the term severe asthma with fungal sensitization (SAFS) was introduced to describe this particular phenotype of severe asthma |18|. A case of SAFS is defined by:

- Severe asthma (i.e. British Thoracic Society step 4 or worse) |18|.
- Exclusion of ABPA (i.e. total IgE <1000 IU/ml).
- Evidence of sensitization to one or more fungi, by skin prick test or RAST test.

By utilizing this terminology, both improved diagnostics and directed treatment become possible, although the concept and diagnostic criteria could change as more is understood. Based on limited epidemiological work, around 4–8% of adult asthmatics have SAFS.

Clinical features

Patients with SAFS have troublesome asthma. All described patients are adults and may be male or female, with a mean age at diagnosis of ~50 years with a wide spectrum. Their pulmonary function measured by forced expiratory volume in one second (FEV_1) or peak flow varies from 20–120% predicted, depending on how well their disease is controlled. Many have significant nasal symptoms with runny nose, sneezing and hay fever-like symptoms. They do not produce plugs of sputum, as ABPA patients do, although CT scans may show some mucus in airways. Eosinophilia is common. Most are completely dependent on high-dose inhaled corticosteroids, with intermittent courses of oral steroids required for exacerbations, and some are on continuous oral steroids.

Persistent asthma typically leads to deterioration in pulmonary function over time often characterized as chronic obstructive pulmonary disease.

Diagnosis

Patients with SAFS have severe asthma as defined by the British Thoracic Society |19| and evidence of sensitization to one or more fungi. Sensitization can be determined with SPT or RAST tests (Table 3.3). While some patients are sensitized to many fungi, the majority only react to one or two fungi. The commonest fungi that patients are sensitized to are *A. fumigatus* and *C. albicans*, with *A. alternata*, *Trichopyton* spp., *C. herbarum*, *P. chrysogenum* and *B. cinerea*. SPT results are often not concordant with RAST results. RAST titres (to *A. fumigatus*) are much lower than titres in patients with ABPA. Patients have total serum IgE values below 1000 IU/ml, and often close to or in the normal range. Some patients (~25%) have weakly positive *A. fumigatus* IgG antibody titres or precipitins detectable.

Pathogenesis and genetics

Sensitization and/or exposure to mould allergens are clearly associated with asthma severity [16–18]. For example, a recent cross-sectional study published in the *British Medical Journal* in 2002 of 1132 adults with asthma found that sensitization to *Alternaria* spp. or *Cladosporium* spp. is strongly associated with severe asthma (odds ratio of 3.2 for *Cladosporium*) in Europe and Australia, New Zealand and in Oregon, USA [20]. No such association was found for pollens or cats. Eight published studies showed that fungal sensitivity is associated with increased asthma severity, hospital admission and intensive care admissions in adults and with increased bronchial reactivity in children [18]. Skin reactivity to fungal allergens such as *Alternaria* spp. has been reported to be especially common in patients with life-threatening asthma.

High fungal spore concentrations in outdoor air are associated with admission to hospital and asthma severity. There is a strong temporal relationship between high environmental spore counts and asthmatic attacks. For example, asthma deaths, emergency room attendance, hospital admission rates, and wheezing and cough are more likely to occur on days when local mould spore counts are high, in both adults and children. Asthma deaths and admissions in young adults and children in the UK coincide with the summer–autumn peak of ambient mould spores.

In addition to outside air exposure, considerable evidence supports an association between asthma severity and indoor mould exposure. Respiratory symptoms are more commonly reported in damp and/or mouldy houses. Numerous population-based studies have reported one or more positive associations between indoor fungal exposure levels and health outcomes. There are weak associations between measured dampness and respiratory symptoms. A Scottish study reported that asthmatic patients were more than twice as likely as control patients to live in a house that was considered damp or mouldy by a building surveyor. Rising indoor exposure to *Cladosporium* significantly increased the risk of an asthma attack. All these features are consistent with asthma severity being determined partly by continuous, or intermittent exposure to airborne fungi.

Treatment and outcome

Patients with SAFS are highly experienced asthmatic patients, usually on multiple medications. Long-term inhaled and frequent courses of oral corticosteroids usually control patients' worst symptoms, but at the long-term cost of well-known adverse events. These patients are usually already taking short- or long-acting beta 2 agonists, with some benefit. Many are also taking leukotriene antagonists. Antifungal therapy with itraconazole (200 mg twice daily) is beneficial in having a major effect on pulmonary and nasal symptoms [21]. Therapeutic drug monitoring is advised for itraconazole to optimize exposure to itraconazole, which may require switching between capsules and oral solution, and sometimes raising or lowering the dose. Fluconazole may be beneficial in those sensitized to *Trichophyton* spp. |22|. The duration of antifungal therapy is uncertain. Omalizumab, anti-IgE therapy, has not been studied in SAFS specifically.

Thunderstorm asthma

There is also an association between high spore counts, thunderstorms and severe asthma attacks, so called 'thunderstorm asthma', first noted in 1985 |23|. The hypothesis is that increased humidity coupled with high winds triggers increased spore release and dissemination. Some outbreaks have implicated grass pollen, but not measured fungal spores. However, several allergens are common to fungi and grasses, so it could be a mutually synergistic effect. Several fungi have been implicated including *Didymella exitialis, Sporobolomyces* and *Alternaria* |24|. No long-term follow-up on affected patients has been reported to indicate what action to take or the outcome after the acute attack is over. Only conventional therapy has been used in these episodes, not antifungal therapy, presumably because there is no immediate means of establishing the diagnosis with certainty.

Occupational asthma and extrinsic allergic alveolitis caused by fungi

Numerous examples of extrinsic allergic alveolitis (EAA) (hypersensitivity pneumonitis or more correctly bronchioloalveolitis) |25,26| caused by fungi are described (Table 3.4). While most cases of EAA are related to bacterial exposure, some other occupational pulmonary problems such as 'grain fever' or 'organic dust syndrome' have a fungal component to them. A 'pure' cause and effect relationship with any specific agent can be difficult to define. Whilst the occupational causes of the EAA are many and varied, there are a few reports of occupational asthma caused by fungi, and unusual environmental fungi at that. Occupational asthma is under-diagnosed and any (fungal) exposure is often obscure, suggesting that these few examples represent a more common problem than is realized. A well-documented example includes an outbreak among workers producing citric acid from *Aspergillus niger* in which many of the symptomatic workers had skin-prick positivity to *Aspergillus* |27|. Other case examples include:

● Asthma in a mushroom worker with no evidence of alveolitis, but with immunological (IgE and IgG) reactivity to the spores of *Pleurotus cornucopiae*.
● Occupational asthma confirmed in 2 women working in condom manufacture where *Lycopodium clavatum* was used as a dusting agent.
● A research microbiologist developed occupational asthma with specific IgE antibodies, while working with the slime mould, *Dictyostelium discoideum*.

Table 3.4 Well-described allergic extrinsic bronchioloalveolitis caused by fungi

Disease name	Fungus implicated	Process
Farmer's lung	*Penicillium brevicompactum/ olivicolor*	Turning or storing damp hay, opening bales for feeding livestock, threshing mouldy grain
Mushroom worker's lung	*Agaricus bisporus, Pleurotus osteatus, Lentinus edodes*	Exposure in spawning sheds
Malt worker's lung	*Aspergillus clavatus*	Handling grain
Suberosis	*Penicillium frequentans*	Storage of hot damp cork
Maple bark stripper's lung	*Cryptospora corticale*	Stripping bark from logs
Sequoiosis	*Aureobasidium pullulans*	Damp saw mill dust
Wood pulp worker's lung	*Alternaria* species	Pulping contaminated wood
Wine grower's lung	*Botrytis cinerea*	Mould contamination
Cheese worker's lung	*Penicillium casei/roqueforte*	Cleaning mould off cheese
Tobacco worker's lung	*Aspergillus fumigatus*	Handling contaminated tobacco

- A coal miner in a mine contaminated with *Rhizopus nigricans* developed occupational asthma with specific IgE antibodies to the organism.
- A plywood factory worker whose case was confirmed by specific challenge to a *Neurospora* species, which was isolated in the air. The individual was IgE RAST positive and skin positive to this organism.
- An orchid grower developed sensitivity to *Cryptostroma corticale*, found in the wood chips used in cultivating the orchids.

There are no data published as to whether antifungal therapy is of any value for either EAA or occupational asthma related to fungi. Generally avoidance is recommended, but for some patients this has significant economic consequences.

Conclusion

There are considerable data indicating that particular genetic factors provide the seedbed for disease related to fungal exposure, which is especially true for ABPA. Different genetic factors are likely to be contributory for SAFS, EAA and other disease entities related to fungal exposure. Numerous fungi are implicated, suggesting that some common allergens may be implicated, although certain individuals may be sensitized to only one fungus or allergen. Current diagnostic approaches are fairly crude and narrow in scope, especially as patients with SAFS may have relatively normal total IgE concentrations, and negative RAST or negative SPT tests. The role of antifungal therapy, as a component of the total care package delivered, requires further study, but data showing considerable improvement are convincing for ABPA and SAFS.

References

1. Lass-Flörl C, Salzer GM, Schmid T, *et al.* Pulmonary Aspergillus colonization in humans and its impact on management of critically ill patients. *Br J Haematol* 1999; **104**(4): 745–7.

2. Ponikau JU, Sherris DA, Kern EB, *et al.* The diagnosis and incidence of allergic fungal sinusitis. *Mayo Clin Proc* 1999; **74**(9): 877–84.

3. Hope WW, Walsh TJ, Denning DW. The invasive and saprophytic syndromes due to *Aspergillus* spp. *Med Mycol* 2005; **43**(Suppl 1): S207–38.

4. Denning DW. Invasive aspergillosis. *Clin Infect Dis* 1998; **26**: 781–805.

5. Bowyer P, Fraczek M, Denning DW. A comparative genomic analysis of fungal allergens reveals the presence of multiple cross reactive proteins. *BMC Genomics* 2006; **7**: 251.

6. Nierman W, Pain A, Anderson MJ, *et al.* Genomic sequence of the pathogenic and allergenic filamentous fungus *Aspergillus fumigatus*. *Nature* 2005; **438**: 1151–6.

7. Donnelly S, Dalton JP, Loukas A. Proteases in helminth- and allergen- induced inflammatory responses. *Chem Immunol Allergy* 2006; **90**: 45–64.

8. Virnig C, Bush RK. Allergic bronchopulmonary aspergillosis: a US perspective. *Curr Opin Pulm Med* 2007; **13**(1): 67–71.

9. Stevens DA, Moss RB, Kurup VP, *et al.* Allergic bronchopulmonary aspergillosis in cystic fibrosis—state of the art: Cystic Fibrosis Foundation Consensus Conference. *Clin Infect Dis* 2003; **37**(Suppl 3): S225–64.

10. Donnelly SC, McLaughlin H, Bredin CP. Period prevalence of allergic bronchopulmonary mycosis in a regional hospital outpatient population in Ireland 1985–88. *Ir J Med Sci* 1991; **160**(9): 288–90.

11. Knutsen AP. Genetic and respiratory tract risk factors for aspergillosis: ABPA and asthma with fungal sensitization. *Med Mycol* 2006; **44**(Suppl): 61–70.

12. Sambatakou H, Pravica V, Hutchinson I, Denning DW. Cytokine profiling of pulmonary aspergillosis. *Int J Immunogenetics* 2006; **33**: 297–302.

13. Stevens DA, Schwartz HJ, Lee JY, *et al.* A randomized trial of itraconazole in allergic bronchopulmonary aspergillosis. *N Engl J Med* 2000; **11**: 756–62.

14. Wark PA, Hensley MJ, Saltos N, *et al.* Anti-inflammatory effect of itraconazole in stable allergic bronchopulmonary aspergillosis: a randomized controlled trial. *J Allergy Clin Immunol* 2003; **111**: 952–7.

15. Denning DW, Riniotis K, Dobrashian R, Sambatakou H. Chronic cavitary and fibrosing pulmonary and pleural aspergillosis: Case series, proposed nomenclature and review. *Clin Infect Dis* 2003; **37**(Suppl 3): S265–80.

16. Kauffman HF, van der Heide S. Exposure, sensitization, and mechanisms of fungus-induced asthma. *Curr Allergy Asthma Rep* 2003; **3**(5): 430–7.

17. O'Driscoll BR, Hopkinson LC, Denning DW. Mould sensitisation is common amongst patients with severe asthma requiring multiple hospital admissions in North West England. *BMC Pulmonary Medicine* 2005; **5**: 4.

18. Denning DW, O'Driscoll BR, Hogaboam CM, *et al.* The link between fungi and asthma – a summary of the evidence. *Eur Resp Journal* 2006; **27**: 615–26.

19. http://www.brit-thoracic.org.uk/asthma-guideline-download.html

20. Zureik M, Neukirch C, Leynaert B, *et al.* Sensitisation to airborne moulds and severity of asthma: cross sectional study from European Community respiratory health survey. *Br Med J* 2002; **325**: 411–15.

21. Denning DW, O'Driscoll BR, Powell G, *et al.* Randomized controlled trial of oral antifungal treatment for severe asthma with fungal sensitisation (SAFS), the FAST study. *Am J Respir Crit Care Med* 2008. In press.

22. Ward GW Jr, Woodfolk JA, Hayden ML, *et al.* Treatment of late-onset asthma with fluconazole. *J Allergy Clin Immunol* 1999; **104**: 541–6.

23. Packe GE, Ayres JG. Asthma outbreak during a thunderstorm. *Lancet* 1985; **2**: 199–204.

24. Dales RE, Cakmak S, Judek S, *et al.* The role of fungal spores in thunderstorm asthma. *Chest* 2003; **123**(3): 745–50.

25. Jacobs RL, Andrews CP, Coalson JJ. Hypersensitivity pneumonitis: beyond classic occupational disease-changing concepts of diagnosis and management. *Ann Allergy Asthma Immunol* 2005; **95**(2): 115–28.

26. Fink JN, Ortega HG, Reynolds HY, *et al.* Needs and opportunities for research in hypersensitivity pneumonitis. *Am J Respir Crit Care Med* 2005; **171**(7): 792–8.

27. Topping MD, Scarisbrick DA, Luczynska CM, *et al.* Clinical and immunological reactions to *Aspergillus niger* among workers at a biotechnology plant. *Br J Ind Med* 1985; **42**(5): 312–18.

Additional information and images

www.aspergillus.org.uk
www.doctorfungus.org

Managing rhinitis

GLENIS SCADDING

KEY POINTS

1. Rhinitis is often the first manifestation of allergy in the teenager or young adult.

2. Rhinitis is classified into mild or moderate to severe depending on whether the symptoms interfere with quality of life, and into intermittent or persistent depending on the time course.

3. Allergic rhinitis is much more that sneezing, rhinorrhoea and nasal obstruction; it is associated with poor quality sleep, problems with academic performance and behaviour, and a detrimental effect on examination performance in teenagers.

4. The diagnosis of allergic rhinitis is based upon a typical history of allergic symptoms and diagnostic tests that demonstrate the presence of allergen-specific IgE.

5. The majority of asthmatic patients have rhinitis; the presence of allergic rhinitis in such patients may exacerbate asthma, and appropriate treatment of rhinitis may facilitate better asthma control.

Introduction

Our noses are the gatekeepers of our airways. The nose is responsible for filtering, warming and humidifying 10 000 litres of air daily. Nasal functions also include olfaction and immune defence. The adjacent sinuses are probably needed for skull lightening, vocal resonance and production of nitric oxide at microbicidal levels.

Rhinitis is frequently disregarded by clinicians. This is a mistake since not only are the symptoms of running, blocking, itching and sneezing of importance to many patients, they can sometimes be so severe as to prevent normal work or school attendance. Quality of life is considerably reduced by rhinitis, even more so by rhinosinusitis, which has effects comparable to those of angina or severe arthritis [1].

Rhinitis is often the first manifestation of allergy in the teenager or young adult. This may progress to persistent symptoms with resultant nasal congestion which impacts on adjacent structures such as the sinuses, throat, middle ear and lower respiratory tract [2]. Rhinitis, both allergic and non-allergic is a risk factor for the development of asthma with an odds ratio of 3 [3]. It is also implicated in otitis media with effusion in childhood [4] and in sinusitis [5], which should rightly be termed rhinosinusitis since sinus inflammation occurring other than via the nose is a rarity. More recently there has been recognition that rhinitis results in poor quality sleep and in consequent problems with academic performance and behaviour [6].

Therefore it is worth taking rhinitis seriously and managing it well. This demands close co-operation with the patient and, if the patient is a child, their parents or carers.

Recently, synergy has been demonstrated between allergy and infection in children with asthma. Asthmatic children who get a rhinoviral cold are 20 times more likely to be hospitalized if they are allergic and exposed to their relevant allergen [7]. This phenomenon is probably also operative in otitis media with effusion and rhinosinusitis. Allergic children have been shown to have more infections and more problems with those infections. Adequate treatment of the underlying allergic disease helps to diminish these problems.

Is it rhinitis?

The clinical definition of rhinitis is of nasal running, sneezing and itching and blocking. The Allergic Rhinitis and its Impact on Asthma (ARIA) guidelines [8] classify rhinitis into mild or moderate to severe depending on whether these symptoms interfere with quality of life and into intermittent or persistent depending on the time course (Table 4.1).

Table 4.1 Classification of allergic rhinitis according to ARIA (with permission from [8])
1. 'Intermittent' means that the symptoms are present
<4 days a week
Or for <4 consecutive weeks
2. 'Persistent' means that the symptoms are present
More than 4 days a week
And for >4 consecutive weeks
3. 'Mild' means that none of the following items are present:
Sleep disturbance
Impairment of daily activities, leisure and/or sport
Impairment of school or work
Symptoms present but not troublesome
4. 'Moderate/severe' means that one or more of the following items are present:
Sleep disturbance
Impairment of daily activities, leisure and/or sport
Impairment of school or work
Troublesome symptoms

Rhinitis has several underlying causes, which can be grouped into three categories—allergic, infective and other |8|. Allergic rhinitis is remarkably common affecting some 25% of the population. In children, recurrent viral colds are the major differential diagnosis. These are not usually accompanied by significant itching or conjunctivitis. Other less common differential diagnoses are primary ciliary dyskinesia |9| (which involves continual unremitting rhinorrhoea present since birth, usually together with a wet cough) and, in adults, cerebrospinal fluid (CSF) rhinorrhoea which is predominantly unilateral, increases on bending forwards and in which condition nasal fluid tests positive for beta transferrin. Nasal obstruction in children can be caused by structural problems such as choanal atresia, encephalocoeles and meningocoeles or by nasal polyps, which should elicit tests for cystic fibrosis |10|.

The diagnosis of an allergic form of rhinitis rests on taking an adequate detailed history and supplementing this by examination and, if necessary, specific allergy tests.

History

The history should include the areas noted in Table 4.2. The timing of symptoms in relation to possible allergen exposure is of primary relevance. A questionnaire is helpful in that it allows the patient and family to focus their attention on the disorder and possible causes.

Table 4.2 Allergic triggers for rhinitis

Trigger types	Origin/specific example of trigger	Type of rhinitis caused
Mites	House dust mite, storage mite allergen in mite faecal pellets	Main causes of perennial rhinitis
Pollens	Trees, grasses, shrubs, weeds	Main causes of seasonal rhinitis Cross-reactivity among pollens
Animals	Cats, dogs, horses	Allergen in sebaceous glands and saliva
	Mice, rats	Allergen mainly in urine
Moulds	*Cladosporium, Alternaria, Aspergillus*	Seasonal and/or perennial symptoms
Occupation-induced	Flour, latex, laboratory animals, wood dust, enzymes, other airborne proteins	Reversible with early diagnosis and avoidance but becomes chronic and irreversible if the exposure is prolonged
		May progress to asthma. Diagnosis based on symptom diary cards and provocation tests
Occupation-aggravated	Smoke, cold air, formaldehyde, sulphur dioxide, ammonia, glues, solvents etc	Pre-existing rhinitis can be aggravated by work-place irritants

Nasal and palatal itch together with sneezing suggest an allergic cause. If this is seasonal then pollens or mould spores are likely causes, if occurring mainly at home then house dust mite, pets or mould could be causative. Symptoms occurring at work usually relate to occupational allergens such as latex, wheat flour, animal allergens etc. Remission of these symptoms on holiday suggests an environmental cause.

Rhinorrhoea can be anterior or can occur predominantly into the nasopharynx as a post-nasal drip. If clear then infection is unlikely. Thick yellow secretions can be caused by allergy with eosinophilic infiltration and do not necessarily represent infection. When secretions are green there are usually neutrophils involved and an underlying infection is likely, although this may be complicating an allergic diaphysis. Blood stained secretions if unilateral should suggest ENT referral for investigation of tumour or possibly foreign body, these can however also be caused by misapplication of nasal sprays on to the septum or nose picking. Severe bilateral crusting and bleeding suggests an underlying granulomatous disorder or bleeding diathesis, cocaine use or extensive nasal picking.

Nasal obstruction, if unilateral, is often related to septal deviation but can also be caused by foreign bodies, especially in childhood, antrochoanal polyps and various tumours. Unilateral choanal atresia can also occur. Bilateral obstruction is most likely due to nasal polyposis or significant rhinitis. Obstruction that alternates from nostril to nostril over several hours occurs when a degree of nasal congestion reveals the normal nasal cycle.

Olfaction is important as the original brain was a smell brain and there is still remarkable radiation of impulses from the olfactory receptors around the brain, particularly to the limbic areas, which relate to memory. Hyposmia can occur with almost any form of rhinitis. Complete persistent anosmia has multiple other causes including anterior cranial fossa tumours and endocrine dysfunction. Patients should be referred for investigation. Hyposmia may also be the initial presentation of neurodegenerative diseases such as Parkinson's disease or Alzheimer's dementia.

Pain alone is almost never due to allergy or to any form of rhinosinusitis. It can, if accompanied by discharge and poor sense of smell accompany an infective rhinosinusitis. Bilateral symmetrical symptoms of pressure around the nasal bridge without any other symptoms are regarded as mid-facial segment pain and are a version of tension headache [11].

Conjunctivitis usually occurs in association with seasonal allergic rhinitis, but can be a feature of perennial rhinitis.

Concomitant symptoms from other areas of the respiratory tract should be sought. These include snoring, sleep problems, vocal difficulties, hearing problems. Some patients may reveal food reactions to fresh fruits and vegetables in association with seasonal allergic rhinitis. This is the oral allergy syndrome and is caused by ingestion of food antigens that cross-react with those of pollen. The foods are often tolerated if cooked, since a major cross-reacting allergen (profiling) is heat labile [12].

Disorders of the lower respiratory tract are common in patients with rhinitis, especially in those with more severe rhinosinusitis. A history of cough, wheeze, shortness of breath, sputum production and haemoptysis should therefore be sought.

A family history of atopy, seasonal rhinitis or asthma makes a diagnosis of allergic rhinitis more likely.

A detailed social history is needed to look for possible allergens. Inhalant allergens are frequently involved, but food ones rarely. Exceptions are the oral allergy related ones, gustatory rhinitis which is probably neurological rather than allergic, non-IgE mediated symptom exacerbation by aspirin–related foodstuffs such as preservatives, E numbers, alcohol, spices, herbs and dried fruit and in small children with skin and /or gut allergies IgE mediated reactions to milk, eggs, soya etc.

A drug history should be taken looking both for drugs as a cause of rhinitis (alpha blockers, other antihypertensives, overuse of topical sympathomimetics, aspirin, non-steroidal anti-inflammatory drugs [NSAIDs]) and also for rhinitis therapies which have been tried. It is important to ask how these were used and for how long since many patients will have tried a nasal spray briefly and ineptly.

Examination

A brief external visual assessment may provide clues to the diagnosis of rhinitis. A horizontal crease (allergic crease) is produced by constant rubbing of the nose (the allergic salute), which may itself be seen. Other significant abnormalities include the widened nasal bridge due to polyposis, depression of the nasal bridge, which can occur post-operatively or be caused by Wegener's granulomatosis or misuse of cocaine. A purple tip to the nose is seen in sarcoidosis (lupus pernio). The facies may be those of hypothyroidism, which is a cause of nasal obstruction.

Internal nasal examination can be achieved with a head mirror and Thudichum's speculum, but is more simply done with an otoscope. In specialist clinics the nasendoscope is more likely to be used and gives better quality information especially at middle turbinate level. Chest physicians may use fibre optic bronchoscopes via the nose and these can provide adequate nasal information.

The turbinate appearance should be noted. These may be hypertrophied, pale and wet in allergy. Any secretions present, plus their colour and consistency should be described together with the presence of any nasal polyps. Large polyps can be distinguished from inferior turbinate by their lack of sensitivity, yellowish grey colour and the fact that it is possible to separate them from the sidewall of the nose. Any deviation of the septum can contribute to obstruction, particularly as there is often compensatory hypertrophy of the opposite turbinate.

Crusting and granulations raise the possibility of a granulomatous disease such as Wegener's or sarcoidosis. A septal perforation is most commonly caused by previous surgery but can be due to regular use of vasoconstrictors such as cocaine or a vasculitis. Extensive nose picking and possible steroid sprays are much rarer causes.

Tests

Skin prick tests should be carried out routinely to determine if the rhinitis is allergic or non-allergic. These need interpretation in the light of the clinical history, since some 15% of people with positive skin prick tests do not develop symptoms on exposure to the relevant allergens. They are however sensitized, and are at risk of doing so at some point in the future. Skin prick tests have a high negative predictive

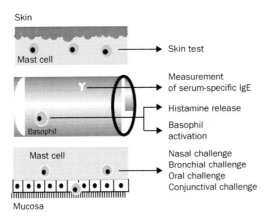

Fig. 4.1 Diagnosis of IgE-mediated allergy (with permission from |8|).

value. Care must be taken if the patient has been taking antihistamines, tricyclic antidepressants or topical corticosteroids all of which can suppress the skin prick test results. Care must also be taken in patients with a history of anaphylaxis, and skin prick tests in such patients are inadvisable outside specialist clinics |13|.

Specific IgE in serum may be requested if skin tests are not possible or when skin tests together with a history give equivocal results. Skin prick tests are more sensitive to inhalants such as cat, mould and grass pollen. Currently available skin prick tests and immunoassays show similar sensitivity to house dust mite.

Other tests may be necessary in order to establish a putative diagnosis or to assess the patency of the nasal airway.

The tests used to diagnose IgE-mediated allergy are outlined in Figure 4.1 (for further details, see Chapter 1).

Treatment of rhinitis

Figure 4.2 shows an algorithm for the treatment of allergic rhinitis. Grades of recommendations of various interventions are given in Table 4.3.

Education

In any chronic disorder where the patient needs to take prolonged measures and therapy, adequate education about the disease itself, the measures to be taken, the nature, mode of application and safety of the treatment is vital in order to achieve concordance. Standardized allergy education has been shown to improve disease-specific quality of life. It is also important to educate patients about the possible complications and comorbid associations of rhinitis together with their recognition and possible treatments.

Allergen avoidance

If adequate, then this is remarkably effective: hay fever patients are not symptomatic outside the hay fever season. Avoidance has shown clear benefit in domestic pet,

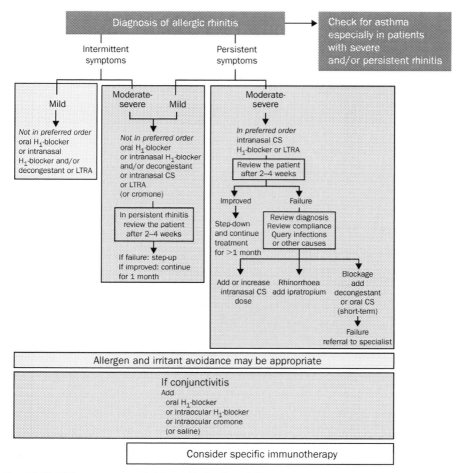

Fig. 4.2 Rhinitis management (with permission from |8|).

horse, laboratory animals and latex allergy. Trials of house dust mite avoidance have proved negative |14,15|; however, no high quality trial has used a variety of measures to reduce all domestic allergens (for details, see Chapter 14). A recent brief open study using carpet removal, decluttering, pet removal and extensive superheated steam cleaning followed by repeated domestic cleaning showed significant improvement in 10 children with allergic rhinitis and asthma over 2 months. A properly controlled prospective trial is needed. Nasal air filters have been shown to be useful in seasonal allergic rhinitis, but increase nasal obstruction and can be uncomfortable.

Irritant avoidance

Many rhinitic patients exhibit nasal (and bronchial) hyperreactivity to irritants such as smoke, perfume, dust, pollutants and temperature change. Avoidance of these is likely to cause a reduction in symptoms.

Table 4.3 Level of evidence for different interventions in allergic rhinitis (with permission from [8])

Intervention	Seasonal rhinitis		Perennial rhinitis (mostly applies for studies ≤4 weeks)*		Persistent rhinitis[†]
	Adults	**Children**	**Adults**	**Children**	
H₁-antihistamine					
Oral	A	A	A	A	A
Intranasal	A	A	A	A	No data
Intraocular	A	A	B	B	No data
Glucocorticosteroid					
Intranasal	A	A	A	A	No data
Oral	A	B	B	B	No data
IM	A	B	B	B	No data
Cromones					
Intranasal	A	A	A	B	No data
Intraocular	A	A	B	B	No data
NAAGA (topical)	B	C	C	C	No data
Antileukotriene	A	A over 6 years			No data
Decongestant					
Intranasal	C	C	C	C	No data
Oral	A				No data
Oral + H₁-antihistamine	A	B	B	B	No data
Anticholinergic			A	A	No data
Homeopathy	D	D	D	D	No data
Acupuncture	D	D	D	D	No data
Phytotherapy	B	D	D	D	No data
Other CAM	D	D	D	D	No data
Specific immunotherapy: rhinoconjunctivitis					
Subcutaneous	A	A	A	A	No data
Sublingual‡	A	A	A	A	No data
Intranasal‡	A				No data
Specific immunotherapy: asthma					
Subcutaneous	A	A	A	A	
Sublingual‡	A	A	A	A	
Anti-IgE	A	A over 12 years	A	A over 12 years	No data

Intervention	Seasonal rhinitis		Perennial rhinitis (mostly applies for studies ≤4 weeks)*		Persistent rhinitis†
	Adults	Children	Adults	Children	
Allergen avoidance					
House dust mites	D	D	D	D	No data
Other indoor allergens	D	D	D	D	No data
Total avoidance of occupational agent			A (for asthma)		No data
Partial avoidance of latex			B		No data

* Very few studies longer than 4 weeks.

† Applies to treatments only carried out in studies with persistent rhinitis.

‡ Applies to high-dose treatment.

Nasal douching

A recent review suggests that douching is effective in rhinitis and rhinosinusitis |16|. It reduces symptoms in children and adults with seasonal rhinitis and is safe and inexpensive. Isotonic saline solutions are usually used. Hypertonic solutions can disrupt thick mucus more effectively but are more irritating to the nasal mucosa. Nasal douching may also be helpful in primary ciliary dyskinesia.

Topical corticosteroids

Topical corticosteroids are the treatment of choice for anything more than mild rhinitis and have been shown by meta-analysis to be superior to antihistamines in controlling rhinitis symptoms |17|. They act by suppressing inflammation at multiple points in the inflammatory cascade. They reduce rhinitis symptoms by about 50% with a variable effect on associated allergic conjunctivitis. They are effective both in allergic and some forms of non-allergic rhinitis.

Patients need to be warned that the clinical effects may not be apparent for several days and that regular repeated use is necessary. Treatment should be started some 2 weeks prior to a known allergen season as this delays the onset of symptoms and improves efficacy.

The first generation of topical corticosteroids (betamethasone, dexamethasone) are significantly absorbed and are not suitable for long-term use. There is moderate absorption from molecules such as beclomethasone and budesonide. The former has been shown to decrease childhood growth if used twice daily. Systemic absorption is negligible with mometasone and fluticasone both of which have been shown to be safe used once daily in children over a 1-year period |18,19|. Concomitant treatment with CYP3A inhibitors such as itraconazole or ritonavir may increase the systemic bioavailability of intranasal corticosteroids.

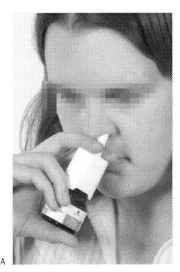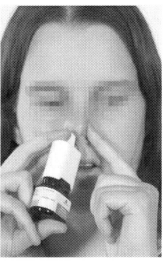

A   B

Fig. 4.3 Use of nasal sprays. A. Correct: the opposite hand is used to spray towards the lateral wall of the nose. The spray should *not* be sniffed hard back but should be allowed to remain in the nose where mucociliary clearance will spread it slowly over the lining and back towards the back of the throat over 10–20 minutes after which it is swallowed. B. Incorrect: using the ipsilateral hand and pushing the opposite side of the nose allows the spray to land on the nasal septum which is likely to become sore and may bleed.

Side-effects of local nasal irritation, sore throat and minor epistaxis occur in about 1 in 10 users. These can be minimised by correct use (Figure 4.3). Septal perforation is an extremely rare complication. Care is needed if patients with glaucoma are treated and eyeball pressure monitoring should be frequent and regular.

Nasal drops are preferable for nasal polyposis and probably also for chronic rhinosinusitis [20]. These are used in the 'head upside down position' in order to reach the osteomeatal complex at which the sinuses drain. Care should be taken in children who may be receiving corticosteroids at three sites: nose, lung and skin for rhinitis, asthma and eczema. Childhood growth, which is very sensitive to corticosteroids, should be monitored.

Systemic glucocorticosteroids

These are rarely indicated for rhinitis except if nasal obstruction is very severe or as short-term rescue for uncontrolled symptoms of seasonal rhinitis at important times. They should always be used briefly and in combination with a topical nasal corticosteroid. A suggested regime for adults is 0.5mg per kg orally in the morning with food for 5 days.

Injectable corticosteroids

These are not recommended, as the risk benefit profile is poor compared to other available treatments. Injection of the inferior turbinate with corticosteroid has resulted in blindness and is therefore not recommended.

Antihistamines

Antihistamines reduce total nasal symptom scores by a mean of 30% compared to placebo and are predominantly effective on neurally mediated symptoms such as itching, sneezing and running. They are useful alone in mild to moderate rhinitis and are also of benefit when added to topical corticosteroids in moderate to severe rhinitis, if steroids alone fail to control the symptoms.

Given orally they improve allergic symptoms at sites other than the nose, e.g. conjunctiva, palate, skin and lower airways.

A Cochrane meta-analysis shows that they cause a small improvement in nasal obstruction |21|. This may be more marked in the recent molecules (desloratadine, fexofenadine, cetirizine and levocetirizine).

Antihistamines, like topical nasal corticosteroids have been shown to significantly improve quality of life in rhinitis and to be cost-effective |22,23|.

Side-effects

First-generation antihistamines cause sedation and psychomotor retardation and are associated with a decrease in academic performance so are not suitable for rhinitis therapy |24,25|. Second-generation antihistamines are less sedating with fexofenadine having the least sedative effects. Terfenadine and astemizole were found to prolong the cardiac QT interval if higher doses were used or if hepatic metabolism was competitively inhibited by other drugs. The presently available second-generation antihistamines (acrivastine, cetirizine, desloratadine, fexofenadine, levocetirizine, loratadine, mizolastine) do not cause significant QT prolongation at normal therapeutic doses and do not have any major significant drug interactions. Some patients are hypersensitive to antihistamines and this is usually a problem with the whole class of drugs.

Topical nasal antihistamines

These have therapeutic effects similar, or slightly superior, to those of oral antihistamines in the nose but do not improve symptoms at other sites. They have the advantage of fast onset of action, usually within 15 min (the fastest oral antihistamine levocetirizine takes around 30 min). Topical antihistamines are therefore useful as rescue therapy but may also help in non-allergic rhinitis.

Side-effects

Local irritation and taste disturbances with azelastine are the major problems encountered. Their place in therapy is similar to that of the oral antihistamines.

Antileukotrienes

These are of two kinds, receptor antagonists (LTRAs, e.g. montelukast and zafirlukast) and synthesis inhibitors (e.g. zileuton). Around 50% of rhinitis patients respond to these drugs; however, this responsiveness is not easy to predict at present. Their therapeutic profile is similar to antihistamines, with an efficacy comparable to loratadine in seasonal allergic rhinitis |26|. They are less effective than topical nasal corticosteroids. The combination of antileukotriene plus antihistamine does not improve efficacy compared to either alone to an extent which is clinically relevant |27|. The combination is not superior to a topical corticosteroid alone |28|. At present their place is in patients with seasonal allergic rhinitis and asthma.

Side-effects

These drugs are usually well tolerated with occasional headaches, gastrointestinal symptoms or rashes at frequencies similar to that seen with placebo in clinical trials. There have been occasional reports of the Churg-Strauss Syndrome developing in patients treated with antileukotrienes. However this may relate to steroid withdrawal and further long-term evaluation is needed.

Antileukotrienes may also be useful in patients with asthma and persistent rhinitis or nasal polyposis |29|.

Anticholinergics

Ipratropium bromide decreases rhinorrhoea but has no effect on other nasal symptoms. It needs to be used three times a day. Regular use may be effective in predominant rhinorrhoea conditions, such as old man's drip, or as an add-on for allergic rhinitis when watery rhinorrhoea persists despite topical steroids and antihistamines |30|. It is also useful for autonomic rhinitis when the dominant symptom is profuse watery rhinorrhoea in response to irritants or temperature changes, and it has been shown to be useful in the common cold.

Side-effects

The major side-effects are dry nose and epistaxis. Systemic anticholinergic effects are unusual but urinary retention and glaucoma can occur and caution is advised in the elderly.

Intranasal decongestants

Alpha 1 agonists such as xylometazoline or ephedrine are sympathomimetics that increase nasal vasoconstriction and reduce obstruction in allergic and non-allergic rhinitis. They are used briefly in order to avoid rebound effects of rhinitis medicamentosa (less than 10 days is suggested) |31|. Their use is mainly for Eustachian tube dysfunction when flying, in children with acute otitis media to relieve middle ear pain and pressure, and following a cold to reduce nose and sinus congestion. They can be used at the start of topical nasal steroid therapy to increase nasal patency and allow the topical steroid sprays access to the nasal mucosa. However, it is difficult then to persuade patients to go on with the steroid spray rather than the decongestant spray. Combined therapy with a topical corticosteroid (Dexa-Rhinaspray Duo) is helpful in exacerbations of rhinosinusitis with nasal blockage.

Oral decongestants (pseudoephedrine)

Oral decongestants are weakly effective in reducing nasal obstruction, but do not cause rebound. They have significant side-effects of hypertension, insomnia, agitation and tachycardia and show interaction with antidepressants. For these reasons they are not generally recommended.

Sodium cromoglicate

Used as a nasal spray, sodium cromoglicate inhibits mast cell degranulation and is weakly effective in reducing nasal obstruction. It needs to be used three or four times daily but is generally very well tolerated. There are occasional reports of local irritation and transient bronchospasm or headache.

The place in therapy is mainly for children under four for whom topical intranasal corticosteroids are not available. It may also be useful where rhinitis symptoms are mild and intermittent prior to exposure to a known allergen.

Allergen immunotherapy

Allergen immunotherapy involves the repeated administration of an allergen extract in order to alter the nature of the immune response and reduce allergic symptoms (for details see Chapter 13). This is the only treatment that has been shown to modify the natural history of allergic rhinitis and to offer the potential for long-term disease remission |32|. Immunotherapy can be provided either by injection (subcutaneous immunotherapy, SCIT) or sublingually (SLIT).

SCIT

The quality of allergy and vaccines is important and only standardized extracts should be used. With injection immunotherapy an optimal maintenance dose of 5 to 20 μg of major allergen has been shown to correspond with clinical efficacy. Adverse events include pain and swelling at the site of injection, seen in the majority of patients; systemic reactions (particularly in patients with asthma) include urticaria, angio-oedema, asthma and anaphylaxis and occur in about 10% of injections. Chronic asthma is a contraindication in the UK.

For these reasons, SCIT should only be performed under the supervision of a physician fully trained in the management of allergic disease with immediate access to adrenaline and other resuscitative measures. Each patient needs to be observed for a minimum of 1 h following an immunotherapy injection.

At present in the UK, allergen injection immunotherapy is recommended in patients with IgE-mediated seasonal pollen-induced rhinitis whose symptoms do not respond adequately to pharmacotherapy used pre-seasonally and then regularly throughout the season. It may be considered in a few carefully selected patients with cat or house dust mite allergy.

The long-term benefits include reduction in progression of rhinitis to asthma and reduction of new sensitizations.

SLIT

A recent Cochrane meta-analysis |33| has shown that SLIT is a safe treatment that significantly reduces symptoms and medication requirements in allergic rhinitis. The size of benefit compared to injection immunotherapy is unclear at present. Recent studies with a grass pollen tablet demonstrate a 30% mean reduction in symptoms over the pollen season with a 38% mean reduction in medication requirements. The long-term benefits of sublingual immunotherapy have not yet been assessed in adults. Efficacy in children has recently been reported together with a reduction of seasonal asthmatic symptoms.

Other therapies

Anti-IgE

Anti-IgE is licensed only for severe asthma in patients over 12, but associated allergic rhinitis may benefit. Future use may include a combined treatment with immunotherapy in high-risk patients |34|.

Surgery

Surgery is rarely required in rhinitis, unless there is pharmacotherapy-resistant inferior turbinate hypertrophy, septal deviations with functional relevance or anatomical variations of the bony pyramid with functional or aesthetic relevance. Chronic rhinosinusitis unresponsive to medical therapy may respond to endoscopic sinus surgery. Certain forms of nasal polyposis (antrochoanal or solitary polyps) should be removed for histology. Bilateral allergic type nasal polyposis can be treated medically provided that an ENT surgeon has seen the patient and is happy with the diagnosis. However, from time to time, surgical removal may be necessary when polyps regrow and become resistant to medical treatment. Fungal sinus disease (mycotoma invasive forms allergic fungal sinusitis), are best treated surgically with an attempt to remove all fungal tissue |35|.

Special considerations

Rhinitis of pregnancy

Rhinitis occurs in one in five pregnancies, and can start at any time during the pregnancy. Nasal vascular engorgement secondary to placental growth hormone appears to be involved. Treatment is difficult, since most medications cross the placenta and the risk/benefit ratio should always be considered. Regular nasal douching is important and previously tried and tested drugs such as beclomethasone, fluticasone and budesonide, which are widely used in pregnant asthmatic women, and loratadine and cetirizine, which have been used for many years, are recommended. Cromones are the safest drug in the first three months of pregnancy. Patients started on immunotherapy prior to pregnancy may continue if they have reached the maintenance phase. Initiation and updosing are contraindicated.

Paediatric rhinitis |36|

Allergic rhinitis is common in childhood but differentiation needs to be made from other forms such as infective rhinitis and structural abnormalities. Selection of treatment needs to be considered in the context of the child's needs and response, and the child's and parent's wishes. Treatment options need to be thoroughly explained to both.

Antihistamines used once daily tend to be tolerated. Nasal steroids with the least systemic bioavailability (fluticasone and mometasone) should be used at the lowest possible dose to control symptoms. The child should be taught how to use the nasal spray. Use prior to cleaning the teeth each morning is helpful in ensuring that the spray is remembered and in that tooth-cleaning provides a displacement activity so that spray is not sniffed back quickly into the nasopharynx. Antileukotrienes may be helpful in children with concomitant asthma.

Nasal douching is simple and safe in children and may provide sufficient relief in mild seasonal rhinitis if used alone.

The rhinitis/asthma link |37|

Rhinitis and asthma are both common diseases and are associated with substantial costs both to patients, their employers and to healthcare systems. They frequently coexist, with rhinitis symptoms occurring in roughly 80% of patients with asthma. Medical care costs are higher in those patients with asthma and rhinitis compared to those with asthma alone.

Rhinitis, both allergic and non-allergic is a risk factor for the development of asthma. Allergic rhinitis increases non-specific bronchial hyper-reactivity during allergen exposure (both seasonal and perennial). Conversely, nasal reactivity to cold dry air is higher where rhinitis is associated with asthma compared to rhinitis alone. Bronchial responsiveness is also increased in viral rhinitis and following nasal allergen challenge. Bronchial hyper-reactivity is reversed by intranasal treatment with sodium cromoglicate, nedocromil sodium and with corticosteroids.

Biopsy studies have shown rhinitic changes in asthma patients without nasal symptoms. Eosinophil numbers correlate between the upper and lower respiratory tract.

A systemic link between the nose and bronchi has been demonstrated by local allergen challenge. Nasal allergen challenge increased bronchial inflammation and vice versa. This appears to be related to extravasation of immature eosinophils from the bone marrow, passage in the circulation and extravasation at the site of allergen exposure but also along the remainder of the respiratory tract.

Rhinosinusitis shows an even higher correlation with asthma |38|. In severe asthmatics, 84% of computed tomography (CT) scans are abnormal. The level of abnormality corresponds to eosinophil numbers in sputum and blood and to functional residual capacity. It correlates inversely with transfer factor.

These observations suggest that the respiratory tract responds and should be considered as one organ in asthma and rhinitis. Thus, as recommended by the ARIA guidelines, all asthmatics should be tested for rhinitis and treatment considered and vice versa.

Specific allergen immunotherapy for rhinitis may reduce the development of asthma in children, and reduces non-specific bronchial hyper-reactivity and seasonal asthma in adults with seasonal rhinoconjunctivitis |39,40|.

Patients with comorbid asthma and rhinitis receiving treatment for rhinitis have a significantly lower risk of attending accident and emergency departments and of hospitalizations for asthma |41–43|. A prospective study is awaited.

Rhinosinusitis

Isolated inflammation of the sinus linings rarely occurs, so rhinosinusitis is the preferred term. Symptoms under 12 weeks are regarded as acute, longer as chronic rhinosinusitis |44|. As with rhinitis, allergic, infective and other forms occur. Mixed forms can exist (e.g. allergic rhinosinusitis with superadded infection). Nasal polyposis is considered a form of rhinosinusitis (chronic polypoid rhinosinusitis) and can have an allergic, infective or non-allergic aetiology.

The major symptoms of rhinosinusitis are of nasal obstruction, discharge that is frequently posterior, together with facial pain or pressure and olfactory disturbance. To confirm the diagnosis, these symptoms need to be complemented by either endoscopic signs at the middle meatus: oedema and obstruction of the osteomeatal complex, polyps, mucopurulent discharge and/or changes at this complex or in the sinuses on computerized tomography |44|.

The diagnosis and treatment of this condition is dealt with in the European and American guidelines. In severe forms, the underlying pathogenesis is likely to involve aspirin hypersensitivity, allergic fungal sinusitis or antineutrophil cytoplasmic antibody (ANCA)-associated disease.

References

1. Laforest L, Bousquet J, Pietri G, et al. Quality of life during pollen season in patients with seasonal allergic rhinitis with or without asthma. *Int Arch Allergy Immunol* 2005; **136**: 281–6.

2. Bachert C, Vignola AM, Gevaert P, et al. Allergic rhinitis, rhinosinusitis, and asthma: one airway disease. *Immunol Allergy Clin North Am* 2004; **24**: 19–43.

3. Leynaert B, Bousquet J, Neukirch C, et al. Perennial rhinitis: An independent risk factor for asthma in nonatopic subjects: results from the European Community Respiratory Health Survey. *J Allergy Clin Immunol* 1999; **104**: 301–4.

4. Doyle WJ. The link between allergic rhinitis and otitis media. *Curr Opin Allergy Clin Immunol* 2002; **2**: 21–5.

5. Slavin RG. Complications of allergic rhinitis: implications for sinusitis and asthma. *J Allergy Clin Immunol* 1998; **101**: S357–60.

6. Blaiss MS. Allergic rhinitis and impairment issues in schoolchildren: a consensus report. *Curr Med Res Opin* 2004; **20**: 1937–52.

7. Murray CS, Simpson A, Custovic A. Allergens, viruses, and asthma exacerbations. *Proc Am Thorac Soc* 2004; **1**: 99–104.

8. Bousquet J, Khaltaev N, Cruz AA, et al. Allergic Rhinitis and its Impact on Asthma (ARIA) 2008 update (in collaboration with the World Health Organization, GA(2)LEN and AllerGen. *Allergy* 2008; **63**(Suppl 86): 8–160. PMID: 18331513.

9. Bush A. Primary ciliary dyskinesia. *Acta Otorhinolaryngol Belg* 2000; **54**: 317–24.

10. Yung MW, Gould J, Upton GJ. Nasal polyposis in children with cystic fibrosis: a long-term follow-up study. *Ann Otol Rhinol Laryngol* 2002; **111**: 1081–6.

11. West B, Jones NS. Endoscopy-negative, computed tomography-negative facial pain in a nasal clinic. *Laryngoscope* 2001; **111**: 581–6.

12. Ortolani C, Ispano M, Pastorello E, et al. The oral allergy syndrome. *Ann Allergy* 1988; **61**: 47–52.

13. Reid MJ, Lockey RF, Turkeltaub PC, Platts-Mills TA. Survey of fatalities from skin testing and immunotherapy 1985–1989. *J Allergy Clin Immunol* 1993; **92**: 6–15.

14. Terreehorst I, Hak E, Oosting AJ, et al. Evaluation of impermeable covers for bedding in patients with allergic rhinitis. *N Engl J Med* 2003; **349**: 237–46.

15. Sheikh A, Hurwitz B. House dust mite avoidance measures for perennial allergic rhinitis. *Cochrane Database Syst Rev* 2001; CD001563.

16. Brown CL, Graham SM. Nasal irrigations: good or bad? *Curr Opin Otolaryngol Head Neck Surg* 2004; **12**: 9–13.

17. Weiner JM, Abramson MJ, Puy RM. Intranasal corticosteroids versus oral H1 receptor antagonists in allergic rhinitis: systematic review of randomised controlled trials. *Br Med J* 1998; **317**: 1624–9.

18. Schenkel EJ, Skoner DP, Bronsky EA, *et al.* Absence of growth retardation in children with perennial allergic rhinitis after one year of treatment with mometasone furoate aqueous nasal spray. *Pediatrics* 2000; **105**: E22.

19. Allen DB, Meltzer EO, Lemanske RF Jr, *et al.* No growth suppression in children treated with the maximum recommended dose of fluticasone propionate aqueous nasal spray for one year. *Allergy Asthma Proc* 2002; **23**: 407–13.

20. Aukema AA, Mulder PG, Fokkens WJ. Treatment of nasal polyposis and chronic rhinosinusitis with fluticasone propionate nasal drops reduces need for sinus surgery. *J Allergy Clin Immunol* 2005; **115**: 1017–23.

21. Hore I, Georgalas C, Scadding G. Oral antihistamines for the symptom of nasal obstruction in persistent allergic rhinitis – a systematic review of randomized controlled trials. *Clin Exp Allergy* 2005; **35**: 207–12.

22. Canonica GW, Bousquet J, Van Hammée G, *et al.* Levocetirizine improves health-related quality of life and health status in persistent allergic rhinitis. *Respir Med* 2006; **100**: 1706–15.

23. Bousquet J, Demarteau N, Mullol J, *et al.* Costs associated with persistent allergic rhinitis are reduced by levocetirizine. *Allergy* 2005; **60**: 788–94.

24. Vuurman EF, van Veggel LM, Uiterwijk MM, *et al.* Seasonal allergic rhinitis and antihistamine effects on children's learning. *Ann Allergy* 1993; **71**: 121–6.

25. Walker S, Khan-Wasti S, Fletcher M, *et al.* Seasonal allergic rhinitis is associated with a detrimental effect on examination performance in United Kingdom teenagers: case-control study. *J Allergy Clin Immunol* 2007; **120**: 381–7. Epub 8 Jun 2007.

26. Philip G, Malmstrom K, Hampel FC, *et al.* Montelukast for treating seasonal allergic rhinitis: a randomized, double-blind, placebo-controlled trial performed in the spring. *Clin Exp Allergy* 2002; **32**: 1020–8.

27. Nayak AS, Philip G, Lu S, *et al.* Efficacy and tolerability of montelukast alone or in combination with loratadine in seasonal allergic rhinitis: a multicenter, randomized, double-blind, placebo-controlled trial performed in the fall. *Ann Allergy Asthma Immunol* 2002; **88**: 592–600.

28. Wilson AM, Orr LC, Sims EJ, Lipworth BJ. Effects of monotherapy with intra-nasal corticosteroid or combined oral histamine and leukotriene receptor antagonists in seasonal allergic rhinitis. *Clin Exp Allergy* 2001; **31**: 61–8.

29. Ragab S, Parikh A, Darby YC, Scadding GK. An open audit of montelukast, a leukotriene receptor antagonist, in nasal polyposis associated with asthma. *Clin Exp Allergy* 2001; **31**: 1385–91.

30. Grossman J, Banov C, Boggs P, *et al.* Use of ipratropium bromide nasal spray in chronic treatment of nonallergic perennial rhinitis, alone and in combination with other perennial rhinitis medications. *J Allergy Clin Immunol* 1995; **95**: 1123–30.

31. Scadding GK. Rhinitis medicamentosa. *Clin Exp Allergy* 1995; **25**: 391–4.

32. Durham SR, Walker SM, Varga EM, *et al.* Long-term clinical efficacy of grass-pollen immunotherapy. *N Engl J Med* 1999; **341**: 468–75.

33. Wilson DR, Lima MT, Durham SR. Sublingual immunotherapy for allergic rhinitis: systematic review and meta-analysis. *Allergy* 2005; **60**: 4–12.

34. Kuehr J, Brauburger J, Zielen S, *et al.* Efficacy of combination treatment with anti-IgE plus specific immunotherapy in polysensitized children and adolescents with seasonal allergic rhinitis. *J Allergy Clin Immunol* 2002; **109**: 274–80.

35. Schubert MS. Allergic fungal sinusitis. *Clin Rev Allergy Immunol* 2006; **30**: 205–16.

36. Greiner A, Meltzer EO. In: Graham, Scadding & Bull (eds). *Paediatric Rhinitis in Paediatric ENT*, Springer, 2007.

37. Passalacqua G, Ciprandi G, Pasquali M, *et al.* An update on the asthma-rhinitis link. *Curr Opin Allergy Clin Immunol* 2004; **4**: 177–83.

38. ten Brinke A, Grootendorst DC, Schmidt JT, *et al.* Chronic sinusitis in severe asthma is related to sputum eosinophilia. *J Allergy Clin Immunol* 2002; **109**: 621–6.

39. Moller C, Dreborg S, Ferdousi HA, *et al.* Pollen immunotherapy reduces the development of asthma in children with seasonal rhinoconjunctivitis (the PAT-study). *J Allergy Clin Immunol* 2002; **109**: 251–6.

40. Walker SM, Pajno GB, Lima MT, *et al.* Grass pollen immunotherapy for seasonal rhinitis and asthma: a randomized, controlled trial. *J Allergy Clin Immunol* 2001; **107**: 87–93.

41. Crystal-Peters J, Neslusan C, Crown WH, *et al.* Treating allergic rhinitis in patients with comorbid asthma: the risk of asthma-related hospitalizations and emergency department visits. *J Allergy Clin Immunol* 2002; **109**: 57–62.

42. Adams RJ, Fuhlbrigge A, Guilbert T, *et al.* Inadequate use of asthma medication in the United States: results of the asthma in America national population survey. *J Allergy Clin Immunol* 2002; **110**: 58–64.

43. Corren J, Manning BE, Thompson SF, *et al.* Rhinitis therapy and the prevention of hospital care for asthma: a case-control study. *J Allergy Clin Immunol* 2004; **113**: 415–19.

44. Fokkens W, *et al.* European position paper on rhinosinusitis and nasal polyps. *Rhinol Suppl* 2007; **20**: 1–136.

5

Chronic sinusitis and asthma

JEFFREY CULP, JOHN STEINKE, LARRY BORISH

KEY POINTS

1. Disease within the sinuses is one of the most common healthcare problems, affecting ~16% of the population and having significant adverse impact on quality of life and daily functioning.

2. The majority of patients with chronic sinusitis do not *primarily* have an infectious disorder.

3. Chronic sinusitis comprises numerous disorders including those characterized by chronic inflammation with mucous gland hyperplasia and remodelling, chronic hyperplastic eosinophilic sinusitis and allergic fungal sinusitis.

4. The pathological appearance of chronic hyperplastic eosinophilic sinusitis is very similar to that of asthma and is frequently diagnosed in association with asthma.

5. Pharmacological and surgical interventions which act to reduce systemic effects of chronic hyperplastic eosinophilic sinusitis, including topical corticosteroids, leukotriene modifiers and aspirin desensitization could modulate severity of asthma; however, this linkage at present remains unproven.

Introduction

Definitions and classification of sinusitis

The term sinusitis refers to the presence of inflammation within any of the four pairs of paranasal sinuses. Disease within the sinuses produces one of the most common healthcare problems, affecting ~16% of the population and having significant adverse impact on quality of life and daily functioning [1–3]. The diagnosis and management of sinusitis have been challenging and, to a great extent, unsatisfactory. Sinusitis comprises many conditions with distinct aetiologies and recognition of this has led to increasing appreciation of the importance of categorizing these unique presentations of sinusitis, with the expectation that this will lead to implementing improved, disease-specific therapeutic interventions.

Table 5.1 Classification of sinusitis

Categories	Grouping	Aetiology
Acute sinusitis	Viral sinusitis	Rhinovirus, Metapneumovirus, Influenza A/B
	Acute bacterial sinusitis	*Streptococcus pneumoniae, Moraxella catarrhalis, Haemophilus influenzae*
Subacute sinusitis	Bacterial sinusitis	*Strep. pneumoniae, M. catarrhalis, H. influenzae*
Chronic sinusitis without nasal polyposis	Chronic infectious sinusitis	Immune deficiency, anatomical abnormalities. Secondary infections with anaerobes, Gram-negative organisms, *Staphylococcus aureus*
	Chronic inflammatory sinusitis	Anatomical abnormalities, allergic rhinitis
Chronic sinusitis with nasal polyposis	Chronic hyperplastic eosinophilic sinusitis	Aspirin-tolerant
		Aspirin-exacerbated respiratory disease
	Allergic fungal sinusitis	*Bipolaris spicifera, Curvularia lunata, Aspergillus fumigatus, Fusarium* sp.
	Cystic fibrosis	Infection, bacterial biofilm, possibly AFS

Sinusitis traditionally has been divided into three categories (acute, subacute, and chronic) based on disease duration (Table 5.1). Challenges associated with the appropriate diagnosis of sinusitis are discussed below. Patients with sinus symptoms for less than 4 weeks' duration are considered to have 'acute sinusitis'. 'Subacute sinusitis' comprises patients whose disease is of 4–8 weeks' duration. When the symptoms persist beyond 8 weeks, it is termed 'chronic sinusitis' (CS). Acute and subacute sinusitis typically represent infectious processes that are caused by respiratory viruses and pyogenic bacteria (*Streptococcus pneumoniae, Haemophilus influenza, and Moraxella catarrhalis*). Historically, CS has been managed as an infectious disease thought to be caused by anaerobic bacteria, Gram-negative organisms, *Staphylococcus aureus*, and other unusual bacteria. This concept led to the prominent utilization of antibiotics and surgical drainage as treatment. It is becoming apparent, however, that the majority of patients with CS do not *primarily* have an infectious disorder [4–6]. Unfortunately, physicians continue to prescribe antibiotics to treat CS despite numerous contradictory efficacy studies [7]. With development of CS, patients lose mucociliary clearance and other physiological mechanisms that normally act to maintain the sterility of the sinuses and thereby become colonized with numerous bacteria. When obtaining sinus cultures using appropriate sterilization, sinus puncture, and quantification, studies have demonstrated polymicrobial organisms and non-virulent organisms present at low titre [4,6]. In combination with the prominent absence of neutrophils [8] and the failure to respond to multiple courses of broad-spectrum antibiotics, these observations support the increasing recognition that most patients with CS do not have an infectious process.

Contrasting studies that purported to show that CS is an infectious disorder may have misinterpreted the nature of this colonization. It remains plausible, however, that this bacterial colonization is not completely inert. Bacterial-derived microfilms are likely to be contributing to the severity of the chronic inflammation and, as discussed below, bacterial by-products, such as endotoxin and *Staph*-derived superantigens, can directly exacerbate the immune mechanisms that underlie CS. Finally, while most patients with CS do not *primarily* have an infectious disorder, it is important to appreciate that the development of CS predisposes the patient to recurrent episodes of acute sinusitis. Interestingly, the acute sinusitis that complicates CS is produced by the same spectrum of pyogenic organisms as affects patients without CS |9|. The recognition that most chronic sinusitis is not infectious has instigated efforts to better categorize these disorders.

A summary statement comprising expert opinion within this field argues that CS consists of two disorders. CS without nasal polyps (NPs) is characterized by the presence of a chronic inflammatory infiltrate with or without neutrophils and generally by the absence of NP. CS with NP is a hyperplastic disorder characterized by eosinophils and generally by the presence of NPs |2,3|. A small subset of patients with CS does, in fact, have 'chronic infectious sinusitis'. This typically involves patients with underlying anatomical abnormalities, humoral immune deficiencies, human immunodeficiency virus, Kartaganer syndrome, and cystic fibrosis (CF). Pathologically, these patients are identified by prominent neutrophilia and intense bacterial infiltration ($>10^5$ to 10^6 cfu/ml) within their sinuses. In contrast, most patients in the CS without NP category have a non-infectious inflammatory disorder |10|. 'Chronic inflammatory sinusitis' is thought to result from chronic or recurrent occlusion of the sinus ostia secondary to viral rhinitis, allergic rhinitis, anatomic predisposition, or other causes. These processes lead to recurrent acute (or subacute) bacterial infections possibly in association with barotrauma of the sinus cavities and damage to the respiratory epithelium, ciliary destruction, mucous gland and prominent goblet cell hyperplasia, bacterial colonization, and ultimately the chronic inflammatory changes |11,12|. The inflammatory component of this form of sinusitis consists of a mononuclear cell infiltrate with few, if any, neutrophils. Eosinophils are *not* a feature of chronic inflammatory sinusitis and nasal polyp formation is uncommon. This disease is associated with robust remodelling with dense deposition of collagen and other matrix proteins |13|. When caused by anatomical occlusion, chronic inflammatory sinusitis may be responsive to surgical interventions |14,15|. While chronic infectious and chronic inflammatory sinusitis together comprise the subgroup of patients with 'CS without NP', it should be noted that nasal polyposis can complicate both conditions. For example, nasal polyps are often the presenting complaint in CF.

The other idiopathic immune inflammatory disease is referred to as 'chronic hyperplastic eosinophilic sinusitis' (CHES). This disease is frequently associated with nasal polyps, leading to the consensus group suggesting that CHES be termed 'CS with NP' |2|. Among the disorders producing CS, it is CHES that is uniquely linked to the presence of asthma, and thus, this disorder will be the focus of the chapter. As discussed below, up to 20–30% of patients with CHES who also have NP and asthma demonstrate exacerbation of their upper and lower airway symptoms with exposure to aspirin and other non-steroidal anti-inflammatory drugs (NSAIDs) |16,17|. This has led to the recognition of a distinct subset of patients who have aspirin-exacerbated respiratory disease (AERD or Samter's triad). In contrast to chronic inflammatory sinusitis, CHES acts as a self-propagating syndrome and, as such, does not respond well to surgery alone |14|. The final condition associated with CS is allergic fungal sinusitis (AFS). AFS represents a severe variant of CHES associated with the colonization of fungi within the sinus cavities and the presence of an immunoglobulin (Ig)E and Th2-like lymphocyte-mediated allergic inflammatory response. Immune and allergic mechanisms of AFS are discussed in detail elsewhere |18,19|. The remainder of this chapter will focus on CHES, its association with asthma, its role in contributing to the presence, severity and exacerbations of asthma, and evidence that attenuation of CHES might have therapeutic utility in asthma.

Pathogenesis

Immune mechanisms of chronic hyperplastic eosinophilic sinusitis

CHES is an inflammatory disease characterized by the accumulation of eosinophils, fibroblasts, mast cells, goblet cells, and T helper lymphocytes |1,20|. It is the prominent accumulation of eosinophils, however, which is the diagnostic feature of this condition (Fig. 5.1) |8,13,20–22|. The diagnosis of CHES can only be unambiguously established upon pathological examination of tissue taken from the disease site with histochemical staining for eosinophils or eosinophil-derived mediators (such as eosinophil cationic protein or major basic protein) |8,21,23|. While nasal polyposis frequently occurs with cystic fibrosis and less commonly can occur with chronic inflammatory sinusitis, the presence of nasal polyposis (and also asthma) may be used in practice as presumptive evidence for CHES |2,24–26|.

In CHES, the sinus tissue demonstrates a marked increase in cells (lymphocytes, fibroblasts, and eosinophils) that express cytokines, chemokines, and pro-inflammatory lipid mediators (cysteinyl leukotrienes (CysLTs), 5-oxo-eicosatetraenoic acid (5-oxo-ETE), and others) that are responsible for the development of eosinophilia. Eosinophilic inflammation is a complex process reflecting the need to synthesize these cells, recruit them into the sinus tissue, and activate them to release the toxic cationic granule proteins and other mediators responsible for sinus inflammation. Eosinophilopoiesis reflects primarily the biological activity of the cytokine interleukin (IL)-5. Other cytokines including IL-3, and granulocyte-macrophage colony-stimulating factor (GM-CSF), and the CysLTs synergize with IL-5 in this process. Eosinophil precursors are increased in numbers in both the blood and bone marrow of patients with CHES and asthma |27|. Recruitment of eosinophils into the sinus tissue reflects the synergistic influences of cellular adhesion and chemotaxis. Important to adhesion are the induction on endothelium of P-selectin (CD62P) by cytokines and CysLTs and vascular cell adhesion molecule (VCAM)-1 by IL-4, IL-13, and tumour necrosis factor (TNF)-α. Important chemotactic factors include CCL11 (eotaxin-1) and other eotaxins |28|,

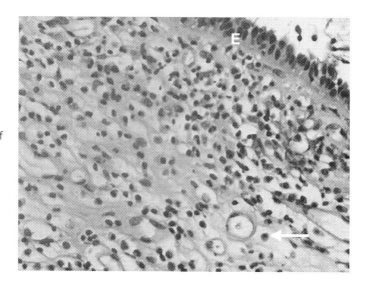

Fig. 5.1 Pathology of CHES (H&E stain): the prominent expression of eosinophils is apparent |13|. E = epithelium; arrow = eosinophil.

platelet-activating factor (PAF), CysLTs |29|, and 5-oxo-HETE. Newly synthesized eosinophils display a limited ability to degranulate in response to inflammatory stimuli. In order for degranulation to occur, the cells need to be 'primed', an effect mediated primarily by IL-3, IL-4, IL-5 and GM-CSF. Within the sinuses, eosinophils are activated by many compounds including CCL5 (RANTES), CCL11, IL-1, IL-3, IL-5, GM-CSF, TNF-α, PAF and the CysLTs |30–36|. Although normally short-lived, many of these factors, including IL-3, IL-5 and GM-CSF, inhibit eosinophil apoptosis and permit the cells to survive for days or even weeks within the inflammatory milieu. Finally, in CHES, the sinuses contain eosinophil- and basophil-specific progenitor cells |37,38|. These eosinophil/basophil progenitors or colony-forming units (Eo/B cfu) are bone marrow-derived mononuclear cells that express CD34, CD35, and IL-5 receptors. In response to appropriate signals (e.g., IL-5 and GM-CSF), these stem cells can mature and allow the autonomous (bone marrow-independent) perpetuation of sinus inflammation |27|. Eosinophils are a prominent source of many of these cytokines and lipid mediators, and this suggests that CHES is a disease of unrestrained inflammation. Once eosinophils are recruited, they provide the growth factors necessary for their further recruitment, proliferation, activation and survival.

The role of bacteria and bacterial-derived immune adjuvants in CHES

As discussed, patients with CHES routinely become colonized with numerous bacteria and are prone to recurrent bacterial infections. Bacteria may be relevant to the pathophysiology of CHES through their ability to provide antigens and immune adjuvants (such as endotoxin). *Staphylococcus aureus* colonizing the sinuses is thought to play a particularly important role in exacerbating CHES through its ability to generate superantigens. The *S. aureus*-derived enterotoxins (SAEs) are a group of superantigens that activate the immune system by cross-linking certain

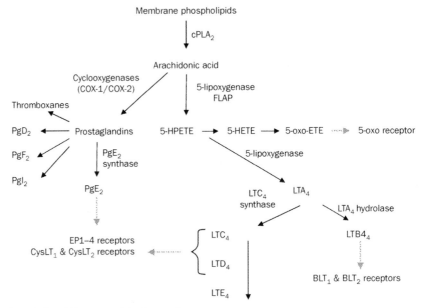

Fig. 5.2 Arachidonate metabolism pathway.

V_β-chains of the T cell receptor on nearby T helper lymphocytes. Binding of SAE leads to the activation of all T cells expressing the target V_β-chains (up to 30% of all T cells) |39|. Superantigens require the existence of pre-existing disease to make available T cells upon which the SAEs can act. *Staph* colonization was present in 66.7% of subjects with 'CS with NP', and when a subgroup of aspirin-sensitive subjects was examined this frequency jumped to 87.5% |40|. This colonization with *Staph* is associated with the demonstration of SAEs in the nasal polyp tissue |41|. These studies support a role for SAEs in exacerbating CHES; however, the critical proof of a role for SAEs in CHES requires data demonstrating over-expression of T cells bearing relevant V_β-chains specific to the SAEs in the sinus tissue |42,43|. Reducing the volume of bacteria in the sinuses, and thereby the concentration of superantigen, could explain the anecdotal benefits ascribed to antibiotics in CHES, without requiring this to be an infectious disorder.

Aspirin-exacerbated respiratory disease

Aspirin-exacerbated respiratory disease reflects a distinct subset of CHES. These patients develop upper respiratory symptoms of nasal congestion, rhinorrhoea, and paroxysmal sneezing, typically with severe exacerbations of their asthma after taking aspirin or other NSAIDs that inhibit cyclooxygenase (COX)-1. Ingestion of these agents leads to a shift in arachidonic acid metabolism from cyclooxygenase products (prostaglandins) to the CysLTs (Fig. 5.2) |44–46|. CysLTs are produced by activated eosinophils, basophils, mast cells, and to a lesser extent by monocytes, dendritic cells, and T cells. CysLTs are metabolites of arachidonic acid, which is liberated from membrane phospholipids in response to cytosolic phospholipase A_2 (Fig. 5.2). For CysLT generation, 5-lipoxygenase (5-LO) acts in concert with the 5-LO-activating protein (FLAP) to convert arachidonic acid to LTA_4. LTA_4 is conjugated to glutathione by LTC_4 synthase (LTC_4S) to form LTC_4. LTC_4 is released and further metabolized by the removal of glutamate to LTD_4 and then by removal of glycine to form LTE_4 [47].

AERD was originally defined by the 'triad' of nasal polyps, aspirin sensitivity, and asthma (Samter's triad). Other features of this disorder are its association with severe CHES, tissue and circulating eosinophilia, and the frequent absence of atopy [16,26,48,49]. Aspirin intolerance occurs in as many as 20% of adult asthmatics and up to 30% of asthmatics with chronic sinusitis or nasal polyposis [16,17]. In many patients, asthma does not develop, thus the current preference for the term AERD rather than aspirin-intolerant asthma or 'triad' asthma.

AERD is explained in part by the over-expression of and over-responsiveness to the CysLTs. AERD subjects display dramatic upregulation of two essential enzymes involved in CysLT synthesis, 5-LO and LTC_4S [25,48,50]. This over-expression makes possible the constitutive over-production of the CysLTs and the life-threatening surge in CysLTs that occurs with ingestion of aspirin and other NSAIDs [45,51]. CysLTs have important pro-inflammatory and pro-fibrotic effects that contribute both to the extensive hyperplastic sinusitis and nasal polyposis that characterize this disorder and to the severity of these patients' asthma [26,47,52,53]. Prostaglandin E_2 (PgE_2) inhibits mast cell and eosinophil activation. It is hypothesized that PgE_2 prevents activation of these allergic inflammatory cells, and that when PgE_2 concentrations are reduced by NSAIDs, they become activated. Support for this concept is derived from the observation that exogenously administered PgE_2 prevents this response from developing [54]. The robust expression of 5-LO and LTC_4S leads to the subsequent surge in CysLT secretion. Aspirin-tolerant subjects have much lower expression of 5-LO and LTC_4S and therefore do not have this surge in CysLT secretion. In general, selective COX-2 inhibitors are well tolerated in these subjects [55,56] suggesting that it is constitutive, COX-1-derived PgE_2 that is necessary for this protective effect.

CysLTs function through their ability to interact with two homologous receptors. The CysLT type 1 receptor is prominently expressed on airway smooth muscle, eosinophils, and other immune cells and these receptors mediate CysLT-induced bronchospasm [57]. CysLT2 receptors are prominently expressed in the heart, prostate, brain, adrenal cells, endothelium and lung [58,59] but are also expressed on eosinophils, monocytes, T and B lymphocytes, and mast cells [60]. Although the precise function of CysLT2 receptors in allergic disease and immunity is not known, they are thought to play a greater role in remodelling and fibrotic processes [47]. Subjects with AERD demonstrate enhanced responsiveness to CysLTs related to impressive over-expression of CysLT receptors on their sinus and NP tissue [61,62].

In addition to modulation of CysLTs and their receptors, the pathophysiology of AERD also involves dysregulation of the prostaglandin synthesis pathway. The expression of cox-2 and PgE_2 are both diminished in AERD [25,63]. NP tissue obtained from AERD patients also displays diminished expression of the anti-inflammatory PgE_2 receptor (EP2) exacerbating the harmful effects of its diminished production |64|. This baseline deficiency in PgE_2 renders AERD patients increasingly susceptible to anaphylaxis in response to its further reduction after aspirin ingestion.

Natural history and epidemiology of asthma in CS

CHES frequently coexists in patients with asthma. When adult asthmatics are evaluated by computed tomography (CT) scan, ~74–90% have some degree of mucosal hyperplasia |65–69|, which in ~30% of asthmatics is sufficiently greater than that observed in healthy controls to be specific to the presence of asthma. Most individuals diagnosed with CHES have asthma, and among non-asthmatics the presence of CHES defines a cohort at high risk for development of asthma. The sinuses are an extension of the respiratory tract and the inflammation observed in CHES/NP has many pathological and immune similarities to that observed in asthma. In addition to the shared eosinophilia and inflammatory mediators, similarity extends to the same prominent basement membrane thickening (Fig. 5.3) |13,21|. These shared features support the view that CHES and asthma represent different manifestations of similar disease processes developing in the upper and lower respiratory tract.

It is generally accepted doctrine that sinusitis contributes to the presence and severity of asthma. This is largely based on anecdotal association studies demonstrating worsening of sinusitis concomitantly with asthma exacerbations and intervention studies alleging that surgical or medical treatment of sinusitis improves asthma. The problem with this argument is that precipitants of asthma are generally also precipitants of sinusitis, and thus, the association of sinusitis with asthma exacerbations may be an epiphenomenon. For example, allergen exposure |70–76| and respiratory viruses |77–79| are the most important precipitants of asthma exacerbations and both produce or worsen sinusitis.

The intervention studies are also problematic insofar as the effect of sinusitis intervention on asthma has *never* been addressed in a controlled study and these patients routinely receive treatments to improve their asthma |80,81|. In addition to the absence of a controlled study, many of the interventions utilized to establish this dogma are unproven in CHES (antibiotics), often ineffective for CS (Caldwell-Luc surgery), or likely to mediate their beneficial effects through direct effects on the airway (macrolide antibiotics). The concept that treatment of CHES might improve asthma is based upon treatments that have not been established to even improve the sinusitis itself! In summary, the present literature is insufficient to categorically conclude that sinusitis directly influences asthma severity and it remains quite plausible that these are merely similar disease processes effecting the upper and lower respiratory tract and sharing similar natural histories. An effort is underway to define effective therapies for CS |2,3|. It should therefore become possible to perform definitive studies to address this important question.

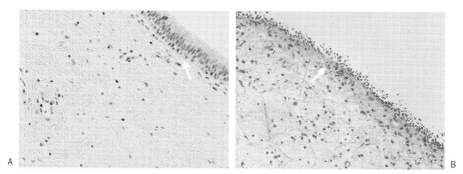

Fig. 5.3 Pathology of CHES (trichrome stain): basement membrane in normal sinus tissue (A) compared to basement membrane thickening in CHES (B) |13|. Arrows = basement membrane.

While it is important to appreciate that the concept regarding a linkage of sinusitis to asthma is unproven, such a linkage is supported by some evidence and remains plausible. For example, a recent study by Ragab and colleagues demonstrated that both medical and surgical treatment of CS was associated with improvement in concomitant asthma |82|. What follows is a discussion of current theories regarding the basis for a connection by which sinusitis could worsen asthma and, by extension, through which sinusitis treatment could ameliorate asthma severity.

Proposed mechanisms linking chronic sinusitis to asthma (Table 5.2)

Neurological reflex

A sinus-bronchial neurological reflex mediated by the cholinergic pathway is supported by some data. There are certainly well-described axonal loops acting in the lungs of asthmatic subjects that contribute to bronchial hyper-reactivity. However, the distinct innervation of the lungs (vagus nerve) and sinuses (trigeminal nerve) is inconsistent with typical reflexes or axonal loops. The neuronal reflexes do not adequately explain the inflammatory processes characterized by activated eosinophils and Th2-like lymphocytes that develop in the lungs in temporal association with sinusitis exacerbations.

Mouth breathing

The nose conditions the inhaled air by providing a tortuous surface over which the air is humidified and warmed, and on which large particles impact and are removed. Nasal congestion developing with CHES could force the patient into mouth breathing. Inhaling unconditioned (cold, dry) air is a known cause of bronchospasm in asthmatics. However, this is unlikely to be a cause of worsening airway inflammation which occurs with concomitant flares of sinusitis and asthma.

Table 5.2 Mechanisms of sinusitis exacerbation of asthma

Coincidental association of similar pathological processes in upper and lower airways	In the absence of controlled studies, there may not be a causal interplay between sinusitis and asthma
Sinus-bronchial reflex	Some evidence, however, of the distinct innervation of the lungs (vagus) and sinuses (trigeminal) is inconsistent with typical reflex or axonal loops as described in bronchial hyper-reactivity (BHR); nor is this likely to explain what is primarily an inflammatory Th2-like lymphocyte eosinophilic disease of the lungs
Mouth breathing	Inhaling unconditioned air could cause bronchospasm but would not exacerbate inflammation
Aspiration	Well-performed studies with instillation of isotope into the sinuses (as opposed to intranasal application) eliminates this as an aetiology in conscious subjects [84]
Vocal cord dysfunction	In contrast to aspiration, mucopurulent posterior pharyngeal drainage could cause laryngeal irritation and produce VCD [85]. Studies connecting sinusitis and asthma may have failed to address confounding effects of VCD.
Humoral recirculation of cytokines and immune cells (T helper lymphocytes, eosinophils, and eosinophil precursors) from the upper airway and sinuses to the lungs	The currently accepted model (Fig. 5.4)

Aspiration

This is the concept that sinus-derived posterior pharyngeal drainage, enriched in inflammatory cells, their secreted by-products, and other irritants, could be aspirated into the airways and thereby exacerbate underlying asthma [83]. However, in well-performed studies using instillation of radioisotopes directly into the sinuses, no evidence for aspiration could be discerned [84]. Conflicting studies showing apparent aspiration of sinus contents into the lungs utilized nasal sprays, and this approach may have allowed direct access of the spray into the airway. While significant aspiration below the larynx is not likely to occur in non-obtunded subjects, posterior pharyngeal drainage is a characteristic feature of CS and this is likely to function as a laryngeal irritant. CS could thereby be a cause of the paradoxical closure of the vocal cords that is responsible for vocal cord dysfunction (VCD or 'paradoxical laryngospasm') [85]. Many of the studies linking CS to asthma may have failed to address the confounding effects of including patients who actually had VCD.

Humoral recirculation

Any link between sinusitis and asthma can best be ascribed to a systemic inflammatory process. The cytokines associated with allergic inflammation do not function hormonally. Thus, T helper lymphocyte-associated cytokines such as IL-4,

IL-5, and IL-13 cannot be identified in serum samples and certainly are unlikely to access the bone marrow at a concentration sufficient to drive haematopoietic differentiation. In contrast, T helper lymphocytes, including those newly differentiated from naïve cells in sinus lymphatic tissue or reactivated memory cells, present within the sinus tissue are capable of migrating to the bone marrow. This is analogous to the migration of T lymphocytes from the asthmatic airway to the bone marrow that has been described in murine asthma models. It is this ability of activated cytokine-expressing cells to circulate that provides the ability of cytokines to function at a distance [86]. Once delivered to the bone marrow, these T helper cells will stimulate the production of inflammatory cells including basophils, eosinophils, and mast cell precursors [27,87,88]. Cells activated in the sinuses also include locally produced eosinophil basophil colony forming units (Eo/B cfu) [89] and these will be released into the circulation where they will mature [27,38,90]. There will be selective recruitment of the newly generated eosinophils (and other inflammatory cells) generated through these mechanisms back into the sinus tissue. However, these cells will also migrate into the lungs of susceptible individuals, specifically individuals with pre-existing asthma. Newly generated eosinophils (and other cells) generated through these mechanisms express adhesion molecules that will direct their migration and adherence to inflamed tissue displaying relevant counter-ligands. For example, very late antigen (VLA)-4 on eosinophils will interact and adhere to endothelial cells expressing the counter-ligand VCAM-1. This will lead to the further influx of eosinophils into the sinuses. However, in the presence of established asthma, vascular endothelium in the lungs will also express the relevant counter-ligands, leading to inflammatory cell adherence. These inflamed organs are rich in chemotaxins such as CCL11, PAF, and CysLTs, that drive the diapedesis and chemotaxis of these cells into the inflamed tissue [20,34,52,91]. Through these systemic humoral mechanisms, inflammation in the sinuses can produce increased inflammation in the lungs including the reported eosinophil influx [27,88,90]. Non-asthmatics do not express the necessary adhesion molecules and chemotaxins in their airways and thus do not have the machinery necessary to recruit inflammatory cells into their lungs during exacerbations of sinusitis. This model is summarized in Figure 5.4.

While this model has never been specifically studied, the concept that CHES could contribute to asthma severity is supported by studies linking CHES to systemic and airway inflammation. Several studies have shown that severity of CHES directly influences circulating eosinophilia and CHES may have a stronger influence on absolute eosinophil counts than does asthma [65,68]. In the most intriguing study, subjects with CHES were divided into groups with limited and more severe disease according to a CT scan-based volumetric measure of hyperplastic tissue content in their sinuses. The severity of sinus disease was linked to increased absolute eosinophil counts (440/μl vs 170/μl), and appeared to influence airway inflammation as shown by eosinophilia in induced sputum samples (7.3% vs 0.7%) [68]. This circumstantial evidence supports a linkage between CHES and asthma. At present, however, the concept that sinusitis directly influences the development or severity of asthma and that sinusitis treatment will improve asthma has

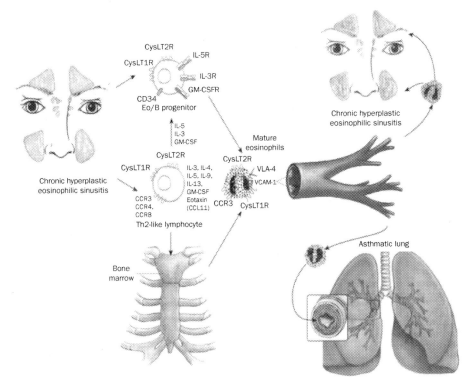

Fig. 5.4 Model giving overview of mechanism by which allergen immune activation can induce inflammation in sinus tissue (see text for details).

not been categorically established. Treatment of CHES may be warranted as part of a treatment plan for the refractory asthmatic and certainly is essential in reducing the morbidity directly ascribable to this disorder. The remainder of this chapter will address current approaches to the treatment of CS.

Clinical course

Therapeutic implications

The management of CS has been disappointing and at present, in the United States at least, there is not a single Federal Drug Administration approved treatment for this disorder. A problem confounding the evaluation of clinical interventions of sinusitis has been the absence of validated criteria to assess the presence and severity of sinusitis. Traditionally, studies have utilized clinical criteria to evaluate the sinuses including presence of such symptoms as purulent anterior or posterior nasal drainage, nasal congestion, frontal headaches, cough, etc. However, none of these criteria are specific for the sinuses because they indirectly reflect the presence of either nasal disease (purulent drainage) or lower respiratory tract disease (cough). The relevance of headaches to sinus disease is unclear as compelling data suggest that most patients with 'sinus headaches' actually suffer from atypical migraines |92,93|. As a result, clinical studies that have compared sinusitis symptom scores with CT scans show that clinical scores are often little better than random when predicting the presence and severity of sinusitis |65–69|. The absence of validated objective criteria for assessing presence of CHES or responsiveness to therapeutic interventions has tempered the value of most sinusitis studies.

Ancillary therapies

Many ancillary therapies are routinely recommended for CS and are similar to those utilized for acute sinusitis (Table 5.3). Interventions designed to increase sinus ostial patency are based on the hypothesis that reducing ostial obstruction should help in the expulsion of retained mucous and infectious materials—mechanisms of dubious benefit in CHES. This approach includes the use of systemic decongestants such as pseudoephedrine. While decongestants reduce nasal resistance, the only study of a systemic decongestant on sinus function was performed with phenylpropanolamine and this agent produced an *insignificant* increase in maxillary ostia |94|. No controlled study with systemic decongestants in CS has been performed and the only controlled study in acute sinusitis demonstrated no clinical benefit |94|. Improved mucociliary clearance can be accomplished by reducing the viscosity of secretions. This can be accomplished with nasal saline irrigation. Saline irrigation must be performed with large volumes of saline, which can be administered with a bulb syringe or other device. Nasal saline irrigation might also provide efficacy in CS through its ability to break up bacterial biofilms. Various mucolytics and expectorants have also been recommended in CS based on the hypothesis that they should ease clearance of tenacious, viscous mucus. While these agents, including iodinated glycerol, guaifenesin, and acetyl cysteine, have some efficacy in COPD, there have been no studies showing efficacy in CS.

Allergen avoidance / immunotherapy: the role of allergy in CHES

A role for allergen avoidance or allergen desensitization immunotherapy is contingent on the extent to which CHES is an allergic disorder. In support of this, CS has been linked to the increased expression of allergic (IgE) sensitization. Thus, allergic rhinitis was seen in 56% of 200 consecutive patients with CS |75|. Similarly, 50% of children with 'recalcitrant' sinusitis were skin test positive as were 78% of patients with 'severe' sinus disease |75|. In another study, slightly less than half of patients with CHES/NP had allergies |70|. The significance of these observations is unclear insofar as the prevalence of allergic rhinitis or positive skin tests in well-matched control populations was not reported and can be highly variable reflecting variables regarding how the skin testing is performed. In fact, a recent extensive National Health Survey in the United States reported the

Table 5.3 Treatment of chronic hyperplastic eosinophilic sinusitis

Category	Proposed mechanism	Role in CHES
Nasal saline irrigation	Diminish viscosity of inspissated secretions—improve mucociliary clearance; dissolution of bacterial biofilms	Useful adjunct therapy
Decongestants (pseudoephedrine, phenylephrine)	Reduced sinus ostial obstruction; promote expulsion of mucous and infectious materials	Unproven Proposed mechanism is of dubious benefit in CHES
Antihistamines (loratadine, fexofenadine, cetirizine)	Reduce oedema and mucus secretion caused by histamine	Ineffective CHES is not an allergic disease and histamine is not a prominent mediator
Expectorants: guaifenesin, potassium iodide, acetyl cysteine	Ease clearance of tenacious, viscous mucous	Unproven Limited efficacy in COPD; this has never been extended to CS
Allergy avoidance / immunotherapy	A role for allergy in CHES is unproven and inconsistent with inability of aeroallergens to access the sinus cavities	Unproven
Systemic corticosteroids	Corticosteroids have potent anti-inflammatory and especially anti-eosinophil efficacy	Effective therapy but inappropriate in the face of long-term treatment requirements
Topical corticosteroids	Reduce eosinophils and cytokines	Reduce size and recurrence of NP Unproven for CHES; efficacy is limited by ability to access sinus cavities
Leukotriene modifiers	Cysteinyl leukotrienes are important pro-inflammatory mediators highly expressed in CHES tissue	LT receptor antagonists are unproven. 5-LO inhibitor zileuton associated with diminished polyp size and reversal of anosmia
Aspirin desensitization	Associated with diminished cysteinyl leukotriene production and responsiveness (CysLT receptor expression)	Reduce frequency of acute sinusitis complications of CHES, polyp recurrence, and anosmia. Only effective in aspirin-intolerant patients
Surgery	Provide drainage of inspissated mucus and inflammatory tissue	Produce instant reduction in CHES biomass. Without follow-up medical therapy disease is likely to recur. Useful adjunct to medical therapies.

prevalence of positive prick skin tests to be 54.3% in healthy adults, not impressively different from that reported in CS |95|. The presence of a positive skin test in a patient with CHES cannot be interpreted as signifying an allergic aetiology. An additional argument against a role for allergy in CHES is the lack of evidence that inhalant allergens access the sinus cavities. In one study, radiolabelled allergen did not access the sinuses |96|. Using a much smaller radioisotope placed on the nasal mucosa, it was shown that isotope could access the sinuses with nose blowing but not with nasal breathing, sneezing, or coughing |97|. These studies were done in healthy volunteers and even this limited potential access of allergens into the sinuses is likely to be reduced in CS secondary to inflamed sinus mucosa and the occlusion of the sinus ostia. Ironically, this natural protection of sinus tissue from inhalant allergens is likely be reversed by sinus surgery.

Despite the unlikelihood that allergens directly access the sinuses, there is intriguing evidence that still supports a role for allergy in CHES. Thus, insufflation of ragweed pollen in sensitive subjects was associated with increased hyperaemia and metabolic activity in the maxillary sinus and similar changes were observed during the ragweed season that became inactive post-seasonally |72,73|. In a different study, either radiographic changes in the maxillary sinuses or symptoms referable to the sinuses were seen in approximately half of the subjects undergoing allergen provocation challenges |74|. The strongest evidence that inhalant allergens could have a role in CHES is derived from studies in which catheters were inserted into both maxillary sinuses. Nasal challenges were performed with grass or ragweed extracts instilled into one nostril after which bilateral sinus lavages were performed. In these studies, nasal allergen challenges triggered eosinophil influx into the ipsilateral, but more impressively, this also occurred in the contralateral maxillary sinus |76|. These data support a role for inhalant allergens in the pathophysiology of CHES, but also suggest that this does *not* necessarily require direct allergen access into the sinuses. Allergic rhinitis activates Th2-like lymphocytes in the nose with subsequent mast cell recruitment and eosinophil activation. It is reasonable to speculate that a systemic inflammatory mechanism similar to that described for the link between sinusitis and asthma could develop between the nares and the sinuses. At present, however, a role for allergies in the aetiology or severity of CHES remains unproven. No clinical studies have shown that either allergen avoidance or immunotherapy has clinical benefit in CHES using validated sinus-specific outcome parameters. Recommendations for allergen avoidance and immunotherapy should be primarily focused on achieving benefit for the underlying allergic rhinitis or asthma.

Systemic corticosteroids

Systemic corticosteroids benefit CHES through their ability to directly attenuate eosinophilia and other components of the inflammation of this disorder |98|. In an attempt to decrease the use of systemic corticosteroids, a recent study showed that a two-week tapering course of oral corticosteroids improved all nasal symptoms, polyp size and nasal flow, and subsequent use of intranasal budesonide maintained these effects |99|. The ability of topical corticosteroids (CCS) to locally reduce cytokine production (including IL-4, IL-5, GM-CSF and TNF-α), inhibit T helper lymphocyte function, and inhibit activation of both eosinophils and eosinophil precursors supports the concept that these agents could provide efficacy in CHES |100,101|. In contrast to allergic rhinitis and asthma, however, it is unlikely that *intranasal CCS* can directly access the sinus cavities in order to achieve that efficacy. Although various manoeuvres have been proposed to promote the access of nasal corticosteroids into the sinuses, the likely presence of occlusion of the ostiomeatal complex precludes their direct access, although this may be partially achieved in subjects who have undergone functional endoscopic sinus surgery

(FESS). In contrast to their lack of proven efficacy for CHES, intranasal CCS can reduce nasal polyps |102|, reflecting their ability to directly access the polyp tissue. The role of intranasal CCS in CHES has not been adequately addressed in a properly performed controlled clinical trial with validated outcome criteria.

Leukotriene modifiers

CHES tissue demonstrates increased presence of CysLTs and metabolic enzymes involved in LT synthesis |25,52|. CysLTs have important pro-inflammatory capabilities including primarily their ability to promote eosinophilic inflammation. Other activities relevant to CHES include their ability to increase vascular permeability, stimulate mucus secretion and decrease mucociliary clearance |52|. Clinical trials of leukotriene modifiers in asthma and allergic rhinitis have shown reductions in both circulating absolute eosinophil counts and tissue eosinophilia |103,104|. Leukotriene modifiers could therefore provide benefit in CHES through direct reduction of eosinophil recruitment and activation in the sinuses. CysLT1 receptor antagonists (zafirlukast and montelukast) have been suggested to have efficacy in CHES in uncontrolled trials |105|. Montelukast has been reported to decrease nasal itching, post-nasal discharge, sneezing, and rhinorrhoea for 1 year in the patients who are status post-endoscopic sphenoethmoidectomy |106|. In the only placebo-controlled trial of an LT modifier in CHES, the 5-LO inhibitor zileuton was shown to reduce polyp size and restore sense of smell |107|. The efficacy of zileuton is intriguing as inhibition of 5-LO has broader implications than use of one of the CysLT1 receptor antagonists. In addition to blocking LTB_4 and the 5-oxo-ETE pathways, reduced synthesis of CysLTs will thereby block inflammation mediated through the CysLT2 as well as CysLT1 receptor.

Antifungal approaches

Recently, it has been suggested that CHES might be caused by the development of a Th2-like lymphocyte-mediated response to fungal colonization of the sinus cavities |108,109|. In addition to the presence of fungi in the sinuses, this concept is supported by the increased production of IL-5 and IL-13 when T lymphocytes derived from CS patients, but not controls, were exposed to fungal extracts |109|. These studies led to the concept that intranasal amphotericin B might be an effective treatment for patients with CS. Although initial uncontrolled studies supported efficacy, more recent controlled studies with amphotericin B nasal lavages have shown either modest improvement in CT scan volumetric scores |110| or, alternatively, no evidence for reduction of the clinical signs and symptoms of CS |111|.

Aspirin desensitization

Aspirin desensitization is a proven therapy in patients with AERD. This technique involves successive ingestion of increasing doses of aspirin over several days, until a therapeutic dose is achieved (generally 650 mg twice a day). This technique is risky and must be done cautiously, ideally in a hospital setting. The use of a leukotriene modifier reduces—but does not eliminate—the risks of aspirin desensitization. Successful aspirin desensitization decreases basal and aspirin-stimulated leukotriene synthesis as well as decreasing sensitivity to cysteinyl leukotrienes by dramatically downregulating expression of CysLT receptors |61,62|. Aspirin desensitization decreases symptoms of sinus disease, reduces courses of antibiotics reflecting reduced numbers of secondary acute sinusitis episodes, decreases need for sinus surgeries, and restores the sense of smell |112|. These beneficial results are tempered, however, by the risks of desensitization and long-term aspirin administration. Aspirin desensitization can also be indicated in patients with AERD who require aspirin treatment for an unrelated medical condition. Selective COX-2 inhibitors can generally be safely administered to individuals with AERD (but these agents do not provide benefit for the sinus disease) |55,56|.

Surgery

No controlled trial of functional endoscopic sinus surgery has been performed; however, FESS has been associated with high reported rates of clinical improvement (up to 97.5% at 2 years) |14|. Unfortunately, patients with extensive disease, multiple sinus involvement, nasal polyposis, asthma or aspirin intolerance have a poor outcome. These observations suggest that FESS may be uniquely useful in patients with chronic inflammatory sinusitis in whom anatomical defects are present that are predisposing the patient to recurrent acute or subacute infections with the subsequent mucociliary damage, remodelling, and chronic inflammation. With CHES, FESS is less unlikely to be curative for what is primarily an immune-mediated hyperplastic disease of the sinuses. In the absence of post-surgical medical management, the immune mechanisms underlying CHES are still extant and the disease is likely to recur. FESS remains a valuable adjunct to the treatment of this disorder, as medical approaches are likely to be more effective in preventing recurrence of CHES and NP than in ameliorating well-established disease.

Newer biotechnology approaches

Given the pathophysiological similarities between CHES and asthma and the likelihood that these are similar or perhaps even identical disease processes affecting the upper and lower airways, respectively, it seems likely that newer biotechnology-derived therapies designed to treat severe asthma are likely to produce similar benefits for CHES. Clinical experience with humanized anti-IgE (omalizumab) in asthma shows that it lessens allergen-induced IgE-mediated activation of mast cells and basophils and thereby attenuates acute allergic reactions |113|. The efficacy of omalizumab in CHES is obviously limited by the extent to which CHES is an IgE-mediated disease. As previously discussed, allergen-specific mechanisms may produce a systemic inflammatory milieu that could contribute to the severity of CHES. It seems less likely, however, that inhaled aeroallergens directly access the sinus cavities and exacerbate CHES in an IgE-dependent fashion that is likely to be ameliorated by omalizumab. In contrast, it is plausible that IgE-dependent reactions could develop in CHES to locally produced allergens. For example, allergic fungal sinusitis is associated with IgE-mediated allergic reactions to fungi colonizing the sinuses and, similarly, specific IgE is known to develop to *Staph*-derived antigens in patients colonized with that microorganism |114|. At present, no clinical data exist to support the use of humanized anti-IgE as a specific treatment for CHES.

Insofar as CHES is defined by the accumulation of activated eosinophils, it seems likely that interventions designed to attenuate eosinophilic inflammation will be particularly beneficial in this disorder. There is convincing evidence regarding the role of eosinophilia in fibrosis and airway remodelling in allergic disease. IL-5 deficient mice have markedly diminished eosinophil numbers and suppression of remodelling |115–118|. More specifically, mice genetically engineered to lack eosinophils continue to display airway hyper-reactivity and increased mucus secretion but do not develop fibrosis and remodelling |119|. The production of transforming growth factor-β, platelet-derived growth factor, fibroblast growth factor, and other growth factors by activated eosinophils contribute to the proliferation of fibroblasts and deposition of connective tissue observed in asthma and CHES |120–122|. The experience with humanized anti-IL-5 (mepolizumab) in asthma supports the ability of this intervention to greatly attenuate both the bone marrow eosinophilopoietic response associated with asthma and airway eosinophilia |123|. Similar to what was observed in the murine model |119|, anti-IL-5 treatment, while markedly reducing eosinophil numbers, had no significant effect on lung function or bronchial hyper-reactivity in human studies. However, anti-IL-5 is associated with diminished deposition of matrix proteins |124|. As a disease characterized by exuberant remodelling and deposition of matrix proteins, CHES could be uniquely responsive to eosinophil-directed therapies, such as with mepolizumab. A recent study using reslizumab (a humanized anti-human IL-5 mAb) showed reduction of nasal polyp size in half of the patients, while nasal levels of IL-5 predicted the response to the anti-IL-5 treatment |125|.

That significant residual tissue eosinophilia was observed in the mepolizumab studies |123| suggests that single target interventions may insufficiently reduce tissue eosinophilia to produce adequate therapeutic benefit in CHES (or asthma). This reflects in part the complementary role of other cytokines, including especially GM-CSF, in promoting activation and differentiation of eosinophilic precursors |126|. This failure may also reflect roles for both constitutive (IL-5-independent) eosinophilopoiesis and perhaps the need to attenuate expression of either eosinophil-specific chemokines (e.g., inhibition of CCL11 [eotaxin] using chemokine receptor CCR3 antagonists) or eosinophil-specific adhesion molecules (e.g., through the use of VLA-4 antagonists) |127|. Arguably, no single agent is likely to be effective for CHES and it will be necessary to synergistically block both the systemic bone marrow component of CHES as well as local factors critical for inflammatory cell recruitment. The shared pathology of CHES with asthma suggests that as newer agents become established for asthma they may subsequently prove to have utility in CHES.

Conclusion

Chronic sinusitis comprises numerous disorders including those characterized by chronic inflammation with mucous gland hyperplasia and remodelling, CHES, and allergic fungal sinusitis. Only very rarely is chronic sinusitis *primarily* an infectious disorder. CHES is characterized by unrestrained proliferation of eosinophils, Th2-like lymphocytes, fibroblasts, goblet cells, and mast cells. The pathological appearance of CHES is very similar to that of asthma and is frequently diagnosed in association with asthma. Exacerbations of CHES occur temporally with worsening of asthma. In the absence of well-controlled studies, this linkage at present remains unproven, as precipitants of asthma exacerbations are capable of concomitantly producing sinusitis episodes. Many mechanisms have been ascribed for the putative linkage of sinusitis to asthma including a neuronally mediated sinus-bronchial reflex, the harmful effects of mouth breathing and inhaling unconditioned air into the lungs, aspiration of sinus contents into the lungs, or the confounding influences of sinusitis as a precipitant of vocal cord dysfunction. The best current explanation for an association of CHES with asthma is that the activation of T helper lymphocytes in the sinuses leads to the differentiation and activation of immune cells including eosinophils and basophils from precursors present in the nasal tissue and bone marrow. In subjects with pre-existing asthma, the presence of specific adhesion molecules, such as VCAM-1, and chemotactic molecules, such as CCL11 (eotaxin) and the CysLTs in the lungs will promote the recruitment of these newly generated cells from the circulation. Finally, pharmacological and surgical interventions which act to reduce systemic effects of CHES, including topical corticosteroids, leukotriene modifiers and aspirin desensitization could modulate severity of asthma, although clinical trials with appropriate outcome measures are needed.

References

1. Kaliner MA, Osguthorpe JD, Fireman P. Sinusitis: Bench to bedside. *J Allergy Clin Immunol* 1997; **99**(6, Part 2): 829.

2. Meltzer EO, Hamilos DL, Hadley JA, *et al.* Rhinosinusitis: establishing definitions for clinical research and patient care. *J Allergy Clin Immunol* 2004; **114**(6 Suppl): 155–212.

3. Slavin RG, Spector SL, Bernstein IL, *et al.* The diagnosis and management of sinusitis: A practice parameter update. *J Allergy Clin Immunol* 2005; **116**(Suppl 6): S13–47.

4. Orobello Jr PW, Park RI, Belcher LJ, *et al.* Microbiology of chronic sinusitis in children. *Arch Otolaryngol Head Neck Surg* 1991; **117**: 980–3.

5. Poole MD. Pediatric sinusitis is not a surgical disease. *ENT Journal* 1992; **71**(12): 622–3.

6. Wald ER. Microbiology of acute and chronic sinusitis in children and adults. *Am J Medical Science* 1998; **316**(1): 13–20.

7. Sharp HJ, Denman D, Puumala S, Leopold DA. Treatment of acute and chronic rhinosinusitis in the United States, 1999–2002. *Arch Otolaryngol Head Neck Surg* 2007; **133**(3): 260–5.

8. Demoly P, Crampette L, Mondain M, *et al.* Assessment of inflammation in noninfectious chronic maxillary sinusitis. *J Allergy Clin Immunol* 1994; **94**: 95–108.

9. Tinkleman DG, Silk HJ. Clinical and bacteriologic features of chronic sinusiti in children. *American J Disease Children* 1989; **143**: 938–41.

10. Van Zele T, Claeys S, Gevaert P, *et al.* Differentiation of chronic sinus diseases by

measurement of inflammatory mediators. *Allergy* 2006; **61**(11): 1280–9.

11. Berger G, Kattan A, Bernheim J, Ophir D. Polypoid mucosa with eosinophilia and glandular hyperplasia in chronic sinusitis: a histopathological and immunohistochemical study. *Laryngoscope* 2002; **112**(4): 738–45.

12. Kountakis SE, Arango P, Bradley D, *et al.* Molecular and cellular staging for the severity of chronic rhinosinusitis. *Laryngoscope* 2004; **114**(11): 1895–905.

13. Early SB, Han JW, Borish L. Histologic examination reveals distinct disease subsets of chronic sinusitis. *J Allergy Clin Immunol* 2007; **119**(1): S243.

14. Kennedy DW. Prognostic factors, outcomes and staging in ethmoid sinus surgery. *Laryngoscope* 1992; **102**(12 Pt 2 Suppl 57): 1–18.

15. Lavigne F, Nguyen CT, Cameron L, *et al.* Prognosis and prediction of response to surgery in allergic patients with chronic sinusitis. *J Allergy Clin Immunol* 2000; **105**(4): 746–51.

16. Szczeklik A, Sanak M. Molecular mechanisms in aspirin-induced asthma. *ACI International* 2000; **12**(4): 171–6.

17. Vally H, Taylor ML, Thompson PJ. The prevalence of aspirin intolerant asthma (AIA) in Australian asthmatic patients. *Thorax* 2002; **57**: 569–74.

18. Schubert MS, Goetz DW. Evaluation and treatment of allergic fungal sinusitis. I. Demographics and diagnosis. *J Allergy Clin Immunol* 1998; **102**(3): 387–94.

19. Ponikau JU, Sherris DA, Kern EB, *et al.* The diagnosis and incidence of allergic fungal sinusitis. *Mayo Clin Proc* 1999; **74**(9): 877–84.

20. Hamilos DL, Leung DYM, Wood R, *et al.* Eosinophil infiltration in nonallergic chronic hyperplastic sinusitis with nasal polyposis (CHS/NP) is associated with endothelial VCAM-1 upregulation and expression of TNF-α. *Am J Respir Cell Mol Biol* 1996; **15**: 443–50.

21. Harlin SL, Ansel DG, Lane SR, *et al.* A clinical and pathologic study of chronic sinusitis: The role of the eosinophil. *J Allergy Clin Immunol* 1988; **81**: 867–75.

22. Ferguson BJ. Eosinophilic mucin rhinosinusitis: a distinct clinicopathological entity. *Laryngoscope* 2000; **110**: 799–813.

23. Ponikau JU, Sherris DA, Kephart GM, *et al.* Striking deposition of toxic eosinophil major basic protein in mucus: implications for chronic rhinosinusitis. *J Allergy Clin Immunol* 2005; **116**(2): 362–9.

24. Mygind N, Dahl R, Bachert C. Nasal polyposis, eosinophil dominated inflammation, and allergy. *Thorax* 2000; **55**(Suppl 2): S79–83.

25. Perez-Novo CA, Watelet JB, Claeys C, *et al.* Prostaglandin, leukotriene, and lipoxin balance in chronic rhinosinusitis with and without nasal polyposis. *J Allergy Clin Immunol* 2005; **115**(6): 1189–96.

26. Mascia K, Borish L, Patrie J, *et al.* Chronic hyperplastic eosinophilic sinusitis as a predictor of aspirin-exacerbated respiratory disease. *Ann Allergy Asthma Immunol* 2005; **94**(6): 652–7.

27. Denburg JA, Sehmi R, Saito H, *et al.* Systemic aspects of allergic disease: bone marrow responses. *J Allergy Clin Immunol* 2000; **106**: S242–6.

28. Braunstahl GJ, Overbeek SE, Kleinjan A, *et al.* Nasal allergen provocation induces adhesion molecule expression and tissue eosinophilia in upper and lower airways. *J Allergy Clin Immunol* 2001; **107**(3): 469–76.

29. Spada CS, Nieves AL, Krauss AH, Woodward DF. Comparison of leukotriene B4 and D4 effects on human eosinophil and neutrophil motility *in vitro*. *J Leukocyte Biol* 1994; **55**: 183–91.

30. Hamilos D, Leung DYM, Wood R, *et al.* Chronic hyperplastic sinusitis: Association of tissue eosinophilia with mRNA expression of granulocyte-macrophage colony-stimulating factor and interleukin-3. *J Allergy Clin Immunol* 1993; **92**: 39–48.

31. Finotto S, Ohno I, Marshall JS, *et al.* TNF-α production by eosinophils in upper airways inflammation (nasal polyposis). *J Immunol* 1994; **153**: 2278–89.

32. Hamilos DL, Leung DYM, Wood R, *et al.* Evidence for distinct cytokine expression in allergic versus nonallergic chronic sinusitis. *J Allergy Clin Immunol* 1995; **96**: 537–44.

33. Bachert C, Wagenmann M, Hauser U, Rudack C. IL-5 synthesis is upregulated in human nasal polyp tissue. *J Allergy Clin Immunol* 1997; **99**: 837–42.

34. Minshall EM, Cameron L, Lavigne F, *et al.* Eotaxin mRNA and protein expression in chronic sinusitis and allergen-induced nasal responses in seasonal allergic rhinitis. *Am J Respir Cell Mol Biol* 1997; **17**: 683–90.

35. Hamilos DL, Leung DYM, Huston DP, *et al.* GM-CSF, IL-5, and RANTES immunoreactivity and mRNA expression in chronic hyperplastic sinusitis with nasal polyposis. *Clin Exp Allergy* 1998; **28**: 1145–52.

36. Steinke JW. Mediator feedback loops: difficulties in treating chronic hyperplastic eosinophilic sinusitis/nasal polyposis. *Recent Res Devel Allergy and Clin Immunol* 2004; **5**: 15–25.

37. Kim YK, Uno M, Hamilos DL, *et al.* Immunolocalization of CD34 in nasal polyposis. Effect of topical corticosteroids. *Am J Respir Cell Mol Biol* 1999; **20**(3): 388–97.

38. Denburg JA. Haemopoietic mechanisms in nasal polyposis and asthma. *Thorax* 2000; **55**(Suppl 2): S24–5.

39. Krakauer T. Immune response to staphylococcal superantigens. *Immunol Res* 1999; **20**(2): 163–73.

40. Van Zele T, Gevaert P, Watelet JB, *et al.* Staphylococcus aureus colonization and IgE antibody formation to enterotoxins is increased in nasal polyposis. *J Allergy Clin Immunol* 2004; **114**(4): 981–3.

41. Bachert C, Gevaert P, Holtappels G, *et al.* Total and specific IgE in nasal polyps is related to local eosinophilic inflammation. *J Allergy Clin Immunol* 2001; **107**(4): 607–14.

42. Schubert MS. A superantigen hypothesis for the pathogenesis of chronic hypertrophic rhinosinusitis, allergic fungal sinusitis, and related disorders. *Ann Allergy Asthma Immunol* 2001; **87**(3): 181–8.

43. Bachert C, Gevaert P, van Cauwenberge P. Staphylococcus aureus superantigens and airway disease. *Curr Allergy Asthma Rep* 2002; **2**(3): 252–8.

44. Picado C, Ramis I, Rosello J, *et al.* Release of peptide leukotriene into nasal secretions after local instillation of aspirin in aspirin-sensitive asthmatic patients. *Am Rev Respir Dis* 1992; **145**: 65–9.

45. Israel E, Fischer AR, Rosenberg MA, *et al.* The pivotal role of 5-lipoxygenase products in the reaction of aspirin-sensitive asthmatics to aspirin. *Am Rev Respir Dis* 1993; **148**: 1447–51.

46. Szczeklik A, Sladek K, Dworski R, *et al.* Bronchial aspirin challenge causes specific eicosanoid response in aspirin-sensitive asthmatics. *Am J Respiratory Critical Care Medicine* 1996; **154**: 1608–14.

47. Kanaoka Y, Boyce JA. Cysteinyl leukotrienes and their receptors: cellular distribution and function in immune and inflammatory responses. *J Immunol* 2004; **173**(3): 1503–10.

48. Cowburn AS, Sladek K, Soja J, *et al.* Overexpression of leukotriene C4 synthase in bronchial biopsies from patients with aspirin-intolerant asthma. *J Clin Invest* 1998; **101**: 834–46.

49. Szczeklik A, Nizankowska E. Clinical features and diagnosis of aspirin induced asthma. *Thorax* 2000; **55**(Suppl 2): S42–4.

50. Sampson AP, Cowburn AS, Sladek K, *et al.* Profound overexpression of leukotriene C4 synthase in bronchial biopsies from aspirin-intolerant asthmatic patients. *Int Archives Allergy Immunology* 1997; **113**: 355–7.

51. Nasser SMS, Patel M, Bell GS, Lee TH. The effect of aspirin desensitization on urinary leukotriene E4 concentrations in aspirin-sensitive asthma. *Am J Respir Crit Care Med* 1995; **151**: 1326–30.

52. Steinke JW, Bradley D, Arango P, *et al.* Cysteinyl leukotriene expression in chronic hyperplastic sinusitis-nasal polyposis: importance to eosinophilia and asthma. *J Allergy Clin Immunol* 2003; **111**(2): 342–9.

53. Mascia K, Haselkorn T, Deniz YM, *et al.* Aspirin sensitivity and severity of asthma: evidence for irreversible airway obstruction in patients with severe or difficult-to-treat asthma. *J Allergy Clin Immunol* 2005; **116**(5): 970–5.

54. Sestini P, Armetti L, Gambaro G, *et al.* Inhaled PgE2 prevents aspirin-induced bronchoconstriction and urinary LTE4 excretion in aspirin-sensitive asthma. *Am J Respir Crit Care Med* 1996; **153**: 572–5.

55. Stevenson DD, Simon RA. Lack of cross-reactivity between rofecoxib and aspirin in aspirin-sensitive patients with asthma. *J Allergy Clin Immunol* 2001; **108**(1): 47–51.

56. Woessner KM, Simon RA, Stevenson DD. The safety of celecoxib in patients with aspirin-sensitive asthma. *Arthritis Rheum* 2002; **46**(8): 2201–6.

57. Lynch KR, O'Neill GP, Liu Q, *et al.* Characterization of the human cysteinyl leukotriene CysLT1 receptor. *Nature* 1999; **399**(6738): 789–93.

58. Sjöström M, Johansson AS, Schroder O, *et al.* Dominant expression of the CysLT2 receptor accounts for calcium signaling by cysteinyl leukotrienes in human umbilical vein endothelial cells. *Arterioscler Thromb Vasc Biol* 2003; **23**(8): E37–41.

59. Heise CE, O'Dowd BF, Figueroa DJ, *et al.* Characterization of the human cysteinyl leukotriene 2 receptor. *J Biol Chem* 2000; **275**(39): 30531–6.

60. Figueroa DJ, Borish L, Baramki D, *et al.* Expression of cysteinyl leukotriene synthetic and signaling proteins in inflammatory cells in active seasonal allergic rhinitis. *Clin Exp Allergy* 2003; **33**: 1380–8.

61. Arm JP, O'Hickey SP, Spur BW, Lee TH. Airway responsiveness to histamine and leukotriene E4 in subjects with aspirin-induced asthma. *Am Rev Respir Dis* 1989; **140**: 148–53.

62. Sousa AR, Parikh A, Scadding G, *et al.* Leukotriene-receptor expression on nasal mucosal inflammatory cells in aspirin-sensitive rhinosinusitis. *New Engl J Med* 2002; **347**(19): 1493–9.

63. Schmid M, Gode U, Schafer D, Wigand ME. Arachidonic acid metabolism in nasal tissue and peripheral blood cells in aspirin intolerant asthmatics. *Acta Otolaryngol* 1999; **119**(2): 277–80.

64. Ying S, Meng Q, Scadding G, *et al.* Aspirin sensitive rhinosinusitis is associated with reduced E-prostanoid 2 (EP2) receptor expression on nasal mucosal inflammatory cells. *J Allergy Clin Immunol* 2006; (in press).

65. Newman LJ, Platts-Mills TAE, Phillips CD, *et al.* Chronic sinusitis. Relationship of computed tomographic findings to allergy, asthma, and eosinophilia. *J Am Med Assoc* 1994; **271**: 363–7.

66. Pfister R, Lutolf M, Schapowal A, *et al.* Screening for sinus disease in patients with asthma: a computed tomography-controlled comparison of A-mode ultrasonography and standard radiography. *J Allergy Clin Immunol* 1994; **94**: 804–9.

67. Bresciani M, Paradis L, Des Rouches A, *et al.* Rhinosinusitis in severe asthma. *J Allergy Clin Immunol* 2001; **107**: 73–80.

68. ten Brinke A, Grootendorst DC, Schmidt JT, *et al.* Chronic sinusitis in severe asthma is related to sputum eosinophilia. *J Allergy Clin Immunol* 2002; **109**: 621–6.

69. Peters E, Hatley TK, Crater SE, *et al.* Sinus computed tomography scan and markers of inflammation in vocal cord dysfunction and asthma. *Ann Allergy Asthma Immunol* 2003; **90**(3): 316–22.

70. Settipane GA, Chafee FH. Nasal polyps in asthma and rhinitis. A review of 6,037 patients. *J Allergy Clin Immunol* 1977; **59**(1): 17–21.

71. Rachelefsky GS, Goldberg M, Katz RM, *et al.* Sinus disease in children with respiratory

allergy. *J Allergy Clin Immunol* 1978; **61**(5): 310–14.

72. Slavin RG, Zilliox AP, Samuels LD. Is there such an entity as allergic sinusitis? *J Allergy Clin Immunol* 1988; **81**: 284A.

73. Borts MR, Slavin RG. Further studies in allergic sinusitis using SPECT. *J Allergy Clin Immunol* 1989; **83**(Suppl 1): 302A.

74. Pelikan Z, Pelikan-Filipek M. Role of nasal allergy in chronic maxillary sinusitis – diagnostic value of nasal challenge with allergens. *J Allergy Clin Immunol* 1990; **86**: 484–91.

75. Rachelefsky GS. National guidelines needed to manage rhinitis and prevent complications. *Ann Allergy Asthma Immunol* 1999; **82**(3): 296–305.

76. Baroody FM, Saengpanich S, deTineo M, *et al.* Nasal allergen challenge leads to bilateral maxillary sinus eosinophil influx. *J Allergy Clin Immunol* 2002; **109**: S84.

77. Gwaltney JM Jr, Phillips CD, Miller RD, Riker DK. Computed tomographic study of the common cold. *N Engl J Med* 1994; **330**: 25–30.

78. Johnston SL, Pattemore PK, Sanderson G, *et al.* Community study of the role of viral infections in exacerbations of asthma in 9–11 year old children. *Br Med J* 1995; **310**: 1225–9.

79. Heymann PW, Carper HT, Murphy DD, *et al.* Viral infections in relation to age, atopy, and season of admission among children hospitalized for wheezing. *J Allergy Clin Immunol* 2004; **114**(2): 239–47.

80. Rachelefsky GS, Katz RM, Siegel SC. Chronic sinus disease with associated reactive airway disease in children. *Pediatrics* 1984; **73**(4): 526–9.

81. Slavin RG. Asthma and sinusitis. *J Allergy Clin Immunol* 1992; **90**: 534–7.

82. Ragab S, Scadding GK, Lund VJ, Saleh H. Treatment of chronic rhinosinusitis and its effects on asthma. *Eur Respir J* 2006; **28**(1): 68–74.

83. Brugman SM, Larsen GL, Henson PM, *et al.* Increased lower airways responsiveness associated with sinusitis in a rabbit model. *Am Rev Respir Dis* 1993; **147**: 314–20.

84. Bardin PG, Van Heerden BB, Joubert JR. Absence of pulmonary aspiration of sinus contents in patients with asthma and sinusitis. *J Allergy Clin Immunol* 1990; **86**: 82–8.

85. Bucca C, Rolla G, Scappaticci E, *et al.* Extrathoracic and intrathoracic airway responsiveness in sinusitis. *J Allergy Clin Immunol* 1995; **95**(1, Part 1): 52–9.

86. Wood LJ, Inman MD, Denburg JA, O'Byrne PM. Allergen challenge increases cell traffic between bone marrow and lung. *Am J Respir Cell Mol Biol* 1998; **18**(6): 759–67.

87. Gaspar Elsas MI, Joseph D, Elsas PX, Vargaftig BB. Rapid increase in bone-marrow eosinophil production and responses to eosinopoietic interleukins triggered by intranasal allergen challenge. *Am J Respir Cell Mol Biol* 1997; **17**(4): 404–13.

88. Inman MD, Ellis R, Wattie J, *et al.* Allergen-induced increase in airway responsiveness, airway eosinophilia, and bone-marrow eosinophil progenitors in mice. *Am J Respir Cell Mol Biol* 1999; **21**(4): 473–9.

89. Linden M, Svensson C, Andersson M, *et al.* Circulating eosinophil/basophil progenitors and nasal mucosal cytokines in seasonal allergic rhinitis. *Allergy* 1999; **54**(3): 212–19.

90. Steinke JW, Borish L. The role of allergy in chronic rhinosinusitis. *Immunol Allergy Clin North Am* 2004; **24**(1): 45–57.

91. Jahnsen FL, Haraldsen G, Aanesen JP, *et al.* Eosinophil infiltration is related to increased expression of vascular cell adhesion molecule-1 in nasal polyps. *Am J Respir Cell Mol Biol* 1995; **12**(6): 624–32.

92. Cady RK, Schreiber CP. Sinus headache or migraine? Considerations in making a differential diagnosis. *Neurology* 2002; **58**(9 Suppl 6): S10–14.

93. Perry BF, Login IS, Kountakis SE. Nonrhinologic headache in a tertiary rhinology practice. *Otolaryngol Head Neck Surg* 2004; **130**(4): 449–52.

94. Zeiger RS. Prospects for ancillary treatment of sinusitis in the 1990s. *J Allergy Clin Immunol* 1992; **90**: 478.

95. Arbes SJ Jr, Gergen PJ, Elliott L, Zeldin DC. Prevalences of positive skin test responses to 10 common allergens in the US population: results from the third National Health and Nutrition Examination Survey. *J Allergy Clin Immunol* 2005; **116**(2): 377–83.

96. Adkins TN, Goodgold HM, Hendershott L, Slavin RG. Does inhaled pollen enter the sinus cavities? *Ann Allergy Asthma Immunol* 1998; **81**(2): 181–4.

97. Gwaltney JM Jr, Hendley JO, Phillips CD, *et al.* Nose blowing propels nasal fluid into the paranasal sinuses. *Clin Infect Dis* 2000; **30**(2): 387–91.

98. Hissaria P, Smith W, Wormald PJ, *et al.* Short course of systemic corticosteroids in sinonasal polyposis: a double-blind, randomized, placebo-controlled trial with evaluation of outcome measures. *J Allergy Clin Immunol* 2006; **118**(1): 128–33.

99. Benitez P, Alobid I, de Haro J, *et al.* A short course of oral prednisone followed by intranasal budesonide is an effective treatment of severe nasal polyps. *Laryngoscope* 2006; **116**(5): 770–5.

100. Barnes PJ. Mechanisms of action of glucocorticoids in asthma. *Am J Respir Crit Care Med* 1996; **154**(2 Pt 2): S21–6; discussion S6–7.

101. Wood LJ, Sehmi R, Gauvreau GM, *et al.* An inhaled corticosteroid, budesonide, reduces baseline but not allergen-induced increases in bone marrow inflammatory cell progenitors in asthmatic subjects. *Am J Respir Crit Care Med* 1999; **159**(5 Pt 1): 1457–63.

102. Small CB, Hernandez J, Reyes A, *et al.* Efficacy and safety of mometasone furoate nasal spray in nasal polyposis. *J Allergy Clin Immunol* 2005; **116**(6): 1275–81.

103. Knorr B, Matz J, Bernstein JA, *et al.* Montelukast for chronic asthma in 6- to 14-year old children: a randomized, double-blind trial. *J Am Med Assoc* 1998; **279**: 1181–6.

104. Pizzichini E, Leff JA, Reiss TF, *et al.* Montelukast reduces airway eosinophilic inflammation in asthma: a randomized, controlled trial. *Eur Respir J* 1999; **14**: 12–18.

105. Parnes SM, Churna AV. Acute effects of antileukotrienes on sinonasal polyposis and sinusitis. *ENT Journal* 2000; **79**(1): 18–21.

106. Mostafa BE, Abdel Hay H, Mohammed HE, Yamani M. Role of leukotriene inhibitors in the postoperative management of nasal polyps. *ORL J Otorhinolaryngol Relat Spec* 2005; **67**(3): 148–53.

107. Dahlen B, Nizankowska E, Szczeklik A, *et al.* Benefits from adding the 5-lipoxygenase inhibitor zileuton to conventional therapy in aspirin-intolerant asthmatics. *Am J Respir Crit Care Med* 1998; **157**(4 Pt 1): 1187–94.

108. Taylor MJ, Ponikau JU, Sherris DA, *et al.* Detection of fungal organisms in eosinophilic mucin using a fluorescein-labeled chitin-specific binding protein. *Otolaryngol Head Neck Surg* 2002; **127**(5): 377–83.

109. Shin SH, Ponikau JU, Sherris DA, *et al.* Chronic rhinosinusitis: an enhanced immune response to ubiquitous airborne fungi. *J Allergy Clin Immunol* 2004; **114**(6): 1369–75.

110. Ponikau JU, Sherris DA, Weaver A, Kita H. Treatment of chronic rhinosinusitis with intranasal amphotericin B: a randomized, placebo-controlled, double-blind pilot trial. *J Allergy Clin Immunol* 2005; **115**(1): 125–31.

111. Ebbens FA, Scadding GK, Badia L, *et al.* Amphotericin B nasal lavages: not a solution for patients with chronic rhinosinusitis. *J Allergy Clin Immunol* 2006; **118**(5): 1149–56.

112. Stevenson DD, Simon RA. Selection of patients for aspirin desensitization treatment. *J Allergy Clin Immunol* 2006; **118**(4): 801–4.

113. Milgrom H. Is there a role for treatment of asthma with omalizumab? *Arch Dis Child* 2003; **88**(1): 71–4.

114. Gevaert P, Holtappels G, Johansson SG, *et al.* Organization of secondary lymphoid tissue and local IgE formation to Staphylococcus aureus enterotoxins in nasal polyp tissue. *Allergy* 2005; **60**(1): 71–9.

115. Blyth DI, Wharton TF, Pedrick MS, *et al.* Airway subepithelial fibrosis in a murine model of atopic asthma: suppression by dexamethasone or anti-interleukin-5 antibody. *Am J Respir Cell Mol Biol* 2000; **23**(2): 241–6.

116. Trifilieff A, Fujitani Y, Coyle AJ, *et al.* IL-5 deficiency abolishes aspects of airway remodelling in a murine model of lung inflammation. *Clin Exp Allergy* 2001; **31**(6): 934–42.

117. Tanaka H, Komai M, Nagao K, *et al.* Role of interleukin-5 and eosinophils in allergen-induced airway remodeling in mice. *Am J Respir Cell Mol Biol* 2004; **31**(1): 62–8.

118. Cho JY, Miller M, Baek KJ, *et al.* Inhibition of airway remodeling in IL-5-deficient mice. *J Clin Invest* 2004; **113**(4): 551–60.

119. Humbles AA, Lloyd CM, McMillan SJ, *et al.* A critical role for eosinophils in allergic airways remodeling. *Science* 2004; **305**(5691): 1776–9.

120. Weller PF. Human eosinophils. *J Allergy Clin Immunol* 1997; **100**: 283.

121. Giembycz MA, Lindsay MA. Pharmacology of the eosinophil. *Pharmacol Reviews* 1999; **51**(2): 213–339.

122. Zagai U, Skold CM, Trulson A, *et al.* The effect of eosinophils on collagen gel contraction and implications for tissue remodelling. *Clin Exp Immunol* 2004; **135**(3): 427–33.

123. Flood-Page PT, Menzies-Gow AN, Kay AB, Robinson DS. Eosinophil's role remains uncertain as anti-interleukin-5 only partially depletes numbers in asthmatic airway. *Am J Respir Crit Care Med* 2003; **167**(2): 199–204.

124. Flood-Page P, Menzies-Gow A, Phipps S, *et al.* Anti-IL-5 treatment reduces deposition of ECM proteins in the bronchial subepithelial basement membrane of mild atopic asthmatics. *J Clin Invest* 2003; **112**(7): 1029–36.

125. Gevaert P, Lang-Loidolt D, Lackner A, *et al.* Nasal IL-5 levels determine the response to anti-IL-5 treatment in patients with nasal polyps. *J Allergy Clin Immunol* 2006; **118**(5): 1133–41.

126. Braccioni F, Dorman SC, O'Byrne PM, *et al.* The effect of cysteinyl leukotrienes on growth of eosinophil progenitors from peripheral blood and bone marrow of atopic subjects. *J Allergy Clin Immunol* 2002; **110**(1): 96–101.

127. Mochizuki A, Tamura N, Yatabe Y, *et al.* Suppressive effects of F-1322 on the antigen-induced late asthmatic response and pulmonary eosinophilia in guinea pigs. *Eur J Pharmacol* 2001; **430**(1): 123–33.

PART III

Skin

6

Eczema

MICHAEL ARDERN-JONES, PETER FRIEDMANN

KEY POINTS

1. There are many types of eczema, most of which do not involve allergy.

2. Allergic contact eczema/dermatitis is a specific T lymphocyte-mediated immune reaction to exogenous chemicals.

3. Allergic causality is established by topical patch tests with suspected chemicals. Tests are read at 48 hours.

4. The predisposition to atopic dermatitis is likely to be genetically determined defects in the skin barrier and immune system.

5. Allergens derived from many environmental substances including dust mite, animal fur and occasionally foods are implicated in the manifestation of atopic dermatitis.

6. Immediate (IgE mediated) reactions are not commonly important triggers of atopic dermatitis.

Introduction

The term eczema (interchangeable term: dermatitis) denotes a pattern of inflammation in the skin. This is characterized microscopically by infiltration predominantly of lymphocytes and the formation of fluid within the epidermis as well as the dermis. Clinically, the lesions of eczema are itchy and consist of tiny erythematous papules, which may coalesce to form ill-defined patches. The fluid may form tiny collections and sometimes coalesce to form bigger blisters, or may simply ooze and 'weep' through the epidermis. Eczema may be differentiated into endogenous (no known predisposition) or exogenous (genetic predisposition to responses to the environment) as defined by the causative factor involved. Eczemas with external causation are classified further as allergic or irritant. Allergic responses are specific to the individual and the allergen involved, whereas irritant responses may occur in any individual and are not specific to the irritant. Eczemas with an external cause include allergic contact eczema, irritant contact eczema, sunlight-induced eczema and atopic eczema. In these exogenous eczemas there is an underlying genetic susceptibility to developing allergy. This chapter will focus on irritant and allergic contact eczema and atopic eczema since these are the conditions in which management of allergy is of crucial importance.

Irritant and allergic contact eczema (dermatitis)

Aetiology and pathogenesis

The skin comes into contact with a wide range of environmental chemical substances on a daily basis. Many of these are potentially toxic and many are capable of inducing T lymphocyte-mediated immunological reactions. Irritants are generally not able to activate specific T cell responses (adaptive immunity) but through their toxic effects they can activate innate immune responses in the form of cytokines and non-specific recruitment of inflammatory processes. Typical irritants are surfactants (soaps and detergents), solvents (petrol, paraffin) or caustics (acids or alkalis). Contact sensitizers are mostly small molecules which, in susceptible individuals, can evoke adaptive immune responses via recognition by T lymphocytes. Once immune sensitization has occurred and clones of specific memory/effector T cells have been generated, then wherever the sensitizer contacts the skin, the T cell-mediated inflammation of contact eczema will be elicited.

Mechanisms of sensitization by contact allergens

Small chemical entities are not visible to T lymphocytes unless they act as haptens, becoming bound to proteins which act as carriers, suitable for mounting in the grooves of major histocompatibility complex (MHC) molecules and hence recognition by T cell receptors. Chemicals vary in their intrinsic sensitizing potency, but their ability to act as immunogens is mainly related to their chemical reactivity and ability to bind to proteins [1–3]. In order to mount a 'positive' immune response to a chemical, the immune system has to receive danger signals that activate dendritic cells—most potent contact sensitizers are also irritants and it is likely that the irritant effects involve activation of the innate immune response. The contact sensitizer has to penetrate to the viable layers of the epidermis where they are taken up by the epidermal dendritic antigen-presenting cells—Langerhans' cells. In response to the danger signals sensed by the keratinocytes and Langerhans' cells in the epidermis, cytokines interleukin-1β and tumour necrosis factor-α (TNFα) are produced which stimulate the Langerhans' cells to migrate down into the dermis carrying whatever substance(s) perturbed their environment (Fig. 6.1) [4,5]. At the same time, the dermis responds to the perturbation by activating mechanisms that facilitate trafficking of T cells into the skin, hence enhancing immune surveillance. Thus, microvascular endothelium increases expression of adhesion molecules intercellular adhesion molecule (ICAM)-1 and E-selectin while chemokines are released which can attract T cells

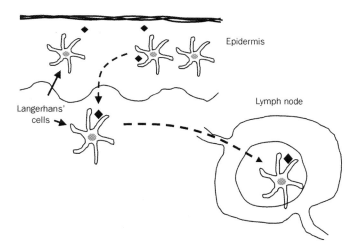

Fig. 6.1 Perturbation of epidermis in response to contact sensitizer. Perturbation by haptens induces migration of Langerhans' cells down into the dermis carrying the perturbing antigen. They then migrate to the regional lymph node to present the antigen to T cells.

passing through the dermal microvessels |6|. The Langerhans' cells migrate to the regional lymph nodes and on the way they mature into more potent antigen presenting cells by augmenting their expression of MHC-class II and costimulatory molecules (CD40, 80 and 86). Upon arrival in the regional nodes they enter the T cell-rich paracortical regions where they present their 'cargo' to the naïve T cells. When a T cell with the appropriate hapten-specific cognate receptor recognizes its target, it is activated by the dendritic cell via the full range of signals, surface costimulatory molecules and cytokines. It undergoes proliferation to generate a clone of memory/effector T cells, which leave the lymph node to enter the systemic circulation. These T cells are able to circulate to the skin and respond to presentation of the sensitizer by antigen presenting cells. However, the majority of cells will undergo apoptosis without further activation. A small fraction of T cells establish long-lived immunological memory for that hapten/sensitizer, so that the next time it is in contact with the skin the T cell response will be recruited to the site over 18–24 h to generate the allergic contact hypersensitivity response which is manifested as allergic contact eczema.

Diagnosis of contact allergy

The first part of the process of diagnosis is the clinical assessment. The rash must be recognized as eczematous and the distribution on the body should be compatible with the pattern of contact with the suspected or possible contact sensitizers. When eczema is confined to the hands, the differential diagnosis will include irritant contact dermatitis, which is usually induced by solvents, soaps/detergents, acids, alkalis and various forms of wet work including handling raw foods. If the eczema is localized to the face and hands (dorsa) it may indicate that sunlight is playing a role as a provoking agent. In some cases, long wavelength ultraviolet (UV-A) light can directly trigger an eczematous reaction—photo-dermatitis. In others, the UV light may interact with chemicals to generate altered photoproducts that may be immunogenic—the condition of photo-allergic dermatitis.

A careful history must be taken to assess the likely exposure to possible sources of contact sensitivity that the individual may experience in day-to-day living. Individuals with contact allergies are often aware of the culprits or they may have suspicions. The time course of exacerbations and ameliorations of the rash in relation to time at work or engagement with hobbies such as gardening or painting may provide important clues. The nature of the occupation is important, as there are particular risks associated with many occupations. Hairdressing, the building industry, the electrical industry, the woodworking and joinery industry are all examples of occupations that have particular occupational exposure risks. Patients with facial eczema may be reacting to personal products applied to the skin or to airborne products including fragrances in aerosols, 'vapours' from house plants or fumes from occupations or hobbies involving soldering or welding. A source of contact allergy that is easily overlooked is the ingredients in topical medicaments—preservatives, stabilizers and even the active drug molecules such as corticosteroids.

Once the clinical diagnosis is suspected, one or more culprit allergens may be evident. However, to prove the patient is allergic to these and to screen for other contact sensitivities, the procedure of contact allergy patch testing should be performed.

Patch testing

The basic procedure involves application of agents to be tested to the skin, usually of the back, in purpose-designed chambers. The most frequently employed are Finn® chambers which are circular aluminium discs moulded to have a central depression or chamber. The substance to be tested is usually mixed in white soft paraffin, which can be placed directly in the chamber; liquids can be dropped onto an absorbent paper disc placed in the chamber. Each chamber is mounted on an adhesive hypoallergenic adhesive tape (Scanpore). Other chambers also available include Hill Top® which are rectangular plastic chambers and T.R.U.E. Test® which are paper discs impregnated with the standard contact allergens and mounted on adhesive tape in strips. The chambers are applied in strips to the upper back over the scapulae if possible. The whole assembly is then carefully marked with indelible marker pen to enable location of the placement of the different allergens after the chambers have been removed. The patches are removed 48 h later and read (Box 6.1) according to the scale devised by the International Contact Dermatitis Research Group (ICDRG) |7|:

Box 6.1 Reading patch test responses as set out by ICDRG |7|.

?+	Doubtful reaction; faint erythema only
+	Weak positive reaction; erythema, infiltration, possibly papules
++	Strong positive reaction; erythema, infiltration, papules, vesicles
+++	Extreme positive reaction; intense erythema and infiltration, coalescing vesicles
IR	Irritant reaction—different types
NT	Not tested

The first patch tests are normally performed using the 'European Standard Battery' (ESB) devised by the ICDRG. This battery comprises 30 tests including metals (nickel cobalt, chromate); dye substances (paraphenylenediamine and other azo dyes used in clothing); rubber chemicals (grouped as a mixture), thiurams (used in the vulcanization of rubber) and the mercapto mix (comprising chemicals used as accelerators in hard rubbers such as shoe soles). In addition, there is a group of excipients used in medicaments and personal products, including preservatives and stabilizers.

While the ESB is often adequate for detecting common contact allergies, it is frequently necessary to use more specialized batteries containing chemicals relevant to particular occupations or situations. When the patch test reactions are read they must be assessed as being either true allergic (type IV hypersensitivity) or irritant reactions. Irritant reactions often have more sharply defined margins and less oedematous swelling than true positive reactions. The next part of the diagnostic procedure is that of determining whether positive responses to patch test challenges are of clinical relevance—are they detecting the causally relevant allergy or are there positive responses which are not causally relevant and which can be discounted?

The process of determining which allergens should be tested and what the responses mean is highly specialized and should be performed by specifically trained staff in dermatology departments with appropriate equipment. Having established that there are clinically relevant contact allergies present, the crucial part of management of allergic contact eczema then becomes the avoidance of the causal allergens. Sometimes this is easy, and can be achieved by changing to a different personal product or medicament. However, frequently, there is a significant implication regarding the person's workplace and their job. Redeploying people within the workplace is one method of avoiding contact with causally important substances, but some individuals have to give up their job, sometimes needing to retrain and enter a completely new profession. One of the hardest groups of allergens to avoid are the rubber accelerators—people with shoe dermatitis can find it remarkably difficult to find shoes that are free of all rubber components—rubber glues are used almost universally in shoe manufacture.

In conclusion, the management of contact eczema involves identification of the causal factors—irritants or sensitizers, avoidance of the culprit and treatment of the skin inflammation with appropriate topical anti-inflammatory corticosteroids and emollients.

Atopic eczema—atopic dermatitis (atopic eczema)

Definition

Atopic dermatitis is widely recognized to be a disease of many clinical appearances. As a result it has not only been described by a number of different names but criteria for diagnosis have varied. Realizing the importance of a strict disease

Table 6.1 The Hanifin and Rajka diagnostic criteria for atopic dermatitis. With permission from |9|

Major criteria	Features
Pruritus	Present
Dermatitis	Affecting flexural surfaces in adults and the face and extensors in infants
Disease pattern	Chronic or relapsing
Personal or family history of atopy	Cutaneous or respiratory atopy
Minor criteria	
Features of the 'atopic face'	Facial pallor or erythema, hypopigmented patches, infraorbital darkening, infraorbital folds or wrinkles, cheilitis, recurrent conjunctivitis, and anterior neck folds
Triggers of atopic dermatitis	Foods, emotional factors, environmental factors, and skin irritants such as wool, solvents and sweat
Complications of atopic dermatitis	Susceptibility to cutaneous viral and bacterial infections, impaired cell-mediated immunity, immediate skin test reactivity, raised serum IgE, keratoconus, anterior subcapsular cataracts.
Others	Early age of onset, dry skin, ichthyosis, hyperlinear palms, keratosis pilaris, hand and foot dermatitis, nipple eczema, white dermatographism, perifollicular accentuation

A diagnosis of AD is made when three of four major and three minor symptoms are present.

Table 6.2 Criteria for the diagnosis of atopic dermatitis. Adapted with permission from |12|

Major criteria	Features
Pruritus	Evidence of itchy skin, or parental report of scratching or rubbing
Minor criteria	
History of a recurrent rash	On the flexures
Personal (or family history) of atopy	Asthma or hay fever (or first-degree relative if under 4 years)
Disease pattern	Onset under 2 years old (not used if child is under 4 years)
Current active dermatitis	In flexures (including cheeks, forehead and lateral aspects of limbs if under 4 years)

A diagnosis of AD is made when one major and three or more minor criteria are present.

definition, Hanifin and Rajka published their seminal diagnostic criteria in 1980 |8|, which Hanifin later revised (Table 6.1) |9|. These contained major and minor criteria for the diagnosis. The criteria were subsequently refined and validated by the UK working party |10–13| to produce evidence-based diagnostic criteria relevant to the outpatient setting (Table 6.2). The criteria are currently purely clinical features from history and examination with no reference to IgE, which creates some confusion when the World Allergy Organization (WAO) diagnosis of atopy is considered in respect of the name 'atopic dermatitis'. To somewhat rectify this apparent disparity, the WAO have suggested a reclassification of dermatitis (Fig. 6.2)

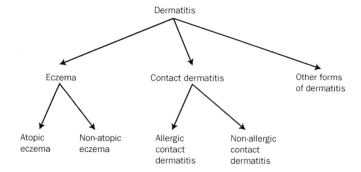

Fig. 6.2 World Allergy Organization classification of dermatitis and eczema |14|.

|14|, which distinguishes eczema from dermatitis of other causes and sub-divides eczema into atopic and non-atopic as defined by immunoglobulin (Ig)E and or skin testing.

Clinical features, natural history

The major symptom of atopic dermatitis is pruritus. However, affected individuals also suffer discomfort from very dry or cracked skin and often have difficulty sleeping. The typical cutaneous features of atopic dermatitis include scaling/xerosis, erythema, papules, vesicles, lichenification and excoriation. These features represent a wide spectrum of overlapping phenotypes. Currently, there is no good model to explain a particular disease pattern in any individual. Typically, infants present with involvement of the forehead and cheeks. In early childhood, the disease may be more flexural including elbows, knees, wrists and ankles. The adult pattern of disease arises at or after puberty and generally affects the face (often peri-orbital and forehead regions), neck, upper back, upper arms and lower legs. Hands and feet are also frequently involved in the teens and adult pattern. Discoid eczema (well demarcated lesions usually on the trunk and limbs) is more common in adult onset disease. Lichenification (thickening of the epidermis) usually predominates as a marker of chronic disease. Acute flares in all age groups will be accompanied by increased inflammation often with associated exacerbation of pruritus. Skin infection is frequent and may present as exudation, crusting and ulceration.

Disease onset is typically in early life, 60% in the first year and 85% before the age of five |15| and it affects both sexes equally. Three disease patterns are recognized: persistent disease (19%), intermittent disease (38%) and remitting disease (43%) |16|. The strongest predictive factors for development of persistent disease include disease severity and a family history of atopy |16|.

Epidemiology

Atopic dermatitis is the most common inflammatory skin disease in the UK, affecting up to 20% of the school age population and 3% of adults. World prevalence is highest in Northern Europe and developed countries |17|. For comparison, prevalence in rural Ethiopia was estimated to be 0.3% in 1996 |18|, yet this was significantly lower than the urban population of the same country (1.5%). A difference in prevalence in populations of the same genetic background separated only by geographical factors, particularly between agricultural and city dwelling populations, is also well documented in developed countries (e.g. in Finland higher prevalence occurs in the industrialized southern region in comparison to the eastern rural areas [19]). Similarly, higher socioeconomic class [20] and smaller family size [21] have been associated as risk factors for atopic dermatitis.

Over the last 50 years, numerous epidemiological studies have demonstrated an increasing prevalence of AD and allergic disease in general (e.g. from 1.3% to 23% in Scandinavia [22]). Disease incidence appears to show corresponding trends: before 1960 incidence ranged from 1.4% to 3.1%; 1960–70, 3.8% to 8.8%; after 1970, 8.9–20.4% [23].

Differential diagnosis

As discussed above, the clinical phenotype of atopic dermatitis is heterogeneous. This occasionally makes clinical diagnosis difficult. Other diseases that may mimic atopic dermatitis include cutaneous superficial fungal infections, infestations (scabies mite), and allergic contact dermatitis. The predilection for hands and feet in some individuals may also make psoriasis difficult to exclude. Facial eczema is usually distinct from seborrhoeic dermatitis but can be similar. Cutaneous lymphoma (mycosis fungoides) may also resemble atopic dermatitis in some individuals.

Histopathology

Histopathology of acute atopic dermatitis lesions demonstrate intra- and intercellular oedema (spongiosis) of the keratinocytes, which occasionally progresses to vesicle formation. Associated with spongiosis is a sparse infiltrate of CD4+ T lymphocytes in the epidermis. There is mild to moderate epidermal hyperplasia and a loose perivascular infiltrate around superficial venules in the papillary dermis.

In chronic eczema the epithelium is irregularly thickened, the papillary dermis is often hyperplastic, and a chronic inflammatory infiltrate, dominated by macrophages and eosinophils, is present in the dermis. The epidermis contains an increased number of IgE-bearing Langerhans' cells. Perineural fibrosis is often present in cutaneous nerves in the superficial portion of these lesions. The reticular dermis is usually unaffected.

Pathogenesis

Genetics

The importance of genetic factors in atopic dermatitis is underlined by the high level of concordance observed in monozygotic versus dizygotic twins (0.72–0.77 vs 0.15–0.23) [24,25]. Candidate genes that have demonstrated disease association include *filaggrin*, *IL-4*, *IL-4R* and *SPINK5*. Genome scans have revealed hot spots at 1q21 [26], 3p24–22 [27] and 3q21 [28]. Interestingly, many of the hot spots do not overlap between atopic conditions; rather there is considerable overlap between atopic dermatitis and psoriasis. This finding suggests that the focus of the genetic influence is on the skin itself [26] rather than on the immune system.

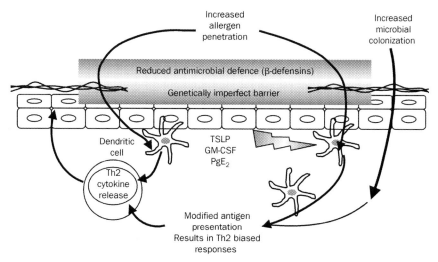

Fig. 6.3 Interaction between the epidermis and immune system in atopic eczema. The epidermis has increased permeability (genetic abnormalities of filaggrin) and reduced innate antimicrobial defences. In addition, production of thymic stromal lymphopoietin (TSLP) and prostaglandin E$_2$ conditions dendritic cells to induce Th2 differentiation. T cell re-encounter with antigen in the skin induces inflammatory Th2 cytokine release and induces down-regulation of genes involved in both antimicrobial defence and skin barrier formation.

Skin function defects

As keratinocytes differentiate towards the skin surface, they change shape (flatten) and eventually lose their nuclear components (corneocytes). Corneocytes are bound together by corneodesmosomes and these are surrounded by a complex mixture of fatty acids and enzymes known as the lipid matrix. The combination of structural and lipid components form the skin barrier, which is essential to keep required nutrients in (e.g. water) and environmental agents out (e.g. microbes). Recently it has been shown that mutations in the gene encoding a key structural protein in the skin (filaggrin) are strongly associated with atopic dermatitis |29|.

AD patients are particularly susceptible to certain cutaneous infections |30|. The most common skin infection is with *Staphylococcus aureus*. However, human papilloma virus-induced warts, fungal infections, viruses (such as HSV1 and 2, vaccinia, coxsackie A and molluscum contagiosum) are also frequent pathogens, in some cases, causing severe complications such as eczema herpeticum.

Defects in innate immune responses made by skin cells have been associated with AD (Fig. 6.3). For example, there are reported reductions in keratinocyte derived antimicrobial peptides (cathelicidin LL-37, β-defensin 2 and β-defensin 3) |31,32|; neutrophil chemoattractant IL-8 |32|; and inducible nitric oxide synthase (iNOS) |32| which mediates pathogen killing through release of NO |33|. Further compromise of antimicrobial defence in AD occurs as a result of defective dermicidin-derived antimicrobial peptides, produced by eccrine glands |34|. Production of IgA, a key epithelial antimicrobial immunoglobulin, is also reduced in the sweat and tears of AD patients |35,36| which may help explain the concordance between staphylococcal growth on both mucosal and skin surfaces in these patients.

Immune defects

In both contact dermatitis (see earlier) and atopic dermatitis, T cells infiltrate the skin early in the disease. One of the principal findings that distinguishes AD from allergic contact dermatitis is the cytokine profile present in acute lesions. In an acute lesion of AD, Th2 cytokines (IL-4, IL-5 and Il-13) predominate |37,38| whereas Th1 cytokines are dominant in allergic contact dermatitis.

T cells, which make IL-4 and IL-13, are able to induce B cell production of allergen-specific IgE. Of individuals with AD, 55–90% have increased total and specific IgE levels in the blood |39|. IgE is cross-linked on the surface of cells following encounter with allergen, this leads to degranulation and release of inflammatory mediators in mast cells and enhanced dendritic cell allergen up-take and subsequent allergen-epitope presentation to T cells. The predisposition to making allergen-specific Th2 responses is therefore thought to be central to the pathogenesis of atopic diseases. Atopic adults make Th2 responses |40,41|, and Th2 skewed responses in cord blood have been found to predict childhood atopic dermatitis |42|. Recently, thymic stromal lymphopoietin (TSLP) produced by keratinocytes has been found to modulate dendritic cell polarization of T cell responses towards Th2 |43|. Further work revealed that transgenic over-expression of TSLP in the skin induces atopic dermatitis in the mouse |44|.

Signalling between innate and adaptive immune systems as a result of mutations in pattern-recognition receptor genes has also been found to be defective in some individuals with AD.

Infection

Unlike controls, most individuals with AD will have *Staphylococcus aureus* identifiable on skin swabs, usually at higher density in lesional skin |45–47|. Treatment resulting in lower staphylococcal loads produces clinical improvement in most cases |47,48|. Furthermore, *S. aureus* present on the skin of atopics is significantly more likely to express superantigen and indeed the levels correlate with disease severity |49–51|. Recent data suggest that staphylococcal superantigen can act to enhance allergen presentation in the skin and also further skew the allergen-specific immune response to a Th2 profile |52|, thus providing a link between infection and allergy.

Hygiene

Strachan |21| first proposed the 'hygiene hypothesis' in 1989. His proposal suggested that smaller family size and increased hygiene in the home contribute to the reduction in childhood cross-infection between siblings and subsequent rise in incidence of allergic disease. However, repeated epidemiological studies have failed to reproducibly demonstrate a reduced infection rate in AD |53–63|.

Neuropeptides

Many patients report an association between stress and exacerbation of their atopic dermatitis. Further work has demonstrated that neuropeptides and nerve

Table 6.3 The frequency of positive patch test responses in patients with atopic eczema

	D. pteronyssinus	D. farinae	Cat	Grass
Adults				
Number tested	31	21	31	22
Number +ve	21	9	16	11
% +ve	68%	43%	54%	50%
Children*				
Number tested	24	15	20	24
Number +ve	14	2	8	6
% +ve	58%	13%	40%	25%

* Children were aged 7 years and above.

fibres are prominently increased in lesions of atopic dermatitis, thus suggesting an influence of efferent nerve mechanism that may regulate inflammation in the skin |64,65|.

Allergy and allergens

The role of immediate hypersensitivity (allergy) to environmental aero and food allergens is still not well established in AD. The presence of allergen-specific immune reactivity can be detected *in vitro* by tests which measure specific IgE (RAST, Immunocap), basophil function (markers of activation, histamine release), lymphocyte function (markers of activation, proliferation, cytokine release, cytotoxicity) and lymphocyte specificity (peptide–MHC conjugates). Unfortunately, most of these tests have not been validated for clinical use so most centres measure only allergen-specific IgE. Augmented immune reactivity (positive allergy tests) can be detected by several types of challenge in response to many allergens but the problem is to establish clinical relevance and causal significance of these responses. Thus, skin prick tests elicit positive weal and flare responses at 15 min, reflecting IgE-dependent, immediate type hypersensitivity. Intradermal injection of allergens elicits a complex triphasic response comprising the immediate 15 min weal and flare, the 6–12 h late phase responses and also delayed 24–48 h responses thought to reflect lymphocyte-mediated allergy |66|. Epicutaneous patch application of aero and food allergens for 48 h may elicit an eczematous response that is indistinguishable from naturally occurring eczema. The frequencies of positive responses to aeroallergen challenge tests in atopic eczema patients are of the order of 90–95% for prick tests and 45–85% for patch tests (Table 6.3). The rate of positive patch test responses depends on the dose of allergen used and whether or not the skin permeability barrier is disrupted by tape stripping |67–69|. The 'Atopy Patch Test', as defined by the European Task Force on Atopic Dermatitis (ETFAD), involves application of 200 'index of reactivity' (IR) units of each allergen on 12 mm diameter Finn Chambers, with no deliberate disruption of the stratum corneum permeability barrier. One hundred IR was designated as the strength of allergenic extract that elicited a weal of geometric mean diameter of 7 mm on skin prick test in 30 subjects sensitive to the corresponding allergen. APT elicits positive responses to house dust mite allergens in up to 45% |69| However, with tape stripping |67| and higher concentrations of allergen, much higher frequencies of positive responses can be obtained (Table 6.3).

Another source of allergic 'drive' for atopic eczema is the skin surface commensal yeast *Malassezia furfur*. This organism is present on the skin of everyone. In a proportion of atopic eczema sufferers, active allergic responses reflected by positive prick tests (specific IgE dependent) and patch tests (T cell-mediated) are present |70,71|.

Allergen avoidance

The main aim of establishing causal relevance of a given allergen for any patient with atopic dermatitis is to ameliorate the skin condition by avoidance of the allergen. However, interpretation of whether positive challenge tests reflect causal significance of the relevant allergens is surprisingly unreliable. Immediate Type 1 responses are generally thought to relate to mucosal symptoms, which many eczema sufferers also experience. While it is generally presumed that cutaneous symptoms are best represented by eczematous responses at 48 h after epicutaneous patch tests, there is little evidence that these responses are good predictors of allergens that would be beneficial to avoid. Clinical responses to oral challenge with milk in 118 children aged 2 to 36 months elicited positive responses in 54% |72|. The children showing positive responses to milk challenge exhibited immediate responses (urticaria, pruritus and exanthemata) in 49% while they were of a delayed-onset eczematous type in 41%. Positive prick tests occurred in 67% of the children with acute onset symptoms, while positive patch tests occurred in 89% of the children with delayed onset symptoms |72|. A number of authors have suggested that after double-blind placebo-controlled food challenges, patch test challenges are the next best method for identifying sensitization by foods |72–74|. However, the number of studies that have linked the outcome of skin tests to the results of avoidance of the provoking foods is very limited |69,75|. Therefore, dietary manipulation to avoid ingestion of causally relevant foods appears still to be best achieved after double-blind placebo-controlled food challenge. 'Hit and miss' omission of foods of choice or suspicion is generally unrewarding.

Of the environmental aero-allergens the house dust mite is the one that is of greatest significance firstly because it elicits positive allergy tests in most atopic eczema patients and secondly, because it is a practical possibility to put into place effective dust mite allergen avoidance regimens. Although many authors have examined the frequency of positive skin tests, both prick tests and patch tests, and found positive responses in the majority of eczema sufferers, the ability to use these results to predict who will benefit from allergen avoidance is low to non-existent. Also, the question of whether dust mite elimination is clinically efficacious is still controversial. The clinical efficacy of dust mite elimination has been clearly shown by three studies |76–78| while others found no clinical benefit |79,80|. Sanda and colleagues used an environmental chamber |77|, Tan and colleagues |78| used a combination of occlusive bedding encasements, a spray containing both tannic acid to denature allergens and an acaricide to kill dust mites as well as a high powered, high filtration vacuum cleaner. They observed highly significant reductions of Der p 1 content on the surface of the mattress and in the domestic environment. This was associated with significant improvements in the atopic eczema scores for both adults and children. Interestingly, neither Gutgesell and colleagues |79| nor Oosting and co-workers |80| observed any clinical benefits. Gutgesell used bedding encasements and high powered vacuum cleaners but not the allergen denaturing spray, and Oosting used only bedding encasements without either the vacuum cleaner or the spray. It seems unlikely that the allergen denaturing spray made the critical difference since in Tan's study, although the reduction in Der p 1 load in the carpets was highly significant, there was no difference between the active (high-powered vacuum plus spray) and placebo—(normal vacuum cleaner only) treatments. The other difference in the study designs was their duration: Tan's study ran over 6 months while those of Gutgesell and Oosting ran over 12 months. In Tan's study, the patients with the worst eczema severity derived the greatest benefits from introduction of dust mite eradication measures.

Colonization and infection of atopic eczema skin with *Staphylococcus aureus* is present in almost 100% of cases. Although commonly viewed as an alternate mechanism of inflammation, recent clinical and molecular investigation has highlighted the potential of staphylococcal superantigen to provide an interaction between the innate and acquired immune systems which may enhance allergic reactivity |52,81|. Such a mechanism may suggest that allergen avoidance in the setting of reducing the antimicrobial load may be more beneficial than either approach alone.

Eczema sufferers who exhibit the pattern of worst involvement on the head, neck and upper torso often derive clinical benefit from use of imidazole antifungal agents to temporarily eradicate the *M. furfur*.

Overall management of atopic eczema

1. *Allergen avoidance*: From the above, it can be seen that allergen avoidance strategies can be applied for foods, dust mites and possibly animal furs and also *M. furfur*. The biggest problem is that although many eczema sufferers give positive skin tests to some or all these allergens, being certain which are the causal ones is unreliable. If anti-dust mite measures are attempted they must be done thoroughly and must include encasing all components of the bed (mattress, duvet and pillows) in mite/dust-proof bags. An alternative for the duvet is to change to 'hospital style' cotton air cell blankets that can be washed frequently. Similarly, the pillows can be given a hot wash and tumble-dry every 3–4 months, or even renewed completely. Most modern 'box construction' vacuum cleaners do a good job of allergen removal. If carpets are present then it is impossible to completely eliminate dust mite allergens and animal fur allergens as they remain stuck in the carpets. The requirement for

allergen denaturing sprays is raised by Tan's study above, but the real value of such sprays is still uncertain.

2. *Treating the skin*: Moisturizing with bland oils, creams or ointments is essential and helps improve the barrier function of the skin as well as soothe itch and dryness. The inflammation of eczema requires topical corticosteroids in a range of potencies. When they fail or if they induce side-effects, then topical calcineurin inhibitors (tacrolimus or pimecrolimus) are indicated. If there is inadequate control of the eczema with topical regimens, then systemic therapy with immunosuppressants such as azathioprine or cyclosporine may be required.

References

1. Basketter D, Dooms-Goossens A, Karlberg AT, Lepoittevin JP. The chemistry of contact allergy: why is a molecule allergenic? *Contact Dermatitis* 1995; **32**(2): 65–73.

2. Lepoittevin J, Benezra C, Sigman C, *et al.* Molecular aspects of allergic contact dermatitis. In: Rycroft R, Menne T, Frosch P (eds). *Textbook of Contact Dermatitis*, 2nd edition. Springer-Verlag, Berlin, 1995, pp 105–19.

3. Weltzien HU, Moulon C, Martin S, *et al.* T cell immune responses to haptens. Structural models for allergic and autoimmune reactions. *Toxicology* 1996; **107**(2): 141–51.

4. Cumberbatch M, Dearman RJ, Kimber I. Langerhans cells require signals from both tumour necrosis factor-alpha and interleukin-1 beta for migration. *Immunology* 1997; **92**(3): 388–95.

5. Cumberbatch M, Tucker S, Dearman R, *et al.* Regulation of human epidermal Langerhans cell migration. *J Leukoc Biol* 1998; D1.

6. Friedmann PS, Strickland I, Memon AA, Johnson PM. Early time course of recruitment of immune surveillance in human skin after chemical provocation. *Clin Exp Immunol* 1993; **91**(3): 351–6.

7. Maibach H, Fregert S. Manual of contact dermatitis. *Contact Dermatitis* 1980; **6**(7): 430–4.

8. Hanifin J, Rajka G. Diagnostic features of atopic dermatitis. *Acta Derm Venereol Suppl (Stockh)* 1980; **92**: 44–7.

9. Hanifin J. Atopic dermatitis. In: Moschella S, Hurley H (eds). *Dermatology*, 3rd edition. WB Saunders Co, Philadelphia, 1992.

10. Williams HC, Burney PG, Hay RJ, *et al.*; The UK Working Party's Diagnostic Criteria for Atopic Dermatitis. I. Derivation of a minimum set of discriminators for atopic dermatitis. *Br J Dermatol* 1994; **131**(3): 383–96.

11. Williams HC, Burney PG, Strachan D, Hay RJ; The UK Working Party's Diagnostic Criteria for Atopic Dermatitis. II. Observer variation of clinical diagnosis and signs of atopic dermatitis. *Br J Dermatol* 1994; **131**(3): 397–405.

12. Williams HC, Burney PG, Pembroke AC, Hay RJ; The UK Working Party's Diagnostic Criteria for Atopic Dermatitis. III. Independent hospital validation. *Br J Dermatol* 1994; **131**(3): 406–16.

13. Williams HC, Burney PG, Pembroke AC, Hay RJ; UK Diagnostic Criteria for Atopic Dermatitis Working Party. Validation of the UK diagnostic criteria for atopic dermatitis in a population setting. *Br J Dermatol* 1996; **135**(1): 12–17.

14. Johansson SG, Bieber T, Dahl R, *et al.* Revised nomenclature for allergy for global use: Report of the Nomenclature Review Committee of the World Allergy Organization, October 2003. *J Allergy Clin Immunol* 2004; **113**(5): 832–6.

15. Kay J, Gawkrodger DJ, Mortimer MJ, Jaron AG. The prevalence of childhood atopic

eczema in a general population. *J Am Acad Dermatol* 1994; **30**(1): 35–9.

16. Illi S, von Mutius E, Lau S, *et al.* The natural course of atopic dermatitis from birth to age 7 years and the association with asthma. *J Allergy Clin Immunol* 2004; **113**(5): 925–31.

17. International Study of Asthma and Allergies (ISAAC) Steering Committee. Worldwide variation in prevalence of symptoms of asthma, allergic rhinoconjunctivitis, and atopic eczema: ISAAC. *Lancet* 1998; **351**(9111): 1225–32.

18. Yemaneberhan H, Flohr C, Lewis SA, *et al.* Prevalence and associated factors of atopic dermatitis symptoms in rural and urban Ethiopia. *Clin Exp Allergy* 2004; **34**(5): 779–85.

19. Poysa L, Korppi M, Pietikainen M, *et al.* Asthma, allergic rhinitis and atopic eczema in Finnish children and adolescents. *Allergy* 1991; **46**(3): 161–5.

20. Williams HC, Strachan DP, Hay RJ. Childhood eczema: disease of the advantaged? *Br Med J* 1994; **308**(6937): 1132–5.

21. Strachan DP. Hay fever, hygiene, and household size. *Br Med J* 1989; **299**(6710): 1259–60.

22. Schultz LF, Diepgen T, Svensson A. The occurrence of atopic dermatitis in north Europe: an international questionnaire study. *J Am Acad Dermatol* 1996; **34**(5 Pt 1): 760–4.

23. Levy RM, Gelfand JM, Yan AC. The epidemiology of atopic dermatitis. *Clin Dermatol* 2003; **21**(2): 109–15.

24. Larsen FS, Holm NV, Henningsen K. Atopic dermatitis. A genetic-epidemiologic study in a population-based twin sample. *J Am Acad Dermatol* 1986; **15**(3): 487–94.

25. Schultz LF. Atopic dermatitis: a genetic-epidemiologic study in a population-based twin sample. *J Am Acad Dermatol* 1993; **28**(5 Pt 1): 719–23.

26. Cookson WO, Ubhi B, Lawrence R, *et al.* Genetic linkage of childhood atopic dermatitis to psoriasis susceptibility loci. *Nat Genet* 2001; **27**(4): 372–3.

27. Bradley M, Soderhall C, Luthman H, *et al.* Susceptibility loci for atopic dermatitis on chromosomes 3, 13, 15, 17 and 18 in a Swedish population. *Hum Mol Genet* 2002; **11**(13): 1539–48.

28. Lee YA, Wahn U, Kehrt R, *et al.* A major susceptibility locus for atopic dermatitis maps to chromosome 3q21. *Nat Genet* 2000; **26**(4): 470–3.

29. Palmer CN, Irvine AD, Terron-Kwiatkowski A, *et al.* Common loss-of-function variants of the epidermal barrier protein filaggrin are a major predisposing factor for atopic dermatitis. *Nat Genet* 2006; **38**(4): 441–6.

30. Baker BS. The role of microorganisms in atopic dermatitis. *Clin Exp Immunol* 2006; **144**(1): 1–9.

31. Ong PY, Ohtake T, Brandt C, *et al.* Endogenous antimicrobial peptides and skin infections in atopic dermatitis. *N Engl J Med* 2002; **347**(15): 1151–60.

32. Nomura I, Goleva E, Howell MD, *et al.* Cytokine milieu of atopic dermatitis, as compared to psoriasis, skin prevents induction of innate immune response genes. *J Immunol* 2003; **171**(6): 3262–9.

33. Bruch-Gerharz D, Fehsel K, Suschek C, *et al.* A proinflammatory activity of interleukin 8 in human skin: expression of the inducible nitric oxide synthase in psoriatic lesions and cultured keratinocytes. *J Exp Med* 1996; **184**(5): 2007–12.

34. Rieg S, Steffen H, Seeber S, *et al.* Deficiency of dermcidin-derived antimicrobial peptides in sweat of patients with atopic dermatitis correlates with an impaired innate defense of human skin in vivo. *J Immunol* 2005; **174**(12): 8003–10.

35. Toshitani A, Imayama S, Shimozono Y, *et al.* Reduced amount of secretory component of IgA secretion in tears of patients with atopic dermatitis. *J Dermatol Sci* 1999; **19**(2): 134–8.

36. Imayama S, Shimozono Y, Hoashi M, *et al.* Reduced secretion of IgA to skin surface of patients with atopic dermatitis. *J Allergy Clin Immunol* 1994; **94**(2 Pt 1): 195–200.

37. Hamid Q, Boguniewicz M, Leung DY. Differential in situ cytokine gene expression in acute versus chronic atopic dermatitis. *J Clin Invest* 1994; **94**(2): 870–6.

38. Hamid Q, Naseer T, Minshall EM, et al. In vivo expression of IL-12 and IL-13 in atopic dermatitis. *J Allergy Clin Immunol* 1996; **98**(1): 225–31.

39. Schmid-Grendelmeier P, Simon D, Simon HU, et al. Epidemiology, clinical features, and immunology of the "intrinsic" (non-IgE-mediated) type of atopic dermatitis (constitutional dermatitis). *Allergy* 2001; **56**(9): 841–9.

40. Wierenga EA, Snoek M, de Groot C, et al. Evidence for compartmentalization of functional subsets of CD2+ T lymphocytes in atopic patients. *J Immunol* 1990; **144**(12): 4651–6.

41. Parronchi P, Macchia D, Piccinni MP, et al. Allergen- and bacterial antigen-specific T-cell clones established from atopic donors show a different profile of cytokine production. *Proc Natl Acad Sci USA* 1991; **88**(10): 4538–42.

42. Lange J, Ngoumou G, Berkenheide S, et al. High interleukin-13 production by phytohaemagglutinin- and Der p 1-stimulated cord blood mononuclear cells is associated with the subsequent development of atopic dermatitis at the age of 3 years. *Clin Exp Allergy* 2003; **33**(11): 1537–43.

43. Soumelis V, Liu YJ. Human thymic stromal lymphopoietin: a novel epithelial cell-derived cytokine and a potential key player in the induction of allergic inflammation. *Springer Semin Immunopathol* 2004; **25**(3–4): 325–33.

44. Yoo J, Omori M, Gyarmati D, et al. Spontaneous atopic dermatitis in mice expressing an inducible thymic stromal lymphopoietin transgene specifically in the skin. *J Exp Med* 2005; **202**(4): 541–9.

45. Leyden JJ, Marples RR, Kligman AM. Staphylococcus aureus in the lesions of atopic dermatitis. *Br J Dermatol* 1974; **90**(5): 525–30.

46. Ring J, Abeck D, Neuber K. Atopic eczema: role of microorganisms on the skin surface. *Allergy* 1992; **47**(4 Pt 1): 265–9.

47. Guzik TJ, Bzowska M, Kasprowicz A, et al. Persistent skin colonization with Staphylococcus aureus in atopic dermatitis: relationship to clinical and immunological parameters. *Clin Exp Allergy* 2005; **35**(4): 448–55.

48. Nilsson EJ, Henning CG, Magnusson J. Topical corticosteroids and Staphylococcus aureus in atopic dermatitis. *J Am Acad Dermatol* 1992; **27**(1): 29–34.

49. Zollner TM, Munk ME, Keller T, et al. The superantigen exfoliative toxin induces cutaneous lymphocyte-associated antigen expression in peripheral human T lymphocytes. *Immunol Lett* 1996; **49**(1–2): 111–16.

50. Zollner TM, Wichelhaus TA, Hartung A, et al. Colonization with superantigen-producing Staphylococcus aureus is associated with increased severity of atopic dermatitis. *Clin Exp Allergy* 2000; **30**(7): 994–1000.

51. Bunikowski R, Mielke ME, Skarabis H, et al. Evidence for a disease-promoting effect of Staphylococcus aureus-derived exotoxins in atopic dermatitis. *J Allergy Clin Immunol* 2000; **105**(4): 814–19.

52. Ardern-Jones MR, Black AP, Bateman EA, Ogg GS. Bacterial superantigen facilitates epithelial presentation of allergen to T helper 2 cells. *Proc Natl Acad Sci USA* 2007; **104**(13): 5557–62.

53. Benn CS, Melbye M, Wohlfahrt J, et al. Cohort study of sibling effect, infectious diseases, and risk of atopic dermatitis during first 18 months of life. *Br Med J* 2004; **328**(7450):1223.

54. McKeever TM, Lewis SA, Smith C, et al. Early exposure to infections and antibiotics and the incidence of allergic disease: a birth cohort study with the West Midlands General Practice Research Database. *J Allergy Clin Immunol* 2002; **109**(1): 43–50.

55. Strachan DP. Family size, infection and atopy: the first decade of the "hygiene hypothesis". *Thorax* 2000; **55**(Suppl 1):S2–10.

56. Bodner C, Godden D, Seaton A. Family size, childhood infections and atopic diseases. The Aberdeen WHEASE Group. *Thorax* 1998; **53**(1): 28–32.

57. Linneberg A, Ostergaard C, Tvede M, *et al.* IgG antibodies against microorganisms and atopic disease in Danish adults: the Copenhagen Allergy Study. *J Allergy Clin Immunol* 2003; **111**(4): 847–53.

58. Wickens KL, Crane J, Kemp TJ, *et al.* Family size, infections, and asthma prevalence in New Zealand children. *Epidemiology* 1999; **10**(6): 699–705.

59. Strachan DP, Taylor EM, Carpenter RG. Family structure, neonatal infection, and hay fever in adolescence. *Arch Dis Child* 1996; **74**(5): 422–6.

60. Forastiere F, Agabiti N, Corbo GM, *et al.* Socioeconomic status, number of silings, and respiratory infections in early life as determinants of atopy in children. *Epidemiology* 1997; **8**(5): 566–70.

61. Nafstad P, Magnus P, Jaakkola JJ. Early respiratory infections and childhood asthma. *Pediatrics* 2000; **106**(3): E38.

62. Matricardi PM, Rosmini F, Ferrigno L, *et al.* Cross sectional retrospective study of prevalence of atopy among Italian military students with antibodies against hepatitis A virus. *Br Med J* 1997; **314**(7086): 999–1003.

63. Ponsonby AL, Couper D, Dwyer T, *et al.* Relationship between early life respiratory illness, family size over time, and the development of asthma and hay fever: a seven year follow up study. *Thorax* 1999; **54**(8): 664–9.

64. Raap U, Kapp A. Neuroimmunological findings in allergic skin diseases. *Curr Opin Allergy Clin Immunol* 2005; **5**(5): 419–24.

65. Nockher WA, Renz H. Neurotrophins in allergic diseases: from neuronal growth factors to intercellular signaling molecules. *J Allergy Clin Immunol* 2006; **117**(3): 583–9.

66. Wistokat-Wulfing A, Schmidt P, Darsow U, *et al.* Atopy patch test reactions are associated with T lymphocyte-mediated allergen-specific immune responses in atopic dermatitis. *Clin Exp Allergy* 1999; **29**(4): 513–21.

67. van Voorst Vader PC, Lier JG, Woest TE, *et al.* Patch tests with house dust mite antigens in atopic dermatitis patients: methodological problems. *Acta Derm Venereol* 1991; **71**(4): 301–5.

68. Ring J, Darsow U, Gfesser M, Vieluf D. The 'atopy patch test' in evaluating the role of aeroallergens in atopic eczema. *Int Arch Allergy Immunol* 1997; **113**(1–3): 379–83.

69. Darsow U, Vieluf D, Ring J. Evaluating the relevance of aeroallergen sensitization in atopic eczema with the atopy patch test: a randomized, double-blind multicenter study. Atopy Patch Test Study Group. *J Am Acad Dermatol* 1999; **40**(2 Pt 1): 187–93.

70. Tengvall LM, Johansson C, Scheynius A, Wahlgren C. Positive atopy patch test reactions to Pityrosporum orbiculare in atopic dermatitis patients. *Clin Exp Allergy* 2000; **30**(1): 122–31.

71. Johansson C, Eshaghi H, Linder MT, *et al.* Positive atopy patch test reaction to Malassezia furfur in atopic dermatitis correlates with a T helper 2-like peripheral blood mononuclear cells response. *J Invest Dermatol* 2002; **118**(6): 1044–51.

72. Isolauri E, Turjanmaa K. Combined skin prick and patch testing enhances identification of food allergy in infants with atopic dermatitis. *J Allergy Clin Immunol* 1996; **97**(1 Pt 1): 9–15.

73. Mehl A, Rolinck-Werninghaus C, Staden U, *et al.* The atopy patch test in the diagnostic workup of suspected food-related symptoms in children. *J Allergy Clin Immunol* 2006; **118**(4): 923–9.

74. Heine RG, Verstege A, Mehl A, *et al.* Proposal for a standardized interpretation of the atopy patch test in children with atopic dermatitis and suspected food allergy. *Pediatr Allergy Immunol* 2006; **17**(3): 213–17.

75. Breuer K, Heratizadeh A, Wulf A, *et al.* Late eczematous reactions to food in children with atopic dermatitis. *Clin Exp Allergy* 2004; **34**(5): 817–24.

76. Clark RA, Adinoff AD. Aeroallergen contact can exacerbate atopic dermatitis: patch tests as a diagnostic tool. *J Am Acad Dermatol* 1989; **21**(4 Pt 2): 863–9.

77. Sanda T, Yasue T, Oohashi M, Yasue A. Effectiveness of house dust-mite allergen avoidance through clean room therapy in patients with atopic dermatitis. *J Allergy Clin Immunol* 1992; **89**(3): 653–7.

78. Tan BB, Weald D, Strickland I, Friedmann PS. Double-blind controlled trial of effect of housedust-mite allergen avoidance on atopic dermatitis. *Lancet* 1996; **347**(8993): 15–18.

79. Gutgesell C, Neumann C. Allergen avoidance in individuals with house-dust mite sensitization. *Allergologie* 1994; **17**: 371–3.

80. Oosting AJ, de Bruin-Weller MS, Terreehorst I, *et al*. Effect of mattress encasings on atopic dermatitis outcome measures in a double-blind, placebo-controlled study: the Dutch mite avoidance study. *J Allergy Clin Immunol* 2002; **110**(3): 500–6.

81. Langer K, Breuer K, Kapp A, Werfel T. Staphylococcus aureus-derived enterotoxins enhance house dust mite-induced patch test reactions in atopic dermatitis. *Exp Dermatol* 2007; **16**(2): 124–9.

7

Angio-oedema and urticaria

BETTINA WEDI, ALEXANDER KAPP

KEY POINTS

1. Exact definition of the respective angio-oedema/urticaria subtype is required to choose the best treatment approach.

2. Most subtypes persist for several years and health-related quality of life is significantly impaired.

3. The aetiology of chronic urticaria is heterogeneous and involves persistent, subclinical bacterial infections, non-allergic hypersensitivity reactions and autoreactivity.

4. Specific and sufficient treatment of identified triggering factors can result in complete remission of angio-oedema/urticaria.

5. First line symptomatic treatment consists of second generation H_1-antihistamines.

6. Flawless studies investigating alternatives are rare.

Introduction

Correct recognition of the diverse clinical subtypes of the common disorders urticaria and angio-oedema facilitates clinical assessment and treatment. Appearance, distribution, duration of (individual) weals and/or angio-oedema, and of additional symptoms is often informative. In most cases urticaria and angio-oedema coexist but may occur separately.

Although rarely life-threatening, angio-oedema and urticaria result in a significant impairment of health-related quality of life. Exact definition of the respective subtype is required to choose an adequate treatment approach. The goal is to maximize quality of life and ability to work or to go to school and to minimize potential side-effects.

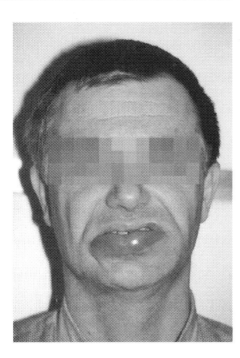

Fig. 7.1 Typical asymmetric non-C1 inhibitor deficient angio-oedema of the lower lips.

What is angio-oedema?

Angio-oedema is defined by sudden, pronounced swelling of the deep dermis and subcutaneous or submucosal tissues and is often more painful than itching |1|. Although angio-oedema can occur anywhere on the body, frequently the eyelids, lips (Fig. 7.1), and genitalia are involved but sometimes also the tongue and laryngo-pharynx, which can be life-threatening. Resolution can take up to three days. The pathomechanism is local vasodilatation and increase in capillary permeability with plasma leakage. Two main types are subclassified, C1 inhibitor deficient and non-C1 inhibitor deficient angio-oedema |2,3|. Most non-C1 inhibitor deficient angio-oedema are caused by histamine release mediated by immunoglobulin (Ig)E- or non-immunological activation of mast cells.

What is urticaria?

Urticaria, also known as hives, is one of the most common dermatological conditions |1|. It is characterized by acute or chronic, superficial swellings of the skin associated with itching (Fig. 7.2). Lifetime incidence is higher than 20%. The itching can be pricking or burning and is usually worse in the evening or at night. The size, number and shape of weals, which are more often rubbed than scratched, vary considerably and can develop anywhere on the body. Systemic symptoms such as fatigue, respiratory, gastrointestinal and arthralgic symptoms may occur. The clinical pictures are of heterogeneous aetiology and therefore subclassified into distinct groups. More than half of the patients with urticaria have concurrent angio-oedema.

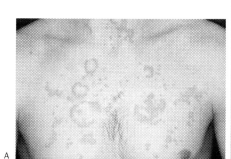
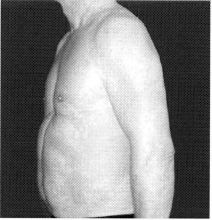

A   B

Fig. 7.2 Typical weal and flare reactions in two patients (A, B) with spontaneous urticaria.

Classification and management of angio–oedema

With or without urticaria?

Depending on the cause, several subtypes of angio-oedema can be classified |2,3|. In most cases angio-oedema (80–90%) is associated with urticaria (Table 7.1). Angio-oedema without weal and flare reaction must be regarded as a separate entity.

Table 7.1 Non-C1 inhibitor deficient angio-oedema

Subtype	Cause	Association with urticaria
1. Allergic	1. IgE-mediated (usually with urticaria)	1. Usually
2. Non-allergic	2. e.g. NSAID-induced	2. Usually
3. Pharmacological	3. ACE inhibitor-induced (class-effect)	3. No
4. Infectious	4. e.g. associated with *H. pylori* infection	4. Usually
5. Physical	5. Exposure to vibration, cold, pressure	5. Possible
6. Idiopathic	6. No identifiable cause	6. Usually

C1 inhibitor deficient?

Angio-oedema without urticaria can be caused by C1 inhibitor deficiency |2,3|, either of hereditary subtype (only 5% of all angio-oedema without urticaria) or acquired angio-oedema (very rare) (Table 7.2).

Hereditary angio-oedema (HAE) is a rare autosomal dominant condition with a prevalence of 1:50,000 in the general population. It is caused by a deficiency (type I, 85%) or dysfunction (type II, 15%) of C1 inhibitor without sex bias. In contrast, type III occurs exclusively in women with quantitatively and function-

Table 7.2 C1 inhibitor deficient angio-oedema (*without* urticaria)

Subtype		Cause, laboratory findings
Hereditary (HAE)	Type I	● C1 inhibitor protein deficiency; low C1 inhibitor, low C4, normal or slightly decreased C1q
	Type II	● C1 inhibitor dysfunction; normal C1 inhibitor protein, but decreased functional C1 inhibitor activity, low C4, normal or slightly decreased C1q
	Type III	● Exclusively in women; normal C1 inhibitor, normal C4, low C1q
Acquired (AAE)	Type I	● Secondary to lymphoma, immune complex-mediated depletion of C1 inhibitor; low C1 inhibitor, low C4, low C1q
	Type II	● Autoimmune; autoantibodies against C1 inhibitor; decreased functional C1 inhibitor activity, low C4, low C1q

ally normal C1 inhibitor activity related to oestrogens (episodes during menstruation, pregnancy and use of contraceptives or hormone replacement therapy).

HAE develops more slowly compared to ordinary angio-oedema, often beginning with a prodrome and can be associated with colicky abdominal pain. It develops spontaneously or after trauma, particularly with dental manoeuvres. Most cases are diagnosed in childhood and have a positive family history. The attacks become worse at puberty and usually decrease in frequency and severity after the age of 50. The main sites involved are face, hands, arms, legs, genitalia and buttocks. Glossal, pharyngeal or laryngeal involvement can be life-threatening and treatment with corticosteroids/antihistamines is ineffective. In one large series, 10% had required intubation or tracheotomy, at least once.

In HAE, laboratory findings reveal a low (<30% normal) functional C1 inhibitor titre and profoundly depressed C4 level. Antigenic (or quantitative) levels of C1 inhibitor are low in type I HAE patients but normal in type II HAE patients. If C1 inhibitor value appears normal or raised (and C4 is low), a test of C1 inhibitor function should be carried out. The absolute levels of C4 or C1 inhibitor function do not change with acute symptoms. Hence, it is not necessary to await an attack of angio-oedema to obtain a diagnostic specimen; the C4 concentration will be <10 mg/dl even during quiescent periods.

Acquired C1 inhibitor deficient angio-oedema (AAE) occurs in the fifth and six decades of life. In type I, C1 inhibitor depletion may the result of circulating immune complexes secondary to malignancy (e.g. B-cell lymphoma, myeloma). In type II, autoantibodies directed against C1 inhibitor itself are generated. Laboratory assessment should include C1 inhibitor protein level and function, and levels of C4 and C1q. The laboratory findings in both types of acquired C1 inhibitor deficient angio-oedema are similar to those in HAE except that C1q levels are also decreased.

Treatment of C1 inhibitor deficient angio-oedema

Treatment of HAE is difficult |2,3|. For acute attacks, C1 inhibitor concentrate or fresh frozen plasma should be administered. Intubation or tracheotomy may be necessary. Corticosteroids and antihistamines are not helpful, epinephrine may be tried. Prophylactic treatment involves anabolic androgens (e.g. danazol) that increase the serum levels of C1 inhibitor and should be prescribed in the lowest effective dosage (hepatotoxicity, liver tumours, hirsutism). In mild HAE, avoidance of provoking factors, angiotensin-converting enzyme (ACE) inhibitors, estrogens together with C1 inhibitor, or fresh frozen plasma prophylactically before dental or surgical procedures may be sufficient.

In 2008, a selective peptidometic bradykinin β_2-receptor antagonist (icatibant) may be available for the treatment of HAE.

Which subtype of non-C1 inhibitor deficient angio-oedema?

Angio-oedema with normal C1 inhibitor function may be of allergic (IgE-mediated), non-allergic (e.g. non-steroidal anti-inflammatory drug [NSAID]-induced), pharmacological (ACE inhibitor-induced), infectious (e.g. *Helicobacter pylori*-induced), physical (e.g. in cold urticaria) or of unknown (idiopathic) nature (Table 7.1). Details of the management of these aetiologies are described under the heading chronic urticaria.

Treatment of non-C1 inhibitor deficient angio-oedema

Antihistamines are of little value in non-C1 inhibitor deficient angio-oedema, but given on a regular basis, they may attenuate severity or frequency of angio-oedema. Randomized controlled trials focusing on recurrent non C1 inhibitor associated angio-oedema without urticaria are not available. Treatment is similar to chronic urticaria but often emergency treatment is needed. A dose of 40–60 mg of prednisone can be used; if needed, the treatment may be extended by an additional 1 or 2 days. For life-threatening episodes, parenteral corticosteroids, epinephrine or even intubation or tracheotomy may be necessary.

Pharmacological non-C1 inhibitor deficient angio-oedema

Angio-oedema occurs in about 0.6% of patients receiving ACE inhibitor treatment, and is more common in African-Americans. In most cases, angio-oedema occurs within three months of starting the drug but occurrence after several years is also possible. The pathomechanism of pharmacological angio-oedema involves accumulation of bradykinin caused by decreased bradykinin degradation secondary to ACE inhibitors, angiotensin II receptor blockers (sartans) or vasopeptidase inhibitors.

In recurrent angio-oedema, ACE inhibitors, sartans and NSAIDS should be avoided. Occasionally, angio-oedema may continue for some weeks or even months after the ACE inhibitor has been withdrawn.

Classification and management of urticaria

Several classifications of urticaria subtypes exist |4–6|. Here, the clinical classification of the European Guideline |6| is used. Other classifications place emphasis on the aetiology (e.g. ordinary urticaria, autoimmune urticaria) or include other diseases such as urticarial vasculitis. Differences have been explained by historical influences, exposure of specialties to different populations with urticaria and most importantly to the complexity, breadth and diversity of the condition with multiple causes, associations and aggravating factors |7|.

Which type of urticaria? Spontaneous, physical or special type?

About 80% of urticaria is spontaneous, 10% physical, and less than 10% of special type (Table 7.3), but two or, rarely, more subtypes can occur in the same patient (e.g. spontaneous chronic urticaria and dermographism). In these cases, urticaria is long persisting and more often difficult to treat.

Table 7.3 Classification of urticaria subtypes

Urticaria type	Subtype
Spontaneous (80%)	Acute
	Chronic
Physical (<10%)	Cold
	Delayed pressure
	Localized heat
	Solar
	Dermographic
	Vibratory
Special type (<10%)	Aquagenous
	Cholinergic
	Contact
	Exercise-induced

Spontaneous urticaria: acute or chronic?

About two-thirds of spontaneous urticaria is acute (allergic or non-allergic), commonly seen in medical emergency service, and about one-third is chronic urticaria (non-allergic). In both types, episodes of angio-oedema are associated in more than 50% of cases.

Acute urticaria is defined as spontaneous weal and flare reaction of less than 6 weeks' duration, most often for one or two weeks, often due to an allergic or viral aetiology.

In contrast, chronic urticaria (lifelong prevalence about 0.5%, most common in middle-aged adult women) is defined by persistence for more than six weeks with nearly daily wealing episodes. Urticaria with less frequently occurring bouts over a long period is called episodic and is more likely to have an identifiable environmental trigger. Chronic urticaria usually persists on average for 3 to 5 years but may be still present even after 20 years. Quality of life is significantly impaired due to intense pruritus, sleep disturbances and secondary psychosocial problems.

Acute urticaria: allergic or non-allergic?

Acute non-allergic urticaria is most frequent and often associated with an acute upper respiratory or genitourinary infection and/or a non-allergic (so-called pseudoallergic) reaction to NSAIDs (particularly preferential cyclooxygenase I inhibitors such as aspirin). In contrast, in atopics, acute allergic urticaria caused by IgE-mediated allergy (e.g. to food allergens, hymenoptera stings, and drugs such as penicillin) can be found more frequently. Diagnosis is based upon a careful history to identify potential triggering factors (ask for atopic diseases, known allergies, drug intake, signs of infections) and physical examination (blood pressure, pulse, lung auscultation).

Treatment of acute urticaria

Causal treatment may include stopping of culprit drug intake or the prescription of antibiotics in bacterial infections. If a cause cannot be primarily identified, no further investigations are recommended due to the self-limiting nature. Inpatient care is recommended in cases of dyspnoea, hypotension, and generalized severe urticaria. Symptomatic treatment consists of low-sedating H_1-antihistamines up to fourfold daily (consider potential side-effects when increasing the dose!) for one to two weeks. In severe cases (associated severe angio-oedema) initial administration of glucocorticosteroids up to 100–250 mg prednisolone (i.v.) and H_1-antihistamine (i.v.) are needed, maybe repeatedly. In progressive cases (anaphylactic shock), administration of epinephrine is advised. It has been suggested that adequate treatment of acute urticaria is able to inhibit progression to chronic urticaria.

How to diagnose and manage chronic urticaria

The diagnosis of chronic urticaria is based upon a thorough history considering potential triggering factors, a physical examination including a test for dermographism, laboratory investigations and, if needed, additional specific procedures. Every attempt should be made to find an underlying aetiology in each patient, because the identification and elimination of causal factors represents the best therapeutic approach. With regard to the long duration of the annoying skin disease, a well-directed work-up based upon a thorough history is indicated. An expert opinion should be sought in severe and unusual cases.

IgE-mediated hypersensitivity is very rarely the cause of symptoms in chronic urticaria. Therefore, routine skin prick tests to inhalant and food allergens are of little value. However, many direct and indirect mast cell releasing factors may be involved such as autoimmune mechanisms, infectious diseases (viral, bacterial, fungal, parasites) |8| particular *Helicobacter pylori*-associated gastritis |9|, pseudoallergic mechanisms and others such as internal diseases and malignancies. Several of these mechanisms can be active in a single patient.

About one-third of patients show evidence for an autoimmune pathogenesis caused by functional mast cell stimulating IgG antibodies against the alpha subunit of the hight-affinity IgE receptor and, more rarely, against IgE itself |10|. Indicative is a positive autologous serum skin test (ASST) although the clinical relevance is far from being clear. ASST may be confirmed by *in vitro* serum-induced basophil activation tests (histamine release, leukotriene production, increase in surface expression of activation markers such as CD63) [11]. In addition, about 30% of chronic urticaria cases are also associated with thyroid antibodies [12].

Aspirin [13], NSAIDs and other mast cell activating drugs like morphine, codeine, muscle relaxants, polymyxin and dextran aggravate symptoms and evoke exacerbations. Rare, non-allergic hypersensitivity reactions to food additives should be proven by a double-blind, placebo-controlled challenge [14].

The treatment goal is to maximize quality of life and ability to work or to attend school and to minimize drug-related side-effects such as sedation.

Unspecific trigger factors should be avoided (Table 7.4). Specific and sufficient treatment of identified persistent bacterial and parasitic infections can result in complete remission.

Long-acting low-sedating antihistamines are the mainstay of symptomatic treatment and can be given the highest grade of recommendation according to the criteria of evidence-based medicine. It is common practice to exceed the licensed dose although available data are limited [15]. The current European Guideline [16] recommends an increase up to fourfold the normal dose while considering the side-effects. Management is better achieved by taking antihistamines regularly, not just when the patient is symptomatic. Due to the long-term duration of the disease, low-sedating H1-antihistamines are preferred, particularly when increased dosage is needed. For chronic urticaria the evidence base is of high quality for azelastine, cetirizine, desloratadine, ebastine, fexofenadine, levocetirizine, loratadine and mizolastine (in alphabetical order) [17]. Replacement of one H1-antihistamine with another should be tried because of individual differences in responsiveness. The primary choice is based on pharmacokinetic properties, side-effects, comorbidity and concomitant treatment [18]. The clinical relevance of additional anti-inflammatory effects that have been demonstrated *in vitro* is considered controversial [19].

How to approach the antihistamine-resistant patient with chronic urticaria

Antihistamines, even in increased off-label dose, fail in a significant number of severely affected patients, particularly in patients with autoimmune urticaria. However, antihistamines are the only drugs approved for chronic urticaria treatment. All alternatives are not licensed for chronic urticaria and the evidence base is limited [16–18,20]. Second-line approaches are summarized in Table 7.4.

Chronic urticaria subgroups (i.e. with positive ASST and/or intolerance to aspirin/food additives) might benefit from addition of leukotriene antagonists [21].

The choice of a combination of an H_1-antihistamine with a H_2-antihistamine is not justified nowadays. The evidence base is poor and mainly exists for first-generation antihistamines. The H_2-antihistamine effect has been explained by interaction with the hepatic cytochrome P450 enzyme system resulting in an indirect increase of the H_1-antihistamine plasma concentration [22].

Table 7.4 Treatment modalities in chronic urticaria

1. Avoidance of unspecific factors	2. Specific treatment	3. Symptomatic, immunomodulating or immunosuppressive treatment	
● Aspirin/other NSAID (in favour of acetaminophen)	● Of persistent bacterial infections with	First-line	*Best evidence, fewer side-effects*
	– *Helicobacter pylori*		Non-/low-sedating H₁-antihistamines:
● Mast cell activating drugs: morphine, codeine, muscle relaxants, polymyxin and dextran	– streptococci		● regularly
	– staphylococci		● up to four times daily (off-label use)
● Alcohol	– yersinia		● consider individual response (try different choices)
● Overheating	● Of dental infections	Second-line* (consult expert)	*Less evidence, fewer side-effects*
● Tight clothing	● Of ear, nose and throat infections		Antileukotrienes, (hydroxy-)chloroquine, dapsone, oral low-dose glucocorticosteroids (omalizumab)
● In case of angio-oedema: ACE inhibitors (often also sartans)	● Of autoimmune thyroiditis		
	● Diet in case of non-allergic hypersensitivity to food additives (proven through controlled challenges)		*Good evidence, but significant side-effects*
			Cyclosporin A
			Less evidence, significant side-effects:
			Doxepin, oxatomide, ketotifen, sulfasalazine, IVIG, plasmapheresis, methotrexate, cyclophosphamide, mycophenolate mofetil, tacrolimus, warfarin, stanozolol

*Usually, combination treatment with non-/low-sedating H₁ antihistamines in adequate dose is recommended

Cyclosporin A |23,24| appears to be of value in severely affected patients although urticaria may reappear after discontinuation.

Randomized controlled trials of the efficacy of glucocorticosteroids have not been published. They should only be used with caution, for example, to achieve short-term control of symptoms in acute exacerbations.

Antidepressants (doxepin), mast cell stabilizers (oxatomide, ketotifen), calcium channel blockers (nifedipine) and sympathomimetics (terbutaline) as well as warfarin and stanozolol were evaluated in randomized controlled trials of poor quality. In light of high rates of side-effects and limited benefit, these drugs cannot be recommended.

Other drugs such as dapsone, sulfasalazine, tacrolimus, methotrexate, mycophenolate mofetil, cyclophosphamide, interferon, and COX-2 inhibitors as well as plasmapheresis and intravenous immunoglobulin (IVIG) infusions have not been studied in randomized controlled trials. Evidence is based on case reports, case series or uncontrolled, open trials. Substances such as colchicines have only been studied in other entities such as hypocomplementemic urticaria vasculitis syndrome (HUVS) or in urticarial vasculitis but not in chronic urticaria.

Based upon our *in vitro* |11| and *in vivo* |17,18| evidence in addition to lower quality randomized controlled trials |25,26| dapsone and (hydroxy-)chloroquine may be worthwhile subjects for future randomized controlled trials.

Potential future treatment options are under investigation or might be interesting including H_4 receptor antagonists or biologicals such as anti-IgE (omalizumab) or anti-CD20 (rituximab).

Treatment side-effects

Discontinuation of antihistamines due to unwanted interactions occurs in few patients. Potential side-effects of antihistamines such as impairment of performance, sedation, interaction with CYP450 enzymes, liver, cardiac side-effects and nephrotoxicity should be considered for the respective choice. For antihistamines metabolized by CYP450 enzymes, co-administration of macrolide antibiotics (e.g. clarithromycin in triple therapy of *Helicobacter pylori*) or imidazole antifungals can prolong the QTc interval and lead to potentially fatal arrhythmias (torsades de pointes).

The risk–benefit profile for each alternative (off-label use) should be carefully considered before treatment. This applies especially to immunosuppressive agents. Table 7.5 demonstrates possible daily doses and drug-related side-effects that should be considered.

How to manage a child with chronic urticaria

It has been shown that 20–30% of children with acute urticaria of which almost all were associated with acute infections progressed into chronic urticaria |27|. Accordingly, persistent chronic, often bacterial, infections (e.g. with streptococci, staphylococci, but also with *Helicobacter pylori*) and sometimes also viral infections (e.g. with Epstein-Barr virus or cytomegalovirus) can be found in childhood chronic urticaria |28|. As in adults, positive ASST indicating autoreactivity can be found in one-third |29|.

Table 7.5 Dosing and potential side-effects of second-line off-label choices (in alphabetical order)

Drug	Possible dose (daily if not otherwise stated)	Side-effects to consider:
Antileukotrienes	e.g. montelukast 10 mg	Gastrointestinal symptoms, diarrhoea, Churg-Strauss syndrome,
Chloroquine	250 mg	Retinopathy, G6PDH deficiency, gastrointestinal symptoms, impaired liver and/or kidney function, skin hyperpigmentation, myopathy
Cyclophosphamide	Increasing until 1500 mg i.v. every 4 weeks	Immunosuppression, bone marrow toxicity, cystitis
Cyclosporin A	2.5–5 mg/kg	Nephrotoxicity, hypertension, immunosuppression, disturbed lipid metabolism
Dapsone (4,4,-diaminodi-phenylsulfone)	100–150 mg (6 days per week)	G6PDH deficiency, haemolytic anaemia, methaemoglobinaemia, impaired liver function, neuropathy, intolerance of sulphonamides, hypersensitivity syndrome
Doxepin	10–50 mg	Sedation, dry mouth, constipation
Glucocorticosteroids	Initially 40–50 mg prednisone equivalent; short course or with gradual tapering by 2.5–5 mg per week, not long-term	Cushingoid changes, diabetes, glaucoma, osteoporosis, hypertension, gastrointestinal ulcers, weight gain
IVIG	0.4–2 g/kg for 5 days	Cost, temporary effect, fever, headache, arthralgia
Ketotifen	2 (up to 4) mg	Sedation, weight gain, impotence
Methotrexate	15–20 mg weekly or 5 mg daily for 2 days per week	Bone marrow and liver toxicity, pulmonary fibrosis, gastrointestinal ulcers
Mycophenolate mofetil	2000 mg	Gastrointestinal symptoms, leukopenia, anaemia, carcinogenicity
Omalizumab	375 mg every 2 weeks	Cost, delayed anaphylaxis
Oxatomide	60 mg	Sedation
Plasmapheresis	Not applicable	Cost, temporary effect, flu-like symptoms, headache, malaise, pyrexia
Stanazolol	4 mg	Androgen effects, impaired liver function
Sulfasalazine	500 mg, increasing by 500 mg each week until 2–4 g	G6PDH deficiency, intolerance of sulphonamides, leukopenia, headaches, photosensitivity, reversible oligospermia
Tacrolimus	Initially 0.1–0.14 mg/kg	Gastrointestinal symptoms, immunosuppression, nephrotoxicity, tremor
Warfarin	Until INR 2.0–2.5	Haemorrhage

Evidence-based recommendations for antihistamines in childhood urticaria do not exist. First-generation antihistamines should be avoided since they are associated with significant impairment of school performance and may also have paradoxical stimulatory central nervous system (CNS) effects. Modern antihistamines show a better safety profile. Cetirizine, levocetirizine, loratadine, desloratadine and fexofenadine are available in paediatric formulations. There is evidence that elimination of antihistamines is more rapid in children compared to adults |30|.

How to manage chronic urticaria in pregnancy

It is best to avoid all antihistamines in pregnancy, particularly in the first trimester, although teratogenic effects have not been proven.

Cetirizine and loratadine belong to Food and Drug Administration (FDA) pregnancy category B (no evidence of harm to the foetus in animal studies but no proof of safety in humans); fexofenadine and desloratadine belong to FDA pregnancy category C (evidence of harm to the foetus, no studies available in animals and no proof of safety in humans) |31,32|. There is some debate that older antihistamines such as chlorphenamine (FDA category B) might be preferred due to longer experience |5|. During lactation, fexofenadine and loratadine might be used.

Differential diagnosis of chronic urticaria

Differentials include scabies, arthropod reactions, urticarial stages of autoimmune bullous skin diseases such as bullous pemphigoid, and early stages of vasculitis and erythema multiforme.

If weals are non-itching, autoinflammatory syndromes with urticaria-like skin lesions should be considered |33|. These are characterized by persistent or recurrent fever and may be hereditary (mutation of CIAS1 on chromosome 1q44 encoding cryopyrin) such as Muckle-Wells syndrome, familial cold autoinflammatory syndrome (FACS), and chronic infantile neurological cutaneous and articular syndrome (CINCA), or may be acquired such as Schnitzler's syndrome. In addition, other immune disorders (e.g. systemic lupus erythematosus, hypocomplementemic urticaria vasculitis syndrome) may present with (often non-itching!) urticaria-like skin lesions.

Classification and management of physical urticarias

Physical urticarias form a distinct group that is caused reproducibly by external physical stimulus and should be clearly differentiated from spontaneous urticaria although both can coexist |34|. Usually the weals resolve within 2 h except in delayed pressure urticaria and delayed dermographic urticaria. Although clinically impressive, to date the pathomechanisms have not been clarified, nor are sufficient data available to recommend treatment schedules based upon current evidence. Most physical urticarias persist for an average of 3–5 years or longer. Physical urticaria is diagnosed by thorough history, clinical examination and provocation procedures using standardized physical tests |34|. Infection as

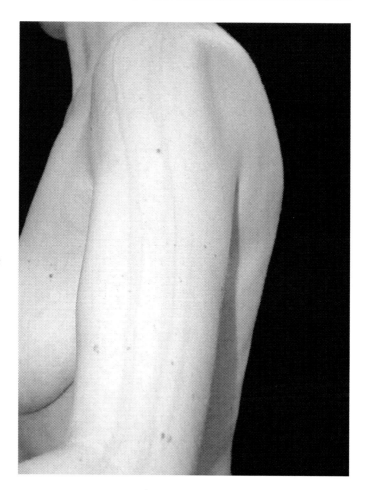

Fig. 7.3 Dermographic urticaria three minutes after firm stroking of the skin.

an aetiology for physical urticaria has been controversial |8|. Autoreactivity, i.e. positive ASST, autoantibodies against IgE-receptor/IgE or against thyroid has not been described.

Dermographic urticaria (factitial urticaria, symptomatic dermographism)

Dermographic urticaria develops within a few minutes after firm stroking of the skin (Fig. 7.3) and presents with intensely itching linear weals. In contrast, urticarial dermographism is asymptomatic. Dermographic urticaria is the most frequent subtype of physical urticaria with a mean duration of 6.5 years and is often combined with spontaneous chronic urticaria. Thorough history guides further investigations to exclude causative agents such as infections. Treatment is similar to chronic urticaria with low-sedating H_1-antihistamines given regularly and at adequate dose (up to fourfold the normal dose). Additionally, some evidence exists for the use of ketotifen |16|.

Delayed pressure urticaria

In delayed pressure urticaria deep, painful swellings develop 6–8 h after sustained pressure and persist for up to 2 days. Typical localizations are the palms and soles, buttocks, back and skin under straps and belts. Systemic symptoms of malaise, arthralgia, myalgia, and leukocytosis can be associated. Delayed pressure urticaria is more common in middle-aged males and persists for an average of 6–9 years, often resulting in disability to work. It may be associated with chronic urticaria.

Diagnostic are standardized pressure tests applying weights in amounts of 0.5 to 1.5 kg/cm^2 for 10 min in different areas (back, ventral and dorsal thigh). Readings should be done at least after 30 min, 3 h, 6 h and 24 h [34]. Only definite raised weals occurring after several hours indicate delayed pressure urticaria. Elicited weals that persist for more than 24 h should be biopsied to exclude vasculitis.

Antihistamines, even in increased doses, often fail; nevertheless, they represent the mainstay of treatment. Some patients benefit from additional low-dose corticosteroids (e.g. 40–20 mg prednisone), others by treatment with dapsone (100–150 mg/d). Moreover, methotrexate (15 mg/week), montelukast, ketotifen plus nimesulide, sulfasalazine or topical clobetasol propionate 0.5% ointment have been tried successfully [16].

Cold urticaria

Acquired cold urticaria and angio-oedema occur mainly in young adults within minutes after contact with cold bodies or cold water, also cold air and sometimes cold food/drinks [35]. Coexistence with cholinergic urticaria has to be considered. The average duration is five years. Generalized systemic, sometimes life-threatening, reactions can follow lowering of the body temperature. Standardized cold provocation should ideally define the threshold temperature. Recently, low-voltage Peltier thermoelectric elements have been developed.

Identified infectious diseases such as syphilis, borreliosis, hepatitis, infectious mononucleosis and HIV infections but also unrecognized bacterial infections have been reported as triggering factors and should be treated adequately. Low-sedating H$_1$-antihistamines are the first line in treatment. In idiopathic cases, antibiotic treatment (e.g. with doxycycline or penicillin, i.m. or p.o.) is worthwhile trying. Other low-evidence alternatives are cyproheptadine, ketotifen, and montelukast [16].

Localized heat urticaria

Rare localized heat urticaria with small sized and fleeting weals develops immediately by direct contact with a warm object such as air or water (eliciting temperature ranges from 38°C to more than 50°C). Ideally, the threshold temperature should be defined. Evidence-based treatment is not available. Skin hardening to heat or chloroquine may be tried [16].

Solar urticaria

Solar urticaria comprises only 4% of all photosensitive skin disorders and affects predominantly women in their third or fourth decades of life. Mostly UV light is the eliciting physical stimulus but wavelengths ranging from 280 to 760 nm have been described. Standardized provocation should use specific wavelengths of a monochromator and, for example, a slide projector (visible light) for 10 min to determine the minimal urticarial dose (MUD). The lesions usually fade 15 min to 3 h after onset. The differential list includes systemic lupus erythematosus, erythropoietic protoporphyria, and more common, polymorphous light eruptions.

Low-sedating H_1-antihistamines are the first line of treatment but often fail. Photo-hardening of the skin may be effective. Otherwise, plasmapheresis, cyclosporinA, photopheresis, plasma exchange, intravenous immunoglobulins or hydroxychloroquine can be tried |16|.

Vibratory urticaria/angio-oedema

Very rarely, strong vibrating forces (e.g. pneumatic hammer) result in vibratory urticaria and/or angio-oedema. In these cases, avoidance of exposure to vibrating forces represents the treatment of choice |16|.

Special types of urticaria

Special types should be differentiated from physical urticaria because they are not (only) caused by an external physical stimulus.

Cholinergic urticaria

Cholinergic urticaria which is common in young adults usually lasting for an average of 5–6 years is caused by a short increase in body temperature that can be the result of physical exercise, passive warmth (hot bath) or emotional stress. Coexistence of cold urticaria should be considered. The weals are fleeting (disappearance within several minutes to one hour) and typically only of pinhead size. Systemic symptoms such as nausea, headache and dizziness may be observed. Provocation by ergometer exercise or by running in place for 5 to 15 min is used for diagnostic purposes. The mainstay of treatment is low-sedating H_1-antihistamines (in increased dose) regularly and/or 60 min before typical triggering situations, but they often fail |16|. It is difficult to achieve exercise tolerance. Optional medications to use are ketotifen or danazol.

Exercise-induced urticaria/angio-oedema

Exercise-induced urticaria and/or angio-oedema is a condition that can occur during or after exercise. Usually, the weals are bigger than in cholinergic urticaria and systemic symptoms, even anaphylactic shock, are more common. Some conditions additionally depend on food intake irrespective of the type, and some depend on specific food intake if IgE-mediated sensitization is present. In these cases, exercise should be avoided for 4 to 6 h after eating. Antihistamines may not be sufficient to prevent symptoms. Exercises should be slowing down or stopped as soon as symptoms start and it is better to exercise with a partner who knows about the condition and can apply emergency medication.

Aquagenic urticaria

In rare aquagenic urticaria, contact to water of any temperature liberates a water-soluble allergen from the stratum corneum that diffuses into the dermis. Weals occurring in the contact area (e.g. to a water compress at body temperature for 30 min) are small-sized. Prophylactic treatment with low-sedating H_1-antihistamines is sufficient in most cases.

Contact urticaria

Contact to an urticant that may cause an immunological (IgE-dependent) or non-immunological reaction (IgE-independent) results in contact urticaria. Allergic contact urticants such as food, latex and animals mainly play a role in atopic individuals (particularly in atopic dermatitis) and can progress to anaphylaxis. Contact to stinging nettles is the most common form of non-allergic contact urticaria. Other non-allergic contact urticants are irritants such as balsam or Peru, benzoic acid and cinnamic aldehyde in cosmetics. Most reactions are work-related therefore details of the patient's employment are essential. If IgE-mediated reactions are suspected, skin prick test and specific IgE measurements are indicated. Other commonly used tests are open application tests with readings at 20, 40, 60 min or chamber tests applied for 15 min with similar reading. Early diagnosis is critical to educate the patient to avoid the contact, because several episodes of contact urticaria can result in protein contact dermatitis.

Conclusion

Urticaria and angio-oedema are common and, if chronic, often persist for years with significant impact on quality of life and occupational ability. There is a clear need for agreement and rationalization of the nomenclature and diagnostic classification of urticaria and angio-oedema at a cross-specialty and international level. To achieve a better understanding of disease aetiopathogenesis and to compare clinical trials, a clear-cut definition of patient subgroups is required. Treatment of most urticaria subtypes is difficult and, apart from the antihistamines, is neither standardized nor 'approved'. Avoidance of identified trigger factors (infections, NSAIDs, mast cell activators) is generally recommended. Low-sedating H1-antihistamines represent the mainstay of treatment. In most cases their dose has to be increased (according to the current European guidelines up to fourfold while considering potential side-effects). The evidence base for treatment alternatives is totally insufficient and the risk–benefit profile of each off-label used drug should be carefully considered. More randomized controlled trials of high quality including carefully characterized urticaria patients are vitally needed.

References

1. Wedi B, Kapp A. Urticaria and angioedema. In: Mahmoudi M (ed). *Allergy: Practical Diagnosis and Management.* Mc Graw Hill, New York, USA, 2007, Chapter 11, pp. 84–94.

2. Gompels MM, Lock RJ, Abinun M, *et al.* C1 inhibitor deficiency: consensus document. *Clin Exp Immunol* 2005; **139**: 379–94.

3. Kaplan AP, Greaves MW. Angioedema. *J Am Acad Dermatol* 2005; **53**: 373–88.

4. Grattan C, Powell S, Humphreys F. Management and diagnostic guidelines for urticaria and angio-oedema. *Br J Dermatol* 2001; **144**: 708–14.

5. Powell RJ, Du Toit GL, Siddique N, *et al.* BSACI guidelines for the management of chronic urticaria and angio-oedema. *Clin Exp Allergy* 2007; **37**: 631–50.

6. Zuberbier T, Bindslev-Jensen C, Canonica W, *et al.* EAACI/GALEN/EDF guideline: definition, classification and diagnosis of urticaria. *Allergy* 2006; **61**: 316–20.

7. Grattan CEH. Towards rationalizing the nomenclature and classification of urticaria: some guidance on guidelines. *Clin Exp Allergy* 2007; **37**: 625–6.

8. Wedi B, Raap U, Kapp A. Chronic urticaria and infections. *Curr Opin Allergy Clin Immunol* 2004; **4**: 387–96.

9. Federman DG, Kirsner RS, Moriarty JP, Concato J. The effect of antibiotic therapy for patients infected with Helicobacter pylori who have chronic urticaria. *J Am Acad Dermatol* 2003; **49**: 861–4.

10. Grattan CE. Autoimmune urticaria. *Immunol Allergy Clin North Am* 2004; **24**: 163–81.

11. Wedi B, Novacovic V, Koerner M, Kapp A. Chronic urticaria serum induces histamine release, leukotriene production, and basophil CD63 surface expression–inhibitory effects of anti-inflammatory drugs. *J Allergy Clin Immunol* 2000; **105**: 552–60.

12. O'Donnell BF, Francis DM, Swana GT, *et al.* Thyroid autoimmunity in chronic urticaria. *Br J Dermatol* 2005; **153**: 331–5.

13. Grattan CE. Aspirin sensitivity and urticaria. *Clin Exp Dermatol* 2003; **28**: 123–7.

14. Zuberbier T, Chantraine-Hess S, Hartmann K, Czametzki BM. Pseudoallergen-free diet in the treatment of chronic urticaria. A prospective study. *Acta Derm Venereol* 1995; **75**: 484–7.

15. Asero R. Chronic unremitting urticaria: is the use of antihistamines above the licensed dose effective? A preliminary study of cetirizine at licensed and above-licensed doses. *Clin Exp Dermatol* 2006; **16**: 1–5.

16. Zuberbier T, Bindslev-Jensen C, Canonica W, *et al.* EAACI/GALEN/EDF guideline: management of urticaria. *Allergy* 2006; **61**: 321–31.

17. Wedi B, Kapp A. Chronic urticaria: assessment of current treatment. *Exp Rev Clin Immunol* 2005; **1**: 459–73.

18. Wedi B, Kapp A. Evidence-based therapy of chronic urticaria. *J Dtsch Dermatol Ges* 2007; **5**: 146–57.

19. Simons FE. Advances in H1-antihistamines. *N Engl J Med* 2004; **351**: 2203–17.

20. Wedi B, Kapp A. Evidence-based treatment of urticaria. *Dtsch Med Wochenschr* 2006; **131**: 1601–4.

21. Di Lorenzo G, Pacor ML, Mansueto P, *et al.* Is there a role for antileukotrienes in urticaria? *Clin Exp Dermatol* 2006; **31**: 327–34.

22. Simons FE, Sussman GL, Simons KJ. Effect of the H2-antagonist cimetidine on the pharmacokinetics and pharmacodynamics of the H1-antagonists hydroxyzine and cetirizine in patients with chronic urticaria. *J Allergy Clin Immunol* 1995; **95**: 685–93.

23. Grattan CE, O'Donnell BF, Francis DM, *et al.* Randomized double-blind study of cyclosporin in chronic 'idiopathic' urticaria. *Br J Dermatol* 2000; **143**: 365–72.

24. Griffiths CE, Katsambas A, Dijkmans BA, *et al.* Update on the use of ciclosporin in immune-mediated dermatoses. *Br J Dermatol* 2006; **155**: 1–16.

25. Baumgart KW, Mullins R. Use of hydroxychloroquine in refractory urticaria. *J Allergy Clin Immunol* 2000; **105**: 795–6.

26. Reeves GEM, Boyle MJ, Bonfield J, *et al.* Impact of hydroxychloroquine therapy on chronic urticaria: chronic autoimmune urticaria study and evaluation. *Int Med J* 2004; **34**: 182–6.

27. Sackesen C, Sekerel BE, Orhan F, *et al.* The etiology of different forms of urticaria in childhood. *Pediatr Dermatol* 2004; **21**: 102–8.

28. Wieczorek D, Raap U, Liekenbröcker T, *et al.* [Chronic urticaria in childhood]. *Hautarzt* 2004; **55**: 357–60.

29. Du Toit G, Prescott R, Lawrence P, *et al.* Autoantibodies to the high-affinity IgE receptor in children with chronic urticaria. *Ann Allergy Asthma Immunol* 2006; **96**: 341–4.

30. Chae KM, Tharp MD. Use and safety of antihistamines in children. *Dermatol Ther* 2000; **13**: 374–83.

31. Schatz M. H1-antihistamines in pregnancy and lactation. *Clin Allergy Immunol* 2002; **17**: 421–36.

32. Simons FE. Advances in H1-antihistamines. *N Engl J Med* 2004; **351**: 2203–17.

33. Hull KM, Shoham N, Chae JJ, *et al.* The expanding spectrum of systemic autoinflammatory disorders and their rheumatic manifestations. *Curr Opin Rheumatol* 2003; **15**: 61–9.

34. Kontou-Fili K, Borici-Mazi R, Kapp A, *et al.* Physical urticaria: classification and diagnostic guidelines. An EAACI position paper. *Allergy* 1997; **52**: 504–13.

35. Siebenhaar F, Weller K, Mlynek A, *et al.* Acquired cold urticaria: clinical picture and update on diagnosis and treatment. *Clin Exp Dermatol* 2007; **32**: 241–5.

PART IV

Systemic

Latex allergy

PAUL CULLINAN

KEY POINTS

1. Allergies to *rubber* take two basic forms: an immediate, type I hypersensitivity to one or more of the several allergenic proteins in latex (this is true latex allergy); or a delayed, type IV allergic response to one or more of the chemical additives, commonly a thiuram, carbamate or benzothiazole (this is *not* latex allergy).

2. Type IV allergic responses to chemical additives in rubber have a slower onset following exposure; such responses tend to be local to the site of direct exposure and are almost exclusively dermal.

3. Several latex allergens have structural homology with fruit, pollen and mould allergens and it is unsurprising that some patients with latex allergy are also allergic to these (e.g. bananas, kiwis, mangos, avocados, chestnuts, walnuts, tomatoes and sweet peppers).

4. A diagnosis of latex allergy should never be made without supportive immunology (skin prick testing and/or the measurement of serum specific IgE antibodies); the diagnostic sensitivity of these tests is well above 95%.

5. The cornerstone of management is avoidance of exposure; the provision of adrenaline for self-administration may be helpful in patients who have suffered anaphylactic reactions to latex contact; ready access to antihistamines is also useful.

Introduction

Latex allergy erupted dramatically about 20 years ago, flared brightly for a decade or so and has now become quite an unusual diagnosis in most European and North American countries. Nonetheless, new cases will continue to be identified and there is a sizeable legacy of the earlier epidemic; moreover, the factors that gave rise to it may give rise to another in the future.

Latex allergy is not a diagnosis to be made lightly since its consequences are serious and far-reaching. Nor is it a particularly difficult diagnosis to make; and the principles of effective management are not complicated. Nonetheless, there is widespread confusion—both within the medical profession and outside—and misdiagnosis remains fairly common.

Background: what is latex and where does it come from?

Much of the misunderstanding arises from confusion between 'latex' and 'rubber' and can be cleared up by understanding how rubber is made and used. The process begins with *Hevea brasiliensis*,[1] the 'rubber tree', whose name reveals its origins in the forests of the Amazon and other parts of southern and central Americas. Early European visitors to these parts of the world—including Christopher Columbus in Haiti—found the inhabitants to be familiar with an elastic substance that they extracted from the rubber tree and fashioned into bouncing balls, unbreakable bottles and even waterproof clothing. However, latex alone is friable, relatively inelastic, dull in appearance and likely to decompose; moreover *Hevea brasiliensis* in its natural habitat grows in solitary stands and is prey to a host of predators and disease, making it difficult to harvest on a large scale.

For many decades the commercial uses and production of latex were thus limited. Three nineteenth-century developments were to change this. First was the recognition by, among others, Charles Macintosh in Glasgow and James Dunlop, a veterinary surgeon from Belfast, that if treated appropriately the material had wide (and eponymous) applications. Second was the accidental discovery of vulcanization by Charles Goodyear in Massachusetts—a process that rendered natural rubber latex more durable but retained its water resistance. Finally, in 1876, Henry Wickham, an English entrepreneur, smuggled several thousand seeds of the rubber tree past the Portuguese customs officers in Belém do Pará at the mouth of the Amazon and shipped them to the glasshouses at Kew in London. There they flourished and within the year had been shipped to the British colonies of Ceylon and subsequently Malaya where they became the foundation of the great rubber plantations of South East Asia (Fig. 8.1)—and a source of far cheaper and purer latex than had ever been produced in the Amazon.

Only the Second World War could halt such progress; the difficulties in extracting and exporting natural rubber occasioned by the war encouraged the development of alternative, artificial elastomers such as nitrile (a polymer of butadiene and acrylonitrile), neoprene, styrene butadiene and silicone rubber. These rapidly gained popularity and remain in common use. Only a global epidemic such as AIDS could subsequently re-stimulate demand for natural rubber latex. The fear of nosocomial cross-infection and the introduction of 'universal precautions' to healthcare—and to an increasing number of other industrial and care sectors—

---

1 A member of the family *Euphorbiaceae*; gardeners will recognize the milky sap from domestic varieties ('spurges') which is a well-known skin irritant. The rubber tree must not be confused with the 'rubber plant'—*Ficus elastica*.

Fig. 8.1 *Hevea brasiliensis* plantation in Malaysia.

Fig. 8.2 Manufacture of latex gloves by 'dipping' process.

stimulated an enormous and worldwide demand for latex gloves and the resurgence of rubber production in South East Asia.

Thus, most rubber tree plantations are now in Malaysia, Sri Lanka, Thailand and West Africa; very little rubber is still produced in the Amazon. Considerable effort has been put into the breeding of high-output strains of *Hevea brasiliensis* and it is speculated that some strains produce a higher-protein and perhaps more allergenic variety of latex. Latex tapping is carried out by hand in the early hours of the morning when the tree sap is rising. The milky fluid is preserved—usually with ammonia—before being processed with a variety of other preservative, plasticizing, vulcanizing and colouring chemicals. Almost all latex is used in the manufacture of 'dry goods' such as car tyres where it is combined with synthetic elastomers and pressed, moulded or extruded into the required shape. Around 10% is used in the production of directly prepared articles from a latex concentrate using a 'dipping technique' (Fig. 8.2). Such articles include gloves, contraceptives and bottle-feeding teats.

Almost all dipping methods involve the use of a powder to facilitate handling of the sticky products; the powder may be removed during manufacture by subsequent washing—or may be further added to aid in the use of the final product. Originally, powdered talc was used—and still is in the manufacture of rubber balloons. The recognition in the 1960s however that talc caused granulomas and encouraged the formation of adhesions after surgery prompted its replacement in surgical and then other gloves with cornstarch. Latex is adsorbed onto starch more readily than it is onto talc and starch-dusted gloves are far more likely to produce airborne latex particles. In recent years much of the manufacture of rubber products—including gloves—has been relocated from Europe and North America to factories closer to the plantations. Latex is now rarely transported across the world in container ships, often at high temperatures; this too may have affected the allergenicity of the raw material.

Other natural rubbers include gutta percha and chicle. The former, derived from the leaves of the *Palaquium gutta* tree is used in endodontic points for dental root work; it does not appear to contain any proteins that cross-react with natural rubber latex allergens. Chicle—a component of early chewing gums—seems similarly unrelated.

The account above provides several lessons—and probably explains several features of the epidemic of latex allergy that occurred in the 1980s–1990s:

- 'Rubber' is not synonymous with 'latex'.
- Rubber is a complex mixture of natural latex and a wide variety of low molecular weight additives.
- Many articles made from rubber contain very little natural latex; often the latex is not in an 'available' form.
- Some articles made from rubber are entirely artificial—and contain no natural latex at all.
- Articles manufactured by a dipping process contain the highest proportion of natural latex; they include many items used routinely in healthcare.
- Most dipped articles have, at some stage, been powdered.
- Powdered articles—especially gloves—readily release latex proteins into the air. Powder-free articles do not.
- There is inevitable variation in the allergenicity of different latex-containing articles—even those manufactured in a single batch.

Rubber allergy

Consequently, allergies to *rubber* take two basic forms (Fig. 8.3):

1. An immediate, type I hypersensitivity to one or more of the several allergenic proteins in latex: this is true latex allergy; or
2. Much more commonly, a delayed, type IV allergic response to one or more of the chemical additives, commonly a thiuram, carbamate or benzothiazole [1]. This is *not* latex allergy. Much rarer sources of Type IV allergy in latex gloves include the antimicrobial cetyl pyridinium chloride [2]. Type IV responses to latex proteins have been described but their existence is debated; certainly they are rare. Dermatitic reactions to glove powder (cornstarch) are usually due to adsorbed thiurams, though protein contact dermatitis may also occur.

Latex allergens

Natural rubber latex is a complex biological material containing more than 200 polypeptides; in total, proteins make up about 2% of its fresh weight—70% of these are water soluble. At present, 13 latex allergens are recognized by the International Union of Immunological Societies and summarized in Table 8.1. More will undoubtedly be identified.

There is some evidence of an immunospecificity in response whereby patients presumed to have different routes of initial sensitization recognize different sets of allergens. Healthcare workers (and children) who are generally sensitized by

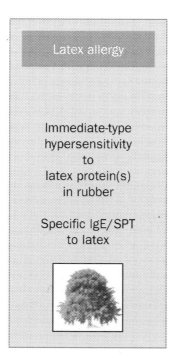

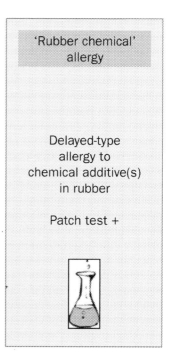

Fig. 8.3 Two kinds of allergy to rubber; only one is 'latex allergy'.

Latex allergy	'Rubber chemical' allergy
Immediate-type hypersensitivity to latex protein(s) in rubber	Delayed-type allergy to chemical additive(s) in rubber
Specific IgE/SPT to latex	Patch test +

inhalation, tend to respond to water-soluble, lutoid proteins including Hev b 2, Hev b 5 and Hev b 6.01, 6.02. Those patients whose sensitization is presumed to have arisen through repeated prolonged catheterization tend to have responses restricted to hydrophobic proteins (Hev b 1 and Hev b 3). Such distinctions are not, however, complete.

Several latex allergens have structural homology with fruit, pollen and mould allergens and it unsurprising that some patients with latex allergy are also allergic to these. Similarly, and almost certainly, some patients with immunological—but not clinical—reactions to latex will not be allergic to latex itself but to one or more cross-reacting proteins. This is important clinically and is discussed more fully below.

Relevant epidemiology

An important starting point in the diagnosis of latex allergy—indeed in the diagnosis of any disease—is consideration of the prior likelihood of the condition in an individual patient. In this respect it is helpful to understand a little of the epidemiology of latex allergy.

Aside from sporadic case reports (some of questionable accuracy), latex allergy was not recognized until the late 1980s. For about a decade afterwards there was an epidemic of reports in the medical literature, reflecting both an increase in the

Table 8.1 Latex allergens currently recognised by the International Union of Immunological Societies. 'Major' allergens are listed in bold

Systematic name	Conventional name	MW (kDa)	Approximate prevalence of specific sensitization in adults with latex allergy [3]	Common associations [4]
Hev b 1	Rubber elongation factor	14.6	20%	
Hev b 2	**β-1,3-glucanase**	**34**	**60%**	Fruit allergy
Hev b 3	Small rubber particle protein	23	20%	
Hev b 4	**Microhelix cyanogenic glucosidase**	**100–115**	**60%**	
Hev b 5	Acidic C-serum protein	16	60%*	Fruit allergy
Hev b 6				
Hev b 6.01	**Prohevein**	**20**	**75%**	
Hev b 6.02	**Hevein**	**4.7**	**75%**	
Hev b 6.03	Prohevein C-domain	14	30%	
Hev b 7	Patatin-like protein	44	40%	Fruit allergy
Hev b 8	Profilin	14	15%	
Hev b 9	Enolase	48	5%†	
Hev b 10	Mn-superoxidase dismutase	25–45	20%†	Mould allergy
Hev b11	Class I chitinase	32	25%†	Mould allergy
Hev b12	Lipid transfer protein	9.3	20%†	
Hev b13	**Lipolytic esterase**	**43**	**75%**	

* = to recombinant protein; † = very few data

incidence of the condition and a growing awareness of prevalent cases. The last decade has seen a dramatic fall in the incidence of new disease and most new diagnoses now will be of previously 'hidden' cases.

Early in the epidemic process two groups were identified as having a particularly high risk of latex allergy:

- First were those whose occupations required them regularly to use latex gloves—in particular those employed in healthcare ('healthcare workers' or HCW) but also factory and construction workers, mechanics, those employed in food production and several others. Dozens of cross-sectional surveys—and a few cohort studies—have been carried out in HCW populations producing prevalence estimates of 'latex allergy' from <1% to over 30%. In fact there has been considerable confusion over the differences between clinical allergy and immunological sensitization—let alone basic epidemiological principles of appropriate population selection and response rates—and the true frequency of latex allergy in these groups is much less clear. Furthermore, it has been remarkably difficult, at anything other than an ecological level, to demonstrate within HCW populations a relationship between risk and glove exposure—probably because of the difficulties in obtaining accurate exposure estimates. Indeed it has been argued that glove wearing is not associated with an increased risk of latex allergy |5|, although this is an argument that few would support |6,7|. Perhaps the clearest demonstration of cause-and-effect in this setting has been the demonstration of a steep reduction in German hospital workers of new cases of allergy following the widespread removal of powdered latex gloves |8|.
- The second group with an identified high risk were those who had undergone repeated urinary catheterization (with latex-containing devices) or surgery—in most cases because of congenital spinal disease or hydrocephalus. Again the risk of new cases has been largely eliminated by the use of latex-free catheters and by constant vigilance.

There is far less information about other groups but surveys of representative 'general' populations suggest that the prevalence of true latex allergy is low. A summary of the better of these surveys is provided in Table 8.2. Several suggest that the general prevalence of sensitization to latex is quite high but this is a conclusion that has to be considered critically. First, it is not clear that some of the surveys were of 'general' populations—blood donors, for example, may contain a high proportion of HCW. Second is the issue of the diagnostic specificity of the immunological methods used—with the further suggestion of cross-reactivity with common antigens, particularly those in pollens. Even an apparently high specificity can, in situations of low prevalence, produce a significant overestimation of the true prevalence of disease |17|. Furthermore, those surveys that have collected clinical information have found a poor correlation between symptoms and specific sensitization suggesting a low specificity for either of these methods in the epidemiological context. It is probable that the true prevalence of clinical latex allergy in general populations is very low.

Table 8.2 Surveys of latex sensitization (and allergy) in 'general' populations

Reference	Source population	#	Country	Response rate	Male	Mean age (years)	Technique	Positive result (%)	Note	Clinical latex allergy: n (%)
[9]	Blood donors	7042	UK	NA	57%	NA	Serum IgE	6.3%	Strong association with pollen sensitization	NA
[10]	Blood donors	1000	USA	NA	53%	38	Serum IgE	3.3%		NA
[11]	Blood donors	1997	USA	NA	56%	NA*	Serum IgE	5.4%–7.6%		NA
[12]	Blood donors	1025	Italy	NA	84%	39	Serum IgE	3.6%	Most also sensitized to pollens	1 (0.09%)
[13]	General population (adult)	5512	USA	NA	NA	Range 17–60	Serum IgE	18.6%		NA
[14]	Attendees for health screening	258	France	35%	48%	32	Serum IgE Skin prick test	3.5% 3%	None sensitized to both methods	4 (1.6%)
[15]	School children	1175	Italy	81%	50%	9	Skin prick test	0.7%		0
[16]	Birth cohort	1877	UK	52%	NS	7	Skin prick test	0.2%		0

NA = not available

A more consistent finding is of an association between atopy and the risk of latex allergy. Thus, the risk is increased in (but not confined to) those with evidence of sensitization, clinical or otherwise, to common protein allergens such as those in pollens or house dust.

Clinical manifestations

In the sensitized person, the clinical manifestations of latex allergy depend on the route of latex exposure. In each case symptoms develop very soon after exposure—within no more than 30 min—as would be expected from an 'immediate-type' allergic response. This brief latency is helpful in distinguishing latex responses from the more delayed effects typical of allergy to the chemical constituents of rubber.

1. Exposure to airborne latex particles—such as those from powdered latex gloves—provokes symptoms typical of a respiratory, protein allergy. These are itching of the eyes, rhinitis and sneezing and sometimes cough and wheeze.
2. Direct exposure to mucous membranes gives rise to local swelling and itching and, if prolonged, to systemic anaphylaxis. Examples of situations where such exposures occur include urinary catheterization, surgery, dental examinations and childbirth.
3. Direct exposure of the skin may provoke local urticaria but this is not common. As with other allergic responses to proteins, hand reactions to latex gloves are said to be more common on the palms ('protein contact dermatitis')—in distinction from the more dorsal features of a 'chemical' contact dermatitis.
4. Because true latex reactions resolve rapidly with treatment or with cessation of the provoking exposure, clinical signs between-times are rare. On the other hand, the rapidity and relative ease with which they can be provoked can be useful diagnostically (see below).

Clinical history

As with most consultations it is useful to begin by letting the patient describe their symptoms ('tell you their diagnosis') without interruption or direction and paying particular attention to their circumstances, timing and nature. Following this, a set of leading questions is helpful; these may include:

- Have you had any reactions at the dentist?
- Have you had any unexpected problems during surgery ...
       ... or childbirth, cervical smear testing etc?
- Have you had any problems with washing up gloves ...
       ... or when blowing up party balloons?
- Have you had any adverse reactions to the use of condoms?[2]
- Have you had any problem after eating fruits or vegetables? Patients with latex allergy often report oral, allergic symptoms to fruits with a very wide range of

---

2 In practice this seems rare with latex allergy.

fruits being implicated. Common examples are bananas, kiwis, mangos, avocados, chestnuts, walnuts, tomatoes and sweet peppers—but dozens of others have been described. On occasion, patients with latex allergy report symptoms when in contact with the 'weeping fig' (*Ficus benjamina*) which is commonly found in homes and offices.

Finally, questions about the frequency and type of regular contact with latex are valuable. These help establish the prior likelihood of latex allergy and serve as a basis for appropriate management if the diagnosis is confirmed. Of particular importance are questions about occupational exposures—in most cases to latex gloves. Traditionally the preserve of HCW, latex gloves are now widely worn by a large number of other occupational groups including nursery staff, mechanics, computer assembly workers and food handlers. Powdered latex gloves are not uncommon in such settings and even if your patient does not use gloves themselves, they may have developed sensitization through vicarious exposure. A history of repeated urinary tract catheterization and/or surgery probably confers an increased risk of latex allergy

Patients with latex allergy—and those who are concerned that they may have latex allergy—commonly fear contact with (and/or report adverse reactions to) a very wide variety of rubber articles. These include many kinds of medical equipment, office articles such as elastic bands, bicycle or car tyres, household furnishings including carpet backings or underlay, party balloons (even when not in direct contact), elasticated clothing and food wrappings. Some will avoid prepared foods such as shop-bought sandwiches for fear that they have been handled by people wearing latex gloves or are packaged in latex-containing wrappings; and many will refrain from eating a long list of fruits and vegetables. It is important to distinguish truly allergic responses from those that arise from anxiety alone. Allergic reactions from latex allergens transferred to foods during handling |18| or from packaging |19|, for example, appear to be very rare. Such concerns however are testament to the widespread use of rubber and to the extensive—and often alarmist—information on latex allergy that is publicly available. In fact, for the reasons outlined earlier, most such fears are unfounded. The majority of rubber articles contain no or very little natural rubber latex; and even if they do, it is often not in a form that is available for the provocation of an allergic response. Nonetheless, fears such as these can be extremely disabling.³

Perhaps the commonest point of diagnostic confusion is between true latex allergy (as above) and allergic responses to the other constituents of rubber. The latter are typical of a delayed-type 'chemical dermatitis'; the distinction is rarely difficult with attentive history-taking:

● Type IV allergic responses to chemical additives in rubber have a slower onset following exposure, although this latency may be blurred if exposure is

---

3 "When I look back on all these worries, I remember the story of the old man who said on his deathbed that he had had a lot of troubles in his life, most of which had never happened." (W. Churchill)

repeated and lengthy—as is often the case, for example, with those who regularly wear rubber gloves at work.

- Such responses tend to be local to the site of direct exposure and are almost exclusively dermal—most commonly on the hands (from glove wearing) but also the feet (rubber trainers), the torso (underwear) or the face (rubber masks). In severe cases a more generalized dermatitis may develop.
- The dermatitis is of an eczematous—rather than urticarial—nature. Because it is of longer duration there may be residual physical signs.

Diagnostic immunology

A diagnosis of latex allergy should never be made without supportive immunology. This is especially the case because of the widespread confusion between 'latex' and 'rubber', the high profile of the condition and the potentially disastrous consequences of a wrong diagnosis.

As with other immunoglobulin (Ig)E-associated allergies the most important immunological methods are skin prick testing and the measurement of serum specific IgE antibodies. In routine practice these are sufficient; more complex tests such as lymphocyte proliferation or basophile histamine release assays are unnecessary and probably useful only in research settings. There are now several, validated, commercial systems for IgE assay and extracts for prick testing; it should not be necessary to use *ad hoc* prick-prick testing which is likely to be both more hazardous and less specific.

Much has been written about the diagnostic efficiency of the various test methods but the arguments are essentially circular in the absence of a credible, alternative 'gold standard' diagnostic method. Moreover, as with all diagnostic tests, their value depends critically on the pre-test probability of disease. The following seems a useful summary:

- Both specific IgE assay and skin prick testing have a very high diagnostic *sensitivity* if performed and interpreted carefully. If comparisons are meaningful then the latter method probably has the edge since levels of circulating serum antibodies may decline if exposure to latex has been avoided.
- In each case, the diagnostic sensitivity is well above 95%. In essence this means that a negative test result makes the diagnosis of latex allergy extremely improbable. Indeed, there are no convincing reports of latex allergy in the presence of negative test results to a battery of IgE assays and skin prick tests.
- It is good practice to use and compare both prick testing and IgE assay although in most cases the results will be in agreement. Some centres routinely employ more than one version of each method.
- The diagnostic *specificity* of these methods *in clinical practice* is probably a little lower with a slightly higher proportion of false positive results. This may be more so for IgE assay than for prick testing. The reasons for this probably lie with cross-reacting antigens in other biological materials such as pollens or moulds.
- Routine testing for IgE-sensitization to common aeroallergens (in particular pollens and moulds) either *in vitro* or by prick test can be useful in the interpretation of apparently false positive findings.

● Where there is an appropriate clinical history the same immunological methods can be used to assess sensitization to fruits and/or vegetables.

There is no convincing evidence that skin prick testing is hazardous in latex allergy but it is prudent to omit it where there is a good history of latex-associated anaphylaxis. Some manufacturers advise the sequential use of test extracts of increasing strength.

Challenge testing

Occasionally it is helpful to proceed to specific provocation testing—particularly when there is discrepancy between the history and immunological findings. It can also be useful as a demonstration to the patient that they are indeed (or more often are *not*) allergic to latex. Provocation testing is hazardous and should only be carried out by those with appropriate experience and in settings where there is ready access to resuscitative equipment.

The principle of provocation testing in this context is the replication of normal exposure to latex under carefully controlled—and preferably 'blind'—conditions. Initial exposures should be of very low intensity and duration; and increased only if no adverse reactions develop. Commonly used methods include:

● Glove wearing.
● (Powdered) glove handling.
● Application of latex (gloves) to the mucous membranes of the mouth or eyes.
● Handling of other latex articles such as balloons.

Most responses indicative of latex allergy develop immediately and are clinically obvious. More refined measures of response include spirometry, non-specific bronchial responsiveness and various techniques for assessing nasal reactions.

Reaching a diagnostic conclusion

It is important, perhaps unusually so, to make a correct diagnosis in this setting. The consequences of a missed (false negative) case are obvious; what is less widely appreciated is the damage that can be caused by a false positive diagnosis. Patients with latex allergy, their families and their employers often need to make major and sometimes costly lifestyle and occupational adjustments; where problems have mistakenly been attributed to latex allergy these adjustments prove useless.

Most cases will fall into one of the following categories (Fig. 8.4)

1. In the context of high prior likelihood, a characteristic history and supportive immunology, a diagnosis of latex allergy can be made without further investigation.
2. In the context of an uncharacteristic history (whatever the prior likelihood) and negative immunological testing, a diagnosis of latex allergy can be ruled out without further investigation.

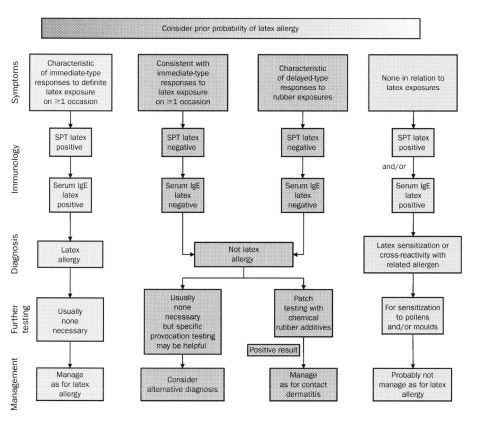

Fig. 8.4 Diagnostic algorithm for latex allergy.

3. In the context of a characteristic history (whatever the prior likelihood) and negative immunological testing, a diagnosis of latex allergy can usually be ruled out without further investigation; however specific provocation testing may be helpful here.

4. In the absence of a characteristic history the interpretation of a positive immunological result can be difficult; again provocation testing may be helpful. In most cases, however, the immunological result is likely to be a false positive one. A search for allergies to cross-reacting antigens is useful in such cases.

Management

As with all immediate-type allergies the cornerstone of management is avoidance of exposure. In most cases, the main route(s) of exposure can be successfully controlled. Thus, for example, latex-free medical equipment is widely available for patients who require it; and there is now good evidence that almost all latex-allergic patients who need to wear gloves at work can continue to do so by switching to non-latex versions |20,21|. In these cases it is important to be sure that colleagues who wear gloves use powder-free types—it is seldom necessary for them also to switch to latex-free gloves but doing so may provide further reassurance. Only rarely is it necessary for a patient to give up their job on account of latex allergy; but in all cases liaison with the patient's occupational health services is invaluable.

More difficulty arises from other latex exposures both in and out of the workplace. Most of these are unlikely to be harmful but there are some that carry a high risk:

1. Patients with latex allergy should be strongly advised to avoid 'internal' exposure to latex. This is most likely to occur during medical, dental and similar procedures including childbirth. Thus, they should advise their health carers of their allergy and ensure that all procedures are carried out with latex-free equipment. It is good advice for them—in case of emergency procedures—to carry identification of their allergy; 'warning bracelets' and the like are easily available.
2. Other exposures—to rubber articles in the wider environment—are less predictably hazardous. As a general principle, most are likely not to provoke allergic responses—either because they contain no latex or because their latex content is not in an 'available' form. Some exposures commonly produce reactions—for instance, wearing washing up gloves and blowing up rubber balloons—but others are best managed on a 'trial and experience' basis. It is in general neither necessary nor helpful to advise a policy of strict avoidance of all rubber articles.
3. Patients who have associated fruit allergies will in any case avoid eating those they have identified as causing problems. As above it is unnecessary (and probably harmful) to advise avoidance of all fruits and vegetables that have been reported elsewhere to cause cross-reacting allergies.

The provision of adrenaline for self-administration may be helpful in patients who have suffered anaphylactic reactions to latex contact; ready access to antihistamines is also useful. Several methods of specific immunotherapy for patients with latex allergy have been described. There are as yet no reports of success in high quality, large-scale blinded and randomized studies; in any case, immunotherapy is likely to have a limited role in the context of a condition where avoidance of exposure is generally successful.

Many patients with latex allergy are frightened by their condition. Sympathy, reassurance and support from an experienced clinician can be very helpful. There is a huge literature on latex allergy, much of which can readily be accessed via the web. It is not necessarily accurate and much is frankly alarmist. Some patients may find more comfort and encouragement from a patient support group. The most established of these are in the UK (Latex Allergy Support Group: *www.lasg.co.uk*) and US (American Latex Allergy Association: *www.latexallergyresources.org*).

References

1. Heese A, Hintzenstern J, Peters K-P, *et al.* Allergic and irritant reactions to rubber gloves in the medical health services. *J Am Acad Dermatol* 1991; **25**: 831–9.

2. Steinkjer B. Contact dermatitis from cetyl pyridinium chloride in latex surgical gloves. *Contact Dermatitis* 1998; **39**: 29–30.

3. Yeang HY. Natural rubber latex allergens: new developments. *Curr Opin Allergy Clin Immunol* 2004; **4**: 99–104.

4. Breiteneder H, Scheiner O. Molecular and immunological characteristics of latex allergens. *Int Arch Allergy Immunol* 1998; **116**: 83–92.

5. Garabrant DH, Schweitzer S. Epidemiology of latex sensitization and allergies in health care workers. *J Allergy Clin Immunol* 2002; **110**(Suppl 2): S82–95.

6. Bousquet J, Flahault A, Vandenplas O, *et al.* Natural rubber latex allergy among health care workers: a systematic review of the evidence. *J Allergy Clin Immunol* 2006; **118**: 447–54.

7. Wartenberg D, Buckler G. Invited commentary: assessing latex sensitization using data from NHANES III. *Am J Epidemiol* 2001; **153**: 523–6.

8. Allmers H, Schmengler J, Skudlik C. Primary prevention of natural rubber latex allergy in the German health care system through education and intervention. *J Allergy Clin Immunol* 2002; **110**: 318–23.

9. Merrett TG, Merrett J, Kekwick R. The prevalence of immunoglobulin E antibodies to the proteins of rubber (*Hevea brasiliensis*) latex and grass (*Phleum pratense*) pollen in sera of British blood donors. *Clin Exp Allergy* 1999; **29**: 1572–8.

10. Ownby DR, Ownby HE, McCullough J, Shafer AW. The prevalence of anti-latex IgE antibodies in 1000 volunteer blood donors. *J Allergy Clin Immunol* 1996; **97**: 1188–92.

11. Saxon A, Ownby D, Huard T, *et al.* Prevalence of IgE to natural rubber latex in unselected blood donors and performance characteristics of AlaSTAT testing. *Ann Allergy Asthma Immunol* 2000; **84**: 199–206.

12. Senna GE, Crocco I, Roata C, *et al.* Prevalence of latex-specific IgE in blood donors: an Italian survey. *Allergy* 1999; **54**: 80–1.

13. Garabrant DH, Roth HD, Parsad R, *et al.* Latex sensitization in health care workers and in the US general population. *Am J Epidemiol* 2001; **153**: 515–22.

14. Porri F, Lemiere C, Birnbaum J, *et al.* Prevalence of latex sensitization in subjects attending health screening: implications for perioperative screening. *Clin Exp Allergy* 1997; **27**: 413–17.

15. Bernadini R, Novembre E, Ingargiola A, *et al.* Prevalence and risk factors of latex sensitization in an unselected pedriatic population. *J Allergy Clin Immunol* 1998; **101**: 621–5.

16. Roberts G, Lack G, Northstone K, Golding J; ALSPAC Study Team. Prevalence of latex allergy in the community at age 7 years. *Clin Exp Allergy* 2005; **35**: 299–300.

17. Yeang HY. Prevalence of latex allergy may be vastly overestimated when determined by in vitro assays. *Ann Allergy Asthma Immunol* 2000; **84**: 628–32.

18. Franklin W, Pandolfo J. Latex as a food allergen. *N Engl J Med* 1999; **341**: 1858.

19. Mak RK, O'Gorman-Lalor O, Croom A, Wakelin SH. An unusual case of latex allergy: contact urticaria from natural rubber latex in chocolate bar wrappers. *Clin Exp Dermatol* 2005; **30**: 190–1.

20. Turjanmaa K, Kanto M, Kautiainen H, *et al.* Long-term outcome of 160 adult patients with natural rubber latex allergy. *J Allergy Clin Immunol* 2002; **110**(Suppl 2): S70–4.

21. Vandenplas O, Jamart J, Delwiche JP, *et al.* Occupational asthma caused by natural rubber latex: outcome according to cessation or reduction of exposure. *J Allergy Clin Immunol* 2002; **109**: 125–30.

9

Managing drug allergy

PASCAL DEMOLY

KEY POINTS

1. Drug hypersensitivity reactions represent up to one-third of adverse drug reactions.

2. Clinical presentations are heterogeneous.

3. Factors other than drugs are mainly responsible for urticaria and maculopapular eruptions.

4. The clinical tools allowing a definite diagnosis include a thorough clinical history, standardized skin tests, reliable biological tests and drug provocation tests.

5. When properly performed in specialized centres, a firm diagnosis is often possible and safe alternative medication can be proposed.

Introduction

Drug hypersensitivity reactions (DHRs) represent the adverse effects of certain drugs which, when taken at a dose tolerated by normal subjects, clinically resemble allergy [1]. Drug allergies are adverse reactions in which antibodies and/or activated T cells are directed against the drug or one of its metabolites. Numerous reactions with symptoms suggestive of allergy are often erroneously considered to be real drug allergies. They occur in a small percentage of patients only and can generally not be predicted. The aetiologies of these reactions include non-specific histamine release (e.g. opiates, radiocontrast media and vancomycin), bradykinin accumulation (angiotensin-converting enzyme inhibitors), complement activation (protamine), induction of leukotriene synthesis (aspirin and non-steroidal anti-inflammatory drugs [NSAIDs]) and bronchospasm (e.g. SO_2 released by drug preparations containing sulphites). In many apparent cases of drug allergy, the underlying disease is the cause of the exanthema (e.g. in the case of an upper respiratory tract infection) or, since drugs are often taken during meals, a food allergy may be involved.

DHRs may represent up to one-third of adverse drug reactions. They can be life-threatening, require or prolong hospitalization and entail changes in the drug prescription |2|. They concern more than 7% of the general population and therefore represent an important public health problem |3|. Both under-diagnosis (due to under-reporting |4,5|) and over-diagnosis (due to the over-use of the term 'allergy' |6|) have to be considered. Misclassification based on the drug allergy history may have consequences on individual treatment choices and can lead to the use of more expensive and less effective drugs. Clinical manifestations are wide and range from maculopapular exanthema to anaphylactic shock, which may be fatal (Table 9.1) |7|.

The diagnosis of immediate and/or delayed hypersensitivity reactions to drugs requires knowledge of the scientific literature with, for the more recently introduced drugs, access to Medline searches and to the Committee on Safety of

Table 9.1 Classification of drug hypersensitivities. Adapted with permission from |7|

Type	Type of immune response	Pathophysiology	Clinical symptoms	Chronology of the reaction
I	IgE	Mast cells and basophil degranulation	Anaphylactic shock, Angio-oedema, Urticaria, Bronchospasm	A few minutes to 1 h after the last intake of the drug
II	IgG and FcR	FcR-dependent cell death	Cytopenia	5–15 days after the start of treatment
III	IgM or IgG and complement or FcR	Deposition of immune complexes	Serum sickness, Urticaria, Vasculitis	7–8 days for serum sickness 7–21 days after the start of treatment for vasculitis
IVa	Th1 (IFN-γ)	Monocytic inflammation	Eczema	5–21 days after the start of treatment
IVb	Th2 (IL-5 and IL-4)	Eosinophilic inflammation	Maculopapular exanthema, bullous exanthema	2–6 weeks after the start of treatment for DRESS
IVc	Cytotoxic T cells (perforin, granzyme B, FasL)	Keratinocyte death mediated by CD4 or CD8	Maculopapular exanthema, bullous exanthema, pustular exanthema	2 days after the start of treatment for fixed drug eruption, 7–21 days after the start of treatment for Stevens-Johnson and TEN
IVd	T cells (IL-8/CXCL8)	Neutrophilic inflammation	Acute generalized exanthematous pustulosis	Less than 2 days

Medicine Reports. The lack of case studies involving a particular compound does not mean that it cannot induce allergic reactions. The diagnosis is indeed based on history, clinical manifestations, and, if possible, on skin tests and biological tests. Few available clinical and biological tools are at our disposal and many of these have not been fully evaluated. Moreover, a definite diagnosis of such a reaction is required in order to institute proper preventive measures.

Under the aegis of the European Academy of Allergology and Clinical Immunology (*www.eaaci.net*), the European Network of Drug Allergy (ENDA) is working towards the establishment of clinical tools in daily practice.

Clinical history

Clinical history should be examined thoroughly and should address the symptomatology (compatible with an allergy?), the chronology of the symptoms (previous exposure, delay between the last dose and the onset of symptoms, effect of stopping treatment), other medication taken (both at the time of the reaction as well as other drugs of the same class taken since) and the medical background of the patient (any suggestion of a previous allergy whether associated with medication or not). Data should be recorded in a uniform format and, in order to harmonize the drug hypersensitivity diagnostic procedures in Europe, members of ENDA have developed a questionnaire |8| available in many different languages (Fig. 9.1). Diagnosis is more difficult when patients are not seen during the acute phase, in which case photographs are helpful. When patients are seen during the reaction, the suspected drugs should be stopped, particularly if danger signs such as bullous or haemorrhagic widespread lesions or mucosal lesions are present (Table 9.2) |9|.

The history is often not reliable since different drugs are frequently taken simultaneously and may account for the symptoms. History can also be imprecise in many cases. Finally, the clinical picture of drug allergy is very heterogeneous, mirroring many distinct pathophysiological events. Thus, for drug allergy diagnosis, many doctors rely on history and various reference manuals. They do not attempt to prove the relationship between the drug intake and the symptoms or to clarify the underlying pathomechanism of the reaction. Such an attitude leads to a misunderstanding of the epidemiology and the pathophysiology of this highly relevant field. In cases where a hypersensitivity reaction is suspected, if the drug is essential and/or frequently prescribed (e.g. β-lactams, paracetamol and NSAIDs), a certified diagnosis should be performed and tests should be carried out in a specialist centre. Only a formal diagnosis of drug hypersensitivity reactions allows the measures required for prevention and treatment to be brought into play. For these drugs, the prudent principle of eviction may be insufficient. This procedure could lead to the elimination of drugs which do not necessarily give rise to reactions and which are widely used. However, this is a valid option until a specialist consultation can be scheduled.

The specific allergy diagnosis should be carried out 4 weeks after the complete clearing of all clinical symptoms and signs. On the other hand, after a time interval of more than 6–12 months, some drug tests may already have turned negative,

DRUG HYPERSENSITVITY QUESTIONNAIRE

INVESTIGATOR: Date of protocol: ....

Name:..Center:..

Address:...Tel/Fax/E-mail:...............................

PATIENT:

Name:...Date of birth:..............................Age:...........years   Weight:..........kg

Height:...........cm

Profession:...Origin:...........................Sex: • M • F

Riskgroups: • Medical staff   • Pharmaceutical Industries   • Farmers   • others (specify).................

CURRENT COMPLAINTS:...

....

....

DRUG REACTION: **DATE OF REACTION:**........................

(Multiple boxes can be ticked; underline the choice if necessary; chronology can be characterized with numbers)

CUTANEOUS SYMPTOMS: **DIFFERENTIAL DIAGNOSIS:**
* Maculopapular exanthema
* Macular exanthema   •...
* Urticarious exanthema
* AGEP (Acute generalized exanthemous pustulosis)   •...
* Eczematoid exanthema
* Erythema exudativum multiforme   •...
* Bullous exanthema
* Stevens Johnson Syndrome / TEN (Lyell)
* Fixed drug exanthema   **CONTRIBUTING FACTORS:**
* Purpura -> Thrombocyte count :................   • Viral infections: • Flu like infection • Other:............
    • palpable   • haemorrhagic-necrotizing   • Fever
    • Visceral organ involvement:...........................   • Suspicion of photosensitivity ? • No • Yes • Unknown
* Contact dermatitis   • Topic cause • Haematogenous cause •   • Stress
* Urticaria vasculitis   • Exercise
* **ONLY** Pruritus   • Other (specify):...
* Urticaria
* Angoedema/Location/s:...............................
* Conjunctivitis   **EVOLUTION:**
* Other (specify):..   **Intensity**

* Morphology/Location/s:...............................

EFFLORESCENCES: Distribution / Dynamics (   )   **h / days**

`• generalized`

GASTROINTESTINAL AND RESPIRATORY SYMPTOMS: **ASSOCIATED SYMPTOMS:**
> Nausea/Emesis   • Involvement of: • Liver • Kidney • Other (specify):......
> Diarrhea   • Fever   ......°C
> Gastro intestinal cramps   • Malaise
                                                               • Pain/Burning • Location/s:.........................
* Cough   • Edema   • Location/s:.........................
* Dysphonia   • Arthralgia/Myalgia • Location/s:...................
* Dyspnea   PEFR or FEV1:............   • Lymphadenopathy
* Wheezing/Bronchospasm   • Other (specify):...................................

* Rhinitis   **CARDIOVASCULAR SYMPTOMS:**
* Rhinorrhea   • Tachykardia   Pulse rate: ..../min
* Sneezing   • Hypotension   Blood pressure: ....mmHg
* Nasal obstruction   • Collapse
* Other (specify):..   • Arrhythmia
                                                               • Other (specify):...................................
PSYCHIC SYMPTOMS:
* Fear/Panic reaction   • Vertigo   **INVOLVEMENT OF OTHER ORGANS :**
* Fainting   *(e.g. peripheral neuropathy, lung involvement, cytopenia....)*
* Paraesthesia/Hyperventilation   •...
* Sweating   •...
* Other (specify):..

Fig. 9.1 Questionnaire for drug hypersensitivities. Adapted with permission from |8|.

SUSPICIOUS DRUGS:

Drug's generic name additives / Indication:	Daily dose / Route of application / Duration of therapy:	Interval between dose and reaction	Previous therapy with this drug:
1.	..............mg/d; ....; ....d		• No • Unknown • Yes -> Symptoms:................................
2.	..............mg/d; ....; ....d		• No • Unknown • Yes -> Symptoms:................................
3.	..............mg/d; ....; ....d		• No • Unknown • Yes -> Symptoms:................................
4.	..............mg/d; ....; ....d		• No • Unknown • Yes -> Symptoms:................................
5.	..............mg/d; ....; ....d		• No • Unknown • Yes -> Symptoms:................................
6.	..............mg/d; ....; ....d		• No • Unknown • Yes -> Symptoms:................................

MANAGEMENT FOLLOWING ACUTE DRUG REACTION: • No therapy
- • Stop of suspicious drugs No.# ....
- • Antihistamines   • local   • systemic
- • Corticosteroids   • local   • systemic
- • Bronchodilatators   • local   • systemic
- • Shock treatment   • Epinephrine   • Plasma expanders   • Other: ....
- • Change to substitute/s:
    - • Type/Name: ....
    - • Tolerance: ....
    - • Other (specify):........................
- • Dosis reduction (Drug........................)........................
- • Other (specify)........................
....

DRUG TAKEN SINCE WITHOUT ANY REACTION:
....
....
....

CURRENT DRUGS: ....   • Antihistamines ....
....   • -Blockers ....
....
....

PERSONAL HISTORY:

1) HAVE SIMILIAR SYMPTOMS BEEN OBSERVED WITHOUT THE INTAKE OF THE SUSPICIOUS DRUGS ? • Yes   • No   • Unknown

2) MEDICAL HISTORY:
- • Asthma
- • Nasal polyposis
- • Cystic fibrosis
- • Diabetes
- • Other/Specification: ....
- • Autoimmune (Sjögren, Lupus, etc)
- • Lymphoprolific (ALL, CLL, Hodgkin, etc.)
- • Intervertebral disk surgery
- • Liver:........................
- • Urticaria pigmentosa / syst. mastocytosis
- • Chronic urticaria
- • HIV positivity
- • Kidney: ....

3) ALLERGIC DISEASES: ....
(eg. pollinosis, atopic dermatitis, food allergy, hymenoptera venom allergy, latex allergy, etc.)

4) DRUG REACTIONS DURING FORMER SURGERY: ....   • Dentist   • Local anaesthesia   • General anaesthesia (No:.....)

5) REACTIONS DURING FORMER VACCINATIONS: ....   • Polio   • Tetanus   • Rubella   • Measles   • Hepatitis B
    • Diphteria   • Other:........................   • Unknown

FAMILY HISTORY: Allergies / Drug allergies:
....
....
....

REMARKS:
....
....
....

Table 9.2   Clinical and biological danger signs suggesting severe cutaneous and/or systemic reactions. Adapted with permission from |9|

Centrofacial oedema

Dysphonia, hypersialorrhea (laryngeal angio-oedema)

Drop in blood pressure

Involvement of extended body surface (>60%)

Painful skin

Atypical target lesions

Positive Nikolsky sign

Epidermolysis, vesicles, bulla

Haemorrhagic or necrotic lesions

Mucosal erosions or aphthous lesions

Systemic signs (high fever, malaise)

Blood cytopenia

Eosinophilia

Affection of internal organs: hepatic cytolysis, proteinuria

Table 9.3   Allergy tests depending on clinical symptoms. Adapted with permission from |9|

Clinical symptoms	Potential pathogenesis	Diagnostic tests
Urticaria	Type I allergy, non-allergic hyper-sensitivity; rarely, type III allergy	Prick, intradermal tests, specific IgE, Mediator release / cellular tests
Angio-oedema		
Anaphylaxis	Type I allergy, non-allergic hyper-sensitivity	Prick, intradermal tests, specific IgE, Mediator release / cellular tests
Maculopapular exanthem	Type IV allergy	Patch, late-reading intradermal tests, LTT
Vesicular-bullous exanthem	Type IV allergy	Patch tests
Pustular exanthem	Type IV allergy	Patch, late-reading intradermal tests, LTT
Fixed drug eruption	Type IV allergy	Patch tests in affected area

LTT = lymphocyte transformation test.

resulting in false negative results. According to the clinical manifestations, a hypothesis on pathogenesis should be generated (Table 9.3) to select appropriate testing procedures |9,10|.

Skin tests

The diagnostic value of skin tests has not been fully evaluated for all drugs, and experience within different centres has rarely been exchanged over the past decades. Skin tests have to be applied depending on the suspected pathomechanism of the hypersensitive drug reactions. Skin prick tests and intradermal tests are particularly important for reactive haptens in order to demonstrate an IgE-dependent mechanism |9|. They should be performed 4 to 6 weeks after the reaction. The prick test is recommended for initial screening due to its simplicity, speed, low cost and high specificity. Intracutaneous tests consist of injecting a sterile, diluted allergen extract superficially into the dermis |10|.

Their sensitivity and predictive values vary, depending on the culprit drug, from excellent (penicillins, myorelaxants, heterologous sera, enzymes) to satisfactory (vaccines, hormones, protamine, opiates, thiopental, cephalosporins, iodine radiocontrast media) to poor or unknown (local anaesthetics, paracetamol, sulfonamides, quinolones, NSAIDs, other anti-infectious agents). Thus, immediate reactions to β-lactams |11|, radiocontrast media |12| or myorelaxants |13|, for example, can be demonstrated by a positive skin prick and/or intradermal test after 20 min. On the other hand, non-immediate reactions manifested by cutaneous symptoms and occurring more than 1 h after the last drug intake, are often T-cell mediated and a positive patch test and/or late-reading intradermal test can be found after several hours or days |9,14|. The tests should follow standard operation procedures and should be performed by trained staff. Unfortunately, apart from allergic reactions to several antibiotics and a few other drugs |15|, for most drug allergens, standardized and validated test concentrations and vehicles have not been elucidated. Sometimes the drug is not available in an adequate reactive form—generally because it is a metabolic derivative which is immunogenic and for which provocation tests are required to confirm the diagnosis.

Provocation tests

A drug provocation test is the gold standard for the identification of an eliciting drug. It is independent of the pathogenesis and takes individual factors into account such as the metabolism and genetic disposition of an individual. Provocation tests have the finest sensitivity, but can only be performed under the most rigorous surveillance conditions and are therefore restricted to certain specialist centres with on-site intensive care facilities |16|. These tests are particularly required for NSAIDs, local anaesthetics, antibiotics other than β-lactams or β-lactams when skin tests are negative. They should be performed after a certain time interval following the hypersensitivity reaction (at least 1 month) using the same drug as in the initial case. The route of administration depends on the suspected drug. The precise challenge procedure varies a great deal from one team to another and guidelines for the performance of provocation tests in drug allergies have recently been proposed |16|. Provocation tests should not be performed if the offending drug is infrequently used. Hypersensitivity reactions are associated with dermal blistering (Stevens-Johnson syndrome, toxic epidermal necrolysis) and/or organ involvements.

Biological tests

It would be highly advantageous to have discriminating biological tests available to establish the nature of the culprit agent, especially for the patient receiving several drugs simultaneously. However, these tests are few in number and, for the most part, not fully validated. It should also be remembered that the interpretation of the results should be determined with caution. A negative test does not exclude the role of the drug, whilst a positive result shows a sensitivity to the drug but does not necessarily confirm that it was responsibe for the reaction.

The demonstration of isolated drug-specific IgE (to penicillins |17|, myorelaxants |18|, chymopapain or tetanus toxoid, for example) does not enable the diagnosis of a drug allergy. However, in conjunction with clinical findings (e.g. typical symptoms of rapid onset), the IgE-dependent mechanism can be pinpointed (particularly if the skin tests to the drug are also positive) |17|. Cross-reactivities between several drugs using quantitative inhibition may also be explored. The absence of specific circulating IgE does not rule out a diagnosis of allergy and this assay is not available for all drugs. The measure of drug-specific IgM or IgG is of interest only in cases of drug-induced cytopenia or allergies to dextrans. The release of histamine from total blood in the presence of the drug correlates well with skin tests and specific IgE for myorelaxants but is not reliable for many other drugs |19|. Moreover, it is costly and requires a high level of technical skill. The usefulness of measuring sulphidopeptide leukotrienes still requires further validation in both IgE-dependent allergies and non-IgE-dependent hypersensitivity reactions |20|. In cases of acute clinical reactions, blood measurements of histamine or tryptase confirm the role played by basophils and mast cells whatever the cause of the degranulation |21|. For drug-induced type II and III allergic reactions, the following tests can be performed: Coombs' test, *in vitro* haemolysis test, determination of complement factors and circulating immune complexes. Studies involving T lymphocytes (lymphocyte transformation/activation tests) remain the domain of a few laboratories |22|. Tests involving basophil degranulation are not trustworthy given the low numbers of circulating basophils. These have been replaced by basophil activation tests, which hold great promise and which are currently undergoing strong evaluation |23–25|.

Conclusion

The diagnosis of hypersensitivity reactions to drugs is often difficult and requires a stereotypic attitude no matter which drug is involved. It remains largely clinical with the help of certain allergy tests that are available for some of the drug classes. Provocation tests are the gold standard but, cumbersome and possibly harmful, are limited to highly specialized centres. New and validated biological tools for diagnosis, available to all clinicians, are necessary in order to improve care for these patients.

A definite diagnosis of hypersensitivity reactions to drugs is required in order to institute proper preventive measures. Whatever the intensity of the clinical reaction, a state of hypersensitivity is shown towards the particular drug with the possibility of a more serious reaction in the future. General preventive measures include a declaration to the Committee on Safety of Medicine Reports. Individual measures include the issue of an 'Allergy Card' specifying the culprit agent(s), the delivery of a list of drugs to avoid and the delivery of a list of possible alternatives. The patient is also asked to make his allergies known prior to all prescriptions and surgical operations and to read the package insert on any drugs to be taken. The lists can never be completely exhaustive, are only indicative and should be frequently updated. Similarly, the questioning (to elicit any history of allergy) of every patient by every clinician prior to issuing a prescription is essential from both a medical and a medico-legal point of view. Preventive measures by pre-medication (e.g. slow injection and preparations with glucocorticosteroids and antihistamines) mainly concern non-allergic hypersensitivity reactions (for example to vancomycin, certain anaesthetics and chemotherapy drugs). The possibility of desensitization should always be considered when the offending drug is essential and when either no alternatives exist or they are unsatisfactory, as in the following cases: sulfonamides in HIV-infected patients |26|, quinolone allergies in some cystic fibrosis patients, serious infections with allergy to penicillins, allergy to tetanus vaccine, haemochromatosis with allergy to desferoxamine, aspirin and NSAID hypersensitivity in patients for whom the necessity for these drugs to treat either a cardiac or rheumatoid illness is clear.

Acknowledgements

The author would like to thank Ms Anna Bedbrook for her help in the preparation of this chapter.

References

1. Johansson S, Bieber T, Dahl R, *et al.* Revised nomenclature for allergy for global use: Report of the Nomenclature Review Committee of the World Allergy Organization, October 2003. *J Allergy Clin Immunol* 2004; **113**: 832–6.

2. Gomes ER, Demoly P. Epidemiology of hypersensitivity drug reactions. *Curr Opin Allergy Clin Immunol* 2005; **5**: 309–16.

3. Gomes E, Cardoso MF, Praça F, *et al.* Self reported drug allergy in a general adult Portuguese population. *Clin Exp Allergy* 2004; **34**: 1597–601.

4. Bäckström M, Mjörndal, Dahlqvist R. Under-reporting of serious adverse drug reactions in Sweden. *Pharmacoepidemiol Drug Saf* 2004; **13**: 483–7.

5. Mittmann N, Knowles SR, Gomez M, *et al.* Evaluation of the extent of under-reporting of serious adverse drug reactions: the case of toxic epidermal necrolysis. *Drug Saf* 2004; **27**: 477–87.

6. Messaad D, Sahla H, Benahmed S, *et al.* Drug provocation tests in patients with a history suggesting an immediate drug hypersensitivity reaction. *Ann Intern Med* 2004; **140**: 1001–6.

7. Pichler WJ. Delayed drug hypersensitivity reactions. *Ann Intern Med* 2003; **139**: 683–93.

8. Demoly P, Kropf R, Bircher A, Pichler WJ. Drug hypersensitivity questionnaire. *Allergy* 1999; **54**: 999–1003.

9. Bircher AJ. Symptoms and danger signs in acute drug hypersensitivity. *Toxicology* 2005; **209**: 201–7.

10. Brockow K, Romano A, Blanca M, *et al.* General considerations for skin test procedures in the diagnosis of drug hypersensitivity. *Allergy* 2002; **57**: 45–51.

11. Torres MJ, Blanca M, Fernandez J, *et al.* Diagnosis of immediate allergic reactions to beta-lactam antibiotics. *Allergy* 2003; **58**: 961–72.

12. Brockow K, Christiansen C, Kanny G, *et al.* Management of hypersensitivity reactions to iodinated contrast media. *Allergy* 2005; **60**: 150–8.

13. Mertes PM, Laxenaire MC, Lienhart A, *et al.* Reducing the risk of anaphylaxis during anaesthesia: guidelines for clinical practice. *J Invest Allergy Clin Immunol* 2005; **15**: 91–101.

14. Romano A, Blanca M, Torres MJ, *et al.* Diagnosis of nonimmediate reactions to beta-lactam antibiotics. *Allergy* 2004; **59**: 1153–60.

15. Barbaud A, Reichert-Penetrat S, Tréchot P, *et al.* The use of skin testing in the investigation of cutaneous adverse drug reactions. *Br J Dermatol* 1998; **139**: 49–58.

16. Aberer W, Bircher A, Romano A, *et al.* Drug provocation testing in the diagnosis of drug hypersensitivity reactions: general considerations. *Allergy* 2003; **58**: 854–63.

17. Fontaine C, Mayorga L, Bousquet PJ, *et al.* Relevance of the determination of serm-specific IgE antibodies in the diagnosis of immediate beta-lactam allergy. *Allergy* 2007; in press.

18. Guéant JL, Mata E, Monin B, *et al.* Evaluation of a new reactive solid phase for radioimmunoassay of serum specific IgE against muscle relaxant drugs. *Allergy* 1991; **46**: 452–8.

19. Demoly P, Lebel B, Messaad D, *et al.* Predictive capacity of histamine release for the diagnosis of drug allergy. *Allergy* 1999; **54**: 500–6.

20. Lebel B, Messaad D, Kvedariene V, *et al.* Cysteinyl-leukotriene release test (CAST) in the diagnosis of immediate drug reactions. *Allergy* 2001; **56**: 688–92.

21. Watkins J, Wild G. Improved diagnosis of anaphylactoid reactions by measurement of serum tryptase and urinary methylhistamine. *Ann Fr Anesth Reanim* 1993; **12**: 169–72.

22. Nyfeler B, Pichler WJ. The lymphocyte transformation test for the diagnosis of drug allergy: sensitivity and specificity. *Clin Exp Allergy* 1997; **27**: 175–81.

23. Kvedariene V, Kamey S, Ryckwaert Y, *et al.* Diagnosis of neuromuscular blocking agent hypersensitivity reactions using cytofluorimetric analysis of basophils. *Allergy* 2006; **61**: 311–15.

24. Sanz ML, Gamboa P, de Weck AL. A new combined test with flowcytometric basophil activation and determination of sulfido-leukotrienes is useful for in vitro diagnosis of hypersensitivity to aspirin and other non-steroidal anti-inflammatory drugs. *Int Arch Allergy Immunol* 2005; **136**: 58–72.

25. Torres MJ, Padial A, Mayorga C, *et al.* The diagnostic interpretation of basophil activation test in immediate allergic reactions to betalactams. *Clin Exp Allergy* 2004; **34**: 1768–75.

26. Demoly P, Messaad D, Sahla H, *et al.* Six-hour trimethoprim-sulfamethoxazole graded challenge in HIV-infected patients. *J Allergy Clin Immunol* 1998; **102**: 1033–6.

Food allergy

JENNIFER MALONEY, HUGH SAMPSON

KEY POINTS

1. Adverse reactions to food include allergic and non-allergic reactions; food allergy is a result of immunological interactions through either IgE or non-IgE-mediated mechanisms, whilst non-allergic adverse food reactions include intolerances that result from host factors.

2. Milk, egg, peanut, wheat and soy are responsible for most food-induced reactions in children, while peanut, tree nuts, fish and shellfish account for most reactions in adults.

3. Pollen-food allergy syndrome (also known as oral allergy syndrome) is a common symptom complex occurring in pollen allergic individuals and usually provokes isolated oral symptoms following exposure to labile proteins in uncooked fruits and vegetables.

4. The double-blind, placebo-controlled food challenge remains the 'gold standard' for diagnosing food hypersensitivities; the positive predictive value of a positive skin prick test is less than 50% when compared to results of double-blind, placebo-controlled food challenges.

5. Dietary avoidance of the causal food allergen is the key element for management of food hypersensitivity.

Introduction

Definition

Food allergy represents one form of adverse food reactions. Adverse reactions to food include food allergic and non-allergic reactions (Fig. 10.1). Immunological interactions, through either immunoglobulin (Ig)E- or non-IgE-mediated mechanisms, result in the development of food allergy. Non-allergic adverse food reactions include intolerances that result from host factors |1|, such as pancreatic insufficiency due to pancreatic enzyme deficit resulting in malabsorption. Toxic

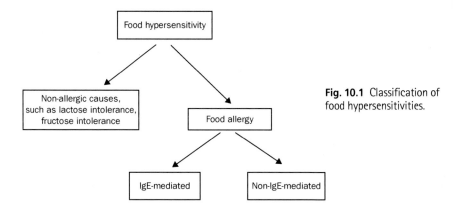

Fig. 10.1 Classification of food hypersensitivities.

food reactions represent a separate category and are due to inherent toxicities or properties of the food, for example, histamine-mediated symptoms due to scromboid fish poisoning or side-effects from caffeine-containing foods |1,2|.

Prevalence

Food allergy affects approximately 6–8% of children under 3 years of age, although the public's perception of food allergy prevalence is greater |3|. A pivotal prevalence study, which followed a cohort of 480 children in a general paediatric practice from birth, determined the prevalence of food reactions in this population. Twenty-eight per cent of the cohort displayed adverse symptoms, which either a physician or family member attributed to food ingestion. Food challenges confirmed food reactions in 8% of the study cohort |3|. In the general American population, it is estimated that the prevalence of food allergy is 3.5–4% |4|.

The estimated frequencies of children who have and percentages of children who outgrow particular food allergies vary depending on the food (Table 10.1). Interestingly, over a five-year period, the rate of peanut allergy in the United States appears to have doubled in young children |5,6|. Similarly, a cohort of children from the Isle of Wight was compared with a previous cohort in terms of peanut clinical reactivity and sensitization, and a twofold increase in clinical reactivity and a threefold increase in peanut sensitization were reported |7|.

Table 10.1	Rates of food allergy. With permission from |3,6,100–107|	
Food	**Percentage of children affected**	**Percentage of children who outgrow the allergy**
Milk	2.5–2.8% of infants in their 1st year of life (~60% IgE-mediated)	85% by age 8.6 years
Egg	1.3–1.6% of children	66% by age 5
Peanut	0.8 of children	~20% of young children

Pollen-food allergy syndrome (also known as oral allergy syndrome) is a common symptom complex occurring in pollen-allergic individuals and usually provokes isolated oral symptoms following exposure to labile proteins in uncooked fruits and vegetables. Of patients with allergic rhinitis, it has been estimated that 23–76% of patients experience oral symptoms to at least one food |8|.

Food allergy commonly presents in patients with or who will develop other atopic diseases. Approximately, one-third of children and adolescents with moderate-severe atopic dermatitis have IgE-mediated food allergy |9|. The presence of food allergy increases the probability of developing allergic airway disease |10,11| and has been shown to be an independent predictor of a persistent wheezing phenotype |12|.

Pathophysiology

Food allergy results from an atypical response of the mucosal immune system to orally consumed antigens. The gastrointestinal (GI) mucosa is an extensive structure responsible for digestion and absorption of nutrients as well as protection from pathogenic organisms. A non-specific physical barrier consisting of epithelial cells, the mucin glycoprotein lining, trefoil factors, proteolytic enzymes and bile salts works with immune and non-immune cells and cytokines to maintain immunological homeostasis |13|.

The mucosal immune system actively defends against pathogens through both the innate and adaptive arms. Peyer's patches (organized lymphoid structures of the small intestine and rectum), sIgA, dendritic cells, antigen-presenting macrophages, MHC class I and II bearing T lymphocytes, intestinal epithelia cells, as well as other cytokine-producing cells, participate in the immunological response |14|. Despite the complex interplay of the mucosal system, approximately 2% of intact food proteins are absorbed through the mature GI tract and reach the lymphatic and portal circulation |15,16|. Infants have augmented vulnerability because their intestinal permeability is increased. Furthermore, infants and young children have decreased gastric acid production and reduced pancreatic and intestinal enzymatic activity |17|. Consequently, there is increased absorption of intact food proteins, which may cause stimulation of the immune system and generation of IgE antibody |17|.

Oral tolerance allows individuals to encounter immense quantities of dietary protein and commensal bacteria without inciting a dynamic immune response. Antigenic factors and host factors are involved in the generation of oral tolerance. Antigenic factors influencing oral tolerance include the form and the dose of the antigen. Soluble antigens are more tolerogenic than particulate antigens |18| and a single high dose or repeated low doses of allergen are tolerogenic compared to a single low dose |19|. Host factors involved in oral tolerance include age, genetics and gastrointestinal flora. Tolerance to food antigens appears to become more effective with increasing age |20|. Host genotypic makeup influences the development of oral tolerance or food hypersensitivity |21,22|. Additionally, commensal gut flora establishes a state of controlled inflammation, which contributes to the homeostasis of the mucosal immune system |13|.

Food allergens

Despite the wide range of foods that humans consume, surprisingly few foods account for the majority of food allergies. Milk, egg, peanut, wheat and soy are responsible for most food-induced reactions in American children, while peanut, tree nuts, fish and shellfish account for most reactions in adults |1|.

Two forms of IgE-mediated food allergy have been proposed. Class 1 food allergy results from sensitization through the gastrointestinal tract |23|. The class 1 food allergens are generally 10–70 kD in size and highly stable; their structure is conserved when subjected to heat, acid or proteases |17|. Examples include milk (caseins), peanut (vicilins), egg (ovomucoid) and non-specific lipid transfer proteins |24|.

Class 2 food allergy results from sensitization to inhalant allergens that are partially homologous to proteins in certain fruits and vegetables. This form of food allergy principally occurs in adolescents and adults. Class 2 allergens are heat labile and susceptible to digestive processes |23|.

Reaction mechanisms

IgE-mediated reactions

IgE-mediated reactions usually occur within minutes to 1 h following ingestion of the causal food. Multiple organ systems may be involved. A review of IgE-mediated food allergic disorders will follow.

Food-induced anaphylaxis

Food-induced anaphylaxis is a severe, potentially fatal, systemic allergic reaction that occurs rapidly after exposure to an allergy-causing food |25|. A retrospective medical review examined the causes of 601 cases of anaphylaxis over a 25-year time period. Twenty-two per cent of the cases were attributed to food allergy |26|.

The majority of anaphylactic events are characterized by cutaneous symptoms, such as urticaria, angio-oedema and flushing, although the absence of skin involvement does not exclude the diagnosis. Cardiovascular collapse with resultant shock may occur without cutaneous symptoms due to decreased blood supply to the skin |27|. In fact, in a report of 13 fatal or near-fatal anaphylactic reactions to foods in children and adolescents (six fatal, seven near-fatal) 38% of reactions were not accompanied by cutaneous symptoms |28|.

As with any IgE-mediated reaction, there may be a late-phase response associated with anaphylaxis. The incidence of biphasic reactions occurs in up to 20% of food-induced events |25|. With biphasic reactions, a period of recovery after the initial reaction is followed by a recurrence of symptoms, which may be severe. The severity of biphasic reactions cannot be predicted based on earlier symptoms.

Food-associated exercise-induced anaphylaxis usually occurs when exercise follows the ingestion of a specific food (such as wheat, shellfish, celery) by approximately 2–4 hours. A less common form of food-associated exercise-induced anaphylaxis occurs with the ingestion of any food prior to exercise. The pathogenesis of food-dependent exercise-induced anaphylaxis is unclear |29,30|.

IgE-mediated cutaneous reactions

Acute urticaria and angio-oedema are the most common manifestations of food-induced allergic reactions (Table 10.2) |1| and symptoms may occur minutes after ingestion. Urticaria also frequently develops in food-allergic patients when their skin has direct contact with the food allergen. Contact reactions are typically localized to areas of direct exposure and are unlikely to provoke systemic reactions, unless inadvertent ingestion occurs |31|. Chronic urticaria and angio-oedema (the presence of symptoms for more than 6 weeks) are infrequently due to food allergy |32|.

Table 10.2 IgE-mediated disease manifestations. With permission from |1,17,31–39|

Involvement	Manifestations
Cutaneous	Erythematous weals/flares, subcutaneous swelling
Respiratory	Rhinoconjunctivitis, laryngeal oedema, cough and bronchospasm
Gastrointestinal anaphylaxis	Acute nausea, abdominal pain, colic, vomiting and/or diarrhoea
Pollen-food allergy syndrome (oral allergy syndrome)	Oropharyngeal pruritus

IgE-mediated respiratory reactions

Food allergy may provoke symptoms affecting the respiratory tract (Table 10.2). Rhinitis and nasal symptoms are commonly seen in patients who have reactions during food challenges |33|. However, food-induced respiratory symptoms usually occur in conjunction with other organ system reactions, and isolated or chronic food-induced asthma or rhinitis are unusual manifestations |34|. Food-induced respiratory symptoms, specifically asthmatic reactions, are risk factors for fatal and near-fatal anaphylactic events |35|.

Allergic reactions can develop as a result of inhalation of airborne proteins from vapours or steams emitted during cooking |36| or from particulate matter from peanut dust when shells are opened |37|. In contrast, exposure of peanut-allergic patients to the smell of peanut butter has not been shown to result in systemic or respiratory symptoms |31|.

IgE-mediated gastrointestinal reactions

Food allergic reactions frequently affect the gastrointestinal tract (Table 10.2). Infants with atopic dermatitis and food allergy who are chronically ingesting the allergen may present with more indolent symptoms, such as intermittent vomiting and failure to thrive |17|.

Pollen-food allergy syndrome occurs in pollen-allergic individuals due to homologous proteins shared between foods and specific airborne pollens (Table 10.2) |38|. The foods are usually tolerated in the cooked form because the allergen's structure (conformation) is lost at high temperatures. Interestingly, although cooking the implicated food results in the loss of IgE binding ability, the cooked

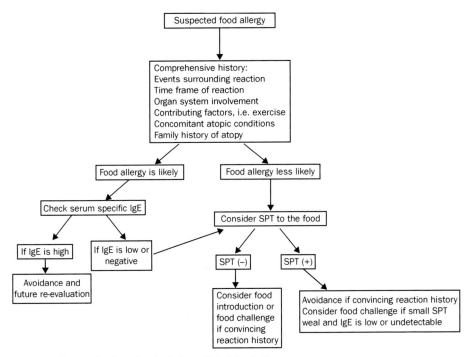

Fig. 10.2 Diagnostic algorithm for IgE-mediated food allergy.

food can activate T cells. Patients with atopic dermatitis and pollen-food allergy syndrome to birch-related foods were evaluated, and following ingestion of cooked birch-related foods, Bet v 1-specific T cells were activated and atopic dermatitis exacerbations occurred |39|.

Diagnosis of IgE-mediated food-allergic disease

The diagnosis of food allergies requires a comprehensive history and targeted testing (Fig. 10.2). Diet diaries may be useful in recognizing patterns of reactivity, in identifying commonly consumed allergens, and in identifying foods that may have 'hidden allergens'.

Diagnostic modalities for IgE-mediated disorders

Skin prick testing is a rapid screening method for IgE-mediated food hypersensitivity. Weals that are 3 mm larger than the negative control are considered positive. Negative skin tests essentially exclude IgE-mediated allergy |40|.

Unfortunately, the positive predictive value of a positive skin prick test is less than 50% when compared to results of double-blind, placebo-controlled food challenges |41|. Furthermore, test results are highly dependent on reagents used (which are not standardized), application technique, area of the body where tests are applied, and interpretation by the physician. Positive skin tests may be helpful especially when a clear-cut history of food reactivity is present. Additionally, when hypersensitivity is suspected to milk, egg or peanut, 'diagnostic SPT levels' have been defined (cow milk ≥ 8 mm, egg ≥ 7 mm, peanut ≥ 8 mm; for children ≤ 2 years of age, cow's milk ≥ 6 mm, egg ≥ 5 mm, peanut ≥ 4 mm) |42|, although the variability in reagents and techniques must be considered when applying these values.

Intradermal skin testing has no place in the diagnosis of food allergy. In addition to having poor specificity and positive predictive value, fatalities have been reported with this diagnostic modality |43|.

Detection of food-specific IgE antibodies (i.e. UniCAP System FEIA, Phadia, Inc.; Uppsala, Sweden) has been shown to be predictive of symptomatic IgE-mediated food allergy |44,45|. The Phadia UniCAP system contrasts with qualitative RAST assays because standardized allergens are used, the dose–response curve is calibrated against the World Health Organization (WHO) IgE standard, and the matrix binds more antigen, which provides a steep dose–response curve |44|. Diagnostic 'decision points' have been generated for common food allergens, namely, milk, egg, peanut and fish (Fig. 10.3). The decision points indicate reaction likelihood, but do not predict reaction severity |44|. As serum specific IgE levels decrease, the likelihood of reaction decreases. However, reactions may still occur for a subset of patients when serum specific IgE levels are undetectable. One study reported that 32/120 (27%) patients (especially young infants), who reacted to milk, egg or peanut challenges had undetectable serum specific IgE levels to the causative food |46|.

The double-blind, placebo-controlled food challenge (DBPCFC) remains the 'gold standard' for diagnosing food hypersensitivities |41|. This approach has minimal patient and/or observer bias. Single-blind challenges and open challenges are other options best utilized for foods that are unlikely to produce a reaction. The decision to pursue a food challenge should be based on the clinical history in conjunction with results of other diagnostic tests. Food challenges are not benign procedures and may result in mild, moderate or severe symptoms requiring medical treatment |47,48|; therefore, a properly equipped environment is essential.

Prior to food challenges, patients should be instructed to avoid antihistamines and β-adrenergic bronchodilators because their use may interfere with the interpretation of results. For IgE-mediated food allergies, the aim is for the patient to eat approximately 8–10 g of dry food mixed within a vehicle |40,47|. A negative blinded challenge must be followed by an open challenge to assure that the patient can ingest the food safely in natural, meal-sized portions.

Mixed and non-IgE-mediated disorders

Several food hypersensitivity disorders exist that are not orchestrated only by IgE antibodies. Cell-mediated reactions, mediated by antigen-sensitized T cells, may be responsible for the manifestations of certain conditions. A few diseases are thought to result from cooperation between cell-mediated and IgE-mediated mechanisms. A discussion of mixed and non-IgE-mediated disorders will follow.

Cutaneous disorders

Atopic dermatitis is a mixed IgE-mediated and cellular disorder (Table 10.3). It is a chronic skin condition that often starts in childhood and is characterized by a

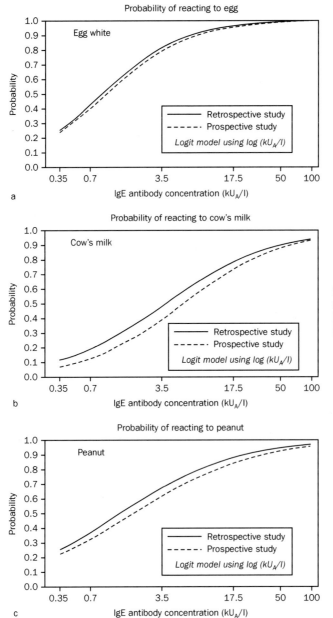

a

b

c

Fig. 10.3 Predictive curves of food allergen specific IgE levels (with permission from |44,45|).

relapsing and remitting course. The cutaneous lesions of atopic dermatitis usually occur on the face, scalp, and extensor surfaces in young children with a distribution shift as children get older to the flexural surfaces of the extremities |49|.

Approximately one-third of children and adolescents with moderate to severe atopic dermatitis have IgE-mediated food hypersensitivity |9|. However, antigen

Table 10.3 Mixed and non-IgE-mediated disease manifestations. With permission from [34,49–81]

Involvement	Disease	Manifestations
Cutaneous	Atopic dermatitis	**Acute**—pruritic, erythematous macular and papulovesicular lesions
		Subacute—erythematous, scaling papules
		Chronic—skin lichenification
	Dermatitis herpetiformis	Pruritic, erythematous, urticarial plaques, papules and vesicles due to gluten sensitivity
	Contact dermatitis	Cell-mediated skin condition due to contact with food, i.e. food handlers
Respiratory	Food-induced pulmonary haemosiderosis	Recurrent pneumonia, haemosiderosis, gastrointestinal blood loss, iron deficiency anaemia, and failure to thrive
Gastrointestinal	AEE	Abdominal pain, spitting-up, vomiting, dysphagia, food refusal, gastro-oesophageal reflux symptoms, food impaction, a poor response to anti-reflux medications
	AEG	Weight loss and failure to thrive, abdominal pain, emesis, nausea, diarrhoea, gastric outlet obstruction in young infants
	Proctocolitis	Blood and mucus in the stool; good overall health without growth delay
	FPIES	Irritability; excessive, vigorous vomiting and diarrhoea a few hours after ingestion of the allergen; hypotension, lethargy, hyponatraemia, acidosis, a 'left-shift', and methemoglobinaemia may occur; stool smears may reveal blood, leucocytes or eosinophils
		A more indolent course, with failure to thrive, hypoalbuminaemia, chronic vomiting and diarrhoea, may occur for young infants chronically eating the allergen
	Coeliac disease	Diarrhoea, abdominal pain, constipation, vomiting, dyspepsia, and mouth ulcers; children may present with failure to thrive, anorexia and short stature; many patients are asymptomatic at diagnosis

specific T cells are likely important regulators of disease pathogenesis [50,51]. T cells from milk-allergic patients with atopic dermatitis were compared with those of milk-allergic patients with gastrointestinal allergy and normal controls. The T cells were incubated with casein, and the proliferating T cells from patients with atopic dermatitis had greater expression of the skin homing receptor cutaneous lymphocyte-associated antigen (CLA) compared with patients with milk-associated allergic gastrointestinal disease and normal control patients [52].

Patients with food allergy-related atopic dermatitis usually have positive food challenges hallmarked by cutaneous symptoms such as pruritic, morbilliform or macular eruptions with a tendency to occur in skin areas affected by atopic dermatitis. The majority of positive food challenges also trigger other organ system involvement. Egg, milk, wheat, peanut, tree nuts and soy are the most frequent foods to cause clinical reactivity |53|, with egg affecting approximately two-thirds of patients with food allergy and atopic dermatitis |54|. If the history reveals food-related symptoms, tests for specific IgE to the food are positive, and an appropriate skin care regimen is ineffective, food elimination may be the best approach. However, caution is needed because although removal of a causal food may improve the skin disease, the patient develops an increased probability of an acute allergic reaction, even anaphylaxis, with abrupt reintroduction of the food |55|.

Respiratory reactions

Food-induced pulmonary haemosiderosis (Heiner's syndrome) is a non-IgE-mediated hypersensitivity reaction primarily due to milk (Table 10.3). Removal of milk from the diet results in symptom resolution |34|.

Gastrointestinal reactions

Allergic eosinophilic oesophagitis and gastroenteritis

Allergic eosinophilic oesophagitis (AEE) and gastroenteritis (AEG) are disorders mediated by IgE-dependent and cell-mediated mechanisms. Eosinophils infiltrate the walls of the oesophagus, stomach and small intestine. Peripheral eosinophilia is found in approximately half of the patients |56|. When evaluating these patients, other known causes of eosinophilia must be excluded |57|. Patients with gastrointestinal eosinophilic disorders have a high incidence of concomitant atopy, with many having sensitizations to foods and environmental allergens |58|.

In a disease-free state, eosinophils are not present in the oesophagus. Eosinophilic oesophagitis may occur at any age. Oesophageal biopsies revealing greater than 20–24 eosinophils per high-powered field have been accepted as criteria for the diagnosis |59|; however, a recent report of three patients meeting biopsy diagnostic criteria of AEE had resolution of disease with proton pump inhibitors, suggesting occasional histopathological overlap with peptic oesophagitis |60|. Oesophageal tissue from AEE may have thickened mucosa, papillary elongation and basal zone hyperplasia. On gross appearance, the oesophagus may have furrowing, mucosal rings, strictures, ulcerations and whitish papules or it may appear normal |56,57,61|.

Allergic eosinophilic gastroenteritis may occur at any age with a wide array of GI symptomatology (Table 10.3) |56–58|. The diagnosis is made through biopsies, which reveal significant eosinophilic infiltration of the gastric and/or duodenal mucosa, with no other identifiable medical cause |62|. A subgroup of patients develops anaemia and hypoalbuminaemia, likely secondary to faecal loss of blood and protein resulting in a protein-losing enteropathy |18|.

Allergic proctocolitis

Allergic proctocolitis is a non-IgE-mediated, eosinophilic disorder that typically presents in the first few weeks to months of life with microscopic or gross blood in the stool (Table 10.3) |63|. Case series reveal that patients with proctocolitis may have peripheral eosinophilia, elevated serum IgE and a family history of atopic disease |64–66|.

Proctocolitis commonly occurs in breast-fed infants (as many as 60% of cases) |65,67,68|, with milk and soy formulas triggering most of the remaining cases |64,66,69|. For infants who develop proctocolitis while breast-feeding, it is believed that cow's milk proteins ingested by the mother are most often the triggering agents in breast milk |70|. Removal of cow's milk from the maternal diet will usually result in gradual symptom resolution |65,67,68|. Alternatively, if rectal bleeding continues, a casein hydrolysate formula, or in rare instances, an amino acid based formula |71| eliminates symptoms, typically within 48–72 h. Many infants who develop proctocolitis from cow's milk formula will also become symptomatic to other foods if introduced in the first 6 months of life, e.g. soy |64,72|.

Food protein-induced enterocolitis syndrome (FPIES)
Food protein-induced enterocolitis syndrome (FPIES) is a non-IgE-mediated food allergy, which usually occurs in formula-fed infants, although it has been reported to occur with a variety of foods (especially cereal grains) in older infants. Symptomatic presentation may be dramatic (Table 10.3) |73–78|. Milk and soy are the most frequent causative foods; however, solid foods (such as oat, barley, rice, chicken and turkey) may be responsible |77,78|. Approximately 50% of patients reactive to milk are also reactive to soy |74,77|; therefore, a casein hydrolysate formula or, in rare instances, an amino acid based formula is required |79|. Food protein-induced enterocolitis syndrome due to grains increases the risk of reactivity to other grains, milk, soy, meats and legumes, necessitating cautious food introduction, especially in the first 6–8 months of life.

Coeliac disease
Coeliac disease is a T cell-mediated disorder in which the body reacts to peptide sequences of the gluten proteins of wheat, rye and barley. Patients develop intestinal villous atrophy, malabsorption and chronic inflammation of the small intestinal mucosa |80|. Features at presentation vary (Table 10.3) |81|. The major HLA-associated haplotypes are DQ2 and DQ8. Removal of gluten from the diet leads to symptom resolution. The diagnostic gold standard is the intestinal biopsy, which illustrates loss of villi, lymphocytic and plasma cell infiltration of the lamina propria and intraepithelial compartments, and crypt lengthening. Enzyme-linked immunosorbent assays for IgA anti-recombinant human tissue transglutaminase can be utilized as a screening tool. IgA anti-gliadin antibodies alone should not be used for screening due to high rates of false positive results |80|. Importantly, testing for coeliac disease, either by biopsy or through serologic studies, must be performed while the patient has a diet that includes gluten; otherwise, false negative results may occur |81|.

Diagnosis of mixed or non-IgE-mediated disorders

The medical history has a poor predictive value for chronic disorders, such as atopic dermatitis and asthma. Whereas skin prick tests and serum specific IgE tests are instrumental in the diagnosis of IgE-mediated food allergy, for cell-mediated and mixed disorders, their diagnostic utility has limited value. Patch testing is a modality being considered for diagnosing delayed hypersensitivity reactions, where T lymphocytes are the major effector cells, e.g. AD, AEE |82,83|. Mehl and colleagues investigated the utility of patch testing when performed in conjunction with serum specific IgE levels and skin prick testing for the diagnosis of symptomatic food allergy. The authors' objective was to find a combination of testing instruments that would make the need for oral food challenges obsolete. Most of the study patients had atopic dermatitis, suggesting a T cell-mediated component of their disease pathogenesis. It was found that the sensitivity of patch testing varied depending on the food (milk, egg, wheat and soy were studied), and testing results varied depending on patient's age. The authors concluded that the lack of uniformity in patch testing results largely eliminates the applicability of this test for daily clinical practice |84|. Although this testing modality may have utility in some situations, lack of patch testing standardization and spurious results (due to skin irritation from the underlying disease and the testing media) makes widespread implementation complex.

The medical history is essential for the diagnosis of allergic proctocolitis and food protein-induced enterocolitis. Resolution of these disorders can only be proven by symptomatic tolerance following oral feeding.

Management of food allergy

Dietary avoidance of the causal food allergen is the key element for management of food hypersensitivity at this time. To practice strict avoidance, patients and their caregivers must be supplied with appropriate educational materials to enable them to prevent ingestion of foods that may have had inadvertent cross-contact with allergens or foods that have hidden allergens. An excellent educational resource for patients and families affected by food allergies is the Food Allergy and Anaphylaxis Network (*www.foodallergy.org*).

Written anaphylaxis action plans should be given to patients and caregivers with explicit explanations regarding the symptoms of anaphylaxis and when epinephrine should be administered. Antihistamines are useful in treating mild symptoms, particularly cutaneous and oral symptoms, but will not reverse systemic reactions. Intramuscular epinephrine should be administered at the first sign of any respiratory symptoms including throat tightness, hoarseness, persistent dry cough, wheezing and or shortness of breath. Epinephrine is the treatment of choice for acute anaphylaxis. Fatalities from anaphylactic events often appear to result from the late administration of epinephrine resulting in irreversible cardiopulmonary complications |27|.

The treatment of eosinophilic disorders requires allergen avoidance. Frequently, multiple foods elicit the disease and must be eliminated from the diet. Corticosteroids result in clinical and histopathological improvement |61,85|; however, the side-effect profile is unacceptable, and the disease returns with discontinuation of the medication. Many patients with eosinophilic gastrointestinal disorders have evidence of sensitization to foods; however, acute reactions to foods are infre-

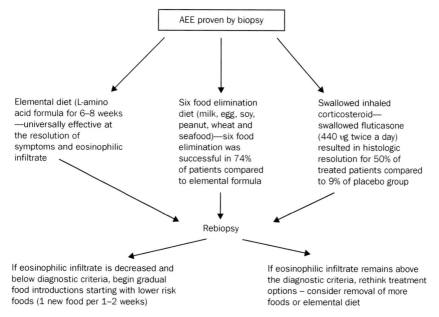

Fig. 10.4 General treatment approach to allergic eosinophilic oesophagitis (AEE) (with permission from |86,87,98,99|).

quently reported. Dietary elimination based on skin prick test and serum specific IgE results alone is frequently insufficient to promote disease resolution |86|.

Placing the patient on an elemental (L-amino acid) formula for 6–8 weeks leads to regression of the gastrointestinal eosinophilic infiltrate |87|. Foods can be slowly reintroduced (one at a time, starting with low-risk foods) into the diet once a biopsy supports that the eosinophils have diminished. For the eosinophilic gastrointestinal disorders, new foods can usually be introduced without physician supervision. A physician-supervised challenge may be necessary if the patient also has evidence of IgE-mediated allergy to the food. Provided that the patient passes the initial challenge, he/she should be instructed to continue eating the food for several days without the introduction of new foods. Several feedings of the food over days to weeks may be necessary to induce symptoms of AEE/AEG |1|. If a causative food is introduced following elimination, the patient usually develops symptoms indistinguishable from those experienced before the elimination diet |86|.

The treatment options practised for AEE have varying success rates (Fig. 10.4). There is much enthusiasm about the possible use of anti-IL-5 (mepolizumab) for AEE. The administration of anti-IL-5 in four adult patients during an open-label phase I/II trial resulted in decreased oesophageal eosinophilia as well as improved clinical scores and quality of life assessments |88|.

For proctocolitis, progression to a normal diet, including the eliminated allergen, is usually possible by 1–2 years of age |56,67|. If the skin prick tests and serum specific IgE levels are negative, gradual allergen introduction typically takes place at home. During food introduction, the parents should be instructed to monitor the stool for visible blood |89|.

For FPIES, action plans must be in place in the event of accidental ingestions. First-line treatment is fluid resuscitation rather than epinephrine and antihistamines (although these medications should be administered if there is concomitant IgE-mediated disease). Corticosteroids should be considered, especially when past history reveals serious reactions. There is a high risk of developing FPIES to multiple foods. For example, up to 50% of patients reactive to milk may react to soy, especially if introduced in the first 6 months of life; up to 65% of patients reactive to grains may react to milk or soy; up to 50% of patients reactive to one grain may react to another grain |90|. More than half of the patients with FPIES due to milk become tolerant by age 3 years. Resolution of FPIES varies by age and is influenced by the primary causative food and the presence of concomitant IgE-mediated disease |90|. To demonstrate whether tolerance has been achieved, oral food challenges in a medically equipped environment are necessary and at least an 18 month reaction-free period is recommended before challenges are considered. During challenges, 0.3–0.6 g of protein per kg of body weight is fed in one or two doses |73|. Reactions are typically delayed, occurring 1–3 h after ingestion of the food. Reactions may be severe with excessive vomiting and possibly resultant hypotension; therefore, intravenous access is necessary prior to the start of the challenge.

Much recent attention has focused on means of altering the immune system to either eliminate food allergy or increase tolerance to the allergenic food. Table 10.4 reviews various treatment approaches.

Table 10.4 Novel therapies. With permission from |108–114|	
Therapy	**Experimental results**
Subcutaneous peanut immunotherapy	Tolerance in 4/6 but intolerable adverse reactions
Sublingual immunotherapy	Trial with hazelnut extract—increased tolerance
Oral desensitization	Increasing doses of cow's milk were administered over a 6-month period—15/21 children tolerated 200 ml of milk/day by the end of the study
Recombinant vaccine	Altered IgE binding epitopes prevent binding of the patient's IgE to the engineered protein within the vaccine
Anti-IgE therapy	Increased tolerance to peanut demonstrated in peanut allergic patients
Traditional Chinese medicine	The Chinese Herbal Medicine Formula has been able to block anaphylaxis in a murine model of peanut allergy

Prevention of food allergy

There is much debate about infant feeding, the appropriate timing of solid food introduction to infants, and how this relates to the development of allergy. Several studies have supported the benefits of breast-feeding, especially if the child is the product of an atopic family |91–94|. Recommendations suggest the delayed introduction of solid foods until at least 4–6 months of age |92,93|, or until greater than 6 months of age for children at high risk for allergy |94|. Additionally, recommendations about the delayed introductions of highly allergenic foods are practised |94|. Despite the recommendations, there are limited data to support precautionary avoidance. One long-term cohort study demonstrated decreased atopic dermatitis and milk allergy with maternal prophylactic avoidance of cow's milk, egg, and peanut during the third trimester and during breast-feeding followed by the delayed introduction of cow's milk to their infants until 1 year, egg until 2 years and peanut until 3 years. A parallel group followed no specific dietary restrictions. Statistically significant differences in atopic disease between the groups did not persist beyond 2 years of age |11,95,96|. Perhaps contradictory to the current recommendations (which suggest delayed introduction of seafood until age 3 years) were the results from a recent study that prospectively followed a birth cohort of children and found that regular fish consumption during the first year of life was associated with a reduced risk of atopic dermatitis, asthma, allergic rhinitis and allergic sensitizations by age 4 years |97|. Unfortunately, the timing of specific food introductions is not well studied and current recommendations are not evidence-based.

Conclusion

Food allergy is a general term that includes a wide range of conditions. The pathogenesis involves IgE-mediated and/or cell-mediated processes with varying manifestations depending on the mechanisms of disease. Diagnosis requires a skillful history, physical examination and targeted diagnostic testing. Treatment requires avoidance of the causal allergen(s). Hopefully, in the future, diagnostic modalities will be more fine-tuned and additional treatment options will be available.

References

1. Sampson HA. Update on food allergy. *J Allergy Clin Immunol* 2004; **113**(5): 805–19; quiz 820.

2. Nowak-Wegrzyn A, Sampson HA. Adverse reactions to foods. *Med Clin North Am* 2006; **90**(1): 97–127.

3. Bock SA. Prospective appraisal of complaints of adverse reactions to foods in children during the first 3 years of life. *Pediatrics* 1987; **79**(5): 683–8.

4. Sicherer SH, Munoz-Furlong A, Sampson HA. Prevalence of seafood allergy in the United States determined by a random telephone survey. *J Allergy Clin Immunol* 2004; **114**(1): 159–65.

5. Sicherer SH, Munoz-Furlong A, Burks AW, Sampson HA. Prevalence of peanut and tree nut allergy in the US determined by a random digit dial telephone survey. *J Allergy Clin Immunol* 1999; **103**(4): 559–62.

6. Sicherer SH, Munoz-Furlong A, Sampson HA. Prevalence of peanut and tree nut allergy in the United States determined by means of a random digit dial telephone survey: a 5-year

follow-up study. *J Allergy Clin Immunol* 2003; **112**(6): 1203–7.

7. Grundy J, Matthews S, Bateman B, *et al.* Rising prevalence of allergy to peanut in children: Data from 2 sequential cohorts. *J Allergy Clin Immunol* 2002; **110**(5): 784–9.

8. Sicherer SH. Clinical implications of cross-reactive food allergens. *J Allergy Clin Immunol* 2001; **108**(6): 881–90.

9. Eigenmann PA, Sicherer SH, Borkowski TA, *et al.* Prevalence of IgE-mediated food allergy among children with atopic dermatitis. *Pediatrics* 1998; **101**(3): E8.

10. Tariq SM, Matthews SM, Hakim EA, Arshad SH. Egg allergy in infancy predicts respiratory allergic disease by 4 years of age. *Pediatr Allergy Immunol* 2000; **11**(3): 162–7.

11. Zeiger RS, Heller S. The development and prediction of atopy in high-risk children: follow-up at age seven years in a prospective randomized study of combined maternal and infant food allergen avoidance. *J Allergy Clin Immunol* 1995; **95**(6): 1179–90.

12. Csonka P, Kaila M, Laippala P, *et al.* Wheezing in early life and asthma at school age: predictors of symptom persistence. *Pediatr Allergy Immunol* 2000; **11**(4): 225–9.

13. Mayer L. Mucosal immunity. *Pediatrics* 2003; **111**(6 Pt 3): 1595–1600.

14. Chehade M, Mayer L. Oral tolerance and its relation to food hypersensitivities. *J Allergy Clin Immunol* 2005; **115**(1): 3–12; quiz 13.

15. Husby S, Foged N, Host A, Svehag SE. Passage of dietary antigens into the blood of children with coeliac disease. Quantification and size distribution of absorbed antigens. *Gut* 1987; **28**(9): 1062–72.

16. Warshaw AL, Walker WA, Isselbacher KJ. Protein uptake by the intestine: evidence for absorption of intact macromolecules. *Gastroenterology* 1974; **66**(5): 987–92.

17. Sampson HA. Food allergy. Part 1: immunopathogenesis and clinical disorders. *J Allergy Clin Immunol* 1999; **103**(5 Pt 1): 717–28.

18. Chehade M, Magid MS, Mofidi S, *et al.* Allergic eosinophilic gastroenteritis with protein-losing enteropathy: intestinal pathology, clinical course, and long-term follow-up. *J Pediatr Gastroenterol Nutr* 2006; **42**(5): 516–21.

19. Friedman A, Weiner HL. Induction of anergy or active suppression following oral tolerance is determined by antigen dosage. *Proc Natl Acad Sci USA* 1994; **91**(14): 6688–92.

20. Eastham EJ, Lichauco T, Grady MI, Walker WA. Antigenicity of infant formulas: role of immature intestine on protein permeability. *J Pediatr* 1978; **93**(4): 561–4.

21. Howell WM, Turner SJ, Hourihane JO, *et al.* HLA class II DRB1, DQB1 and DPB1 genotypic associations with peanut allergy: evidence from a family-based and case-control study. *Clin Exp Allergy* 1998; **28**(2): 156–62.

22. Sicherer SH, Furlong TJ, Maes HH, *et al.* Genetics of peanut allergy: a twin study. *J Allergy Clin Immunol* 2000; **106**(1 Pt 1): 53–6.

23. Breiteneder H, Ebner C. Molecular and biochemical classification of plant-derived food allergens. *J Allergy Clin Immunol* 2000; **106**(1 Pt 1): 27–36.

24. Sicherer SH, Sampson HA. Food allergy. *J Allergy Clin Immunol* 2006; **117**(2 Suppl Mini-Primer): S470–5.

25. Sampson HA, Munoz-Furlong A, Campbell RL, *et al.* Second symposium on the definition and management of anaphylaxis: summary report – Second National Institute of Allergy and Infectious Disease/Food Allergy and Anaphylaxis Network symposium. *J Allergy Clin Immunol* 2006; **117**(2): 391–7.

26. Webb LM, Lieberman P. Anaphylaxis: a review of 601 cases. *Ann Allergy Asthma Immunol* 2006; **97**(1): 39–43.

27. Joint Task Force on Practice Parameters; American Academy of Allergy, Asthma and Immunology; American College of Allergy, Asthma and Immunology; Joint Council of Allergy, Asthma and Immunology. The diagnosis and management of anaphylaxis: an updated practice parameter. *J Allergy Clin Immunol* 2005; **115**(3 Suppl 2): S483–523.

28. Sampson HA, Mendelson L, Rosen JP. Fatal and near-fatal anaphylactic reactions to food in children and adolescents. *N Engl J Med* 1992; **327**(6): 380–4.

29. Johansson SG, Hourihane JO, Bousquet J, et al. A revised nomenclature for allergy. An EAACI position statement from the EAACI nomenclature task force. *Allergy* 2001; **56**(9): 813–24.

30. Sampson HA. Food anaphylaxis. *Br Med Bull* 2000; **56**(4): 925–35.

31. Simonte SJ, Ma S, Mofidi S, Sicherer SH. Relevance of casual contact with peanut butter in children with peanut allergy. *J Allergy Clin Immunol* 2003; **112**(1): 180–2.

32. Greaves M. Chronic urticaria. *J Allergy Clin Immunol* 2000; **105**(4): 664–72.

33. James JM, Bernhisel-Broadbent J, Sampson HA. Respiratory reactions provoked by double-blind food challenges in children. *Am J Respir Crit Care Med* 1994; **149**(1): 59–64.

34. James JM. Respiratory manifestations of food allergy. *Pediatrics* 2003; **111**(6 Pt 3): 1625–30.

35. Bock SA, Munoz-Furlong A, Sampson HA. Fatalities due to anaphylactic reactions to foods. *J Allergy Clin Immunol* 2001; **107**(1): 191–3.

36. Roberts G, Golder N, Lack G. Bronchial challenges with aerosolized food in asthmatic, food-allergic children. *Allergy* 2002; **57**(8): 713–17.

37. Sicherer SH, Furlong TJ, DeSimone J, Sampson HA. Self-reported allergic reactions to peanut on commercial airliners. *J Allergy Clin Immunol* 1999; **104**(1): 186–9.

38. Valenta R, Kraft D. Type 1 allergic reactions to plant-derived food: a consequence of primary sensitization to pollen allergens. *J Allergy Clin Immunol* 1996; **97**(4): 893–5.

39. Bohle B, Zwolfer B, Heratizadeh A, et al. Cooking birch pollen-related food: divergent consequences for IgE- and T cell-mediated reactivity in vitro and in vivo. *J Allergy Clin Immunol* 2006; **118**(1): 242–9.

40. Bock SA, Sampson HA, Atkins FM, et al. Double-blind, placebo-controlled food challenge (DBPCFC) as an office procedure: a manual. *J Allergy Clin Immunol* 1988; **82**(6): 986–97.

41. Sampson HA. Food allergy. Part 2: diagnosis and management. *J Allergy Clin Immunol* 1999; **103**(6): 981–9.

42. Sporik R, Hill DJ, Hosking CS. Specificity of allergen skin testing in predicting positive open food challenges to milk, egg and peanut in children. *Clin Exp Allergy* 2000; **30**(11): 1540–6.

43. Lockey RF. Adverse reactions associated with skin testing and immunotherapy. *Allergy Proc* 1995; **16**(6): 293–6.

44. Sampson HA. Utility of food-specific IgE concentrations in predicting symptomatic food allergy. *J Allergy Clin Immunol* 2001; **107**(5): 891–6.

45. Sampson HA, Ho DG. Relationship between food-specific IgE concentrations and the risk of positive food challenges in children and adolescents. *J Allergy Clin Immunol* 1997; **100**(4): 444–51.

46. Perry TT, Matsui EC, Conover-Walker MK, Wood RA. The relationship of allergen-specific IgE levels and oral food challenge outcome. *J Allergy Clin Immunol* 2004; **114**(1): 144–9.

47. Sicherer SH, Morrow EH, Sampson HA. Dose-response in double-blind, placebo-controlled oral food challenges in children with atopic dermatitis. *J Allergy Clin Immunol* 2000; **105**(3): 582–6.

48. Perry TT, Matsui EC, Conover-Walker MK, Wood RA. Risk of oral food challenges. *J Allergy Clin Immunol* 2004; **114**(5): 1164–8.

49. Blauvelt A, Hwang ST, Udey MC. 11. Allergic and immunological diseases of the skin. *J Allergy Clin Immunol* 2003; **111**(Suppl 2): S560–70.

50. Reekers R, Beyer K, Niggemann B, et al. The role of circulating food antigen-specific lymphocytes in food allergic children with atopic dermatitis. *Br J Dermatol* 1996; **135**(6): 935–41.

51. Werfel T, Ahlers G, Schmidt P, *et al.* Detection of a kappa-casein-specific lymphocyte response in milk-responsive atopic dermatitis. *Clin Exp Allergy* 1996; **26**(12): 1380–6.

52. Abernathy-Carver KJ, Sampson HA, Picker LJ, Leung DY. Milk-induced eczema is associated with the expansion of T cells expressing cutaneous lymphocyte antigen. *J Clin Invest* 1995; **95**(2): 913–18.

53. Burks W. Skin manifestations of food allergy. *Pediatrics* 2003; **111**(6 Pt 3): 1617–24.

54. Sampson HA. Food sensitivity and the pathogenesis of atopic dermatitis. *JR Soc Med* 1997; **90**(Suppl 30): 2–8.

55. Flinterman AE, Knulst AC, Meijer Y, *et al.* Acute allergic reactions in children with AEDS after prolonged cow's milk elimination diets. *Allergy* 2006; **61**(3): 370–4.

56. Sampson HA, Anderson JA. Summary and recommendations: Classification of gastrointestinal manifestations due to immunological reactions to foods in infants and young children. *J Pediatr Gastroenterol Nutr* 2000; **30**(Suppl): S87–94.

57. Rothenberg ME. Eosinophilic gastrointestinal disorders (EGID). *J Allergy Clin Immunol* 2004; **113**(1): 11–28; quiz 29.

58. Guajardo JR, Plotnick LM, Fende JM, *et al.* Eosinophil-associated gastrointestinal disorders: a world-wide-web based registry. *J Pediatr* 2002; **141**(4): 576–81.

59. Blanchard C, Wang N, Rothenberg ME. Eosinophilic esophagitis: pathogenesis, genetics, and therapy. *J Allergy Clin Immunol* 2006; **118**(5): 1054–9.

60. Ngo P, Furuta GT, Antonioli DA, Fox VL. Eosinophils in the oesophagus – peptic or allergic eosinophilic esophagitis? Case series of three patients with esophageal eosinophilia. *Am J Gastroenterol* 2006; **101**(7): 1666–70.

61. Markowitz JE, Liacouras CA. Ten years of eosinophilic oesophagitis: small steps or giant leaps? *Dig Liver Dis* 2006; **38**(4): 251–3.

62. Sampson HA, Sicherer SH, Birnbaum AH. AGA technical review on the evaluation of food allergy in gastrointestinal disorders. American Gastroenterological Association. *Gastroenterology* 2001; **120**(4): 1026–40.

63. Lake AM. Food-induced eosinophilic proctocolitis. *J Pediatr Gastroenterol Nutr* 2000; **30**(Suppl): S58–60.

64. Jenkins HR, Pincott JR, Soothill JF, *et al.* Food allergy: the major cause of infantile colitis. *Arch Dis Child* 1984; **59**(4): 326–9.

65. Pumberger W, Pomberger G, Geissler W. Proctocolitis in breast fed infants: a contribution to differential diagnosis of haematochezia in early childhood. *Postgrad Med J* 2001; **77**(906): 252–4.

66. Goldman H, Proujansky R. Allergic proctitis and gastroenteritis in children. Clinical and mucosal biopsy features in 53 cases. *Am J Surg Pathol* 1986; **10**(2): 75–86.

67. Lake AM, Whitington PF, Hamilton SR. Dietary protein-induced colitis in breast-fed infants. *J Pediatr* 1982; **101**(6): 906–10.

68. Machida HM, Catto Smith AG, Gall DG, *et al.* Allergic colitis in infancy: clinical and pathologic aspects. *J Pediatr Gastroenterol Nutr* 1994; **19**(1): 22–6.

69. Odze RD, Bines J, Leichtner AM, *et al.* Allergic proctocolitis in infants: a prospective clinicopathologic biopsy study. *Hum Pathol* 1993; **24**(6): 668–74.

70. Kilshaw PJ, Cant AJ. The passage of maternal dietary proteins into human breast milk. *Int Arch Allergy Appl Immunol* 1984; **75**(1): 8–15.

71. Vanderhoof JA, Murray ND, Kaufman SS, *et al.* Intolerance to protein hydrolysate infant formulas: an underrecognized cause of gastrointestinal symptoms in infants. *J Pediatr* 1997; **131**(5): 741–4.

72. Odze RD, Wershil BK, Leichtner AM, Antonioli DA. Allergic colitis in infants. *J Pediatr* 1995; **126**(2): 163–70.

73. Powell GK. Food protein-induced enterocolitis of infancy: differential diagnosis and management. *Compr Ther* 1986; **12**(2): 28–37.

74. Powell GK. Milk- and soy-induced enterocolitis of infancy. Clinical features and standardization of challenge. *J Pediatr* 1978; **93**(4): 553–60.

75. Powell GK. Enterocolitis in low-birth-weight infants associated with milk and soy protein intolerance. *J Pediatr* 1976; **88**(5): 840–4.

76. Murray KF, Christie DL. Dietary protein intolerance in infants with transient methemoglobinemia and diarrhea. *J Pediatr* 1993; **122**(1): 90–2.

77. Sicherer SH, Eigenmann PA, Sampson HA. Clinical features of food protein-induced enterocolitis syndrome. *J Pediatr* 1998; **133**(2): 214–19.

78. Nowak-Wegrzyn A, Sampson HA, Wood RA, Sicherer SH. Food protein-induced enterocolitis syndrome caused by solid food proteins. *Pediatrics* 2003; **111**(4 Pt 1): 829–35.

79. Kelso JM, Sampson HA. Food protein-induced enterocolitis to casein hydrolysate formulas. *J Allergy Clin Immunol* 1993; **92**(6): 909–10.

80. James SP. 19. Immunological, gastroenterologic, and hepatobiliary disorders. *J Allergy Clin Immunol* 2003; **111**(Suppl 2): S645–58.

81. McGough N, Cummings JH. Coeliac disease: a diverse clinical syndrome caused by intolerance of wheat, barley and rye. *Proc Nutr Soc* 2005; **64**(4): 434–50.

82. Spergel JM, Beausoleil JL, Mascarenhas M, Liacouras CA. The use of skin prick tests and patch tests to identify causative foods in eosinophilic esophagitis. *J Allergy Clin Immunol* 2002; **109**(2): 363–8.

83. Spergel JM, Andrews T, Brown-Whitehorn TF, *et al.* Treatment of eosinophilic esophagitis with specific food elimination diet directed by a combination of skin prick and patch tests. *Ann Allergy Asthma Immunol* 2005; **95**(4): 336–43.

84. Mehl A, Rolinck-Werninghaus C, Staden U, *et al.* The atopy patch test in the diagnostic workup of suspected food-related symptoms in children. *J Allergy Clin Immunol* 2006; **118**(4): 923–9.

85. Liacouras CA, Wenner WJ, Brown K, Ruchelli E. Primary eosinophilic esophagitis in children: successful treatment with oral corticosteroids. *J Pediatr Gastroenterol Nutr* 1998; **26**(4): 380–5.

86. Kelly KJ, Lazenby AJ, Rowe PC, *et al.* Eosinophilic esophagitis attributed to gastroesophageal reflux: improvement with an amino acid-based formula. *Gastroenterology* 1995; **109**(5): 1503–12.

87. Markowitz JE, Spergel JM, Ruchelli E, Liacouras CA. Elemental diet is an effective treatment for eosinophilic esophagitis in children and adolescents. *Am J Gastroenterol* 2003; **98**(4): 777–82.

88. Stein ML, Collins MH, Villanueva JM, *et al.* Anti-Il-5 (mepolizumab) therapy for eosinophilic esophagitis. *J Allergy Clin Immunol* 2006; **118**(6): 1312–19.

89. Sicherer SH. Clinical aspects of gastrointestinal food allergy in childhood. *Pediatrics* 2003; **111**(6 Pt 3): 1609–16.

90. Sicherer SH. Food protein-induced enterocolitis syndrome: case presentations and management lessons. *J Allergy Clin Immunol* 2005; **115**(1): 149–56.

91. van Odijk J, Kull I, Borres MP, *et al.* Breastfeeding and allergic disease: a multidisciplinary review of the literature (1966–2001) on the mode of early feeding in infancy and its impact on later atopic manifestations. *Allergy* 2003; **58**(9): 833–43.

92. Muraro A, Dreborg S, Halken S, *et al.* Dietary prevention of allergic diseases in infants and small children. Part III: Critical review of published peer-reviewed observational and interventional studies and final recommendations. *Pediatr Allergy Immunol* 2004; **15**(4): 291–307.

93. Host A, Koletzko B, Dreborg S, *et al.* Dietary products used in infants for treatment and prevention of food allergy. Joint Statement of the European Society for Paediatric Allergology and Clinical Immunology (ESPACI) Committee on Hypoallergenic Formulas and the European Society for Paediatric Gastroenterology, Hepatology

and Nutrition (ESPGHAN) Committee on Nutrition. *Arch Dis Child* 1999; **81**(1): 80–4.

94. American Academy of Pediatrics. Committee on Nutrition. Hypoallergenic infant formulas. *Pediatrics* 2000; **106**(2 Pt 1): 346–9.

95. Zeiger RS, Heller S, Mellon MH, *et al.* Effect of combined maternal and infant food-allergen avoidance on development of atopy in early infancy: a randomized study. *J Allergy Clin Immunol* 1989; **84**(1): 72–89.

96. Zeiger RS, Heller S, Mellon MH. Genetic and environmental factors affecting the development of atopy through age 4 in children of atopic parents: a prospective randomized study of food allergen avoidance. *Pediatr Allergy Immunol* 1992; **3**: 110–27.

97. Kull I, Bergstrom A, Lilja G, *et al.* Fish consumption during the first year of life and development of allergic diseases during childhood. *Allergy* 2006; **61**(8): 1009–15.

98. Kagalwalla AF, Sentongo TA, Ritz S, *et al.* Effect of six-food elimination diet on clinical and histologic outcomes in eosinophilic esophagitis. *Clin Gastroenterol Hepatol* 2006; **4**(9): 1097–1102.

99. Konikoff MR, Noel RJ, Blanchard C, *et al.* A randomized, double-blind, placebo-controlled trial of fluticasone propionate for paediatric eosinophilic esophagitis. *Gastroenterology* 2006; **131**(5): 1381–91.

100. Schrander JJ, van den Bogart JP, Forget PP, *et al.* Cow's milk protein intolerance in infants under 1 year of age: a prospective epidemiological study. *Eur J Pediatr* 1993; **152**(8): 640–4.

101. Hide DW, Guyer BM. Cows milk intolerance in Isle of Wight infants. *Br J Clin Pract* 1983; **37**(9): 285–7.

102. Nickel R, Kulig M, Forster J, *et al.* Sensitization to hen's egg at the age of twelve months is predictive for allergic sensitization to common indoor and outdoor allergens at the age of three years. *J Allergy Clin Immunol* 1997; **99**(5): 613–17.

103. Eggesbo M, Botten G, Halvorsen R, Magnus P. The prevalence of allergy to egg: a population-based study in young children. *Allergy* 2001; **56**(5): 403–11.

104. Saarinen KM, Pelkonen AS, Makela MJ, Savilahti E. Clinical course and prognosis of cow's milk allergy are dependent on milk-specific IgE status. *J Allergy Clin Immunol* 2005; **116**(4): 869–75.

105. Boyano-Martínez T, García-Ara C, Díaz-Pena JM, Martín-Esteban M. Prediction of tolerance on the basis of quantification of egg white-specific IgE antibodies in children with egg allergy. *J Allergy Clin Immunol* 2002; **110**(2): 304–9.

106. Hourihane JO, Roberts SA, Warner JO. Resolution of peanut allergy: case-control study. *Br Med J* 1998; **316**(7140): 1271–5.

107. Skolnick HS, Conover-Walker MK, Koerner CB, *et al.* The natural history of peanut allergy. *J Allergy Clin Immunol* 2001; **107**(2): 367–74.

108. Nelson HS, Lahr J, Rule R, *et al.* Treatment of anaphylactic sensitivity to peanuts by immunotherapy with injections of aqueous peanut extract. *J Allergy Clin Immunol* 1997; **99**(6 Pt 1): 744–51.

109. Enrique E, Pineda F, Malek T, *et al.* Sublingual immunotherapy for hazelnut food allergy: a randomized, double-blind, placebo-controlled study with a standardized hazelnut extract. *J Allergy Clin Immunol* 2005; **116**(5): 1073–9.

110. Meglio P, Bartone E, Plantamura M, *et al.* A protocol for oral desensitization in children with IgE-mediated cow's milk allergy. *Allergy* 2004; **59**(9):980–7.

111. Li XM, Srivastava K, Huleatt JW, *et al.* Engineered recombinant peanut protein and heat-killed Listeria monocytogenes coadministration protects against peanut-induced anaphylaxis in a murine model. *J Immunol* 2003; **170**(6): 3289–95.

112. Li XM, Srivastava K, Grishin A, *et al.* Persistent protective effect of heat-killed Escherichia coli producing "engineered," recombinant peanut proteins in a murine model of peanut allergy. *J Allergy Clin Immunol* 2003; **112**(1): 159–67.

113. Leung DY, Sampson HA, Yunginger JW, *et al.* Effect of anti-IgE therapy in patients with peanut allergy. *N Engl J Med* 2003; **348**(11): 986–93.

114. Srivastava KD, Kattan JD, Zou ZM, *et al.* The Chinese herbal medicine formula FAHF-2 completely blocks anaphylactic reactions in a murine model of peanut allergy. *J Allergy Clin Immunol* 2005; **115**(1): 171–8.

Anaphylaxis

PAMELA EWAN

Introduction

Anaphylaxis is becoming more common, particularly amongst children and young adults. Anaphylaxis can be frightening to deal with because of its rapid onset and severity. It can be fatal. Understanding of anaphylaxis and its management is essential for doctors in many fields, particularly those working in general practice and in accident and emergency (A&E) departments. After an anaphylactic reaction, it is important to refer the patients to an allergist so that the cause or type of anaphylaxis can be determined, and an appropriate management package instituted.

Definition

Anaphylaxis means a severe systemic allergic reaction: the term comes from the Greek words ανα ana (against) and φύλαξις phylaxis (protection). There is no universally accepted definition, in part because anaphylaxis comprises a constellation of features not all of which are present in all patients. Argument arises over which clinical features are essential for the diagnosis. A good working definition for practising physicians is that anaphylaxis involves one of the two severe features:

1. Respiratory difficulty (which may be due to laryngeal oedema or asthma); and/or
2. Hypotension (which can present as fainting, collapse, or loss of consciousness) [1].

Several other symptoms (particularly cutaneous) are usually present during the course of anaphylactic reaction. The confusion arises because systemic allergic reactions can be mild, moderate, or severe. For example, generalized urticaria and angio-oedema should not be described as anaphylaxis, as neither respiratory difficulty nor hypotension (i.e. the potentially life-threatening features) are present.

The European Academy of Allergology and Clinical Immunology (EAACI) proposed the following definition: 'Anaphylaxis is a severe, life-threatening, generalized or systemic hypersensitivity reaction'; however, this broad definition will not help facilitate the recognition in primary care and A&E departments [2].

Mechanism

An allergic reaction results from the interaction of an allergen with specific IgE antibodies, bound to Fcε receptors for immunoglobulin (Ig)E on mast cells and basophils. This leads to activation of the mast cell and release of preformed mediators stored in granules (including histamine), as well as of newly formed mediators, which are synthesized rapidly. These mediators are responsible for the clinical features. Rapid systemic release of large quantities of mediators will cause capillary leakage and mucosal oedema, resulting in shock and asphyxia. Airway smooth muscle contraction and mucosal oedema result in asthma-like symptoms.

Anaphylactoid reactions are caused by activation of mast cells and release of the same mediators, but without the involvement of IgE antibodies (for example, certain drugs may act directly on mast cells). This term is no longer used, as for the practical purposes of acute management it is not essential to distinguish an anaphylactic from an anaphylactoid reaction. This difference is relevant only when investigations aiming to identify the cause of the reaction are being considered. Anecdotal evidence from allergy clinic practice appears to suggest that non-IgE-mediated anaphylaxis may be becoming more common.

Incidence

There is a lack of data on the overall incidence of anaphylaxis. However, one can build up a picture from various sources. One of the problems is that anaphylaxis is not always recognized or recorded, so some studies may underestimate the incidence. Another problem relates to variations in definition, so that criteria for inclusion vary in different studies, which can lead to overestimates (for example, in some studies generalized urticaria and angio-oedema were included as anaphylaxis).

A&E data

A retrospective study of anaphylaxis in A&E, identifying only the most severe cases, and relating this number to the population served, estimated that approximately 1 in 3500 patients had an episode of anaphylaxis during the study period in 1993–94 [3].

Incidence rate

A review by a Working Group of the American College of Allergy, Asthma and Immunology, summarized the findings from a number of international epidemiological studies and concluded that the overall frequency of episodes of anaphylaxis lies between 30–60 cases per 100 000 persons at the lower end and 950 cases per 100 000 persons at the higher end |4|.

Lifetime prevalence

The American College of Allergy, Asthma and Immunology Working Group data indicate a lifetime prevalence of between 50 and 2000 episodes/100 000 persons or 0.05–2.0% |4|. More recent UK primary care data concur with the lower end of these estimates, indicating a lifetime age-standardized prevalence of a recorded diagnosis of anaphylaxis of 75.5 per 100 000 in 2005 |5|. Calculations based on these data suggest that approximately 1 in 1333 of the English population have experienced anaphylaxis at some point in their lives. However, this suggests that 45 000 of the UK population have had anaphylaxis, considerably less than suggested by data on specific causes.

Trends

It is clear that anaphylaxis is increasing, and hospital admissions in the UK (representing only a minority of overall cases, as most cases are managed in A&E) showed a 7-fold increase over a 10-year period between 1990 and 2001 |6–9|.

Features of anaphylaxis

The typical features of anaphylaxis are outlined in Table 11.1. Most patients present with cutaneous features, with either respiratory involvement or features of hypotension |1,10|.

Table 11.1   Features of anaphylaxis

Feature	System involved	Severity	Frequency
Erythema, pruritus (generalized), urticaria, angio-oedema	Cutaneous	Minor	Common
Laryngeal oedema, asthma	Airway	Major	Common
Fainting, light-headedness, collapse, loss of consciousness	Cardiovascular	Major	Common
Rhinitis, conjunctivitis, itching of palate or external auditory meatus	Mucosal		Uncommon
Nausea, vomiting, abdominal pain	Gastrointestinal tract		Uncommon
Palpitations	Cardiovascular		Less common
Sense of impending doom			Less common

Pathogenesis

Mast cell mediators have a variety of physiological effects. These include capillary leakage (resulting in urticaria, angio-oedema, laryngeal oedema, hypotension and shock), mucosal oedema (asphyxia and respiratory arrest), and smooth muscle contraction (asthma and abdominal pain).

Aetiology

Foods, drugs and hymenoptera venom are the commonest causes of anaphylaxis |6,11| (Table 11.2). However, although poorly quantitated, non-IgE-mediated (idiopathic) anaphylaxis *seems* much more common. The dominant cause varies with age |12,13| (Table 11.2). In a series of 95 children, the most probable causes were foods (57%), hymenoptera venom (12%), drugs (11%) and exercise (9%). Only 1% was due to latex.

Table 11.2   Common causes of anaphylaxis
● Foods*
● Bee and wasp stings
● Drugs**
● Idiopathic (non IgE-mediated)
*Commonest cause in children; **commonest cause in adults.

Foods are one of the commonest causes of anaphylaxis (33% in Mayo Clinic series and 57% in a series of children |11,13|), and evidence suggests that this is an increasing problem, now well documented for allergies to peanuts and other nuts (Table 11.3). Four per cent of the population have a food allergy and 2% of children in the UK have nut allergy. Insect venom is the next most common cause of anaphylaxis. Drug allergy is an increasing and important cause accounting for most of anaphylaxis in some adult series (Table 11.4). Although latex allergy is common, this is an uncommon cause of anaphylaxis—only a minority of patients with allergy to latex develop anaphylaxis |14|. Latex rubber anaphylaxis—unusually—develops more slowly (up to 30 min from the time of exposure), as the allergen has to be absorbed through the skin or mucosa (for example, during abdominal or gynaecological surgery, vaginal examination, dental work, or simply contact with, or wearing, rubber gloves). Healthcare workers are especially at risk.

Table 11.3   Foods causing anaphylaxis
● Peanuts
● Tree nuts (e.g. brazil nut, almond, hazelnut)
● Fish
● Shellfish
● Egg
● Milk
● Fruit
● Sesame
● Pulses (other than peanuts)
● Others (many other foods)

Table 11.4	Drugs causing anaphylaxis

- Antibiotics (especially penicillin)
- Intravenous drugs used during general anaesthesia (mainly neuromuscular blocking agents)
- Aspirin*
- Non-steroidal anti-inflammatory drugs*
- Intravenous contrast media*
- Opioid analgesics**

*Non-IgE-mediated; **predominantly non-IgE-mediated.

Rare causes include exercise, other physical stimuli, vaccines and semen. Allergen immunotherapy (desensitization) may induce anaphylaxis, and this can rarely occur after skin testing.

Clinical presentations

The clinical presentation of allergic reactions differs between adults and children (for example, adolescents and young adults are the groups most at risk of death). In addition, it is important to recognize that the clinical presentation varies depending on the cause. The information on the time of onset and evolution is also important in determining aetiology. When an allergen is injected systemically (insect stings, intravenous drugs) cardiovascular problems, especially hypotension and shock, predominate. Symptoms are of rapid onset, usually within minutes of an i.v. injection |15|, as at induction of anaesthesia, when large quantities of drug are given as boluses. Foods that are absorbed transmucosally (from the oral mucosa and pharyngeal mucosa as well as stomach) seem especially to cause lip, facial, and laryngeal oedema. Respiratory difficulty therefore predominates |16|. Whilst reactions are of slower onset than with i.v. agents, the symptoms usually occur within 10 min and progression is rapid. In a severe reaction laryngeal oedema, asphyxia and respiratory arrest may occur within 20–30 min. Urticaria/erythema is common in food |16|, venom and drug anaphylaxis |10|.

The clinical pattern of idiopathic anaphylaxis is different and evolves more slowly, usually over a number of hours. Initial symptoms are pruritus of hands and feet, and gastrointestinal symptoms are common.

Case histories: presentations of anaphylaxis

Case 1

Woman aged 30 years; life-threatening anaphylaxis to food.

- *Trigger*: Chinese meal
- *Symptoms and treatment*: one hour after start of multi-course meal
  - felt faint; mild asthma; severe dyspnoea and laryngeal oedema; loss of consciousness; taken to A&E department after 10 min; on arrival cyanosed, respiratory arrest; peri-orbital oedema; salbutamol infusion; cardiac arrest four min later

- adrenaline given; intubated with difficulty and ventilated; required nebulized adrenaline overnight
- *Outcome*: recovered over 8 h
- *Cause*: allergy to green pepper

Case 2

Boy aged 1 year; 'milder' example of food-induced anaphyalxis.

- *Trigger*: tiny quantity of peanut butter
- *Symptoms*: peri-oral blisters; distressed; vomited; slight dyspnoea; urticaria of neck and upper chest. Some improvement after vomiting. Received i.v. chlorpheniramine and hydrocortisone in A&E
- *Outcome*: rapid recovery
- *Cause*: allergy to peanuts

Case 3

Woman aged 62 years; life-threatening anaphylaxis to drug.

- *Trigger*: second tablet of a course of Arthrotec (diclofenac + misoprostol). Drug previously tolerated
- *Symptoms and treatment*: severe life-threatening reaction with, angio-oedema of throat, dyspnoea then loss of consciousness. She was resuscitated in A&E and received adrenaline, other drugs and i.v. fluids. The tryptase taken 90 min after the onset of reaction in A&E was elevated at 53 U/ml (normal range 3–14 ng/l). A baseline tryptase was normal at 6 U/ml
- *Cause*: sensitivity to diclofenac (NSAID; non-IgE-mediated)

Recurrence

The risk of recurrence is high. A prospective study of 432 patients referred to a community-based specialist practice in Australia found that in any 1 year, 1/12 patients who have suffered anaphylaxis will experience recurrence, and 1/50 will require hospital treatment or use adrenaline |17|. In nut allergy where the diagnosis was confirmed, a further nut-induced reaction occurred due to accidental ingestion in 50% of patients over a one-year period |18|.

Mortality

It is difficult to find robust estimates of mortality. Some anaphylactic deaths are not recorded, either because the problem was not recognized or because it was mistaken for asthma. There are approximately 20 anaphylaxis deaths reported each year in the UK, although it is thought that this may be a substantial underestimate. The overall prognosis of anaphylaxis reported in some population-based studies appears good, with a case fatality ratio of less than 1%, but these data are likely biased by the definition of anaphylaxis in case-inclusion |11,19–20|. Risk of death is increased in those with pre-existing asthma, particularly if poorly controlled, and amongst patients who fail to or delay treatment with adrenaline |21,22|. In a series of fatal food-induced anaphylaxis cases, peanuts and tree nuts accounted for more than 90% of the fatalities. Drug reactions and reactions to i.v. agents produce particularly severe reactions, and drug-induced anaphylaxis is an important cause of iatrogenic death during hospital admission. Study of a case series of fatal reactions demonstrated that in fatal anaphylaxis death generally occurred soon after exposure to the allergen |23|. With foods, respiratory arrest usually occurs after approximately 30–35 min, whilst with insect stings death from shock tends to occur 10–15 min following the sting; in the case of anaphylactic reaction to intravenous drugs, death can occur within 10 min. Approximately half of the reported deaths were due to drugs, a quarter food and a quarter bee or wasp stings |23|.

Morbidity

Anaphylaxis creates fear and anxiety, and patients are often concerned about the risk of a further reaction. Avoidance strategies can be difficult for families to cope with initially. Schools need to be involved in a positive way. Involvement of an experienced allergist who can make an accurate diagnosis, has protocols and management plans in place, and can provide reassurance is important.

Immediate investigations

The only immediate test that is useful at the time of reaction is mast cell tryptase |24|. Tryptase is released from mast cells in both anaphylactic and anaphylactoid reactions. It is an indicator of mast cell activation, but does not distinguish mechanisms or help establish the cause. Mast cell tryptase is usually (but not always) raised in severe reactions, especially those with hypotension; however, the level may be within the normal range in less severe systemic reactions. It is important to emphasize that a normal tryptase does not exclude anaphylaxis. As mast cell tryptase is only raised transiently, every effort should be made to collect a blood sample when it peaks (approximately one hour after the onset of the reaction). In addition, it is important also to take a baseline sample when the patient is well. This test remains to be fully evaluated.

Acute management

Adrenaline (epinephrine) is the most important drug in the treatment of anaphylaxis. Adrenaline should be administered intramuscularly. The adult dose is 0.5 ml of 1 in 1000 strength, or 500 μg |25,26|. It is almost always effective. The administration of adrenaline should be followed by chlorpheniramine and hydrocortisone (intramuscular or slow intravenous) |27,28|. This is usually all that is required, provided that treatment is started early. Treatment failure is more likely if administration of adrenaline is delayed. Biphasic reactions have been described but are probably rare; they occur mainly after oral drugs. Administration of hydrocortisone should minimize the risk of late relapse.

Difficulties may arise if the clinical presentation is evolving when the patient is first assessed. Adrenaline should be given to all patients with respiratory difficulties or hypotension. If these features are absent, but other features of a systemic allergic reaction are present, it is appropriate to give chlorpheniramine and hydrocortisone and reassess the patient. If in doubt, give 500 µg adrenaline intramuscularly in an adult or the appropriate dose in a child.

There can be risks associated with intravenous adrenaline. Adrenaline should not be given intravenously except under special circumstances: profound shock (which is immediately life-threatening) or during anaesthesia. Even then, if intravenous adrenaline is given, a dilute solution (1 in 10 000 or 100 µg/ml) must be administered very slowly in aliquots (with an initial dose of 50 µg [i.e., 0.5 ml]) and with cardiac monitoring. Such treatment therefore is rarely indicated outside hospital.

Although myocardial infarction has been reported in the literature as being associated with the use of adrenaline, this probably reflects a bias in reporting, as the effective and safe use of adrenaline is not considered worth reporting. Those with wide experience of its use find adrenaline extremely safe.

β-blockers may increase the severity of an anaphylactic reaction and may antagonize some of the beneficial actions of adrenaline. However, if a patient with anaphylaxis is taking β-blockers this should not prevent the use of adrenaline.

Supporting treatments

If the patient has hypotension then he or she should lie flat with the legs raised, but if respiratory difficulty is the dominant problem it may be better for the patient to sit up. Oxygen should be administered. If the first-line drugs are not rapidly effective for shock, intravenous fluids should be given rapidly.

An inhaled β-2 agonist should be given if asthma is one of the clinical features. Inhaled adrenaline is effective for mild to moderate laryngeal oedema but would not be given if intramuscular adrenaline had already been given as first-line treatment, and it is not a substitute for intramuscular adrenaline.

Drug treatment of anaphylaxis in adults

Intramuscular adrenaline 0.5 ml (500 µg) of 1 in 1000 solution (1 mg/ml)

Chlorpheniramine 10 mg given by intramuscular or slow intravenous injection

Hydrocortisone 200 mg given by intramuscular or slow intravenous injection

---

Doses of adrenaline

Adrenaline i.m. dose—adults

0.5 mg i.m. (= 500 µg = 0.5 ml of 1:1000)

Adrenaline i.m. dose—children

The scientific basis for the recommended doses is weak. The recommended doses are based on what is considered to be safe and practical to draw up and inject in an emergency [29].

(The equivalent volume of 1:1000 adrenaline is shown in brackets).

>12 years: 500 µg i.m. (0.5 ml) i.e. same as adult dose

                    300 µg i.m. (0.3 ml) if child is small or prepubertal

>6–12 years:	300 µg i.m. (0.3 ml)
>6 months–6 years:	150 µg i.m. (0.15 ml)
<6 months:	150 µg i.m. (0.15 ml)

From UK Resuscitation Council guidelines |26|.

Key to management of anaphylaxis
Awareness
Recognize it (consider in differential diagnosis)
Treat quickly

Early recognition and treatment are important for good outcome, and if these can be achieved, anaphylaxis is mostly easily reversible.

Long-term management

Patients are commonly sent home from A&E departments without further advice or are given a preloaded adrenaline syringe without instruction. This is of little value and unfortunately may be seen as the episode having been dealt with. It is important to refer patients to an allergist, with expertise in anaphylaxis. It is important to make an accurate diagnosis and to determine the cause. Advice can then be given on avoidance to prevent further attacks.In addition, appropriate treatment for self-management in case of a further reaction needs to be arranged. This 'management package' has a number of facets, requires broad expertise and experience and is time-consuming |30,31|.

Identifying the cause

In clinical practice, the identification of the cause in the case of IgE mediated reactions is usually based on clinical history of severe reaction following exposure, combined with positive skin prick test and/or elevated specific serum IgE antibody. The causal allergen is sometimes obvious from the history (e.g. a reaction with typical features and appropriate timing after ingestion of a known allergen with no confounding factors). Most food-induced reactions are IgE-mediated, as is latex and venom anaphylaxis.

Double-blind, placebo-controlled challenge is considered the gold standard for diagnosis of food-induced allergy. However, there are several drawbacks to this procedure. Firstly, it may put a patient at a risk of severe anaphylactic reaction, and is thus stressful to patient and parents. Secondly, it is time-consuming and expensive.

The level of specific serum IgE antibody or the size of skin prick test weal diameter may be used to predict the likelihood of patients having a clinical reaction. In general, skin prick tests are most valuable when they are negative (negative predictive value is in excess of 95%, with the positive predicted value being only 50%). Sporik *et al.* reported that in a group of 95 children with a history of clinical reactivity to peanut, mean weal diameter ≥8 mm on skin prick testing predicted clinical reactivity with 100% certainty [32]. However, three out of 18 children with negative skin tests also reacted. Similarly, negative specific serum IgE result has a very high negative predictive value, with positive result having a low specificity. Quantitative measurement of peanut-specific IgE antibodies can improve specificity, and for patients with peanut-specific IgE above 15 kU/l there is more than 95% probability for clinical reactivity [33].

Some anaphylactic reactions are non-IgE-mediated. This group includes certain drugs (e.g. non steroidal anti-inflammatory drugs [NSAIDs], aspirin, opiates), idiopathic anaphylaxis and physical anaphylaxis. The diagnosis is then made, once all other causes of anaphylaxis have been excluded, by history and if necessary challenge testing. Reactions to NSAIDs are not IgE-mediated, but due to excess leukotriene generation, so skin prick testing is not relevant. In physical anaphylaxis, the diagnosis should be made from the history, and may be confirmed by scratch tests, ice cube test etc.

For many substances including drugs, e.g. colloids or patent blue V dye, there are no data on validation of tests, so it is important these are concentrated in specialist centres so data can be built up [34].

Avoidance of the trigger

If a cause is identified, detailed advice should be given on avoidance. This may be simple (e.g. a particular i.v. drug) or more difficult (e.g. nuts or milk). Cross-reactivity adds to the complexity. For example, children allergic to peanut should avoid all nuts because of the increased risk of developing tree nut allergy [35]. In contrast, in adults only the nut to which the patient is allergic needs to be avoided. Patients with penicillin allergy have to avoid all penicillins, but in addition other drugs such as cephalosporins may need to be avoided. In oral allergy syndrome with allergy to fruit, the fruit can be tolerated if well cooked.

In the case of reaction to cyclo-oxygenase (COX) 1 inhibitors, it needs to be determined whether COX 2 inhibitors can be tolerated.

If complete avoidance can be instituted effectively, there will be no further anaphylactic reactions.

Drugs for self-treatment

In the case of inadvertent exposure, or if there is no avoidable trigger (e.g. in idiopathic anaphylaxis), drugs for self-treatment must be available. Early self-treatment is highly effective, and reactions can usually be stopped easily. Syringes preloaded with adrenaline are easy for patients to use and readily available. They deliver fixed intramuscular doses and are available in two strengths: for adults (containing 0.3 ml of 1 in 1000 strength, or 300 µg) and for children (0.3 ml of 1 in 2000, or 150 µg). A 0.5 ml or 500 µg i.m. auto-injector has been introduced. The appropriate self-treatment varies and may include other drugs, particularly oral antihistamines. This should be determined by a specialist, as once a cause is determined and avoidance measures are in place, further reactions after inadvertent exposure are usually less severe. A written treatment plan should be provided by the allergist, and the patient (and relatives) should be taught how and when to use the treatments provided. Trainer syringes are available and real practice is essential, as is regular re-training. In the case of a child, school and nursery staff must be trained in avoidance, recognition of reactions and administration of treatment; this is best delivered by community paediatric teams |36|. This requires expertise and these models are gradually being adopted. If there is no local allergist the general practitioner should provide the auto-injector for self-treatment, but it is essential that these are given with the appropriate advice and training. Practice nurses should have trainer syringes for this purpose. However, the expertise required to diagnose the cause and provide the full management package would not be expected in or appropriate for a primary care setting.

Who needs an adrenaline auto-injector?

This is a difficult question. There are no UK national guidelines, but these are in preparation. Those who have had anaphylaxis and where there is likelihood of a further reaction should carry adrenaline. If the cause can be avoided (e.g. certain prescribed drugs including all intravenous drugs), adrenaline is not needed by the patient. A more difficult area is where the diagnosis (e.g. nut allergy), has a spectrum of severities with a risk of severe reactions. If a child has mild nut allergy, it is difficult to estimate a risk of a severe reaction with a great level of certainty. Data are available on a large series of children and adults with nut allergy where adrenaline for self-use was prescribed according to criteria |31,32|. These were: any reaction involving the airway; any mild (cutaneous) reaction to a trace amount of nut (on the grounds that severity to a larger exposure could not be predicted); any patient with ongoing asthma requiring regular inhaler therapy. Using these criteria, about 70% of patients presenting to an allergy clinic were given adrenaline. The outcome was good, but it should be noted this was part of a comprehensive management package. Advice on avoidance, which is a cornerstone of management, was given and patients were aware, families trained and all carried oral antihistamines.

Efficacy of management plans

There is evidence that comprehensive management plans substantially reduce the incidence and severity of further reactions. Three studies of management plans delivered by specialist allergists in a large number of patients with nut allergy (567, 747 and 798 respectively) over the median follow-up of 48 months, revealed a low incidence (14–21%) of further reactions; furthermore, most of those that occurred were mild requiring either no treatment or only oral antihistamines |31,32|. There was a 60-fold reduction in severe reactions |32|. Few (e.g. 3/798 in one of the series) required adrenaline, and when this was needed a single injection was always effective. Further moderate or severe reactions occurred more often in young adults than in children |32|. The corollary is that in the absence of accurate diagnosis of the cause and appropriate management including avoidance, further anaphylaxis is common. In nut allergy, a further reaction occurs about once every 2 years even when the diagnosis is known—but without specialist advice.

A study in France of personalized care plans (PCPs) for children in schools delivered by an allergist was reviewed in 39 children, and evaluated over 25 months; 33% had a further reaction |37|. Peanut was the most common allergy.

What to do after an anaphylactic reaction

Action	Aim
Immediate: take blood at 1–2 h for measurement of mast cell tryptase	To confirm anaphylactic reaction
Later: refer to an allergy clinic	
– to determine cause	To prevent further attacks
– to organize self-treatment of future reactions (early treatment is the key)	To prevent morbidity

Adapted with permission from [1].

Some patients who have had an anaphylactic reaction wear a medic alert bracelet or necklet: the inscription provided by the allergist alerts other doctors of the anaphylaxis risk should there be a future reaction, thus increasing the prospect of early treatment, as well as aiding avoidance e.g. of a drug or latex rubber.

Practice parameters on the diagnosis and management of anaphylaxis

In the US, the most recent set of practice parameters for the diagnosis and management of anaphylaxis was issued by the Joint Task Force on Practice Parameters in Allergy, Asthma, and Immunology in 2005 [38].

References

1. Ewan PW. Anaphylaxis. *Br Med J* 1998; **316**: 1442–5.

2. Johansson SG, Hourihane JO, Bousquet J, *et al*; EAACI (the European Academy of Allergology and Clinical Immunology) nomenclature task force. A revised nomenclature for allergy. An EAACI position statement from the EAACI nomenclature task force. *Allergy* 2001; **56**(9): 813–24.

3. Stewart AG, Ewan PW. The incidence, aetiology and management of anaphylaxis presenting to an Accident & Emergency department. *Q J Med* 1996; **89**: 859–64.

4. Lieberman P, Camargo CA, Bohlke K, *et al.* Epidemiology of anaphylaxis: findings of the American College of Allergy, Asthma and Immunology Epidemiology of Anaphylaxis Working Group. *Ann Allergy Asthma Immunol* 2006; **97**: 596–602.

5. Sheikh A, Hippisley-Cox J, Newton J, Fenty J. Trends in national incidence, lifetime prevalence and adrenaline prescribing for anaphylaxis in England. *J Roy Soc Med* (in press).

6. Shiekh A, Alves B. Trends in hospital admissions for anaphylaxis. *Br Med J* 2000; **320**: 1441.

7. Gupta R, Sheikh A, Strachan D, Anderson HR. Increasing hospital admissions for systemic allergic disorders in England: analysis of national admissions data. *Br Med J* 2003; **327**: 1142–3.

8. Gupta R, Sheikh A, Strachan D, Anderson HR. Burden of allergic disease in the UK: secondary analyses of national databases. *Clin Exp Allergy* 2004; **34**: 520–6.

9. Gupta R, Sheikh A, Strachan D, Anderson HR. Time trends in allergic disorders in the UK. *Thorax* 2007; **62**: 91–6.

10. Sampson HA, Munoz-Furlong A, Campbell RL, et al. Second symposium on the definition and management of anaphylaxis: summary report – second National Institute of Allergy and Infectious Disease/Food Allergy and Anaphylaxis Network symposium. *Ann Emerg Med* 2006; **47**(4): 373–80.

11. Yocum MW, Butterfield JH, Klein JS, et al. Epidemiology of anaphylaxis in Olmstead County, a population-based study. *J Allergy Clin Immunol* 1999; **104**: 452–6.

12. Alves B, Sheikh A. Age specific aetiology of anaphylaxis. *Arch Dis Child* 2001; **85**: 348.

13. Novembre E, Cianferoni A, Bernardini R, et al. Anaphylaxis in children: clinical and allergologic features. *Pediatrics* 1998; **101**(4): E8.

14. Turjanmaa K, Alenius H, Makinen-Kiljunen S, et al. Natural rubber latex allergy. *Allergy* 1996; **51**: 593–602.

15. Fisher MM, Baldo BA. The incidence and clinical features of anaphylactic reactions during anaesthesia in Australia. *Ann Fr Anesth Reanim* 1993; **2**: 97–104.

16. Ewan PW. Clinical study of peanut and nut allergy in 62 consecutive patients: new features and associations. *Br Med J* 1996; **312**: 1074–8.

17. Mullins RJ. Anaphylaxis: risk factors for recurrence. *Clin Exp Allergy* 2003; **33**: 1033–40.

18. Bock SA, Atkins FM. The natural history of peanut allergy. *J Allergy Clin Immunol* 1989; **83**(5): 900–4.

19. Bohlke K, Davis RL, DeStefano F, et al. Epidemiology of anaphylaxis among children and adolescents enrolled in a health maintenance organization. *J Allergy Clin Immunol* 2004; **113**: 536–42.

20. Brown AF, McKinnon D, Chu K. Emergency department anaphylaxis: a review of 142 patients in a single year. *J Allergy Clin Immunol* 2001; **108**: 861–6.

21. Pumphrey RSH, Gowland MH. Further fatal allergic reactions to food in the United Kingdom, 1999–2006. *J Allergy Clin Immunol* 2007; **119**: 1018–19.

22. Bock SA, Muñoz-Furlong A, Sampson HA. Fatalities due to anaphylactic reactions to foods. *J Allergy Clin Immunol* 2001; **107**(1): 191–3.

23. Pumphrey RS. Lessons for management of anaphylaxis from a study of fatal reactions. *Clin Exp Allergy* 2000; **30**: 1144–50.

24. Schwartz LB. Diagnostic value of tryptase in anaphylaxis and mastocytosis. *Immunol Allergy Clin North Am* 2006; **26**(3): 451–63.

25. Emergency medical treatment of anaphylactic reactions. Project Team of The Resuscitation Council (UK). *Resuscitation* 1999; **41**(2): 93–9.

26. Emergency treatment of anaphylactic reactions. Guidelines for healthcare providers. Working Group of the Resuscitation Council UK. *Resuscitation* 2008 (in press).

27. Rowe BH, Spooner C, Ducharme FM, et al. Early emergency department treatment of acute asthma with systemic corticosteroids. *Cochrane Database Syst Rev* 2001; **1**: CD002178.

28. Smith M, Iqbal S, Elliott TM, et al. Corticosteroids for hospitalised children with acute asthma. *Cochrane Database Syst Rev* 2003; **2**: CD002886.

29. Simons FE, Chan ES, Gu X, Simons KJ. Epinephrine for the out-of-hospital (first-aid) treatment of anaphylaxis in infants: is the ampule/syringe/needle method practical? *J Allergy Clin Immunol* 2001; **108**(6): 1040–4.

30. Ewan PW, Clark AT. Long-term prospective observational study of patients with peanut and nut allergy after participation in a management plan. *Lancet* 2001; **357**(9250): 111–15.

31. Ewan PW, Clark AT. Efficacy of a management plan based on severity assessment in longitudinal and case-controlled studies of 747 children with nut allergy: proposal for good practice. *Clin Exp Allergy* 2005; **35**(6): 751–6.

32. Sporik R, Hill DJ, Hosking CS. Specificity of allergen skin testing in predicting positive open food challenges to milk, egg and peanut in children. *Clin Exp Allergy* 2000; **30**(11): 1540–6.

33. Sampson HA. Utility of food-specific IgE concentrations in predicting symptomatic food allergy. *J Allergy Clin Immunol* 2001; **107**(5): 891–6.

34. Ewan PW. Adverse reactions to colloids. *Anaesthesia* 2001; **56**(8): 771–2.

35. Clark AT, Ewan PW. The development and progression of allergy to multiple nuts at different ages. *Pediatr Allergy Immunol* 2005; **16**(6): 507–11.

36. Vickers DW, Maynard L, Ewan PW. Management of children with potential anaphylactic reactions in the community: a training package and proposal for good practice. *Clin Exp Allergy* 1997; **27**(8): 898–903.

37. Moneret-Vautrin DA, Kanny G, Morisset M, *et al.* Food anaphylaxis in schools: evaluation of the management plan and the efficiency of the emergency kit. *Allergy* 2001; **56**(11): 1071–6.

38. Lieberman P, Kemp SF, Oppenheimer J, *et al.* The diagnosis and management of anaphylaxis: An updated practice parameter. *J Allergy Clin Immunol* 2005; **115** (issue 3): S483–523; DOI: 10.1016/j.jaci.2005.01.010)

Principles of pharmacotherapy of allergic disease

MARTIN CHURCH

KEY POINTS

1. With the exception of immunotherapy, at the present time there is no drug that will cure allergy; the best we can do is to try to relieve the symptoms of acute episodes or flare-ups and to control the underlying inflammation.

2. Drugs used to treat allergic diseases include anti-IgE, chromones, anti-inflammatory drugs (corticosteroids), antihistamines, anti-leukotrienes and bronchodilators (β_2-stimulants).

3. Meta-analyses and systematic reviews have been increasingly used to provide information about the effectiveness of drugs; while yielding very useful information, they have a major disadvantage of being based on statistical analyses of large patient populations, thus predicting efficacy against 'Mr Average Patient' and being biased against drugs (e.g. chromones), which are very effective, but only in a minority of patients.

Introduction

Even though allergy comprises a wide spectrum of conditions affecting many organs, such as asthma, allergic rhinitis, allergic conjunctivitis and urticaria, each of which may require treatment with different drugs, the principles of immunotherapy and pharmacotherapy of all allergic diseases are essentially the same. In order to describe these, readers are referred to Figure 12.1, which is a simplified diagram of an allergic response in a mucosal membrane. The sites at which immunotherapy or pharmacotherapy are capable of modulating allergic disease are denoted by numbers in the diagram. These sites, which denote the subdivisions of this chapter, are: 1. Immunotherapy; 2. Anti-IgE; 3. Chromones; 4. Antiinflammatory drugs—corticosteroids; 5. Antihistamines; 6. Anti-leukotrienes; 7. Bronchodilators—β_2-stimulants.

With the exception of immunotherapy, it must be stressed at the outset that at the present time there is no drug that will cure allergy. The best we can do is to try to relieve

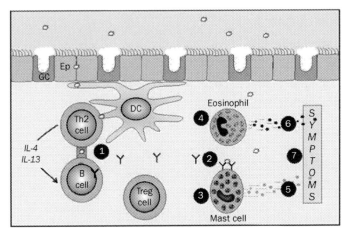

Fig. 12.1 Simplified diagram of an allergic response in a mucosal membrane. Abbreviations for the cells illustrated in the diagram are: Ep, ciliated epithelial cell; GC, goblet cell secreting mucus; DC, dendritic cell; Th2 cell, Th2 lymphocyte; B cell, B lymphocyte; Treg cell, regulatory T cell. The 'Y' symbols represent IgE. Allergen can be seen as small multi-pointed stars above the epithelium, within the DC, Th2 cell and B cell and cross-linking the IgE molecules attached to the mast cell. The numbers refer to the sites where immunotherapy or pharmacotherapy may be applied to modulate the response. These are defined in the text.

the symptoms of acute episodes or flare-ups and to control the underlying inflammation, which exacerbates the symptoms, particularly in chronic allergic diseases.

Site 1: Immunotherapy

In the upper left of Figure 12.1, allergen is seen penetrating the epithelium and being taken up by the dendritic cell. Recognizing the allergen as being foreign, this cell migrates to the lymphoid tissue where it presents the processed allergen to T lymphocytes, in this case a Th2 cell. The Th2 cell then passes the allergen epitope to a B cell. This, together with a cytokine instruction to make immunoglobulin (Ig)E, stimulates the B cell to transform into a plasma cell and secrete large amounts of IgE antibody, which arms the mast cells to stimulate the allergic response on subsequent exposure to allergen. This whole process is held in check by cytokines released by regulatory T cells. The influence of immunotherapy on these immune cells to reduce allergic sensitization is covered in detail in Chapter 13.

Site 2: Anti-IgE

Anti-IgE (omalizumab) was approved by the Food and Drug Administration (FDA) in the United States in 2003 for the treatment of patients with moderate-to-severe persistent asthma which is inadequately controlled with inhaled

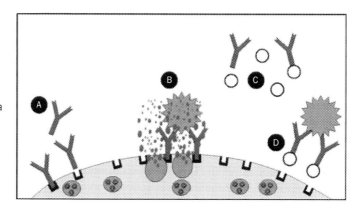

Fig. 12.2 Mechanism of action of anti-IgE in inhibiting activation of a mast cell (see text for a detailed description).

corticosteroids and who have a positive skin test or *in vitro* reactivity to a perennial aeroallergen |1|.

Principle of activity

Prevention of the binding of IgE antibodies to mast cells and basophils thereby inhibits their activation by allergen.

Mechanism of action

In area A of Figure 12.2, the 'Y' shaped IgE antibody molecules are seen binding to high affinity FcεR1 receptors on the mast cell membrane. Area B shows that cross-linkage of two mast cell-bound IgE molecules results in mast cell activation and degranulation. Anti-IgE, shown as white circles in area C, is a humanized IgG1 monoclonal antibody that recognizes and binds to the Fc portion of IgE. Area D shows that this IgE can no longer bind to its receptor on the mast cell and s ineffective even if its Fab portion is cross-linked with allergen. In addition, the long-term removal of free IgE results in a marked downregulation of the expression of high-affinity IgE receptors on basophils, mast cells and dendritic cells thus exerting an anti-inflammatory effect |2|.

Uses

In many clinical trials, omalizumab reduced the incidence of asthma exacerbations, severity of exacerbations, the use of rescue medication, and improved both symptoms and quality of life (QOL) |3|. More recently, largely because of its high cost, the target group patients for omalizumab has become focused on severe asthmatics who are still symptomatic after being treated with high-dose inhaled corticosteroids plus long-acting β-agonists |4|. Another suggested use is a steroid sparing effect in children even though the present minimum age for omalizumab administration is 12 years of age |5|.

Omalizumab has also been shown to be useful in the treatment of severe allergic rhinitis |6| but its use in atopic dermatitis is equivocal |7|. In addition, it is effective in anaphylaxis in patients with systemic mastocytosis. Another anti-IgE product, TNX-901 which will never be marketed following a legal dispute with the manufacturers of omalizumab, significantly and substantially increased the threshold of sensitivity to peanut on oral food challenge from a level equal to approximately half a peanut (178 mg) to one equal to almost nine peanuts (2805 mg), an effect that should translate into protection against most unintended ingestions of peanuts |8|. Finally, omalizumab has been successfully used to prevent unwanted effects during immunotherapy for beekeeper's anaphylaxis |9|.

Unwanted effects

On 21st February 2007, the FDA issued a black box warning following reports of anaphylaxis with omalizumab treatment in at least 0.1% of ~39 500 patients. Consequently, they notified asthmatic patients and healthcare professionals of new reports of serious and life-threatening allergic reactions (anaphylaxis) in patients after treatment with omalizumab. Anaphylaxis may occur after any dose of omalizumab (including the first dose), even if the patient had no allergic reaction to the first dose. The FDA recommended that patients should be fully informed about the signs and symptoms of anaphylaxis, their chance of developing delayed anaphylaxis following omalizumab treatment, and how to treat it when it occurs |10|.

Omalizumab in pregnancy and children: Asthma is estimated to affect up to 4% of pregnancies and aggressive treatment should be considered because asthma during pregnancy can lead to poor outcomes for both mother and child unless controlled adequately |11|. For pregnant women with persistent asthma, the use of inhaled sodium cromoglycate or inhaled budesonide should be considered as first-line agents. Short-acting β-agonists can be used as needed in all asthma categories. Other agents such as salmeterol, leukotriene modifiers, newer inhaled corticosteroids, and omalizumab may be considered in women who showed a good response to these agents before pregnancy.

Safety and effectiveness of omalizumab in paediatric patients below the age of 12 have not been established.

Site 3: Chromones

Sodium cromoglycate was originally introduced as a mast cell stabilizer for the treatment of asthma |12,13| while nedocromil sodium was marketed as a drug to reduce allergic inflammation |14|. More recently, both drugs have become widely used as topical therapies for allergic rhinitis and conjunctivitis.

Principle of activity

Introduced as mast cell stabilizers but now known to also reduce allergic inflammation and to prevent sensory nerve activation.

Mechanism of action

The ability of chromones to reduce histamine release in allergic responses in the bronchi |15|, nose |16| the eye |17| and the intestine |18| supports their mast cell stabilizing action.

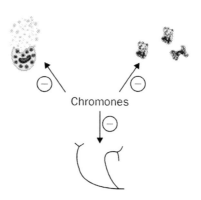

Fig. 12.3 Inhibition by chromones of mast cell activation, eosinophil migration and activation and sensory nerve activation.

Chromones

Besides inhibiting the early-phase response, chromones also protect against allergen-induced late-phase responses, which, in asthma, are associated with the acquisition of bronchial hyper-responsiveness. As these events are associated with the accumulation and activation of inflammatory cells, particularly eosinophils, an inhibitory effect on these aspects of allergic disease must be considered [19]. *In vitro*, activation of eosinophils, neutrophils, and macrophages is reduced by sodium cromoglycate and nedocromil sodium, the latter again being approximately 10 times more potent [20,21]. *In vivo* studies have shown that chromones inhibit eosinophil migration into the lung following allergen challenge [22] in allergic asthma [23] and in aspirin-intolerant asthma [24].

While in asthma an action on mast cells may explain the action of chromones on bronchoconstriction induced by allergen, exercise, and cold air, the effect on that induced by irritant agents, such as sulphur dioxide, is unlikely to be mast cell-mediated. To explain these results, an effect on neuronal reflexes, possibly involving C-fibre sensory neurons, has been postulated [25,26]. The ability of nedocromil sodium to inhibit bronchoconstriction induced by bradykinin and capsaicin would support this theory [27,28]. Interestingly, the effects of chromones in asthma are mimicked by the diuretic drugs, frusemide and bumetanide [29,30], which inhibit a Na-K-Cl co-transporter in the loop of Henle to reduce chloride and sodium reabsorption by the kidney [31]. This co-transporter has since been shown to be involved in mast cell activation [32,33] and in the activation of sensory nerves [17,34,35]. Thus, inhibition of a unique chloride channel is now thought to be the primary target for the actions of chromones.

Uses

Both sodium cromoglycate and nedocromil sodium are acidic drugs with pKa values of 1.0–2.5 and, consequently, exist almost exclusively in the ionized form at physiological pH (~7.4). These physicochemical characteristics mean that the drugs have negligible absorption from the gastrointestinal tract and must be given topically. Aerosols are available for asthma, both drops and sprays for rhinitis, and drops for conjunctivitis. In addition, oral solutions have been suggested for the topical treatment of gastrointestinal allergy. A major advantage of the drugs existing almost exclusively in the ionized form is that any drug absorbed systemically remains in the extracellular compartment thus giving negligible toxicity.

Chromones achieved a well-established place in the control of mildly to moderately severe asthma in the 1980s and 1990s, particularly in children. When used for the prevention of an early-phase allergic response, a single prophylactic inhaled dose has been shown repeatedly to be effective. Their ability to treat both immediate and late-phase bronchoconstrictor events and to prevent the acquisition of bronchial hyper-responsiveness has led to their use in chronic asthma. However, in recent years, meta-analyses and systematic reviews have been increasingly used to provide information about the effectiveness of drugs. Perhaps the most authoritative of these, the Cochrane Database Systematic Reviews, concluded that, in children, the evidence of efficacy of sodium cromoglycate over placebo was not proven |36|. About nedocromil sodium, a similar report concluded that its efficacy in children was equivocal. However, it also concluded that nedocromil sodium had a very good safety profile with no significant short-term or long-term adverse side-effects |37|. While these types of review yield very useful information, they have one great weakness; they are based on statistical analyses of large populations of patients and, therefore, predict efficacy against 'Mr Average Patient'. As such, analyses of this type will always be biased against drugs such as chromones, which are effective only in a minority of patients. Clinical practice over the last three decades has shown that these drugs are of great benefit in some patients. Unfortunately, we have no way of predicting which patients are likely to respond to chromone therapy and herein may lie the weakness of the drugs. However, skilled management of patients with sodium cromoglycate or nedocromil sodium may provide a single asthma therapy, which is free from the potential hazards associated with β-stimulants, corticosteroids, or theophylline.

Sodium cromoglycate and nedocromil sodium drops and nasal sprays have found a place in the treatment of allergic rhinitis and are often the drugs of first choice in children. They are also effective in the treatment of allergic conjunctivitis, particularly as an adjunct to systemic antihistamines.

Unwanted effects

The great advantage of chromones is their excellent safety profile with no significant short-term or long-term adverse side-effects.

Site 4: Anti-inflammatory drugs—corticosteroids (glucocorticoids)

Allergic diseases, particularly those of a more chronic nature, give rise to allergic inflammation, which exacerbates the symptoms. Thus, the inflammation can be visualized as an iceberg (Fig. 12.4). Attacking the iceberg of allergic inflammation with corticosteroids reduces its size and, consequently, the overall severity of the clinical symptoms. Their ability to reduce allergic inflammation has led to the widespread use of corticosteroids in all allergic diseases, including those of the

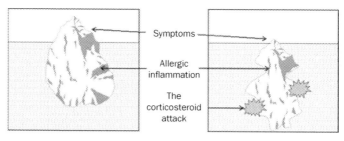

Fig. 12.4 The iceberg of allergic inflammation.

nose, eye, skin, and gastrointestinal tract. However, it must be stressed that glucocorticoids have potentially debilitating, unwanted effects when used incorrectly or inappropriately.

Principle of activity

Corticosteroids reduce allergic inflammation by downregulating the transcription of pro-inflammatory cytokines.

Mechanism of action

Corticosteroids are highly lipophilic and are largely bound to either of two plasma proteins: transcortin, a specific corticosteroid-binding globulin which binds glucocorticoids with high affinity; and albumin, which binds all steroids with low affinity [38]. Free steroid molecules diffuse across the cell membrane where they interact with glucocorticoid receptors (GR) in the cytoplasm. The intracellular actions of corticosteroids are mediated through the activated glucocorticoid receptor which diffuses into the nucleus where it interacts with a specific glucocorticoid response element (GRE) on the chromatin of the DNA to influence transcription and, consequently, *de novo* synthesis of steroid-susceptible proteins [39].

The major anti-inflammatory effects of glucocorticoids appear to be due largely to downregulation of the pro-inflammatory transcription factors nuclear factor-κB (NF-κB) and activator protein-1 (AP-1). The glucocorticoid receptor achieves this effect by epigenetic mechanisms (Fig. 12.5) [40,41]. Briefly, resting DNA is tightly wound around a core of histone proteins in its deacetylated form. When the specific areas encoding for pro-inflammatory adhesion molecules and cytokines are activated by NF-κB or AP-1 during the development of allergic inflammation, the histone core becomes acetylated allowing the DNA to unwind from the histone core and become available for transcription DNA. The presence of the glucocorticoid receptor within the nucleus reduces histone acetylation, causing the DNA to rewind and become inactive.

Glucocorticoids can also switch on gene expression. Activated glucocorticoid receptors translocate to the nucleus where they bind to GREs in the promoter region of glucocorticoid-sensitive genes. This leads to recruitment and activation of transcriptional co-activator molecules, such as CREB-binding protein, that have intrinsic histone acetyltransferase activity and thus cause DNA winding as in panel B of Figure 12.5. Genes which are switched on by this mechanism include the genes for β_2-adrenergic receptor, lipocortin-1/annexin-1 gene (phospholipase

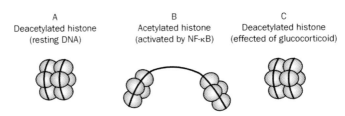

A	B	C
Deacetylated histone	Acetylated histone	Deacetylated histone
(resting DNA)	(activated by NF-κB)	(effected of glucocorticoid)

Fig. 12.5 The effects of transcription factors and glucocorticoids on DNA coiling. In panel **A** resting DNA is tightly coiled around a deacetylated histone core. In panel **B** the effect of a transcription factor, such as NF-κB, has acetylated the histone core allowing the DNA to unwind and transcribe pro-inflammatory adhesion molecules and cytokines. In panel **C** the effect of the activated glucocorticoid receptor, once translocated to the nucleus, is to reduce histone acetylation thus causing the DNA to rewind and become inactive.

A_2 inhibitor), IL-1R2 (decoy receptor), IκBα (inhibitor of NF-κB), CD163 (scavenger receptor) and MAP kinase phosphatase 1 (MKP-1) |40|.

Uses

The anti-inflammatory properties of corticosteroids underpin the majority of their beneficial effects in allergic disease. Guidelines for the use of corticosteroids in asthma have now been formulated in many countries |42,43|. Briefly, they suggest the introduction of inhaled preparations even in relatively mild asthma, increased inhaled doses as asthma becomes more severe, and the use of oral therapy only when the disease cannot be controlled satisfactorily by inhaled therapy. In addition, it is now recommended that corticosteroids be administered together with long-acting β_2-receptor agonists to prevent downregulation of β_2-receptors in the airways |44|. In rhinitis, corticosteroid nasal sprays, such as beclomethasone dipropionate and fluticasone propionate, are used to reduce the influx of mast cells and other inflammatory cells into the nasal mucosa. As they do not inhibit mast cell degranulation, they do not provide immediate relief. For maximal benefit in seasonal rhinitis, topical corticosteroid therapy should be instituted 2–3 weeks before the hay fever season. Unwanted effects are negligible with conventional doses. Systemic therapy should only be used in extremely debilitating conditions.

As allergic rhinitis is very common in patients with asthma, several retrospective database studies in the United States and in Europe have examined the benefits of treating allergic rhinitis in patients with asthma. The results indicate that, for patients with asthma, the presence of comorbid allergic rhinitis is associated with higher total annual medical costs, greater prescribing frequency of asthma-related medications, as well as increased likelihood of asthma-related hospital admissions and emergency visits. Therefore, they suggest an aggressive treatment of allergic rhinitis in patients with concomitant asthma as it is likely to enhance asthma outcomes and quality of life |45,46|.

Corticosteroid eye drops are very effective in the treatment of many forms of conjunctivitis, including allergic conjunctivitis. In extreme conditions, the drug may also be given systemically. However, in eye disease, steroids should only be used under expert medical supervision because of their local unwanted effects.

In the skin, steroid creams and ointments are used for a wide variety of inflammatory conditions, including eczema and atopic dermatitis. They act to suppress symptoms and are in no sense curative, rebound exacerbations often occurring on cessation of treatment. Because of their skin-thinning effects and their ability to be absorbed through the skin and cause systemic effects, steroids should not be the drugs of first choice but reserved for the more problematic conditions. Even then, the lowest strength of the least potent steroids should be used. Also, short courses are recommended wherever possible. The use of topical steroids in the skin of children is discouraged because of the systemic effects.

Unwanted effects

The intracellular events that are responsible for the anti-inflammatory effects of glucocorticoids cannot be separated from their effects on glucose, protein and lipid metabolism and their suppressive effects on the hypothalamo-pituitary-adrenal (HPA) axis. All glucocorticoids, whether natural or synthetic, will exert these effects when present in the systemic circulation. Furthermore, the magnitude of the side-effects is dependent on the dose of the drug absorbed systemically, the potency and duration of the systemic effect and the duration of treatment.

In conclusion, steroids afford effective therapy in allergic disease when the appropriate formulations are given and the physician observes with diligence the basic rules to avoid unwanted effects.

Site 5: Antihistamines

Histamine, released from mast cells and basophils, plays a major role in the pathophysiology of all allergic diseases, including rhinitis, urticaria, asthma, and systemic anaphylaxis. Although there four distinct receptors for histamine, H_1, H_2, H_3 and H_4, in allergic disease, it is the H_1-antihistamines, which are of primary benefit and so it is this class only which will be considered here.

Principle of activity

H_1-antihistamines are inverse agonists of the histamine-H_1 receptor causing inhibition of the effects of histamine.

Mechanism of action

H_1-antihistamines are not receptor antagonists as previously thought, but are inverse agonists. To understand this, we should visualize the receptor as a two-state model (Fig. 12.6) [47]. In this model, an equilibrium exists between the receptor isoforms. Histamine cross-links trans-membrane domain (TM) III and TM V to activate the receptor 24 while H_1-inverse agonists cross-link amino acids on TM IV and TM VI to stabilize the receptor in the inactive form [48].

In addition to stimulating the classical histamine H_1-receptor-mediated effects, histamine acting through the H_1-receptor may also activate the transcription factor NF-κB [49]. As mentioned above, NFκB is a key pro-inflammatory cytokine that is involved in the production of pro-inflammatory adhesion molecules and

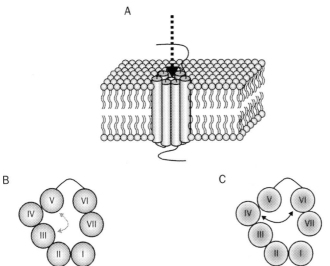

Fig. 12.6 The binding of histamine and cetirizine to the H$_1$-receptor. **A** The ligand–binding site for GPCR is within the transmembrane (TM) domains. **B** Histamine links TMs III and V to stabilize the receptor in the active state. **C** An H$_1$-antihistamine links TMs IV and VI to stabilize the receptor in the inactive state.

cytokines. The reduction of NF-κB activation by H$_1$-antihistamines |50–52| may well explain their long-term effects against allergic inflammation and nasal block-age |53–55|.

Uses

First-generation H$_1$-antihistamines penetrate readily into the brain, in which they occupy 50–95% of the H$_1$-receptors, as shown by positron emission tomography (PET) |56,57|. The result is CNS sedation, which severely compromises the use of these drugs in ambulatory patients. However, the sedative effect of first-generation H$_1$-antihistamines has often been used in the treatment of night-time exacerbations of allergy responses, especially in children. But is this an appropriate use of these drugs? A consensus document produced by American allergists states categorically that first-generation H$_1$-antihistamines should not be used as sedatives |58|. This conclusion is supported by a recent study |59| in which a single dose of 6 mg of chlorpheniramine increased the time to the onset and reduced the duration of rapid eye movement (REM) sleep at night, and the following morning impaired divided attention, vigilance, working memory and sensory-motor performance. The potential of first-generation H$_1$-antihistamines to enhance the central effects of alcohol and other CNS sedatives further limits their use. In addition, many of these drugs also have actions that reflect their poor receptor selectivity, including an atropine-like effect and blockade of both α-adrenergic and 5-hydroxytryptamine receptors.

Second-generation H$_1$-antihistamines penetrate the CNS poorly and are relatively free of sedating effects. Their propensity to occupy H$_1$-receptors in the CNS varies from 0% for fexofenadine to 30% for cetirizine |60|. The main postulated mechanism for their failure to penetrate into the brain is that they are actively pumped out by P-glycoprotein (Pgp), an organic anion transporting protein that is expressed on the luminal surfaces of vascular endothelial cells in the blood vessels that constitute the blood–brain barrier (BBB) |61,62|. The potential of Pgp to limit the passage of fexofenadine, cetirizine, loratadine, and terfenadine across the BBB has been confirmed recently using a canine kidney cell line transfected with human Pgp |63|. However, the brain penetration of fexofenadine and cetirizine, but not that of terfenadine and loratadine, remained poor even under conditions of Pgp inhibition suggesting that there are additional unknown mechanisms that also control brain penetration of these drugs.

Comparative studies between second-generation antihistamines have shown them all to have minimal sedation and no significant effects on a variety of cognitive, psychomotor and driving tests |64,65|. Currently, desloratadine, fexofenadine and loratadine are the H_1-antihistamines for which pilots can receive a waiver for use from the Federal Aviation Administration |66|.

All H_1-receptor antagonists are well absorbed from the gastrointestinal tract after oral dosage, symptomatic relief is observed within 1 to 3 h and their duration of action is generally around 24 h. No tolerance is observed with usage for up to six months |53|. Residual suppression of skin-test reactivity to allergens may last for up to seven days after the discontinuation of an H_1-antihistamine.

In patients with allergic rhinitis, H_1-antihistamines are useful in ameliorating sneezes, itching, and nasal discharge but are less effective in relieving nasal blockage. However, regular usage of H_1-antihistamines does provide relief of nasal blockage |53|.

Histamine can reproduce all of the symptoms of urticaria, including weal, flare, and itching |67|. Consequently, H_1-antihistamines are first-line medications in acute and chronic urticaria with weals of short duration and are very effective in providing symptomatic relief. In atopic dermatitis, itching is one of the major symptoms and scratching often causes a worsening of the lesion. Since histamine is a major pruritogen, the use of H_1-antihistamines relieves pruritus, reduces scratching, and seems to have glucocorticoid-sparing effects.

Unwanted effects

All of the first-generation H_1-antagonists and some of the second-generation antihistamines are oxidatively metabolized by the hepatic cytochrome P450 system, the main exceptions being levocetirizine and cetirizine and fexofenadine. Levocetirizine and cetirizine are excreted largely unchanged in urine and fexofenadine is excreted largely in the faeces |68|. Hepatic metabolism has several implications: prolongation of the serum half-life in patients with hepatic dysfunction and those receiving concomitant cytochrome P450 inhibitors, such as ketoconazole and erythromycin. Also, longer duration of action is found in elderly patients who have reduced liver function. In these patients there is a possibility of precipitating serious unwanted cardiac or CNS effects. Such adverse effects are more likely to occur when first-generation antihistamines are used than when second-generation antihistamines are used.

Some of first-generation H_1-antihistamines may cause sinus tachycardia, reflex tachycardia and supraventricular arrhythmia, and prolongation of the QT interval in a dose-dependent manner. The potential of unwanted serious cardiac effects of astemizole and terfenadine, which are not marketed now, have been described previously [69].

Some of oral H_1-antihistamines including cetirizine, loratadine, and emedastine, are considered relatively safe for use during pregnancy (FDA category B: no adverse effect in animals, but no data in human, or adverse effects in animals but no adverse effects in humans).

Site 6: Anti-leukotrienes—leukotriene receptor antagonists and synthesis inhibitors

Leukotrienes (LTs) are important inflammatory lipid mediators derived from arachidonic acid following its oxidation by 5-lipoxygenase (5-LO) on the nuclear envelope. There are two types of LTs, the dihydroxy acid LTB_4 and the cysteinyl LTs (cysLTs: LTC_4, LTD_4, LTE_4). Eosinophils predominantly produce cysLTs whereas neutrophils mainly produce LTB_4 [70].

CysLTs show activities through two different receptors, $cysLT_1$ and $cysLT_2$ receptor. The $CysLT_1$ receptor seems to be very important for the induction of asthmatic reaction as it induces constriction of airway smooth muscle, increased microvasculature leakage and secretion of bronchial mucosa, and induces the inflammation of the airways, including eosinophil infiltration, and finally hypertrophy of bronchial smooth muscle [71]. In addition, the $cysLT_1$ receptor appears to have roles in other allergic reactions, such as allergic rhinitis, atopic dermatitis, and chronic urticaria [72–74].

Principle of activity

The LT receptor antagonists (LTRAs), montelukast, zafirlukast, and pranlukast prevent the stimulation by leukotrienes of $cysLT_1$ receptors. Zileuton is a leukotriene synthesis inhibitor.

Mechanism of action

LTRAs have been developed to prevent the interaction of LTC_4 and LTD_4 at $cysLT_1$ receptors which are expressed on peripheral blood leucocytes (eosinophils, subsets of monocytes, macrophages, basophils and pre-granulocytic CD34+ cells), lung smooth muscle cells and interstitial macrophages, and spleen and less strongly in small intestine, pancreas and placenta [71]. The primary actions of LTRAs in allergic diseases are to suppress airway inflammation, including eosinophil infiltration, and bronchoconstriction in asthma. In contrast, zileuton is an antioxidant inhibitor of 5-lipoxygenase, a critical enzyme in the synthesis of both cysLTs and LTB_4.

Uses

The primary use of LTRAs is in the treatment of mild to severe asthma. In addition to beneficial effects on pulmonary functions, LTRAs reduce airway inflammation |71,75|. Whereas LTRAs have been suggested to have steroid-sparing activity, inhaled steroids at a dose of 400 μg/day of beclomethasone or equivalent are more effective than anti-leukotriene agents given in the usual licensed doses |76|. Therefore, indiscriminate replacement of steroid therapy with an LTRA is not without risk of loss of good asthma control.

LTRAs may have a particular role in aspirin-induced asthma |77|. In this condition, patients show increased production of cysteinyl leukotrienes because of a genetic polymorphism in the promoter for the cysLT1 receptor. Indeed, this polymorphism has been suggested as a useful genetic marker for predicting LTRA requirements in the long-term management of patients with aspirin-induced asthma |78|.

In seasonal rhinitis, there have been many reports that LTRAs improve the symptoms of allergic rhinitis, particularly nasal blockage |79|. However, two meta-analyses have concluded that LTRAs are modestly better than placebo but less effective than nasal corticosteroids in improving symptoms and quality of life in patients with seasonal allergic rhinitis. Furthermore, LTRAs plus H_1-antihistamines are more effective than H_1-antihistamines alone but inferior to intranasal corticosteroids |80,81|.

In the skin, the evidence for the effectiveness of LTRAs in primary cold urticaria, delayed pressure urticaria and dermographism is mainly anecdotal whereas there is no evidence for efficacy in other physical urticarias, including cholinergic, solar and aquagenic urticarias, vibratory angio-oedema and exercise-induced urticaria |82|.

Unwanted effects

Because LTRAs have relatively high receptor selectivity they are generally safe and well tolerated. The incidence of adverse effects of LTRAs in asthma patients is similar to those seen in placebo in double-blind, placebo-controlled trials. However, there have been reports of the very rare occurrence of Churg-Strauss Syndrome, a rare vasculitic disorder that generally occurs in patients with bronchial asthma, which improves after discontinuation of LTRA therapy |83|.

The antioxidant action of the leukotriene synthesis inhibitor, zileuton, is not entirely specific as it inhibits some other oxidizing enzymes, such as hepatic microsomal cytochrome enzyme, CYP1A2 |84|. As a consequence there were concerns about its liver toxicity. Certainly, elevations of alanine aminotransferase (ALT) and aspartate aminotransferase (AST) have been reported but these have resolved with cessation of treatment |85,86|. As CYP1A2 is involved in the metabolism of many drugs, including theophylline, phenytoin and warfarin, care must be used when co-prescribing such drugs |84|.

Site 7: Bronchodilators—β_2-stimulants

Bronchodilators, or β-adrenoceptor stimulants as they are more correctly called, have been used in the treatment of bronchial asthma for almost 40 years. All β-stimulants are derived from epinephrine in which chemical modifications have increased β-receptor selectivity and extended the duration of action.

Principle of activity

β-stimulants are functional antagonists of bronchoconstriction increasing cyclic AMP levels within bronchial smooth muscle to induce relaxation.

Mechanism of action

More is probably known about the biochemical mechanism of action of β-adrenoceptor stimulants than any other of the drugs used in the treatment of allergic diseases. Their interaction with β-adrenoceptors results in the generation of cyclic AMP, which acts as an intracellular messenger to activate many intracellular biochemical events, including the potent relaxation of bronchial smooth muscle.

Uses

β-stimulants are the first-line treatment used on an 'as required' basis for the reversal of acute asthmatic attacks. In all but the most severe asthmatics, inhalation of an aerosol provides an effective topical treatment by delivering the drug directly to the luminal surface of the bronchus from where it can gain ready access to the bronchial smooth muscle. The onset of action is rapid, within 5–15 min, a vital factor when trying to reverse a developing or established bronchoconstriction. The duration of action of 4–5 h of the short-acting bronchodilators is not long enough to allow the nocturnal asthmatic a full night's sleep. However, the prolonged duration of the long-acting β-agonists (LABAs) has overcome this problem. The major drawbacks to inhalation therapy are problems of poor administration techniques by the patients, particularly young children and geriatric patients, and poor drug penetration into the airways of patients with severe obstruction.

Recently, much debate has raged about the suitability of LABAs to suppress the long-term bronchial inflammation associated with asthma. The consensus of opinion, at present, is that they mask the worsening of bronchial inflammation in asthma |87,88|. However, studies in subjects receiving combination therapy with LABAs plus inhaled corticosteroids suggest that, if anything, there is an enhanced anti-inflammatory action with the combination superior to that achieved with inhaled corticosteroids alone |88|. Consequently, the FDA has issued a public health advisory to highlight recommendations about use of a LABA medicine for asthma |89|. This advisory states:

1. LABAs should not be the first medicine used to treat asthma. LABAs should be added to the asthma treatment plan only if other medicines do not control asthma, including the use of low- or medium-dose corticosteroids.

2. Do not stop using your LABA or other asthma medicines that your health-care professional has prescribed for you unless you have discussed with your healthcare provider whether or not to continue treatment.

3. Do not use your LABA to treat wheezing that is getting worse. Call your health-care professional right away if wheezing worsens while using a LABA.

4. LABAs do not relieve sudden wheezing. Always have a short-acting bron-chodilator medicine with you to treat sudden wheezing.

Unwanted effects

The main problems with β-stimulants result from their over-usage, a point which must be stressed to patients. These side-effects include skeletal muscle tremor to which tolerance develops, hyperglycaemia in diabetes, cardiovascular effects (cardiac arrhythmias acutely and a possibility of myocardial ischaemia in the long term) and hypokalaemia. The dangers of the use of LABAs in the absence of inhaled corticosteroid therapy are described above.

References

1. Hussar DA. New drugs of 2003. *J Am Pharm Assoc* 2004; **44**: 168–206.

2. Holgate S, Casale T, Wenzel S, *et al.* The anti-inflammatory effects of omalizumab confirm the central role of IgE in allergic inflamma-tion. *J Allergy Clin Immunol* 2005; **115**: 459–65.

3. Nowak D. Management of asthma with anti-immunoglobulin E: a review of clinical trials of omalizumab. *Respir Med* 2006; **100**: 1907–17.

4. Walters EH, Walters JA, Wood-Baker R. Anti-IgE and chemotherapy: a critical appraisal of treatment options for severe asthma. *Expert Opin Pharmacother* 2007; **8**: 585–92.

5. Walker S, Monteil M, Phelan K, *et al.* Anti-IgE for chronic asthma in adults and chil-dren. *Cochrane Database Syst Rev* 2006; CD003559.

6. Casale TB. Omalizumab: an effective anti-IgE treatment for allergic asthma and rhinitis. *Drugs Today (Barc)* 2004; **40**: 367–76.

7. Lane JE, Cheyney JM, Lane TN, *et al.* Treat-ment of recalcitrant atopic dermatitis with omalizumab. *J Am Acad Dermatol* 2006; **54**: 68–72.

8. Leung DY, Sampson HA, Yunginger JW, *et al.* Effect of anti-IgE therapy in patients with pea-nut allergy. *N Engl J Med* 2003; **348**: 986–93.

9. Schulze J, Rose M, Zielen S. Beekeepers ana-phylaxis: successful immunotherapy covered by omalizumab. *Allergy* 2007; **62**(8): 963–4. Epub 30 Apr 2007.

10. Cox L, Platts-Mills TA, Finegold I, *et al.* American Academy of Allergy, Asthma & Immunology American College of Allergy, Asthma and Immunology Joint Task Force Report on omalizumab-associated anaphy-laxis. *J Allergy Clin Immunol* 2007; **120**: 1373–7.

11. Blaiss MS. Management of asthma during pregnancy. *Allergy Asthma Proc* 2004; **25**: 375–9.

12. Cox JSG, Beach JE, Blair AMJN. Disodium cromoglycate (Intal). *Adv Drug Res* 1970; **5**: 115–96.

13. Cox JSG, Altounyan REC. Nature and modes of action of disodium cromoglycate (Lomudal). *Respiration* 1970; **27**(Suppl): 292–309.

14. Edwards AM, Auty RM, Clarke AJ, Orr TSC. Nedocromil sodium: a new modulator of inflammation for the treatment of asthma. *J Allergy Clin Immunol* 1985; **75**: 199.

15. Holgate ST, Benyon RC, Howarth PH, *et al.* Relationship between mediator release from human lung mast cells in vitro and in vivo. *Int Arch Allergy Appl Immunol* 1985; **77**: 47–56.

16. Onda T, Nagakura T, Uekusa T, *et al.* Drug effects on antigen-induced release of high molecular weight-neutrophil chemotactic activity and histamine in nasal secretion from children with allergic rhinitis. *Allergy Proc* 1990; **11**: 235–40.

17. Ahluwalia P, Anderson DF, Wilson SJ, *et al.* Nedocromil sodium and levocabastine reduce the symptoms of conjunctival allergen challenge by different mechanisms. *J Allergy Clin Immunol* 2001; **108**: 449–54.

18. Okayama Y, Benyon RC, Rees PH, *et al.* Inhibition profiles of sodium cromoglycate and nedocromil sodium on mediator release from mast cells of human skin, lung, tonsil, adenoid and intestine. *Clin Exp Allergy* 1992; **22**: 401–9.

19. Auty RM. The clinical development of a new agent for the treatment of airway inflammation, nedocromil sodium (Tilade). *Eur J Respir Dis* 1986; **69**(Suppl 147): 120–31.

20. Moqbel R, Walsh GM, Macdonald AJ, Kay B. Effect of disodium cromoglycate on activation of human eosinophils and neutrophils following reversed (anti-IgE) anaphylaxis. *Clin Allergy* 1986; **16**: 73–83.

21. Moqbel R, Cromwell O, Walsh GM, *et al.* Effects of nedocromil sodium (Tilade) on the activation of human eosinophils and neutrophils and the release of histamine from mast cells. *Allergy* 1988; **43**: 268–76.

22. Venge P, Dahl R, Peterson CG. Eosinophil granule proteins in serum after allergen challenge of asthmatic patients and the effects of anti-asthmatic medication. *Int Arch Allergy Appl Immunol* 1988; **87**: 306–12.

23. Manolitsas ND, Wang J, Devalia JL, *et al.* Regular albuterol, nedocromil sodium, and bronchial inflammation in asthma. *Am J Respir Crit Care Med* 1995; **151**: 1925–30.

24. Amayasu H, Nakabayashi M, Akahori K, *et al.* Cromolyn sodium suppresses eosinophilic inflammation in patients with aspirin-intolerant asthma. *Ann Allergy Asthma Immunol* 2001; **87**: 146–50.

25. Dixon M, Jackson DM, Richards IM. The action of sodium cromoglycate on 'C' fibre endings in the dog lung. *Br J Pharmacol* 1980; **70**: 11–13.

26. Jackson DM, Eady R, Farmer J. The effect of nedocromil sodium on non-specific bronchial hyperreactivity in the dog. *Eur J Respir Dis* 1986; **69**(Suppl 147): 217–19.

27. Dixon CMS, Barnes PJ. Bradykinin induced bronchoconstriction: inhibition by nedocromil sodium and sodium cromoglycate. *Br J Clin Pharmacol* 1989; **27**: 831–6.

28. Collier JG, Fuller RW. Capsaicin inhalation in man and the effects of sodium cromoglycate. *Br J Pharmacol* 1984; **81**: 113–17.

29. Anderson SD, Rodwell LT, Daviskas E, *et al.* The protective effect of nedocromil sodium and other drugs on airway narrowing provoked by hyperosmolar stimuli: a role for the airway epithelium? *J Allergy Clin Immunol* 1996; **98**: S124–34.

30. Prandota J. Furosemide: progress in understanding its diuretic, anti-inflammatory, and bronchodilating mechanism of action, and use in the treatment of respiratory tract diseases. *Am J Ther* 2002; **9**: 317–28.

31. Haas M, Forbush B, III. The Na-K-Cl cotransporters. *J Bioenerg Biomembr* 1998; **30**: 161–72.

32. Franzius D, Hoth M, Penner R. Non-specific effects of calcium entry antagonists in mast cells. *Pflugers Arch* 1994; **428**: 433–8.

33. Alton EW, Norris AA. Chloride transport and the actions of nedocromil sodium and cromolyn sodium in asthma. *J Allergy Clin Immunol* 1996; **98**: S102–5.

34. Ahluwalia P, McGill JI, Church MK. Nedocromil sodium inhibits histamine-induced itch and flare in human skin. *Br J Pharmacol* 2001; **132**: 613–15.

35. Willis EF, Clough GF, Church MK. Investigation into the mechanisms by which nedocromil sodium, frusemide and bumetanide inhibit the histamine-induced itch and flare response in human skin in vivo. *Clin Exp Allergy* 2004; **34**: 450–5.

36. van der Wouden JC, Tasche MJ, Bernsen RM, *et al.* Inhaled sodium cromoglycate for asthma in children. *Cochrane Database Syst Rev* 2003; CD002173.

37. Sridhar AV, McKean M. Nedocromil sodium for chronic asthma in children. *Cochrane Database Syst Rev* 2006; **3**: CD004108.

38. Frey BM, Frey FJ. Clinical pharmacokinetics of prednisone and prednisolone. *Clin Pharmacokinet* 1990; **19**: 126–46.

39. Necela BM, Cidlowski JA. Mechanisms of glucocorticoid receptor action in noninflammatory and inflammatory cells. *Proc Am Thorac Soc* 2004; **1**: 239–46.

40. Adcock IM, Ito K, Barnes PJ. Glucocorticoids: effects on gene transcription. *Proc Am Thorac Soc* 2004; **1**: 247–54.

41. Adcock IM, Ford P, Barnes PJ, Ito K. Epigenetics and airways disease. *Respir Res* 2006; 7:21.

42. British Guideline on the Management of Asthma. *Thorax* 2003; **58**(Suppl 1):i1–94.

43. Asthma Management and Prevention in Children. 2006; GINA Website at *www.ginasthma.org*

44. Usmani OS, Ito K, Maneechotesuwan K, *et al.* Glucocorticoid receptor nuclear translocation in airway cells after inhaled combination therapy. *Am J Respir Crit Care Med* 2005; **172**: 704–12.

45. Corren J. The connection between allergic rhinitis and bronchial asthma. *Curr Opin Pulm Med* 2007; **13**: 13–18.

46. Thomas M. Allergic rhinitis: evidence for impact on asthma. *BMC Pulm Med* 2006; **6**(Suppl 1):S4.

47. Leurs R, Church MK, Taglialatela M. H1-antihistamines: inverse agonism, anti-inflammatory actions and cardiac effects. *Clin Exp Allergy* 2002; **32**: 489–98.

48. Wieland K, Laak AM, Smit MJ, *et al.* Mutational analysis of the antagonist-binding site of the histamine H(1) receptor. *J Biol Chem* 1999; **274**: 29994–30000.

49. Bakker RA, Schoonus SB, Smit MJ, *et al.* Histamine H(1)-receptor activation of nuclear factor-kappa B: roles for G beta gamma- and G alpha(q/11)-subunits in constitutive and agonist-mediated signaling. *Mol Pharmacol* 2001; **60**: 1133–42.

50. Arnold R, Rihoux J, Konig W. Cetirizine counter-regulates interleukin-8 release from human epithelial cells (A549). *Clin Exp Allergy* 1999; **29**: 1681–91.

51. Wu RL, Anthes JC, Kreutner W, *et al.* Desloratadine inhibits constitutive and histamine-stimulated nuclear factor-kappaB activity consistent with inverse agonism at the histamine H1 Receptor. *Int Arch Allergy Immunol* 2004; **135**: 313–18.

52. Matsubara M, Tamura T, Ohmori K, Hasegawa K. Histamine H1 receptor antagonist blocks histamine-induced proinflammatory cytokine production through inhibition of Ca2+-dependent protein kinase C, Raf/MEK/ERK and IKK/I kappa B/NF-kappa B signal cascades. *Biochem Pharmacol* 2005; **69**: 433–49.

53. Bachert C, Bousquet J, Canonica GW, *et al.* Levocetirizine improves quality of life and reduces costs in long-term management of persistent allergic rhinitis. *J Allergy Clin Immunol* 2004; **114**: 838–44.

54. Patou J, De Smedt SH, van Cauwenberge P, Bachert C. Pathophysiology of nasal obstruction and meta-analysis of early and late effects of levocetirizine. *Clin Exp Allergy* 2006; **36**: 972–81.

55. Canonica GW, Tarantini F, Compalati E, Penagos M. Efficacy of desloratadine in the treatment of allergic rhinitis: a meta-analysis of randomized, double-blind, controlled trials. *Allergy* 2007; **62**: 359–66.

56. Yanai K, Ryu JH, Watanabe T, *et al.* Histamine H1 receptor occupancy in human brains after single oral doses of histamine H1 antagonists measured by positron emission tomography. *Br J Pharmacol* 1995; **116**: 1649–55.

57. Tagawa M, Kano M, Okamura N, *et al.* Neuroimaging of histamine H1-receptor occupancy in human brain by positron emission tomography (PET): a comparative study of ebastine, a second-generation antihistamine, and (+)-chlorpheniramine, a classical antihistamine. *Br J Clin Pharmacol* 2001; **52**: 501–9.

58. Casale TB, Blaiss MS, Gelfand E, *et al.* First do no harm: managing antihistamine impairment in patients with allergic rhinitis. *J Allergy Clin Immunol* 2003; **111**: S835–42.

59. Boyle J, Eriksson M, Stanley N, *et al.* Allergy medication in Japanese volunteers: treatment effect of single doses on nocturnal sleep architecture and next day residual effects. *Curr Med Res Opin* 2006; **22**: 1343–51.

60. Tashiro M, Mochizuki H, Iwabuchi K, *et al.* Roles of histamine in regulation of arousal and cognition: functional neuroimaging of histamine H1 receptors in human brain. *Life Sci* 2002; **72**: 409–14.

61. Chishty M, Reichel A, Siva J, *et al.* Affinity for the P-glycoprotein efflux pump at the blood-brain barrier may explain the lack of CNS side-effects of modern antihistamines. *J Drug Target* 2001; **9**: 223–8.

62. Polli JW, Baughman TM, Humphreys JE, *et al.* P-glycoprotein influences the brain concentrations of cetirizine (Zyrtec), a second-generation non-sedating antihistamine. *J Pharm Sci* 2003; **92**: 2082–9.

63. Obradovic T, Dobson GG, Shingaki T, *et al.* Assessment of the first and second generation antihistamines brain penetration and role of P-glycoprotein. *Pharm Res* 2007; **24**: 318–27.

64. Ridout F, Hindmarch I. The effects of acute doses of fexofenadine, promethazine, and placebo on cognitive and psychomotor function in healthy Japanese volunteers. *Ann Allergy Asthma Immunol* 2003; **90**: 404–10.

65. Verster JC, Volkerts ER. Antihistamines and driving ability: evidence from on-the-road driving studies during normal traffic. *Ann Allergy Asthma Immunol* 2004; **92**: 294–303.

66. FAA Accepted Medications, 2007. Updated 11/1/07. *www.leftseat.com/medcat1 htm*

67. Kapp A, Pichler WJ. Levocetirizine is an effective treatment in patients suffering from chronic idiopathic urticaria: a randomized, double-blind, placebo-controlled, parallel, multicenter study. *Int J Dermatol* 2006; **45**: 469–74.

68. Molimard M, Diquet B, Strolin-Benedetti M. Comparison of pharmacokinetics and metabolism of desloratadine, fexofenadine, levocetirizine and mizolastine in humans. *Fundam Clin Pharmacol* 2004; **18**: 399–411.

69. Taglialatela M, Castaldo P, Pannaccione A, *et al.* Cardiac ion channels and antihistamines: possible mechanisms of cardiotoxicity. *Clin Exp Allergy* 1999; **29**(Suppl 3): 182–9.

70. Sampson AP. The leukotrienes: mediators of chronic inflammation in asthma. *Clin Exp Allergy* 1996; **26**: 995–1004.

71. Sampson AP, Pizzichini E, Bisgaard H. Effects of cysteinyl leukotrienes and leukotriene receptor antagonists on markers of inflammation. *J Allergy Clin Immunol* 2003; **111**: S49–59.

72. Nayak A, Langdon RB. Montelukast in the treatment of allergic rhinitis: an evidence-based review. *Drugs* 2007; **67**: 887–901.

73. Kagi MK. Leukotriene receptor antagonists – a novel therapeutic approach in atopic dermatitis? *Dermatology* 2001; **203**: 280–3.

74. Wedi B, Kapp A. Pathophysiological role of leukotrienes in dermatological diseases: potential therapeutic implications. *BioDrugs* 2001; **15**: 729–43.

75. Busse W, Kraft M. Cysteinyl leukotrienes in allergic inflammation: strategic target for therapy. *Chest* 2005; **127**: 1312–26.

76. Ducharme FM. Inhaled corticosteroids versus leukotriene antagonists as first-line therapy for asthma: a systematic review of current evidence. *Treat Respir Med* 2004; **3**: 399–405.

77. Salvi SS, Krishna MT, Sampson AP, Holgate ST. The anti-inflammatory effects of leukotriene-modifying drugs and their use in asthma. *Chest* 2001; **119**: 1533–46.

78. Kim SH, Ye YM, Hur GY, *et al.* CysLTR1 promoter polymorphism and requirement for leukotriene receptor antagonist in aspirin-intolerant asthma patients. *Pharmacogenomics* 2007; **8**: 1143–50.

79. Jiang RS. Efficacy of a leukotriene receptor antagonist in the treatment of perennial allergic rhinitis. *J Otolaryngol* 2006; **35**: 117–21.

80. Wilson AM, O'Byrne PM, Parameswaran K. Leukotriene receptor antagonists for allergic rhinitis: a systematic review and meta-analysis. *Am J Med* 2004; **116**: 338–44.

81. Rodrigo GJ, Yanez A. The role of antileukotriene therapy in seasonal allergic rhinitis: a systematic review of randomized trials. *Ann Allergy Asthma Immunol* 2006; **96**: 779–86.

82. Di Lorenzo G, Pacor ML, Mansueto P, *et al.* Is there a role for antileukotrienes in urticaria? *Clin Exp Dermatol* 2006; **31**: 327–34.

83. Cuchacovich R, Justiniano M, Espinoza LR. Churg-Strauss syndrome associated with leukotriene receptor antagonists (LTRA). *Clin Rheumatol* 2007; **26**: 1769–71.

84. Lu P, Schrag ML, Slaughter DE, *et al.* Mechanism-based inhibition of human liver microsomal cytochrome P450 1A2 by zileuton, a 5-lipoxygenase inhibitor. *Drug Metab Dispos* 2003; **31**: 1352–60.

85. Watkins PB, Dube LM, Walton-Bowen K, *et al.* Clinical pattern of zileuton-associated liver injury: results of a 12-month study in patients with chronic asthma. *Drug Saf* 2007; **30**: 805–15.

86. Wenzel S, Busse W, Calhoun W, *et al.* The safety and efficacy of zileuton controlled-release tablets as adjunctive therapy to usual care in the treatment of moderate persistent asthma: a 6-month randomized controlled study. *J Asthma* 2007; **44**: 305–10.

87. Koopmans JG, Lutter R, Jansen HM, van der Zee JS. Clinically masked increases in bronchial inflammation in guideline-treated persistent asthma. *Pulm Pharmacol Ther* 2006; **19**: 397–403.

88. Nelson HS. Long-acting beta-agonists in adult asthma: Evidence that these drugs are safe. *Prim Care Respir J* 2006; **15**: 271–7.

89. FDA Public Health Advisory, Serevent Diskus (salmeterol xinafoate inhalation powder), Advair Diskus (fluticasone propionate & salmeterol inhalation powder), Foradil Aerolizer (formoterol fumarate inhalation powder), 2006. *wwwfdagov/cder/drug/infopage/LABA/default htm*

13

Immunotherapy

ANTHONY FREW

KEY POINTS

1. Specific allergen immunotherapy (SIT) is effective in allergic rhinitis and in anaphylaxis to wasp and bee venom.

2. The role of SIT is asthma is controversial: it works but is potentially dangerous.

3. The mechanisms of successful SIT are not fully understood: induction of T regulatory cells is thought to be important.

4. Sublingual immunotherapy is also effective and may be easier for patients to comply with.

5. Future developments are aiming to deliver simpler, safer regimes and improved efficacy, both in those who currently respond and those who do not respond to standard SIT.

Introduction

Specific allergen immunotherapy (SIT) is the process of administering allergenic molecules or extracts to modify or abolish symptoms associated with atopic allergy. Before starting SIT it is essential to follow the general principles of managing allergic conditions, namely to make an accurate diagnosis, to identify relevant trigger factors, and to institute appropriate interventions which will reduce the impact of those triggers and control both symptoms and disease progression. Many patients with allergies have mild disease, which may be controlled by allergen avoidance and simple drug therapy, but these treatments only work as long as they are taken, so there is clearly a need for additional and long-lasting therapy. SIT is the only current therapy that modifies the immune response to allergens. The treatment is targeted at those allergens recognized by the patient and physician as responsible for symptoms. While claims have been made for wider benefits, there is little convincing evidence that treating for one allergen will improve symptoms caused by another allergen. Before using SIT it is therefore essential to assess patients carefully, with particular emphasis on the role of allergic triggers.

SIT was first described in 1911 by Noon and Freeman from St Mary's Hospital, London [1] and then developed in North America and in Europe, but with some differences in practice either side of the Atlantic. In particular, American allergists tend to treat for all sensitivities identified on skin testing, using mixtures of extracts prepared from bulk vials, whereas in Europe patients are normally only treated with a single allergen, which is supplied direct from the manufacturer. Mixed allergen extracts are available and used in some parts of Europe, but only as custom mixtures from manufacturers. Another difference in manufacturing is that the allergen extracts used in Europe are usually dialysed to remove low molecular weight components, and are standardized according to their ability to elicit a weal, while in the US, extracts may not be dialysed and standardisation is based on ability to elicit erythema rather than weal.

In conventional SIT, patients are started on a very low dose of allergen, and the dose is then increased, usually at weekly intervals until the maintenance dose is achieved. Maintenance doses are then given at 4–6 weekly intervals for 3 to 5 years (2–4 weeks in the USA). Sometimes it is not possible to achieve the maintenance dose, due to side-effects, in which case the maximum tolerated dose may be given instead. Alternative induction regimes can be used either giving several doses on each day (semi-rush or modified rush protocols), or the whole series of incremental injections in a single day (rush protocol). The main drawback to rush and semi-rush protocols is the risk of adverse reactions, which are much commoner than in conventional protocols. On the other hand, full protection against stings can be attained in a few days as compared to the three months required in the conventional regime. Normally SIT is given by subcutaneous injection, but in recent years there has been an upsurge of interest in alternative routes of administration, especially the sublingual route.

Mechanisms

Despite many years of research we still do not know precisely how SIT works. Several mechanisms have been proposed, but it is not clear which of these are simply a predictable immunological response to injected proteins and which are actually responsible for delivering the clinical benefit. Following subcutaneous injection of allergen extracts, the allergenic material is taken up by phagocytic cells and about 1% of an injected dose ends up in the regional lymph nodes. It has long been known that SIT induces allergen-specific immunoglobulin (Ig) G antibodies, which increase progressively over the course of treatment. It has been suggested that these antibodies may intercept the allergen and 'block' the allergic response. In patients treated for hymenoptera venom allergy, the development of allergen-specific IgG antibody correlates with clinical efficacy, but for other allergens the magnitude of the IgG response is not closely related to the degree of efficacy. Moreover, the rise in IgG follows the onset of clinical benefit, rather than preceding it. Over the first few months of SIT, allergen-specific IgE antibodies increase, but the usual rise in IgE seen during natural seasonal exposure is blunted |2|. As the SIT course continues, allergen-specific IgE titres decline, but do not disappear. In keeping with this, SIT has little effect on immediate skin test responses to allergen. In contrast, the late-phase skin test response is virtually abolished after successful SIT. Similar patterns are observed for late-phase nasal and airway responses |3|. This suggests that the beneficial effects of SIT may relate to uncoupling the immediate allergic reaction from its downstream consequences. Both in the skin and in the nose, successful SIT is accompanied by a reduction in T cell and eosinophil recruitment in response to allergen challenge.

As well as inducing allergen-specific IgG, SIT alters the function of allergen-specific T cells (Fig. 13.1). This can be seen both in proliferation assays and in sites challenged with allergen. Th2 cytokine expression is not affected but an increased proportion of the T cells recruited after allergen express the Th1 cytokines interleukin (IL)-2, interferon-gamma (IFN-γ) and IL-12 |4,5|. In addition there is induction of allergen-specific CD4+ T-regulatory cells, which express CD25, Fox p3 and IL-10 |6|. IL-10 has several relevant properties including modulation of IL-4-induced B cell IgE production in favour of IgG4, inhibition of IgE-dependent mast cell activation, inhibition of human eosinophil cytokine production and survival, suppression of IL5, and induction of antigen-specific anergy. Taken together, it seems that SIT modulates allergen-specific T cells, which may explain why the clinical and late-phase responses are attenuated without much impact on

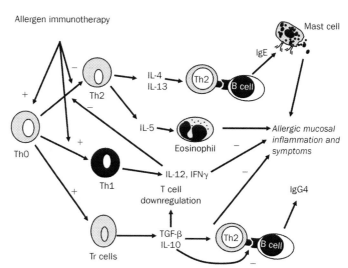

Fig. 13.1 Possible mechanisms of specific immunotherapy. SIT induces both a Th1 response and T-regulatory cells, which have direct and indirect effects on IgE production, Th2 function and the expression of allergic inflammation. Allergen-specific IgG$_4$ production is stimulated via IL-10, although its significance remains uncertain.

allergen-specific IgE antibody titres. One line of current research is focusing on finding more efficient ways of inducing allergen-specific T-regulatory cells.

SIT for venom anaphylaxis

Anaphylaxis to hymenoptera venom is relatively rare, but can be fatal and has a large impact on affected individuals and their quality of life. After a sting, venom-specific IgE antibodies can be found in 30–40% of adults for a few months, but these usually disappear by six months after the sting. Some individuals react more vigorously with high concentrations of venom-specific antibodies, which may persist for many years without further exposure to stings. This group of patients are at risk of anaphylaxis to subsequent stings and a small number die from anaphylaxis each year: a figure of 10-20 deaths per year in the USA has been cited. Before offering venom immunotherapy, physicians need to assess the patient carefully and take into account both the natural history of venom allergy and the risk of re-exposure |7|. Patients who have experienced systemic symptoms after a sting are at much greater risk of anaphylaxis on subsequent stings, as compared to patients who have only had large local reactions. The frequency of systemic reactions to stings in children and adults with a history of large local reactions is about 5–10%, whereas the risk in patients with a previous systemic reaction is between 30 and 70%. In general, there is a lower risk of repeated systemic reactions in children, and in those with a history of milder reactions. In adults the risk of systemic reaction to field stings diminishes over 10–20 years towards 15–30% but probably does not return to the background prevalence in the general population (3%). In contrast, the risk of anaphylaxis to stings in children with a history of cutaneous systemic reactions is less than 5%. At present there is no test that can accurately predict the outcome of the next sting. Live sting challenges have been used for research purposes but are not sufficiently definitive or acceptable for use in clinical practice. Unfortunately, patients can still occasionally react to field stings even if they tolerate a sting challenge under laboratory conditions. In deciding whether to recommend venom SIT, account needs to be taken of factors that alter the likelihood of future stings. Wasp (or yellow jacket) stings are an occupational hazard for bakers, gardeners, outdoor caterers and greengrocers, while honeybee stings are much commoner in beekeepers, their families and neighbours.

Immunization with venom accelerates the process of risk reduction and confers rapid protection against both field and laboratory stings. Severe reactions are very unlikely after completing venom SIT but a low risk of a mild systemic reaction (about 10%) seems to remain for many years. In children, the chance of a sting-induced systemic reaction after SIT is less than 5% and protection seems to last for at least 20 years after completing the course. These percentages need to be considered carefully when deciding whether to offer venom SIT patients injectable epinephrine or other anti-allergic medication for use in the event of a sting during and after therapy.

SIT for allergic rhinitis

Allergic rhinitis is the principal indication for SIT. As with other uses of SIT, appropriate patient selection is essential. The allergic basis of the rhinitis should be carefully assessed on history and skin or blood tests for IgE, while other relevant causes should be excluded. Specific nasal sensitivity to allergens is not assessed in routine clinical practice but may be useful in clinical trials.

The effectiveness of SIT in seasonal allergic rhinitis has been confirmed in many trials, using grass, ragweed and birch pollen. Moreover, SIT has been shown to be clinically effective even in patients with severe seasonal rhinitis that is resistant to conventional drug therapy |8|. The mean level of efficacy in double-blind, placebo-controlled studies is a reduction in symptom scores and rescue medication of around 30–40% over and above that which is achievable with drug therapy alone. Large-scale trials have not been done with multiple allergen SIT of the type widely practised in the US. This is partly because the treatment is individualized, whereas the European single allergen vaccines are easier to study in large groups of patients. Importantly, patients who are multiply sensitized but have grass pollen allergy as their main problem will respond at least as well to grass pollen desensitization as those who are monosensitized to grass pollen (Fig. 13.2). Relatively limited data are available from clinical trials regarding the long-term efficacy of SIT for allergic rhinitis, but the effects last for at least three years after discontinuing therapy |9|. Longer-term studies are difficult to conduct, but open studies and anecdotal clinical evidence suggest that some benefits can extend for as long as 10 years.

The benefits of SIT for perennial rhinitis are less well established than for seasonal rhinitis. In part this reflects the difficulty in determining whether allergy is responsible for perennial symptoms. For example, many people are sensitized to house

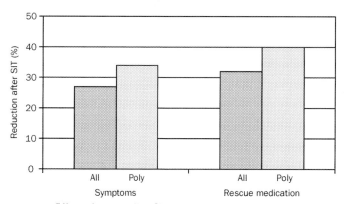

Fig. 13.2 Effect of grass pollen SIT on symptom scores and medication use in a clinical trial of 410 subjects. Percentage reduction in symptom and medication scores during pollen season shown for whole group (all) and polysensitized subjects (poly) (data adapted with permission from |8|).

dust mite as judged by skin tests, but by no means all have symptoms. Moreover, there are several other causes of perennial rhinitis including vasomotor instability, infection, aspirin sensitivity etc. Nevertheless, clinical trials have shown a definite benefit in perennial rhinitis in appropriately selected subjects |10|. SIT definitely works in rhinitis due to allergy to cats, but there is less evidence in dog allergy. In part this may reflect the difference in persistence of cat allergens in the environment, and the high level of endotoxin found in homes with dogs |11|.

The risks and cost-effectiveness of SIT need to be assessed in each individual patient. Mild disease can often be controlled with simple therapies, but about 60% of patients with seasonal allergic rhinitis report inadequate symptom control, even when taking maximal doses of antihistamines and intranasal steroids. Others experience nosebleeds from intranasal steroids and drowsiness from antihistamines. Moreover, we are now more aware of the adverse effects of rhinitis and antihistamines on patients' quality of life. SIT offers a logical approach to dealing with the underlying problem and dealing definitively with the condition rather than simply suppressing it.

SIT for asthma

Immunotherapy is widely used to treat allergic asthma in some parts of the world, but is not regarded as an appropriate treatment for asthma in the UK. This difference of opinion reflects UK experience prior to 1986 when a number of severe adverse reactions were encountered, including a small number of fatalities. This has been blamed partly on poor patient selection and partly on deficiencies in managing the adverse events, but patients with asthma do appear to be at a higher risk of adverse reactions to SIT |11,12|. Current drug therapies for asthma aim to suppress the airways inflammation and smooth muscle contraction that are characteristic features of asthma. None of these treatments are curative and asthma recurs rapidly on ceasing treatment. Moreover, none of the current drug therapies is directed against agents that might cause asthma. Allergen avoidance has been proposed as a potentially useful manoeuvre in those with allergic asthma, but while asthma control can be improved by extreme forms of allergen avoidance (e.g. admission to hospital, sending children to holiday homes at altitude), there is little evidence that similar benefits can be achieved using the type of allergen avoidance that can be achieved in suburban homes. There is thus scope for improving asthma care and for identifying allergen-specific therapies. SIT offers the possibility of deviating the immune response away from the allergic pattern and towards a more protective or less damaging response, but its place still needs to be confirmed in appropriate clinical trials with current allergen extracts.

The efficacy of SIT in adult asthma has been assessed in many trials over the last 50 years. Many of these studies are difficult to interpret, mainly because of poor study design. Most were small, many were not placebo-controlled and they were often open or single-blind. A recent meta-analysis identified 75 papers published between 1954 and 2001. Thirty-six of these were for mite allergy, 20 for pollen allergy, ten for animal dander allergy, 2 for mould allergy, 1 for latex allergy and 6 used combinations of allergens. Concealment of allocation was adequate in only 15 trials. A wide variety of different measurements were made, which makes it difficult to reach a firm view on the overall effectiveness of SIT. Symptom scores improved in the treated groups; exacerbations were reduced in frequency—it was necessary to treat four patients to prevent one exacerbation and to treat five to prevent one from needing an increase in medication |13|. In laboratory tests, SIT reduced the airways response to inhalation of specific allergen and also improved non-specific bronchial reactivity. However, the role of allergic sensitization in ongoing asthma is less clear than for allergic rhinitis, and this leaves residual questions about the wisdom of using a therapy targeted at specific allergens.

The majority of clinical trials of SIT for asthma have compared SIT either with untreated historical controls or with a matched placebo-treated group. To date, the effectiveness of SIT in asthma has rarely been compared with conventional management (avoidance measures and inhaled or oral anti-asthma drugs). One recent study assessed US-style multiple allergen SIT in asthmatic children receiving conventional drug therapy and found no additional benefit in patients who were already receiving optimal drug therapy |14|. There are some flaws in the design of this study and further work of this type is urgently needed.

Effects of SIT on the natural history of allergic disease

A proportion of patients with allergic rhinitis go on to develop asthma each year. The annual rate of progression has been estimated at 5% |15| but this is not universally accepted. It has been suggested that SIT may prevent or modify the development of asthma in children with allergic rhinitis who have not yet developed asthma. In a key study of 205 children aged 6–14, without previously diagnosed asthma, SIT for birch or grass pollen allergy was given in an open randomized design. Three years after completing treatment, 45% of the untreated group had developed asthma while only 26% of the treated group had asthma. These results have been sustained out to seven years after completing therapy. Thus four children had to be treated to prevent one case of asthma |16|. An early open study suggested that SIT may also modify the progression of established asthma |12|. About 70% of treated children lost their asthma after four years' therapy, compared to about 19% of untreated controls. The proportion of children whose asthma was severe at age 16 was also much lower in the treated group |12|. By modern standards, this study was not well designed, and it needs repeating with modern SIT extracts in an up-to-date trial design.

SIT can also prevent the development of new allergic sensitizations |10|. In both open and double-blind studies, monosensitized children were much less likely to acquire new sensitivities, as shown by skin tests, than comparable control groups. In terms of mechanism, it seems unlikely that SIT with house dust mite could directly affect B cells that recognize cat or grass pollen epitopes, but by treating the dust mite allergy, SIT may reduce nasal inflammation and hence reduce the likelihood of exposure to other allergens proceeding to sensitization. There is as yet no evidence to support claims that SIT is different from drug therapy in terms of influencing the evolution of established asthma. In part this reflects the reluctance of physicians to use SIT to treat severe asthma. Studies that have investigated withdrawal of therapy have found fairly rapid recurrence of asthma symptoms although rhinitis symptoms seem to show much more sustained relief after SIT.

Safety

The main factor preventing the wider adoption of standard SIT is the risk of serious adverse reactions. SIT is generally safe in patients who do not have asthma, but significant numbers of deaths have been reported in the UK and the US, among patients with unstable asthma treated by SIT |17|. The incidence of systemic reactions in patients receiving SIT for asthma varies between 5% and 35% in different series. This compares with a rate of serious systemic reactions in patients with rhinitis of about 1 in 500 injections. Systemic reactions are much more likely if the patient has an intercurrent viral illness so doses should be delayed if the patient is unwell or has any signs of active asthma.

In general, immunomodulatory treatments should not be used in patients with autoimmune disorders or malignant disease. While there is no hard evidence that SIT is actually harmful, it seems unwise to manipulate the immune system in such patients, not least because of the risk that spontaneous and unrelated variations in the autoimmune disorder or cancer may be blamed on SIT. Other contraindications to SIT include significant coexistent cardiac disease, and treatment with β-blockers. Although these patients are not at increased risk of adverse reactions, their physiological response to anaphylaxis will be impaired, and they may not respond to epinephrine.

Alternative forms of immunotherapy

While conventional SIT is effective, it is by no means perfect. First, most patients only achieve partial remission, second the course of treatment is long and requires frequent attendance at the clinic, and third there are the safety issues discussed above. Over the past 15 years, there has been an increasing interest in sublingual immunotherapy, in which allergen extracts are placed under the tongue. It is well established that allergens applied to the mucosal surface are handled differently from allergens given by injection, leading to a form of immunological tolerance. In animal models IgE responses to allergens can be reduced or prevented by oral administration of allergen. The precise mechanism of 'oral tolerance' remains unclear, but the route of allergen processing and presentation appears to be critical in determining the subsequent T cell response. In mice, locally administered allergen is taken up by mucosal dendritic cells and then presented to T cells together with IL-12, biasing the response towards a Th1 profile and away from the pro-IgE Th2 profile. It is less clear whether this mechanism can suppress established allergic responses. In contrast to the animal models, the immunological response to SLIT in human studies is relatively modest. Some changes have been found in skin sensitivity but most studies have not reported any change in serum concentrations of allergen-specific IgE or IgG.

After initial scepticism, a considerable amount of evidence has accumulated that sublingual immunotherapy (SLIT) can be effective, with up to 30–40% reductions in symptom scores and rescue medication usage in seasonal allergic rhinitis |18|. Some treatment regimes involve a build-up phase but others start immediately with the full maintenance dose. A recent meta-analysis of SLIT found 22 studies in which 979 patients received active therapy. While many of these studies were small and inconclusive, the combined results indicate that SLIT is indeed effective, with an estimated power of about two-thirds of that seen in comparable studies of injection SIT. Local side-effects were common, but well tolerated. Systemic side-effects were relatively rare, and none of the side-effects were judged to be life-threatening. Since the publication of that meta-analysis, several large trials have been conducted with a grass pollen tablet, which showed a similar level of efficacy. These trials contain more patients than all the earlier studies that were considered in the meta-analysis, and will therefore dominate any future combined assessment of efficacy. Only limited data are available in children, but on present information sublingual immunotherapy would appear to be less effective in children than in adults. SLIT is used routinely in some parts of Europe (especially Italy and France, and increasingly in Germany), but the doses and regimes being prescribed are often different from those used in the clinical trials. Overall, SLIT is likely to widen the scope of SIT and bring in additional prescribers. As with all forms of immunotherapy, patient selection will be the key to ensuring that therapy is targeted to those who are likely to benefit from it.

Future directions

Further improvements in SIT should be possible. Conventional SIT vaccines could be improved through using recombinant allergens, which would allow better standardization, as well as opening the possibility of individualized vaccines for patients with unusual patterns of reactivity. Regulatory and licensing frameworks may present some difficulty for this approach, as under current rules each individual component has to be tested separately for efficacy and safety, as well as any mixtures. Initial trials with cocktails of recombinant allergens have shown efficacy |19|, but it has not yet reached a stage where recombinant SIT vaccines can be compared with conventional allergen extracts.

Another alternative approach with standard extracts is to inject the allergens directly into lymph nodes, under ultrasound guidance. Since less than 1% of injected allergen reaches the lymphatic system after subcutaneous injection, it should be possible to achieve the same clinical effect by giving about 1% of the standard SIT dose. Initial trials have shown comparable immunological and clinical efficacy with just three intranodal injections [20], and further follow-up data are eagerly awaited.

Since the epitopes recognized by IgE molecules are three-dimensional while T cell epitopes are short linear peptide sequences, it is possible to modify allergens or create peptide fragments, which modulate T cells without risking anaphylaxis. Cross-linking allergen proteins with aldehydes reduces their allergenicity while preserving their T cell reactivity. Such allergoids have been shown to be effective in rhinitis due to grass pollen or house dust mite [21]. This approach can also be combined with new adjuvants, for example, the monophosphoryl lipid A derived from salmonella endotoxin, which activates toll-like receptor (TLR)-4 and promotes a Th1-pattern response to the injected allergen [22]. Another alternative adjuvant uses CpG oligodeoxynucleotides (ODN), which stimulate TLR-9. In humans, coupling ragweed allergen to CpG-ODN reduces its IgE binding and deviates the subsequent response towards a Th1-pattern [23]. Initial trials were promising but this has not been sustained in subsequent larger-scale studies [24].

Short peptide sequences can also be used as vaccines that are not recognized by IgE antibodies [25]. Peptide vaccines can either be natural sequences or altered peptide ligands. If high doses of natural peptides are given, these deceive the T cell into high-dose tolerance [26]. Altered peptide ligands induce anergy by providing an incomplete activation signal. Both approaches will be affected by the MHC type of the individual undergoing treatment. By sequential alteration of peptides from *Dermatophagoides pteronyssinus*, it is possible to suppress proliferation of T cell clones recognizing native peptides from the same source, as well as suppressing their expression of CD40 ligand and their production of IL-4, IL-5 and IFN-γ. These anergic T cells do not provide help for B cells to switching class to IgE, and importantly this anergy cannot be reversed by providing exogenous IL-4. In humans, the main focus has been on cat allergen (Fel d 1) peptides, which can reduce the level of symptoms on exposure to cat dander [27]. Similar work has also been reported with peptides of phospholipase A2 (PLA2—a major allergen in bee venom). However, peptide vaccines have not yet shown any greater efficacy than conventional vaccines.

A completely different concept is the use of monoclonal antibodies directed against IgE to reduce the risk of side-effects, and perhaps to increase efficacy. When anti-IgE was given in combination with conventional SIT, the effects were additive against seasonal allergic rhinitis [28]. In theory, concurrent administration of anti-IgE should modify the fate of injected allergen, by preventing IgE-facilitated antigen presentation and altering the response of effector cells. However, for the time being, the high cost of anti-IgE and the need for regular injection are likely to limit its use to patients with severe allergic disease that cannot be managed by other means.

Conclusion

SIT is a useful treatment for allergic rhinitis and for venom hypersensitivity; it can be used in allergic asthma but the risks are higher and careful patient selection is essential. When used appropriately, SIT is effective and acceptably safe, but care is needed to recognize and treat adverse reactions. Appropriate training of allergists and SIT clinic support staff is essential. Despite a century of use, the precise mechanisms of action of SIT remain uncertain. Current emphasis on the role of T regulatory cells is leading to renewed attempts to simplify SIT regimes and reduce its risks. Future directions in SIT include the development of vaccines that are better standardized, and the use of recombinant allergens, both of which should improve the safety profile of SIT. In parallel, the use of better adjuvants may allow us to improve the efficiency and scope of SIT. This might allow increased efficacy in those who already respond, to achieve efficacy in those who do not currently respond at all, or to achieve current levels of efficacy and durability with shorter courses or lower doses. In the longer term, there is a need for more general immunomodulatory therapies, which would be particularly advantageous for those patients sensitized to multiple allergens.

References

1. Freeman J. Vaccination against hay fever: report of results during the first three years. *Lancet* 1914; 1: 1178.

2. Creticos P, Van Metre TE, Mardiney MR, *et al.* Dose-response of IgE and IgG antibodies during ragweed immunotherapy. *J Allergy Clin Immunol* 1984; 73: 94–104.

3. Iliopoulos O, Proud D, Adkinson NF, *et al.* Effects of immunotherapy on the early, late and rechallenge nasal reaction to provocation with allergen: changes in inflammatory mediators and cells. *J Allergy Clin Immunol* 1991; 87: 855–66.

4. Durham SR, Ying S, Varney VA, *et al.* Grass pollen immunotherapy inhibits allergen-induced infiltration of CD4+ T-lymphocytes and eosinophils in the nasal mucosa and increases the number of cells expressing mRNA for interferon-gamma. *J Allergy Clin Immunol* 1996; 97: 1356–65.

5. Ebner C, Siemann U, Bohle B, *et al.* Immunological changes during specific immunotherapy of grass pollen allergy: reduced lymphoproliferative responses to allergen and shift from Th2 to Th1 in T-cell clones specific for Phl p1, a major grass pollen allergen. *Clin Exp Allergy* 1997; 27: 1007–15.

6. Jutel M, Akdis M, Blaser K, Akdis CA. Mechanisms of allergen specific immunotherapy – T-cell tolerance and more. *Allergy* 2006; 61: 796–807.

7. Golden DB, Kagey-Sobotka A, Norman PS, *et al.* Outcomes of allergy to insect stings in children, with and without venom immunotherapy. *N Engl J Med* 2004; 351: 668–74.

8. Frew AJ, Powell RM, Corrigan CJ, Durham SR. Efficacy and safety of specific immunotherapy with SQ allergen extract in treatment-resistant seasonal allergic rhinoconjunctivitis. *J Allergy Clin Immunol* 2006; 117: 319–25.

9. Durham SR, Walker SM, Varga EM, *et al.* Long-term clinical efficacy of grass pollen immunotherapy. *N Engl J Med* 1999; 341: 468–75.

10. Bousquet J, Lockey RF, Malling H-J. Allergen immunotherapy: therapeutic vaccines for allergic diseases. *J Allergy Clin Immunol* 1998; 102: 558–62.

11. Varney VA, Edwards J, Tabbah K, *et al.* Clinical efficacy of specific immunotherapy to cat dander: a double blind placebo controlled trial. *Clin Exp Allergy* 1997; 27: 860–7.

12. Johnstone DE, Dutton A. The value of hypo-sensitization therapy for bronchial asthma in children – a 14-year study. *Pediatrics* 1968; **42**: 793–802.

13. Abramson MJ, Puy RM, Weiner JM. Allergen immunotherapy for asthma. *Cochrane Database Syst Rev* 2003; **4**: CD001186.

14. Adkinson NF, Eggleston PA, Eney D, *et al.* A controlled trial of immunotherapy in allergic children. *N Engl J Med* 1997; **336**: 324–31.

15. Horak F. Manifestation of allergic rhinitis in latent sensitised patients. A prospective study. *Arch Otorhinolaryngol* 1985; **242**: 242–9.

16. Niggemann B, Jacobsen L, Dreborg S, *et al.* Five-year follow-up on the PAT study: specific immunotherapy and long-term prevention of asthma in children. *Allergy* 2006; **61**: 855–9.

17. Bernstein DI, Wanner M, Borish L, Liss GM. Twelve-year survey of fatal reactions to allergen injections and skin testing: 1990–2001. *J Allergy Clin Immunol* 2004; **113**: 1129–36.

18. Wilson DR, Lima MT, Durham SR. Sublingual immunotherapy for allergic rhinitis: systematic review and meta-analysis. *Allergy* 2005; **60**: 4–12.

19. Jutel M, Jaeger L, Suck R, *et al.* Allergen-specific immunotherapy with recombinant grass pollen allergens. *J Allergy Clin Immunol* 2005; **116**: 608–13.

20. Senti G, Prinz-Vavricka B, Erdmann I, *et al.* Intralymphatic allergen administration renders specific immunotherapy shorter and safer. *Allergy* 2007; **62**(S83): 34.

21. Corrigan CJ, Kettner J, Doemer C, *et al.* Efficacy and safety of preseasonal-specific immunotherapy with an aluminium-adsorbed six-grass pollen allergoid. *Allergy* 2005; **60**: 801–7.

22. Puggioni F, Durham SR, Francis JN. Monphosphoryl Lipid A (MPL) promotes allergen-induced immune deviation in favour of Th1 responses. *Allergy* 2005; **60**: 678–84.

23. Tighe H, Takabayashi K, Schwartz D, *et al.* Conjugation of immunostimulatory DNA to the short ragweed allergen Amb a1 enhances its immunogenicity and reduces its allergenicity. *J Allergy Clin Immunol* 2000; **106**: 124–34.

24. Creticos PS, Schroeder JT, Hamilton RG, *et al.* Immunotherapy with a ragweed-TLR9-agonist vaccine for allergic rhinitis. *N Engl J Med* 2006; **355**: 1445–55.

25. Larche M. Peptide immunotherapy. *Immunol Allergy Clin North Am* 2006; **26**: 321–32.

26. O'Hehir RE, Yssel H, Verma S, *et al.* Clonal analysis of differential lymphokine production in peptide and superantigen-induced T-cell anergy. *Int Immunol* 1991; **3**: 819–26.

27. Norman PS, Ohman JL, Long AA, *et al.* Treatment of cat allergy with T-cell reactive peptides. *Am J Respir Crit Care Med* 1996; **154**: 1623–8.

28. Rolinck-Werninghaus C, Hamelmann E, Keil T, *et al.* The co-seasonal application of anti-IgE after preseasonal specific immunotherapy decreases ocular and nasal symptom scores and rescue medication use in grass pollen allergic children. *Allergy* 2004; **59**: 973–9.

14

Allergen avoidance

ADNAN CUSTOVIC

KEY POINTS

The general consensus is that allergen avoidance should lead to an improvement of symptoms in allergic patients. However, for adult asthma there is little evidence to support the use of simple physical or chemical methods as single interventions to control dust mite or pet allergen levels. In contrast, several trials of allergen-impermeable bed encasings and more comprehensive environmental interventions in asthmatic children reported benefits. For rhinitis and eczema, the most recent well-designed studies on single mite avoidance measures failed to demonstrate a clear clinical benefit. Until unequivocal evidence from definitive trials for all age groups and all allergens is available, the following should be used as a guide for a pragmatic approach to allergen avoidance:

1. Use a comprehensive environmental intervention to achieve as great a reduction in allergen exposure as possible.

2. Tailor the intervention to the patient's sensitization and exposure status.

3. If unable to assess the exposure, use the level of allergen-specific IgE antibodies or the size of skin test weal as an indicator.

4. Start the intervention as early in the natural history of the disease as possible.

Introduction

Sensitization to inhalant allergens is a major risk factor for asthma, rhinitis and eczema [1]. Amongst patients with allergic disease, personal exposure to high levels of allergens to which they are sensitized causes exacerbation of symptoms and worsening of the underlying inflammatory process [2–9]. In some sensitized individuals complete cessation of exposure may improve symptoms. For example, patients with hay fever have no symptoms in the absence of pollen, and in occupational asthma complete cessation of exposure to the causal allergen may be associated with an improvement in symptoms and occasionally cure [10]. Similarly, removal of allergic asthmatics to the low allergen environment of hospitals [11] or high altitude sanatoria |12,13| reduces asthma severity in a proportion of patients. However, studies of occupational asthma also suggest that the resolution of symptoms occurs only if complete cessation of exposure is achieved early in the course of disease |14| (i.e. if exposure continues for a prolonged period of time, removal may not result in the symptomatic improvement, and the asthmatic process appears to become self-perpetuating); the failure to improve after cessation of exposure is associated with airway inflammation at follow-up |15|. The duration of this 'window of opportunity' appears to differ markedly between different individuals.

Based on these observations, the guiding principles of allergen avoidance in the management of allergic disease are:

- Achieve major reduction in exposure.
- Commence the intervention early in the natural history of the disease.
- Identify patients who are likely to benefit from the intervention.

How to achieve a major reduction in exposure

Dust mites

Depending on the site of contamination, different measures are used to reduce mite allergens in the home (Table 14.1; reviewed in references |16–21|).

Bed and bedding

Cover the mattress, duvet and pillows with encasings that are impermeable to mite allergens. Various covers differ markedly in their ability to reduce mite exposure, and the most effective solution is covers made of finely woven fabrics |22|. Bedding should be washed regularly (e.g. once a week). Although low temperature washing removes allergen, dust mites can survive it. The bedding should therefore be washed in a hot cycle (above 55°C) if possible.

Carpets and upholstered furnishings

Replace carpets with hard floor coverings (e.g. wooden or linoleum floor). If carpets remain in place, several methods have been suggested (e.g. exposing carpets to direct strong sunlight |18|, steam cleaning |23|, use of acaricides or tannic acid, freezing with liquid nitrogen etc.). However, all of these methods are only partially effective.

Upholstered furniture may be designed with an impermeable barrier below the fabric cover; alternatively, use leather covers.

Other sources of mite allergen exposure

Replace fabric curtains with Venetian blinds; freeze soft toys, then wash to remove allergens and dead mites.

Controlling humidity

Although high levels of humidity are required for mite survival and growth, this approach critically depends on the local climate and housing design. Central

Table 14.1   Measures for reducing dust mite, pet, fungal and cockroach allergen levels

House dust mite

Bed and bedding

   Encase mattress, pillow and quilt in allergen impermeable covers (preferably finely-woven fabric)

   Wash bedding weekly. Use hot cycle (55–60°C) if possible

Replace carpets with hard flooring

Minimize upholstered furniture/replace with leather furniture

Replace curtains with blinds

Minimize dust accumulating objects; keep in closed cupboards

Remove soft toys (if impossible, hot wash/freeze soft toys)

Reduce indoor humidity if possible

Cat / dog

Remove cat/dog from the home

Fungi

Reduce indoor humidity

HEPA air filters in main living areas and bedrooms

Fungicides on heavily contaminated surfaces

Minimize upholstered furniture

Replace carpets with hard flooring (e.g. linoleum or wood)

Ensure regular inspection of heating and air conditioning units to prevent contamination

Cockroaches

Remove food and water sources

Use suitable pesticide in bait form

Remove all dead carcasses and frass

Wash down all surfaces, floors and walls with detergent

Seal cracks in walls and plaster work to reduce further access

Wash all bedding, clothing and curtains

mechanical ventilation heat recovery units and portable dehumidifiers are more effective in reducing indoor humidity in the geographical areas where outdoor humidity is low and home insulation is good, but have not proved effective in areas in which outdoor humidity is high and homes are poorly insulated |**24,25**|. It is important to have in mind that reducing relative humidity of the air alone may not be sufficient to effectively reduce humidity in the mite microhabitats (e.g. in the mattress or deep within carpets) |**25,26**|.

Comprehensive environmental control

Major reduction in personal exposure can only be achieved by a comprehensive strategy combining the most effective measures appropriate for the individual patient, household and geographical area; simple, single measures are unlikely to attain the desired effect. A stringent comprehensive environmental control regime can achieve and maintain a low allergen environment over a prolonged period of time |27|, but is costly and some patients may consider it unacceptable.

Pet allergen avoidance measures

The only way to effectively reduce exposure to cat or dog allergen is not to have one in the home |16|. Even after permanent removal of the pet, allergen levels persist in the home environment for long periods (months to years) |28|.

Controlling pet allergen levels with pet in situ

Air cleaning units with high efficiency particulate arrest (HEPA) filters can reduce the airborne concentration of cat and dog allergens in homes with pets |29|, but the level of reduction in inhaled allergen is relatively small |30|.

Pet washing has been suggested as a practical method to reduce allergen levels |31–33|, but it is unlikely that a modest reduction in allergen exposure achieved by cat and dog washing translates into clinical benefit.

Vacuum cleaners with built-in HEPA filters and double thickness bags do not leak pet allergens in the experimental chamber. However, a real-life study which monitored personal exposure during vacuum cleaning demonstrated an increase in the amount of cat allergen inhaled while using high-efficiency vacuum cleaners |34|. Since the measures to control pet allergen levels with the pet in the home are relatively ineffective, pet removal remains the only advice to pet-sensitized patients who experience symptoms on exposure.

Cockroach allergen reduction

Physical and chemical procedures can be used to control cockroach populations in infested houses |35–37|. Household cleaning is an essential adjunct to successful allergen removal. Sealing cracks and holes in plasterwork and floors can restrict cockroach access. Several pesticides are available, either in a gel or bait form. Before applying insecticide, all possible food sources should be removed; further cleaning should be delayed for a week to avoid removal of insecticides.

Allergen avoidance in the treatment of allergic disease

Attempts to ascertain the clinical benefits of allergen control measures in patients' homes have provided conflicting results (for review, see references |16,19–21,38–40|. The controversy is not whether allergen avoidance works (as outlined previously, in certain situations complete cessation of exposure may be of benefit); the practical questions are how to achieve a sufficient real-life reduction in personal inhaled allergen exposure which can be translated into clinical benefit and how to identify patients who would benefit from an *effective* intervention.

Mite allergen avoidance

The evidence whether the use of measures mentioned in the previous section has any impact on asthma or rhinitis in real life remains equivocal.

Systematic reviews

Updates of the Cochrane meta-analysis of dust mite avoidance studies (the most recent one included 3002 patients from 54 trials |41|) reported no effect of the interventions, and concluded that current methods of mite allergen avoidance should not be recommended to mite-sensitive asthmatics (Fig. 14.1) |41,42|. The authors suggested that the most likely explanation for the lack of clinical effect is that the avoidance methods used in the reviewed studies did not sufficiently reduce mite allergen levels (pointing out that 'it seems inherently implausible to suggest that complete removal of a major provoking agent would be ineffective') |42|. Furthermore, the review emphasized that mite-sensitive asthmatics are usually sensitized to other allergens, raising the question whether focusing on one allergen is the right approach to the environmental control.

Another review of the clinical trials registered by the Cochrane Collaboration and Cochrane Airways Group attempted to study the effect of home dehumidification on asthma control |43|. Only one trial, which compared mechanical ventilation with or without high-efficiency vacuum cleaners, met the inclusion criteria,

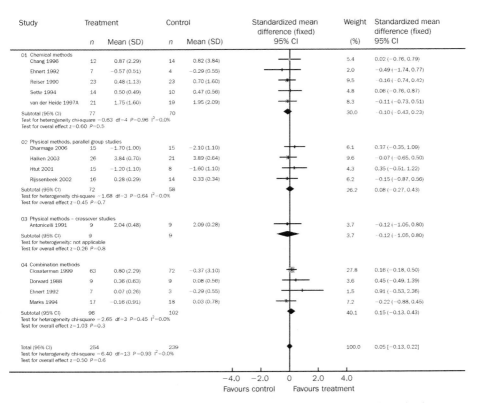

Fig. 14.1 House dust mite control measures for asthma, comparing house dust mite reduction versus control: outcome measure = PC_{20} (provocative concentration for 20% fall in FEV_1) (with permission from |41|).

reflecting poor quality of the studies in this area |44|. The trial failed to show any clinical benefit (however, these findings are inconclusive due to the open design and the small sample size).

Results of a Cochrane systematic review of mite avoidance measures in the management of perennial allergic rhinitis mirror the findings of the meta-analysis in asthma—there was little evidence that a reduction in mite exposure by using physical or chemical measures leads to a sustained improvement in disease control |45|. However, in contrast to the large number of patients included in the meta-analysis of asthma studies, only four small trials satisfied the inclusion criteria of the rhinitis systematic review; furthermore, all of these were judged to be of poor quality. Thus, at the time that the systemic review was carried out, in 2001, published trials had been small and of poor methodological quality, making it impossible to propose any definitive recommendations on the role of mite avoidance measures in the management of mite-sensitive perennial allergic rhinitis |45|.

Systematic review on the effect of mite avoidance measures in patients with eczema has not as yet been carried out.

Beyond systematic review

Adult asthma

Three studies investigating mite avoidance in the treatment of asthma in adults, which demonstrated a clinical benefit, have been much cited as proof that mite allergen avoidance should be a part of the management of mite-sensitive patients |46–48|. However, these studies were of a very different design, used markedly different interventions and recruited a total of only 98 mite-allergic patients in the three studies combined. In contrast, the largest randomized, double-blind, placebo-controlled trial on the effectiveness of mite-impermeable bed covers as a single intervention, involving over 1000 adult asthmatics, found no benefits of the intervention in any of the primary or secondary outcome measures (lung function, treatment requirements, symptoms scores, quality of life, etc.) (Fig. 14.2) |49|. Furthermore, in this study, the *post hoc* analysis of the subgroup of 130 patients who would be expected to benefit most from the intervention (by virtue of having high mite-specific IgE and high baseline mite allergen exposure) showed no differences in any of the outcomes between the active and placebo groups. This was confirmed by a smaller study of 55 mite-sensitized asthmatics who were exposed to high levels of dust mite allergen |50|. These two studies demonstrated convincingly that a single intervention with mite-impermeable covers for the mattress, duvet and pillows is ineffective in the management of asthma in adults, even in individuals who are highly allergic to dust mite *and* exposed to high levels of mite allergens.

Two further studies in the Netherlands investigated the effectiveness of mite-impermeable bed covers. The larger study which recruited 224 mite-sensitized patients with asthma and/or rhinitis and/or eczema, showed no effect of the intervention on the quality of life |51|. In contrast, a small study of 52 mite-sensitized asthmatics suggested some improvement in peak expiratory flow rate (PEFR) in the active group, despite a very short intervention period (9 weeks) |52|.

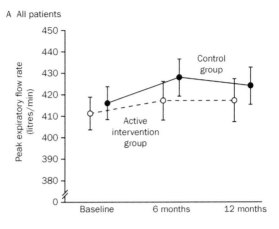

A All patients

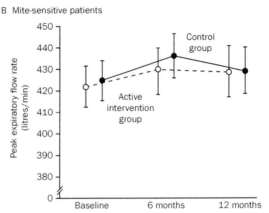

B Mite-sensitive patients

Fig. 14.2 No effect of covering mattress, pillow and quilt with allergen impermeable covers amongst adults with asthma.
Mean morning peak expiratory flow rate in the active intervention and control groups at baseline, 6 months, and 12 months among all patients (Panel A) and among mite-sensitive patients (Panel B) (with permission from |49|).

Asthma in children

Several studies in children with asthma have suggested that simple allergen avoidance measures may improve airway reactivity |53| and lung function |54|, reduce acute emergency room visits |55| or reduce inhaled corticosteroid dose |56| amongst mite-sensitized patients. A much more comprehensive approach to environmental control was adopted by the largest study on the effectiveness of environmental manipulation in children (The Inner-City Asthma Study). This study adopted a wide-ranging intervention |57|. The home environment was evaluated at the start of the study (including measurement of indoor allergen), and the intervention was tailored using information on the children's sensitization and exposure status. The comprehensive intervention focused on the education of the parent/guardian and included advice on the reduction of passive smoke exposure if appropriate. Mattress and pillow encasings and a high-filtration vacuum cleaner were supplied to all homes and additional products required for the tailored intervention (e.g. air filters) were supplied free of charge. The study randomized 937 children aged 5–11 years with poorly controlled asthma and at least

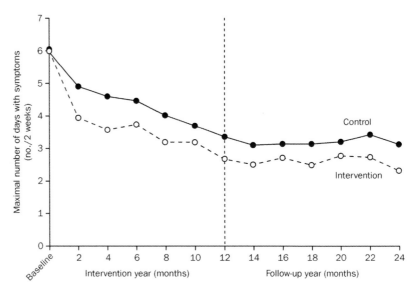

Fig. 14.3 Environmental control is effective amongst children with asthma. mean maximal number of days with symptoms for every two-week period before a follow-up assessment during the two years of the study. The difference between the environmental intervention and control group was significant in both the intervention year ($P < 0.001$) and the follow-up year ($P < 0.001$) (with permission from [57]).

one positive skin test living in inner city areas with high levels of poverty (more than half of the households had an annual income of less than US$ 15,000). The intervention resulted in significantly fewer days with asthma symptoms, which was apparent within 2 months and was sustained over the two-year study period (Fig. 14.3) [57]. The number of emergency room visits was also reduced. This important study demonstrated that allergen levels can be reduced in poor, inner city homes, and also estimated the size of the potential beneficial effect: an environmental intervention costing US$ 2000 per child was associated with an additional 34 symptom-free days over a two-year period, which is cost-effective within the context of the US healthcare system [58].

Rhinitis
The results of the large randomized, double-blind, placebo-controlled study of environmental control measures in patients with perennial allergic rhinitis were published subsequent to the systematic review [59]. In this study, 279 subjects sensitized to dust mite with a positive nasal challenge with mite extract were randomized to receive either active or placebo covers for their beds. There was no beneficial effect of the intervention in any of the outcome measures, although a marked decrease in symptom scores during the 12-month follow-up period was observed in both groups [59].

Eczema

Two recent studies reported no effect of mite-impermeable encasings on quality of life |51| or eczema symptom severity |60|. A further small study in 20 patients also failed to show any improvement in eczema activity with the use of mite-impermeable encasings and acaricides |61|. In contrast, an earlier study, which used a more comprehensive intervention including a combination of bed covers, acaricides and high-filtration vacuum cleaners for 6 months, demonstrated a significant improvement in the severity score and area affected by eczema in the intervention compared to the control group |62|. It is worth noting that approximately half of the participants were children.

Pet allergen avoidance

Clearly, a double-blind, randomized study of pet removal from the home is not feasible. Thus, with respect to the appropriate advice to pet-sensitized pet owners who experience symptoms upon exposure, the advice to remove the pet from the home is based upon common sense, rather than evidence obtained within the context of a rigorous trial. Based on clinical experience and observational studies |63|, it is generally accepted that amongst cat- or dog-allergic patients there should be a clinical improvement associated with the absence of contact with the pet. Given the patients' reluctance to remove their pet from the home, there have been several attempts to study the effect of various regimes of cat and dog allergen avoidance in pet-sensitized pet owners who live with a pet in the home. Of three such studies, two suggested small improvements in asthma-related outcomes |64,65|, but one did not |66|.

Systematic review

A recent systematic review by the Cochrane Airways Group emphasized the paucity of evidence on this topic |67|. The review aimed to determine the clinical efficacy of pet allergen control measures in the homes of patients with pet-allergic asthma by assessing only randomized, controlled trials, which compared an active intervention with control. Due to the limited amount of data available, no meta-analysis was possible. Only two small studies (22 and 35 participants respectively) met the inclusion criteria for the analysis |65,66|. The review concluded that both studies reported no significant differences between the active intervention and control on the primary and secondary outcomes, but that the available trials were too small to provide unequivocal evidence for or against the use of air filtration units in the management of pet-allergic asthma |67|. No trials of other allergen reduction measures (e.g. pet washing or pet removal) were identified. Thus, much larger studies are needed before any recommendations can be made.

How to identify patients who may benefit from effective intervention

In research studies and in clinical practice allergic sensitization is usually considered as a 'yes–no' phenomenon, i.e. individuals are labelled as either sensitized or not based on arbitrary cut-off points on either skin tests or measurement of specific serum IgE. However, recent data indicate that, both in asthma and rhinitis, IgE-mediated sensitization is not a simple 'all-or-nothing' phenomenon—the probability of wheezing, and rhinitis symptoms in childhood increases with increasing specific IgE antibody levels or the size of weal on skin tests |68,69|. Application of these findings to the choice of patients suitable for environmental control is unclear. It is possible that a high level of specific IgE antibodies or a large skin test weal may better identify individuals who may benefit from allergen avoidance, compared to just the presence of sensitization.

Environmental control in the prevention of allergic disease

Several recent review articles reviewed the topic of whether successful reduction in exposure to allergens early in life can reduce the risk of subsequent development of sensitization and symptoms of allergic disease |70–73|. The primary prevention studies are, by design, long-term and will take many years to report the definitive findings. Seven ongoing studies have published results to date. All studies focused on children at high risk of developing allergic disease, but the definition of 'high risk' differed between the studies. Furthermore, the studies used different allergen avoidance approaches (e.g. four of the studies included a dietary intervention in addition to dust mite allergen avoidance) and assessed different primary outcomes at different ages. Thus, the results are not directly comparable.

Isle of Wight Study
This study implemented an intervention designed to reduce exposure to inhalant allergens as part of a primary prevention programme |74–77|. At age 1 year there was a reduction in sensitization and in wheeze in the intervention group |74|, but at ages 2 |75| and 4 years |76| differences in respiratory symptoms failed to reach statistical significance. At age 8 years, sensitization to mite was reduced by more than 50% in the active group, despite modest reductions in mite allergen levels |77|. In the multivariate analysis, children in the active group were significantly less likely to have current wheeze, nocturnal cough, wheeze with bronchial hyper-responsiveness and atopy |77|. Overall, the combined intervention used in this study resulted in a marked reduction in atopic phenotypes during childhood |78|. However, it is impossible to ascertain which part of the intervention programme is responsible for the effect.

Canadian Asthma Primary Prevention Study
This study used a multifaceted intervention including measures to reduce exposure to inhalant and food allergens |79,80|. Mite allergens were significantly reduced in the parental bed throughout the study. At age 2 years, significantly fewer children had asthma in the intervention compared to the control group (16.3% vs 23%), but there was no difference in sensitization |79|. At age 7 years, the prevalence of physician-diagnosed asthma was significantly lower in the intervention group than in the control group (14.9% vs 23.0%), whilst there was no difference in allergic rhinitis, eczema, atopy and bronchial hyper-responsiveness |80|. In this

study, the multifaceted intervention programme appeared effective in reducing the prevalence of asthma in high-risk children at 7 years of age |80|.

The Study on the Prevention of Allergy in Children in Europe
This study directed the multifaceted intervention towards both inhalant and food allergens. Results reported at age 1 year showed a reduction in mite sensitization, but no difference in the proportion of children who had wheezed (21% both groups) |81|. However, at age 2 years, there was no difference between the control and intervention groups in the prevalence of mite sensitization (8.4% control vs 6.1% intervention) or asthma, eczema or rhinitis |82|. In this study, mite avoidance did not have a protective effect on the development of mite sensitization or symptomatic allergy in children at age 2 years.

The Childhood Asthma Prevention Study (CAPS)
This was a multicentre, parallel-group, randomized controlled trial in Sydney, Australia |83–85|. In this study, there was no effect of mite allergen avoidance on sensitization rates at age 18 months |83|. By age 3 years, significantly fewer children were mite-sensitized in the mite allergen avoidance group, but there was no effect on wheeze |84|. At age 5 years, the prevalence of eczema was higher in the active mite avoidance group (26% vs 19%), and mite sensitization and wheeze did not differ between the groups |85|.

The Primary Prevention of Asthma in Children Study
This study in the Netherlands reported that the incidence of asthma-like symptoms during the first two years of life was similar in the intervention and control groups |86|. Furthermore, there were no significant differences in the total and specific IgE |86|. The intervention used in this study was not effective in reducing asthma-like symptoms in high-risk children during the first two years of life, although some modest effect was observed at age 2 years |86|.

The Prevention and Incidence of Asthma and Mite Allergy Study
This was a multicentre, population-based cohort study with a nested intervention study amongst 810 high-risk infants |87,88|. At age 2 years, the only significant difference in clinical outcomes between groups was a reduction in night-time cough without a cold in the active group |87|. At age four years, sensitization and allergic symptoms were similar in both groups |88|. Thus, in this study, there was no effect of mite allergen-impermeable mattress covers on sensitization and symptoms suggestive of allergic disease at age four years.

The Manchester Asthma and Allergy Study (MAAS)
This was a whole population birth cohort study of more than 1000 children, with a nested intervention study in the high-risk group |89,90|. The comprehensive environmental control regime included the fitting of mite-proof encasings to the parental mattress, duvet and pillows by the 16th week of pregnancy, advice to hot wash bedding weekly at over 55°C, supply of a high-filtration vacuum cleaner and

Acarosan to apply to dust reservoirs with high mite allergen levels. Just before the birth of the child, a custom-made cot and carrycot mattresses (made of allergen-impermeable fabric) were supplied to the family, carpets were removed from the nursery and a vinyl cushion floor was fitted. A hot washable toy was also supplied. A significant and sustained reduction in exposure to mite, cat and dog allergens was observed in the homes of children in the active group |91|. At age one year, there was slightly more atopy in the intervention group compared with the control group (17% vs 14%), but this did not reach statistical significance |89|. Asthma-like symptoms were consistently lower in the intervention compared to the control group, and this reached statistical significance for attacks of severe wheeze with shortness of breath, prescribed medication for wheezy attacks, and wheeze after playing or exertion. No difference between the groups was seen for eczema.

However, counter-intuitive results were reported at the follow-up at age 3 years, suggesting that stringent environmental control was associated with *increased* risk of sensitization to dust mite, but *better* lung function |90|. Thus, in the MAAS, stringent environmental control was associated with increased risk of mite sensitization, but better lung function at age three years.

Conclusion

Although the general consensus is that environmental control should lead to an improvement of symptoms in susceptible patients, there is little evidence to support the use of simple physical or chemical methods as single interventions to control dust mite or pet allergen levels in adults with established asthma. It remains likely that a multifaceted intervention in appropriately selected patients could have beneficial effect, but this has not as yet been addressed in an adequately designed study.

In contrast, several trials of allergen-impermeable bed encasings and more comprehensive environmental interventions in asthmatic children reported benefits. The reasons for the apparent differences in response between adults and children are not clear. For rhinitis and eczema, the most recent well-designed studies on single mite avoidance measures failed to demonstrate a clear clinical benefit.

Until unequivocal evidence from definitive trials for all age groups and all allergens is available, the pragmatic approach to environmental control should incorporate the following recommendations:

● Single avoidance measures are ineffective.
● Use a comprehensive environmental intervention to achieve as great a reduction in personal exposure as possible.
● Tailor the intervention to the patient's sensitization and exposure status.
● If unable to assess the exposure, use the level of allergen-specific IgE antibodies or the size of skin test weal as an indicator.
● Start the intervention as early in the natural history of the disease as possible.

With respect to the use of environmental control in the prevention of allergic disease, although clinical outcomes reported from different intervention studies appear inconsistent, some of the results are encouraging. However, it is becoming clear from recent data that no single primary prevention strategy will be applicable to the whole population, but only to individuals within the population with a particular susceptibility |92|. With respect to the advice on prevention strategies using environmental control, we need to move away from the concept of blanket advice aimed at the whole population, to tailor-made individualized measures targeting individuals with specific susceptibilities who will benefit from a particular intervention |93|.

References

1. Simpson BM, Custovic A, Simpson A, *et al.* NAC Manchester Asthma and Allergy Study (NACMAAS): risk factors for asthma and allergic disorders in adults. *Clin Exp Allergy* 2001; **31**(3): 391–9.

2. Lowe LA, Woodcock A, Murray CS, *et al.* Lung function at age 3 years: effect of pet ownership and exposure to indoor allergens. *Arch Pediatr Adolesc Med* 2004; **158**(10): 996–1001.

3. Langley SJ, Goldthorpe S, Craven M, *et al.* Exposure and sensitization to indoor allergens: association with lung function, bronchial reactivity, and exhaled nitric oxide measures in asthma. *J Allergy Clin Immunol* 2003; **112**(2): 362–8.

4. Langley SJ, Goldthorpe S, Craven M, *et al.* Relationship between exposure to domestic allergens and bronchial hyperresponsiveness in non-sensitised, atopic asthmatic subjects. *Thorax* 2005; **60**(1): 17–21.

5. Rosenstreich DL, Eggleston P, Kattan M, *et al.* The role of cockroach allergy and exposure to cockroach allergen in causing morbidity among inner-city children with asthma. *N Engl J Med* 1997; **336**(19): 1356–63.

6. Tunnicliffe WS, Fletcher TJ, Hammond K, *et al.* Sensitivity and exposure to indoor allergens in adults with differing asthma severity. *Eur Respir J* 1999; **13**(3): 654–9.

7. Murray CS, Poletti G, Kebadze T, *et al.* Study of modifiable risk factors for asthma exacerbations: virus infection and allergen exposure increase the risk of asthma hospital admissions in children. *Thorax* 2006; **61**(5): 376–82.

8. Simpson A, Custovic A, Pipis S, *et al.* Exhaled nitric oxide, sensitization, and exposure to allergens in patients with asthma who are not taking inhaled steroids. *Am J Respir Crit Care Med* 1999; **160**(1): 45–9.

9. Custovic A, Taggart SC, Francis HC, *et al.* Exposure to house dust mite allergens and the clinical activity of asthma. *J Allergy Clin Immunol* 1996; **98**(1): 64–72.

10. Chan-Yeung M, Malo JL. Occupational asthma. *N Engl J Med* 1995; **333**(2): 107–12.

11. Platts-Mills TA, Tovey ER, Mitchell EB, *et al.* Reduction of bronchial hyperreactivity during prolonged allergen avoidance. *Lancet* 1982; **2**(8300): 675–8.

12. Peroni DG, Piacentini GL, Costella S, *et al.* Mite avoidance can reduce air trapping and airway inflammation in allergic asthmatic children. *Clin Exp Allergy* 2002; **32**(6): 850–5.

13. Milanese M, Peroni D, Costella S, *et al.* Improved bronchodilator effect of deep inhalation after allergen avoidance in asthmatic children. *J Allergy Clin Immunol* 2004; **114**(3): 505–11.

14. Malo JL, Cartier A, Ghezzo H, *et al.* Patterns of improvement in spirometry, bronchial hyperresponsiveness, and specific IgE antibody levels after cessation of exposure in occupational asthma caused by snow-crab

processing. *Am Rev Respir Dis* 1988; **138**(4): 807–12.

15. Maghni K, Lemiere C, Ghezzo H, *et al.* Airway inflammation after cessation of exposure to agents causing occupational asthma. *Am J Respir Crit Care Med* 2004; **169**(3): 367–72.

16. Custovic A, Murray CS, Gore RB, Woodcock A. Controlling indoor allergens. *Ann Allergy Asthma Immunol* 2002; **88**(5): 432–41; quiz 442–3, 529.

17. Tovey ER, Kemp AS. Allergens and allergy prevention: where to next? *J Allergy Clin Immunol* 2005; **116**(1): 119–21.

18. Tovey E, Marks G. Methods and effectiveness of environmental control. *J Allergy Clin Immunol* 1999; **103**(2 Pt 1): 179–91.

19. Custovic A, Simpson A, Chapman MD, Woodcock A. Allergen avoidance in the treatment of asthma and atopic disorders. *Thorax* 1998; **53**(1): 63–72.

20. Platts-Mills TA. Allergen avoidance. *J Allergy Clin Immunol* 2004; **113**(3): 388–91.

21. Gore RB, Custovic A. Is allergen avoidance effective? *Clin Exp Allergy* 2002; **32**(5): 662–6.

22. Mahakittikun V, Boitano JJ, Tovey E, *et al.* Mite penetration of different types of material claimed as mite proof by the Siriraj chamber method. *J Allergy Clin Immunol* 2006; **118**(5): 1164–8.

23. Cain G, Elderfield AJ, Green R, *et al.* The effect of dry heat on mite, cat, and dog allergens. *Allergy* 1998; **53**(12): 1213–15.

24. Custovic A, Taggart SC, Kennaugh JH, Woodcock A. Portable dehumidifiers in the control of house dust mites and mite allergens. *Clin Exp Allergy* 1995; **25**(4): 312–16.

25. Fletcher AM, Pickering CA, Custovic A, *et al.* Reduction in humidity as a method of controlling mites and mite allergens: the use of mechanical ventilation in British dometic dwellings. *Clin Exp Allergy* 1996; **26**(9): 1051–6.

26. Simpson A, Woodcock A, Custovic A. Housing characteristics and mite allergen levels: to humidity and beyond. *Clin Exp Allergy* 2001; **31**(6): 803–5.

27. Custovic A, Simpson BM, Simpson A, *et al.* Manchester Asthma and Allergy Study: low-allergen environment can be achieved and maintained during pregnancy and in early life. *J Allergy Clin Immunol* 2000; **105**(2 Pt 1): 252–8.

28. Wood RA, Chapman MD, Adkinson NF Jr, Eggleston PA. The effect of cat removal on allergen content in household-dust samples. *J Allergy Clin Immunol* 1989; **83**(4): 730–4.

29. Green R, Simpson A, Custovic A, *et al.* The effect of air filtration on airborne dog allergen. *Allergy* 1999; **54**(5): 484–8.

30. Gore RB, Bishop S, Durrell B, *et al.* Air filtration units in homes with cats: can they reduce personal exposure to cat allergen? *Clin Exp Allergy* 2003; **33**(6): 765–9.

31. de Blay F, Chapman MD, Platts-Mills TA. Airborne cat allergen (Fel d I). Environmental control with the cat in situ. *Am Rev Respir Dis* 1991; **143**(6): 1334–9.

32. Avner DB, Perzanowski MS, Platts-Mills TA, Woodfolk JA. Evaluation of different techniques for washing cats: quantitation of allergen removed from the cat and the effect on airborne Fel d 1. *J Allergy Clin Immunol* 1997; **100**(3): 307–12.

33. Hodson T, Custovic A, Simpson A, *et al.* Washing the dog reduces dog allergen levels, but the dog needs to be washed twice a week. *J Allergy Clin Immunol* 1999; **103**(4): 581–5.

34. Gore RB, Durrell B, Bishop S, *et al.* High-efficiency particulate arrest-filter vacuum cleaners increase personal cat allergen exposure in homes with cats. *J Allergy Clin Immunol* 2003; **111**(4): 784–7.

35. Eggleston PA. Cockroach allergen abatement in inner-city homes. *Ann Allergy Asthma Immunol* 2003; **91**(6): 512–14.

36. Eggleston PA, Arruda LK. Ecology and elimination of cockroaches and allergens in the home. *J Allergy Clin Immunol* 2001; **107**(Suppl 3): S422–9.

37. Eggleston PA, Butz A, Rand C, *et al.* Home environmental intervention in inner-city asthma: a randomized controlled clinical

trial. *Ann Allergy Asthma Immunol* 2005; **95**(6): 518–24.

38. Custovic A, Wijk RG. The effectiveness of measures to change the indoor environment in the treatment of allergic rhinitis and asthma: ARIA update (in collaboration with GA(2) LEN). *Allergy* 2005; **60**(9): 1112–15.

39. Marinho S, Simpson A, Custovic A. Allergen avoidance in the secondary and tertiary prevention of allergic diseases: does it work? *Prim Care Respir J* 2006; **15**(3): 152–8.

40. Simpson A, Custovic A. The role of allergen avoidance in the secondary prevention of atopic disorders. *Curr Opin Allergy Clin Immunol* 2005; **5**(3): 223–7.

41. Gotzsche P, Johansen H. House dust mite control measures for asthma. *Cochrane Database Syst Rev* 2008; **2**: CD001187.

42. Gotzsche PC, Johansen HK, Schmidt LM, Burr ML. House dust mite control measures for asthma. *Cochrane Database Syst Rev* 2004; **4**: CD001187.

43. Singh M, Bara A, Gibson P. Humidity control for chronic asthma. *Cochrane Database Syst Rev* 2002; **2**: CD003563.

44. Warner JA, Frederick JM, Bryant TN, *et al.* Mechanical ventilation and high-efficiency vacuum cleaning: A combined strategy of mite and mite allergen reduction in the control of mite-sensitive asthma. *J Allergy Clin Immunol* 2000; **105**(1 Pt 1): 75–82.

45. Sheikh A, Hurwitz B. House dust mite avoidance measures for perennial allergic rhinitis. *Cochrane Database Syst Rev* 2001; **4**: CD001563.

46. Walshaw MJ, Evans CC. Allergen avoidance in house dust mite sensitive adult asthma. *Q J Med* 1986; **58**(226): 199–215.

47. van der Heide S, Kauffman HF, Dubois AE, de Monchy JG. Allergen reduction measures in houses of allergic asthmatic patients: effects of air-cleaners and allergen-impermeable mattress covers. *Eur Respir J* 1997; **10**(6): 1217–23.

48. Htut T, Higenbottam TW, Gill GW, *et al.* Eradication of house dust mite from homes of atopic asthmatic subjects: a double-blind

trial. *J Allergy Clin Immunol* 2001; **107**(1): 55–60.

49. Woodcock A, Forster L, Matthews E, *et al.* Control of exposure to mite allergen and allergen-impermeable bed covers for adults with asthma. *N Engl J Med* 2003; **349**(3): 225–36.

50. Luczynska C, Tredwell E, Smeeton N, Burney P. A randomized controlled trial of mite allergen-impermeable bed covers in adult mite-sensitized asthmatics. *Clin Exp Allergy* 2003; **33**(12): 1648–53.

51. Terreehorst I, Duivenvoorden HJ, Tempels-Pavlica Z, *et al.* The effect of encasings on quality of life in adult house dust mite allergic patients with rhinitis, asthma and/or atopic dermatitis. *Allergy* 2005; **60**(7): 888–93.

52. van den Bemt L, van Knapen L, de Vries MP, *et al.* Clinical effectiveness of a mite allergen-impermeable bed-covering system in asthmatic mite-sensitive patients. *J Allergy Clin Immunol* 2004; **114**(4): 858–62.

53. Ehnert B, Lau-Schadendorf S, Weber A, *et al.* Reducing domestic exposure to dust mite allergen reduces bronchial hyperreactivity in sensitive children with asthma. *J Allergy Clin Immunol* 1992; **90**(1): 135–8.

54. Carswell F, Birmingham K, Oliver J, *et al.* The respiratory effects of reduction of mite allergen in the bedrooms of asthmatic children – a double-blind controlled trial. *Clin Exp Allergy* 1996; **26**(4): 386–96.

55. Carter MC, Perzanowski MS, Raymond A, Platts-Mills TA. Home intervention in the treatment of asthma among inner-city children. *J Allergy Clin Immunol* 2001; **108**(5): 732–7.

56. Halken S, Host A, Niklassen U, *et al.* Effect of mattress and pillow encasings on children with asthma and house dust mite allergy. *J Allergy Clin Immunol* 2003; **111**(1): 169–76.

57. Morgan WJ, Crain EF, Gruchalla RS, *et al.* Results of a home-based environmental intervention among urban children with asthma. *N Engl J Med* 2004; **351**(11): 1068–80.

58. Kattan M, Stearns SC, Crain EF, *et al.* Cost-effectiveness of a home-based environmental intervention for inner-city children with asthma. *J Allergy Clin Immunol* 2005; **116**(5): 1058–63.

59. Terreehorst I, Hak E, Oosting AJ, *et al.* Evaluation of impermeable covers for bedding in patients with allergic rhinitis. *N Engl J Med* 2003; **349**(3): 237–46.

60. Oosting AJ, de Bruin-Weller MS, Terreehorst I, *et al.* Effect of mattress encasings on atopic dermatitis outcome measures in a double-blind, placebo-controlled study: the Dutch mite avoidance study. *J Allergy Clin Immunol* 2002; **110**(3): 500–6.

61. Gutgesell C, Heise S, Seubert S, *et al.* Double-blind placebo-controlled house dust mite control measures in adult patients with atopic dermatitis. *Br J Dermatol* 2001; **145**(1): 70–4.

62. Tan BB, Weald D, Strickland I, Friedmann PS. Double-blind controlled trial of effect of housedust-mite allergen avoidance on atopic dermatitis. *Lancet* 1996; **347**(8993): 15–18.

63. Shirai T, Matsui T, Suzuki K, Chida K. Effect of pet removal on pet allergic asthma. *Chest* 2005; **127**(5): 1565–71.

64. Francis H, Fletcher G, Anthony C, *et al.* Clinical effects of air filters in homes of asthmatic adults sensitized and exposed to pet allergens. *Clin Exp Allergy* 2003; **33**(1): 101–5.

65. van der Heide S, van Aalderen WM, Kauffman HF, *et al.* Clinical effects of air cleaners in homes of asthmatic children sensitized to pet allergens. *J Allergy Clin Immunol* 1999; **104**(2 Pt 1): 447–51.

66. Wood RA, Johnson EF, Van Natta ML, *et al.* A placebo-controlled trial of a HEPA air cleaner in the treatment of cat allergy. *Am J Respir Crit Care Med* 1998; **158**(1): 115–20.

67. Kilburn S, Lasserson TJ, McKean M. Pet allergen control measures for allergic asthma in children and adults. *Cochrane Database Syst Rev* 2003; **1**: CD002989.

68. Simpson A, Soderstrom L, Ahlstedt S, *et al.* IgE antibody quantification and the probability of wheeze in preschool children. *J Allergy Clin Immunol* 2005; **116**(4): 744–9.

69. Marinho S, Simpson A, Soderstrom L, *et al.* Quantification of atopy and the probability of rhinitis in preschool children: a population-based birth cohort study. *Allergy* 2007; **62**(12): 1379–86. Epub 5 Sept 2007.

70. Simpson A, Custovic A. Allergen avoidance in the primary prevention of asthma. *Curr Opin Allergy Clin Immunol* 2004; **4**(1): 45–51.

71. Simpson A, Custovic A. The role of allergen avoidance in primary and secondary prevention. *Pediatr Pulmonol* 2004; **26**(Suppl): 225–8.

72. Gore C, Custovic A. Preventive measures and their effects. Results from cohort studies. *Paediatr Respir Rev* 2002; **3**(3): 205–18.

73. Gore C, Custovic A. Can we prevent allergy? *Allergy* 2004; **59**(2): 151–61.

74. Arshad SH, Matthews S, Gant C, Hide DW. Effect of allergen avoidance on development of allergic disorders in infancy. *Lancet* 1992; **339**(8808): 1493–7.

75. Hide DW, Matthews S, Matthews L, *et al.* Effect of allergen avoidance in infancy on allergic manifestations at age two years. *J Allergy Clin Immunol* 1994; **93**(5): 842–6.

76. Hide DW, Matthews S, Tariq S, Arshad SH. Allergen avoidance in infancy and allergy at 4 years of age. *Allergy* 1996; **51**(2): 89–93.

77. Arshad SH, Bateman B, Matthews SM. Primary prevention of asthma and atopy during childhood by allergen avoidance in infancy: a randomised controlled study. *Thorax* 2003; **58**(6): 489–93.

78. Arshad SH, Bateman B, Sadeghnejad A, *et al.* Prevention of allergic disease during childhood by allergen avoidance: the Isle of Wight prevention study. *J Allergy Clin Immunol* 2007; **119**(2): 307–13.

79. Becker A, Watson W, Ferguson A, *et al*. The Canadian asthma primary prevention study: outcomes at 2 years of age. *J Allergy Clin Immunol* 2004; **113**(4): 650–6.

80. Chan-Yeung M, Ferguson A, Watson W, *et al*. The Canadian Childhood Asthma Primary Prevention Study: outcomes at 7 years of age. *J Allergy Clin Immunol* 2005; **116**(1): 49–55.

81. Halmerbauer G, Gartner C, Schierl M, *et al*. Study on the Prevention of Allergy in Children in Europe (SPACE): allergic sensitization at 1 year of age in a controlled trial of allergen avoidance from birth. *Pediatr Allergy Immunol* 2003; **14**(1): 10–17.

82. Horak F Jr, Matthews S, Ihorst G, *et al*. Effect of mite-impermeable mattress encasings and an educational package on the development of allergies in a multinational randomized, controlled birth-cohort study – 24 months results of the Study of Prevention of Allergy in Children in Europe. *Clin Exp Allergy* 2004; **34**(8): 1220–5.

83. Mihrshahi S, Peat JK, Marks GB, *et al*. Eighteen-month outcomes of house dust mite avoidance and dietary fatty acid modification in the Childhood Asthma Prevention Study (CAPS). *J Allergy Clin Immunol* 2003; **111**(1): 162–8.

84. Peat JK, Mihrshahi S, Kemp AS, *et al*. Three-year outcomes of dietary fatty acid modification and house dust mite reduction in the Childhood Asthma Prevention Study. *J Allergy Clin Immunol* 2004; **114**(4): 807–13.

85. Marks GB, Mihrshahi S, Kemp AS, *et al*. Prevention of asthma during the first 5 years of life: a randomized controlled trial. *J Allergy Clin Immunol* 2006; **118**(1): 53–61.

86. Schonberger HJ, Dompeling E, Knottnerus JA, *et al*. The PREVASC study: the clinical effect of a multifaceted educational intervention to prevent childhood asthma. *Eur Respir J* 2005; **25**(4): 660–70.

87. Koopman LP, van Strien RT, Kerkhof M, *et al*. Placebo-controlled trial of house dust mite-impermeable mattress covers: effect on symptoms in early childhood. *Am J Respir Crit Care Med* 2002; **166**(3): 307–13.

88. Corver K, Kerkhof M, Brussee JE, *et al*. House dust mite allergen reduction and allergy at 4 yr: follow up of the PIAMA-study. *Pediatr Allergy Immunol* 2006; **17**(5): 329–36.

89. Custovic A, Simpson BM, Simpson A, *et al*. Effect of environmental manipulation in pregnancy and early life on respiratory symptoms and atopy during first year of life: a randomised trial. *Lancet* 2001; **358**(9277): 188–93.

90. Woodcock A, Lowe LA, Murray CS, *et al*. Early life environmental control: effect on symptoms, sensitization, and lung function at age 3 years. *Am J Respir Crit Care Med* 2004; **170**(4): 433–9.

91. Simpson A, Simpson B, Custovic A, *et al*. Stringent environmental control in pregnancy and early life: the long-term effects on mite, cat and dog allergen. *Clin Exp Allergy* 2003; **33**(9): 1183–9.

92. Simpson A, John SL, Jury F, *et al*. Endotoxin exposure, CD14, and allergic disease: an interaction between genes and the environment. *Am J Respir Crit Care Med* 2006; **174**(4): 386–92.

93. Custovic A, Simpson A. Environmental allergen exposure, sensitisation and asthma: from whole populations to individuals at risk. *Thorax* 2004; **59**(10): 825–7.

New therapeutic targets in asthma

BINITA BHOWMICK, DAVE SINGH

KEY POINTS

1. More effective anti-inflammatory drugs need to be developed for asthma.

2. Anti-eosinophil approaches include targeting cytokines (anti-IL4 and -13, anti-IL5) or chemokine receptors (CCR3).

3. Anti IL4 and -13 therapies show efficacy in allergen challenge but longer studies are needed.

4. Anti-IL5 may be useful to reduce eosinophil-associated exacerbations but do not improve airway response to allergen.

5. Anti TNF-alpha therapies show some clinical efficacy but their use may be confined to severe asthmatics due to concerns about side effects.

6. PDE4 inhibitors show good clinical efficacy but are limited by gastrointestinal side effects.

Introduction

Inhaled corticosteroids are the most widely used anti-inflammatory treatment for asthma. However, these drugs can cause significant side-effects, and do not cure asthma. Furthermore, many patients remain symptomatic despite high-dose inhaled corticosteroid treatment even in combination with long-acting β-agonists [1]. The reasons for such 'difficult to treat asthma' are varied, ranging from psychological factors to true drug resistance [2]. Improving the clinical care of such patients therefore requires a multidisciplinary approach. The development of new and effective drugs is one part of this approach.

Any new asthma treatments targeted at inflammation should offer advantages over current treatment regimes. Currently, perhaps the greatest unmet need is the treatment of persistent inflammation that is not adequately controlled by corticosteroids. New therapies for persistent inflammation that can be used with, or instead of, corticosteroids are needed. Asthma patients have heterogeneous inflammatory profiles in the airways |3,4|. The development of inflammatory biomarkers to define specific asthma phenotypes may in future be useful for guiding the specific use of new therapies e.g. anti-eosinophil drugs may be most successfully targeted at patients with the highest levels of eosinophilic airway inflammation.

In asthma patients with more severe disease, it is likely that we will use combination approaches to therapy in future, combining different anti-inflammatory drugs to hit multiple molecular targets. This concept is well established in the treatment of autoimmune diseases such as rheumatoid arthritis and systemic lupus. However, it is important that these drugs are shown to be safe and well tolerated in large clinical trials before being brought to the marketplace.

There are other avenues to improve on current anti-inflammatory therapies for asthma, even in patients with milder disease. These include improved therapeutic index oral treatments, as these are preferred by many patients, and disease-modifying or curative treatments. In this chapter we will focus mainly on new therapies for asthma and allergy that currently have published data from clinical trials, as these are the most likely to be seen in clinical practice in the next decade. We will review more briefly novel molecules with therapeutic potential at an earlier stage of clinical development.

Anti-cytokine therapies

Asthma is characterized by increased activity of Th2 cytokines including interleukin (IL)-4, IL-5 and IL-13. These cytokines, as well as other cytokines involved in inflammation such as tumour necrosis factor alpha (TNFα), represent plausible therapeutic targets in asthma. One of the most common strategies for inhibiting the activities of these cytokines is the use of monoclonal antibodies developed with specificity against the cytokine of interest. The potential advantages and disadvantages of such an approach are listed in Table 15.1. Clearly, a high degree of caution is needed in the design of a clinical development programme to ensure volunteer safety with monoclonal antibodies that may induce acute or long-term side-effects through regulation of the immune system. A major limiting factor in determining the efficacy of any of these approaches is the concept of 'redundancy', whereby inflammatory processes may be driven by multiple cytokines, so inhibition of one cytokine may not be effective because a different cytokine simply takes over. This

Table 15.1 Advantages and disadvantages of monoclonal antibody therapies

Advantages	Disadvantages
Specific cytokine targeting	Development of antibodies to drug
Different mechanism of action to glucocorticoids	Acute anaphylaxis
	Unpredictable acute onset immune dysregulation
Long duration of action	Long-term immunosupression; increasing infection or cancer risk
	Cytokine redundancy

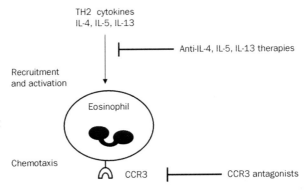

Fig. 15.1 Specific anti-eosinophil therapies. Th2 cytokines IL-4, IL-5 and IL-13 activate eosinophils. CCR3 is a chemokine receptor on the cell surface of eosinophils that plays an important role in chemotaxis.

example is well illustrated for eosinophil activation, where IL-4, IL-5 and IL-13 play overlapping roles (Fig. 15.1).

The rationale for choosing which cytokine to inhibit in human asthma is often based on animal models that inhibit the cytokine of interest, coupled with human data confirming high-level expression of the cytokine. However, even with this information, it is difficult to predict with any degree of certainty the effects in humans. The clinical trial results for anti-cytokine therapies have often shown efficacy that has been below the level of expectation generated by promising animal model data coupled with knowledge of human biology. Some of this may be attributed to redundancy. To overcome the issue of redundancy, it is possible that multiple cytokine targeting is needed. The clinical data regarding anti-cytokine therapies now reviewed have advanced our understanding of the role of specific cytokines in asthma pathophysiology. These clinical trials are summarized in Table 15.2.

Anti-IL-5

Increased numbers of eosinophils are present in the airways of patients with asthma[3], implicating this cell in disease pathogenesis. Eosinophils are known to release a number of pro-inflammatory mediators, and the possible therapeutic effectiveness of inhibiting eosinophils has been evaluated using anti-IL-5 monoclonal antibodies. IL-5 is involved in all stages of eosinophil development, differentiation, trafficking and activation, from the bone marrow to the tissue [5].

A single-dose study by Leckie and colleagues [6] found that mepolizumab significantly reduced eosinophil levels in the peripheral blood and induced sputum of mild atopic asthmatics, but had no effect on histamine airway hyper-reactivity or the late asthmatic response after allergen challenge. However, the trial had a small sample size and was underpowered to detect changes in either of these clinical endpoints [7]. A further study in mild asthmatics found that multiple doses of mepolizumab caused significant reductions in blood (100%) and bronchoalveolar lavage fluid (79%) eosinophils, but had less effect on eosinophil numbers in the bone marrow and bronchial mucosa (52% and 55% reduction, respectively) [8]. Again, there was no effect on lung function and bronchial hyper-reactivity. It is

Table 15.2 Summary of trials using anti-cytokine therapies

Class of drug (name)	No. of patients	Mean FEV$_1$ (% pred)	ICS?	Double-blind, randomized, placebo-controlled trial?	Primary endpoint(s)	Key finding(s)
Intravenous anti-IL-5 (mepolizumab) [6,8]	24	82	No	Yes	LAR	No effect on LAR Reduced blood eosinophils
	24	87	No	Yes	% change in eosinophils	Eosinophils reduced in: blood (100%), BALF (79%), BM (52%), ABM (55%)
Intravenous anti-IL-5 (SCH55700) [10]	18	49.3	Yes	Yes	Safety	Safe 52% reduction in blood eosinophils
Subcutaneous soluble TNFα receptor (etanercept) [18,23]	17	68.3	Yes	No Open-label, no placebo	Asthma control	Improved symptoms, FEV$_1$ (320 ml) and BHR
	10	62	Yes	Yes	BHR QOL score	Improved BHR and QOL score
Anti-TNFα (infliximab) [25]	15	64	Yes	Yes	Change in morning PEFR	No change in morning PEF Reduced exacerbations
Nebulized soluble IL-4 receptor (IL-4R) [11,12]	25	80	Withdrawn	Yes	Safety	Safe No worsening of symptoms or FEV$_1$
	62	75	Withdraw	Yes	Safety FEV$_1$	Safe No worsening of symptoms or FEV$_1$

% pred = % predicted; ABM = airway bronchial mucosa; BALF = bronchoalveolar lavage fluid; BM = bone marrow; FEV$_1$ = forced expiratory volume in 1 second; ICS = inhaled corticosteroids; LAR = late asthmatic response (post inhaled allergen challenge); PEFR = peak expiratory flow rate; QOL = quality of life.

clear from these studies that blocking IL-5 clears eosinophils from the circulation and airway lumen, but does not completely prevent tissue-based eosinophils persisting in the airways. These residual cells may contribute to continued airway inflammation. This study suggests that the degree of pulmonary tissue eosinophilia in asthma is not completely controlled by IL-5, and a network of inflammatory mediators is probably involved with other candidates such as IL-4, IL-13 and granulocyte-macrophage colony-stimulating factor (GM-CSF). Further data have shown that eosinophil-related transforming growth factor beta (TGFβ) activity is reduced in the airways by mepolizumab [9], suggesting a possible role for this therapy in preventing airway remodelling.

In a small pilot dose-ranging study, another monoclonal antibody to IL-5, SCH55700 [10] was found to be safe when administered to severe asthmatics. There was a small increase in forced expiratory volume in one second (FEV$_1$) at 24 h post dose compared with placebo, but this benefit was not sustained. This study was not statistically powered to detect lung function changes, and larger studies are needed to address this issue.

These studies show that anti-IL5 monoclonal antibodies can be administered safely to patients with asthma, and confirm that IL-5 does play a major role in eosinophil traffic. However, tissue-based eosinophils appear to be controlled by other inflammatory mediators as well, and if this is the case, then it may be more beneficial to use anti-IL-5 drugs in combination with other anti-eosinophil agents. Furthermore, eosinophilic inflammation appears to be absent in some patients with symptomatic asthma |3|. Anti-IL-5 therapy should be directed against patients with significant airway eosinophilia and a key issue for anti-eosinophil therapies is patient selection. The precise role of eosinophils in asthma remains unclear due to the small sample sizes of the studies conducted to date, although there is evidence that bronchial hyper-reactivity is not improved by reducing pulmonary eosinophil numbers. Further properly powered studies are needed that evaluate a range of relevant clinical endpoints, such as lung function and exacerbations.

Anti-IL-4 and IL-13

IL-4 plays a role in eosinophil trafficking, IgE isotype switching and Th2 lymphocyte differentiation |5|. A soluble IL-4 receptor (IL-4R) has been developed for inhaled delivery that would in theory 'neutralize' this cytokine. After an initial single safety and dose-ranging study |11|, a multiple-dose, placebo-controlled, parallel-group clinical trial was performed in patients with corticosteroid-dependent asthma in which the IL-4R was administered weekly over 12 weeks after corticosteroid withdrawal |12|. The results are difficult to interpret due to the high withdrawal rate of approximately 50%. There was some evidence for superiority of the 3 mg IL-4R dose compared to placebo for lung function and symptoms. While this study suggests promise for the strategy of IL-4R therapy, larger clinical studies in milder population groups to aid patient retention would be informative. Studies that aid our understanding of the biological effects of blocking IL-4 on airway inflammation are also needed, e.g. does this approach inhibit the activity of pulmonary eosinophils and/or Th2 lymphocytes?

IL-13 has similar actions to IL-4, being involved in eosinophil trafficking as well as the development of allergen induced airway hyper-reactivity in animal models |13,14|. While IL-13 and IL-4 share a common receptor |15|, they seem to signal through different pathways.|16| IL-13 is present in increased concentrations in the airways of asthma patients |17|, suggesting it may play an important role in asthma pathophysiology. Approaches to blocking the effects of this cytokine through a humanized receptor or a monoclonal antibody are being evaluated in clinical trials.

Anti-TNFα

TNFα is a pro-inflammatory cytokine implicated in the pathogenesis of a number of chronic inflammatory human diseases. There is evidence that TNFα plays an important role in the pathophysiology of asthma that does not respond to conventional therapy ('refractory asthma') |18|. TNFα is thought to be derived predominantly from mast cells in the asthmatic airways |19|, but is also produced by

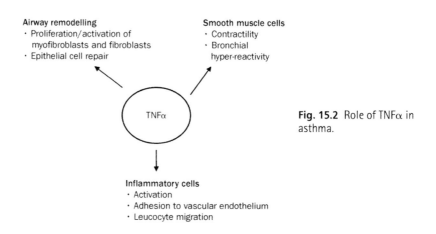

Airway remodelling
· Proliferation/activation of
  myofibroblasts and fibroblasts
· Epithelial cell repair

Smooth muscle cells
· Contractility
· Bronchial
  hyper-reactivity

TNFα

Inflammatory cells
· Activation
· Adhesion to vascular endothelium
· Leucocyte migration

Fig. 15.2 Role of TNFα in asthma.

other cell types |20|. This cytokine is capable of promoting airway inflammation by a variety of mechanisms. These include the upregulation of adhesion molecule expression, thereby promoting inflammatory cell influx, and the direct activation of inflammatory cells (Fig. 15.2). Furthermore, TNFα is known to promote bronchial hyper-reactivity *in vitro* and *in vivo* |21,22|. Anti-TNFα therapies have been effectively used in conditions such as Crohn's disease and rheumatoid arthritis, raising the hope that these drugs may also be effective in patients with refractory asthma. Preliminary evidence for the efficacy of this approach came from an uncontrolled study in 17 refractory asthma patients using the recombinant soluble TNFα receptor etanercept |18|. There was a significant improvement in symptoms, lung function and bronchial hyper-reactivity. However, the lack of a placebo group made interpretation of the data difficult. A randomized, double-blind, placebo-controlled, crossover study using etanercept was subsequently performed, and showed that 10 weeks of treatment significantly improved bronchial hyper-reactivity, FEV_1 and quality of life scores in refractory asthmatics (Fig. 15.3) |23|. However, etanercept did not reduce exhaled nitric oxide levels or sputum eosinophils. The lack of relationship between bronchial hyper-reactivity and airway eosinophilia has similarities to the observations in the anti-IL-5 studies, where a reduction in eosinophil numbers did not change bronchial hyper-reactivity |6,8|. Mast cells play a prominent role in determining airway smooth muscle activity in severe asthma |24| and are probably a key target of anti-TNFα therapy in asthma.

Monoclonal antibody approaches to block the activity of TNFα are also possible. A double-blind, placebo-controlled study of the monoclonal antibody infliximab in 38 patients with moderate to severe asthma showed no effect on the primary endpoint of morning peak expiratory flow rate (PEFR) |25|. However, there was a reduction in exacerbations and sputum TNFα levels in the active treatment group, suggesting that the therapeutic usefulness of this agent needs to be further evaluated.

The role of anti-TNFα drugs in asthma is at present uncertain. The incidence of severe side-effects such as re-activation of infections such as tuberculosis makes

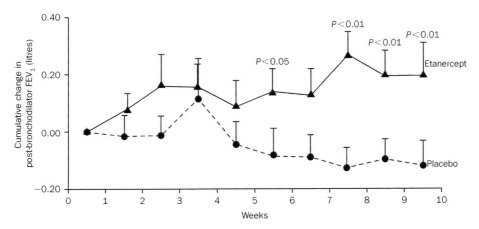

Fig. 15.3 10 weeks of treatment with etanercept significantly improved bronchial hyper-reactivity to methacholine in severe asthmatics (n = 10) (with permission from |23|: © 2006 Massachusetts Medical Society. All rights reserved).

the therapeutic index an important issue to consider, and so it is likely that this approach will only be useful for refractory asthma, probably as an add-on therapy. Larger studies are now needed to fully assess clinical benefit.

Cytokine therapies

An alternative approach to the development of therapies against pro-inflammatory cytokines is the use of cytokines themselves as therapies to inhibit inflammation. An example of this approach is the Th1 cytokine interferon gamma (IFNγ), which is known to inhibit Th2 activity, thus reducing levels of the key asthmatic mediators IL-4, IL-5 and IL-13. Subcutaneous delivery of IFNγ was not clinically effective in antibiotics, suggesting that exogenous IFNγ delivery is not the best approach |26|. Immunotherapy is known to increase IFNγ levels |27| providing an alternative method to boost endogenous IFNγ production rather than delivering exogenous cytokine.

IL-12 upregulates IFNγ production, and is thus involved in controlling the balance between Th1 and Th2 cytokine profiles. Human recombinant IL-12 has been administered to patients with mild allergic asthma for 4 weeks. There was evidence of clinical efficacy, as the peripheral blood eosinophil count was reduced by IL-12 compared to placebo as well as post-allergen challenge sputum eosinophil counts |28|. However, there was no effect on post-allergen challenge lung function or histamine reactivity, and there was a high drop-out rate in the active treatment group due to side-effects including abnormal liver function tests and flu-like symptoms. Minimizing these side-effects is a challenge for cytokine therapies. IL-10 is an anti-inflammatory cytokine that is produced by T-regulatory cells. The administration of this cytokine has produced clinical benefits in psoriasis |29|, and this may be a promising approach for asthma. Again, the therapeutic index including the side-effect profile will have to be evaluated very carefully.

PDE4 inhibitors

Phosphodiesterases (PDEs) are a family of metallophosphohydrolases that hydrolyse cyclic adenosine monophosphate (cAMP) and cyclic guanosine monophosphate (cGMP) into their inactive substrates. Inhibition of PDEs results in an increase in intracellular cAMP and cGMP, promoting smooth muscle relaxation and reduced inflammation (Fig. 15.4). Theophylline is a weak, non-selective PDE inhibitor with a poor side-effect profile. The PDE4 isoform is expressed on inflammatory cells relevant to asthma, such as eosinophils, neutrophils and lymphocytes [30]. This enzyme has been targeted for the treatment of asthma in the hope of improving the therapeutic index offered by theophylline, both by increasing clinical benefits and reducing side-effects. Animal models of asthma have shown promise for this approach [31,32]. In human studies, it has been shown that the PDE4 inhibitor CDP840 reduced the late asthmatic response (LAR) after allergen challenge by 30% [33]. However, there was no improvement in the early asthmatic response (EAR) or bronchial hyper-reactivity to histamine. In contrast, roflumilast seems to be more potent, as it inhibited both the EAR and LAR, by up to 28% and 43% respectively [34]. Previous studies using inhaled corticosteroids have not always demonstrated inhibition of the EAR [35,36], while inhibition of the LAR is generally of the same order of magnitude or greater than that observed with rofumilast [35,37]. In a recent study, it was reported that roflumilast and the

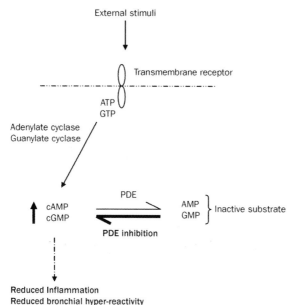

Fig. 15.4 PDE inhibition. The second messengers cyclic adenosine monophosphate (cAMP) and cyclic guanosine monophosphate (cGMP) transduce many cellular effects. They are synthesized from ATP and GTP by adenylate cyclase and guanylate cyclase in response to extracellular stimuli. PDE inhibition causes increased intracellular cAMP and cGMP, which has an anti-inflammatory effect.

inhaled corticosteroid beclomethasone dipropionate caused improvements in pulmonary function |38|. These studies, showing that the clinical effects of roflumilast are comparable with those of inhaled corticosteroids, are encouraging for this class of drugs. Further evidence supporting the potential role of PDE4 inhibition in the therapy of asthma comes from the inhibition of exercise-induced bronchoconstriction by roflumilast |39|.

The PDE4 inhibitors that have been most extensively evaluated in clinical trials of asthma and chronic obstructive pulmonary disease (COPD) are cilomilast and roflumilast. Unfortunately, these drugs still cause gastrointestinal side-effects, which are limiting their clinical development. It is possible that even more selective inhibitors are needed to overcome this problem, as the enzyme subtype PDE4D may mediate nausea and vomiting |40|, while PDE4B may mediate inflammation |41|. Inhaled delivery is an alternative way to limit side-effects.

Inhibition of intracellular signalling mechanisms

Extracellular pro-inflammatory stimuli, such as cytokines, bacterial lipopolysaccharide and antigens, signal through complex intracellular signalling pathways, culminating in the upregulation of inflammatory gene expression. These signal transduction pathways are obvious potential therapeutic targets in inflammatory diseases. An advantage of targeting signalling pathways is that they control inflammatory gene expression in multiple cell types, so this approach can cover a range of relevant inflammatory cells. Also, a number of downstream pro-inflammatory genes can be targeted. However, it is possible that these relatively non-selective approaches will result in clinically important immunosuppression, which needs to be carefully evaluated in clinical trials. It is possible that these drugs may therefore be best used in patients with more severe disease in whom side-effects may be more acceptable.

Signalling pathway inhibitors are currently undergoing clinical trials in a variety of inflammatory diseases including asthma, COPD and rheumatoid arthritis. The signalling pathways of most importance in asthma are shown in Fig. 15.5. nuclear factor-κB (NF-κB) is a key transcription factor in asthma |42|, inducing the transcription of inflammatory genes in the airways. The efficacy of corticosteroids in asthma has been attributed to their ability to repress the activity of NF-κB |43|, indicating that potent targeting of NF-κB is a sensible approach in asthma. IKK2 deactivates the NF-κB inhibitor IκB. Inhibitors of the NF-κB pathway are in clinical development, such as IKK2 inhibitors.

The mitogen-activated protein kinases (MAP kinases) constitute signalling cascades activated by a range of inflammatory stimuli, resulting in upstream kinase activation. There are three major downstream MAP kinases: P38 kinase, c-Jun N-terminal kinase (JNK) and extracellular signal-related kinase (ERK) |44|. These can regulate inflammatory gene expression through modulation of transcription factor activity, including NF-κB and activator protein 1 (AP-1). P38 kinase and JNK inhibition are of most interest in airway diseases |45|. It has been postulated

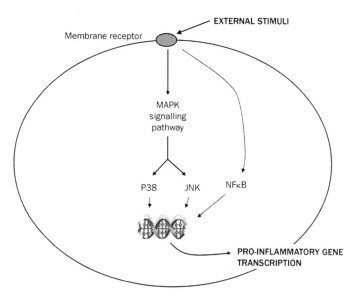

Fig. 15.5 Intracellular signalling pathways. External stimuli activate intracellular signalling pathways via transmembrane receptors. Mitogen activated protein kinase (MAP kinase) pathways include the c–Jun N-terminal kinase (JNK) and P38 MAPK cascades, which activate downstream transcription factors to promote inflammatory gene transcription. NF-κB is a transcription factor important in pro-inflammatory gene transcription in asthma, and is activated by a number of intracellular pathways.

that corticosteroid effects are reduced in some asthma patients because of defective MAP kinase phosphatase-1 activity, which inhibits P38 kinase |43|. Small molecule P38 kinase inhibitors may therefore be most useful as a combination therapy with corticosteroids to maximize anti-inflammatory effects.

Chemokine receptor antagonists

Chemokines are proteins involved in the recruitment of inflammatory cells from the circulation, and their positioning within tissues. Chemokines signal through G-protein coupled receptors. Antagonism of chemokine receptor activity is a potentially attractive way of preventing inflammatory cell traffic into the lungs, allowing targeting of specific cell types. Small molecule inhibitors and monoclonal antibodies against chemokine receptors are in clinical development.

The majority of chemokine receptors are classified into the CCR and CXCR families. Eosinophil recruitment is regulated by CCR3 activation by chemokines such as eotaxin and eotaxin-2 found at increased levels in the airways of asthmatics |46|. CCR3 is therefore a possible target to reduce eosinophilic inflammation in asthma (Fig. 15.1). CCR3 is also expressed on other cell types involved in asthmatic inflammation, such as lymphocytes. Alternative targets include CCR2, which is expressed on lymphocytes and mast cells, and CCR4, which is expressed on Th2 lymphocytes.

Specific targeting of atopy

Drugs targeted specifically at the pathophysiological mechanisms responsible for atopy may have usefulness in atopic asthma or other atopic conditions. Examples of the success of this approach in clinical practice include sodium cromoglycate and anti-IgE. Novel approaches include blockade of the co-stimulatory molecules involved in Th2 lymphocyte activation such as CD28 |47|, and inhibition of the IgE receptor CD23 |48|. An alternative approach to the treatment of established atopy is the *primary prevention* of atopy. While much research is focused on non-pharmacological interventions to achieve this aim, there are also possibilities for pharmacological strategies. For example, the skewing of lymphocyte responsiveness towards Th1 and away from Th2 by neonatal BCG vaccination for prevention of tuberculosis is associated with a lower prevalence of asthma |49|. An alternative strategy may be to amplify T-regulatory cell activity to suppress the development of a Th2 profile |50|. The limiting factor for the clinical development and safety of such strategies is the potential long-term danger of such early-life alterations of the natural balance of the immune system.

Conclusion

The next 5–10 years is likely to see continued efforts to develop and bring to the marketplace novel classes of drugs for the treatment of asthma. While there have been notable examples of effective new classes of drugs in asthma in the last decade, such as leukotriene antagonists and anti-IgE therapy, the mainstay of anti-inflammatory treatment in asthma continues to be inhaled corticosteroids. This situation is likely to remain for the foreseeable future, as the novel drugs most advanced in clinical development such as anti-TNFα and anti-IL-5 will probably be used as add-on therapy in difficult-to-treat asthma cases. Clinical data on PDE4 inhibition suggest considerable promise for this approach, and we await the publication of clinical data on the effectiveness of strategies to inhibit cell signalling such as through the P38 kinase system.

Targeting novel therapies to the most appropriate subgroups of patients is a major challenge, and will be dependent on basic research into biomarkers that define distinct disease characteristics associated with increased drug responsiveness. While these new drugs are being developed, the near future will probably see corticosteroids with improved therapeutic indices and long-acting β-agonists that are more potent and/or longer-acting compared to the currently available drugs being brought to the marketplace.

References

1. Bateman ED, Boushey HA, Bousquet J, et al. Can guideline-defined asthma control be achieved?: the Gaining Optimal Asthma ControL Study. Am J Respir Crit Care Med 2004; **170**: 836–44.

2. Peters SP, Ferguson G, Deniz Y, et al. Uncontrolled asthma: A review of the prevalence, disease burden and options for treatment. Respir Med 2006; **100**: 1139–51.

3. Wenzel SE, Schwartz LB, Langmack EL, et al. Evidence that severe asthma can be divided pathologically into two inflammatory subtypes with distinct physiologic and clinical characteristics. Am J Respir Crit Care Med 1999; **160**: 1001–8.

4. Pavord ID, Brightling CE, Woltmann G, et al. Non-eosinophilic corticosteroid unresponsive asthma. Lancet 1999; **353**: 2213–14.

5. Rothenberg ME, Hogan SP. The eosinophil. Annu Rev Immunol 2006; **24**: 147–74.

6. Leckie MJ, ten Brinke A, Khan J, et al. Effects of an interleukin-5 blocking monoclonal antibody on eosinophils, airway hyper-responsiveness, and the late asthmatic response. Lancet 2000; **356**: 2144–8.

7. O'Byrne PM, Inman MD, Parameswaran K. The trials and tribulations of IL-5, eosinophils, and allergic asthma. J Allergy Clin Immunol 2001; **108**: 503–8.

8. Flood-Page PT, Menzies-Gow AN, Kay AB, et al. Eosinophil's role remains uncertain as anti-interleukin-5 only partially depletes numbers in asthmatic airway. Am J Respir Crit Care Med 2003; **167**: 199–204.

9. Flood-Page P, Menzies-Gow A, Phipps S, et al. Anti-IL-5 treatment reduces deposition of ECM proteins in the bronchial subepithelial basement membrane of mild atopic asthmatics. J Clin Invest 2003; **112**: 1029–36.

10. Kips JC, O'Connor BJ, Langley SJ, et al. Effect of SCH55700, a humanized anti-human interleukin-5 antibody, in severe persistent asthma: a pilot study. Am J Respir Crit Care Med 2003; **167**: 1655–9.

11. Borish LC, Nelson HS, Lanz MJ, et al. Interleukin-4 receptor in moderate atopic asthma. A phase I/II randomized, placebo-controlled trial. Am J Respir Crit Care Med 1999; **160**: 1816–23.

12. Borish LC, Nelson HS, Corren J, et al. Efficacy of soluble IL-4 receptor for the treatment of adults with asthma. J Allergy Clin Immunol 2001; **107**: 963–70.

13. Venkayya R, Lam M, Willkom M, et al. The Th2 lymphocyte products IL-4 and IL-13 Rapidly induce airway hyperresponsiveness through direct effects on resident airway cells. Am J Respir Cell Mol Biol 2002; **26**: 202–8.

14. Luttmann W, Knoechel B, Foerster M, et al. Activation of human eosinophils by IL-13. Induction of CD69 surface antigen, its relationship to messenger RNA expression, and promotion of cellular viability. J Immunol 1996; **157**: 1678–83.

15. Kotowicz K, Callard RE, Friedrich K, et al. Biological activity of IL-4 and IL-13 on human endothelial cells: functional evidence that both cytokines act through the same receptor. Int Immunol 1996; **8**: 1915–25.

16. Laporte JC, Moore PE, Baraldo S, et al. Direct effects of interleukin-13 on signaling pathways for physiological responses in cultured human airway smooth muscle cells. Am J Respir Crit Care Med 2001; **164**: 141–8.

17. Berry MA, Parker D, Neale N, et al. Sputum and bronchial submucosal IL-13 expression in asthma and eosinophilic bronchitis. J Allergy Clin Immunol 2004; **114**: 1106–9.

18. Howarth PH, Babu KS, Arshad HS, et al. Tumour necrosis factor (TNF-alpha) as a novel therapeutic target in symptomatic corticosteroid dependent asthma. Thorax 2005; **60**: 1012–18.

19. Bradding P, Roberts JA, Britten KM, et al. Interleukin-4, -5, and -6 and tumor necrosis factor-alpha in normal and asthmatic airways: evidence for the human mast cell as a

source of these cytokines. *Am J Respir Cell Mol Biol* 1994; **10**: 471–80.

20. Mukhopadhyay S, Hoidal JR, Mukherjee TK. Role of TNF-alpha in pulmonary pathophysiology. *Respir Res* 2006; **7**: 125.

21. Pennings HJ, Kramer K, Bast A, *et al*. Tumour necrosis factor-alpha induces hyperreactivity in tracheal smooth muscle of the guinea-pig in vitro. *Eur Respir J* 1998; **12**: 45–9.

22. Thomas PS, Heywood G. Effects of inhaled tumour necrosis factor alpha in subjects with mild asthma. *Thorax* 2002; **57**: 774–8.

23. Berry MA, Hargadon B, Shelley M, *et al*. Evidence of a role of tumor necrosis factor alpha in refractory asthma. *N Engl J Med* 2006; **354**: 697–708.

24. Brightling CE, Bradding P, Symon FA, *et al*. Mast-cell infiltration of airway smooth muscle in asthma. *N Engl J Med* 2002; **346**: 1699–705.

25. Erin EM, Leaker BR, Nicholson GC, *et al*. The effects of a monoclonal antibody directed against tumor necrosis factor-alpha in asthma. *Am J Respir Crit Care Med* 2006; **174**: 753–62.

26. Boguniewicz M, Schneider LC, Milgrom H, *et al*. Treatment of steroid-dependent asthma with recombinant interferon-gamma. *Clin Exp Allergy* 1993; **23**: 785–90.

27. Larche M, Akdis CA, Valenta R. Immunological mechanisms of allergen-specific immunotherapy. *Nat Rev Immunol* 2006; **6**: 761–71.

28. Bryan SA, O'Connor BJ, Matti S, *et al*. Effects of recombinant human interleukin-12 on eosinophils, airway hyper-responsiveness, and the late asthmatic response. *Lancet* 2000; **356**: 2149–53.

29. Friedrich M, Docke WD, Klein A, *et al*. Immunomodulation by interleukin-10 therapy decreases the incidence of relapse and prolongs the relapse-free interval in psoriasis. *J Invest Dermatol* 2002; **118**: 672–7.

30. Torphy TJ. Phosphodiesterase isozymes: molecular targets for novel antiasthma agents. *Am J Respir Crit Care Med* 1998; **157**: 351–70.

31. Kanehiro A, Ikemura T, Makela MJ, *et al*. Inhibition of phosphodiesterase 4 attenuates airway hyperresponsiveness and airway inflammation in a model of secondary allergen challenge. *Am J Respir Crit Care Med* 2001; **163**: 173–84.

32. Deng Ym, Xie Qm, Tang HF, *et al*. Effects of ciclamilast, a new PDE 4 PDE4 inhibitor, on airway hyperresponsiveness, PDE4D expression and airway inflammation in a murine model of asthma. *Eur J Pharmacol* 2006; **547**: 125–35.

33. Harbinson PL, MacLeod D, Hawksworth R, *et al*. The effect of a novel orally active selective PDE4 isoenzyme inhibitor (CDP840) on allergen-induced responses in asthmatic subjects. *Eur Respir J* 1997; **10**: 1008–14.

34. van Schalkwyk KE, Strydom K, Williams Z, *et al*. Roflumilast, an oral, once-daily phosphodiesterase 4 inhibitor, attenuates allergen-induced asthmatic reactions. *J Allergy Clin Immunol* 2005; **116**: 292–8.

35. Leigh R, Vethanayagam D, Yoshida M, *et al*. Effects of montelukast and budesonide on airway responses and airway inflammation in asthma. *Am J Respir Crit Care Med* 2002; **166**: 1212–17.

36. Palmqvist M, Bruce C, Sjostrand M, *et al*. Differential effects of fluticasone and montelukast on allergen-induced asthma. *Allergy* 2005; **60**: 65–70.

37. Inman MD, Watson RM, Rerecich T, *et al*. Dose-dependent effects of inhaled mometasone furoate on airway function and inflammation after allergen inhalation challenge. *Am J Respir Crit Care Med* 2001; **164**: 569–74.

38. Bousquet J, Aubier M, Sastre J, *et al*. Comparison of roflumilast, an oral antiinflammatory, with beclomethasone dipropionate in the treatment of persistent asthma. *Allergy* 2006; **61**: 72–8.

39. Timmer W, Leclerc V, Birraux G, *et al*. The new phosphodiesterase 4 inhibitor roflumilast is efficacious in exercise-induced asthma and leads to suppression of LPS-stimulated TNF-alpha ex vivo. *J Clin Pharmacol* 2002; **42**: 297–303.

40. Lamontagne S, Meadows E, Luk P, *et al.* Localization of phosphodiesterase-4 isoforms in the medulla and nodose ganglion of the squirrel monkey. *Brain Res* 2001; **920**: 84–96.

41. Jin S-LC, Conti M. Induction of the cyclic nucleotide phosphodiesterase PDE4B is essential for LPS-activated TNF-alpha responses. *Proc Natl Acad Sci USA* 2002; **99**: 7628–33.

42. Wright JG, Christman JW. The role of nuclear factor kappa B in the pathogenesis of pulmonary diseases: implications for therapy. *Am J Respir Med* 2003; **2**: 211–19.

43. Barnes PJ. Corticosteroid effects on cell signalling. *Eur Respir J* 2006; **27**: 413–26.

44. Kumar S, Boehm J, Lee JC. p38 MAP kinases: key signalling molecules as therapeutic targets for inflammatory diseases. *Nat Rev Drug Discov* 2003; **2**: 717–26.

45. Adcock IM, Chung KF, Caramori G, *et al.* Kinase inhibitors and airway inflammation. *Eur J Pharmacol* 2006; **533**: 118–32.

46. Ying S, Meng Q, Zeibecoglou K, *et al.* Eosinophil chemotactic chemokines (eotaxin, eotaxin-2, RANTES, monocyte chemoattractant protein-3 (MCP-3), and MCP-4), and C-C chemokine receptor 3 expression in bronchial biopsies from atopic and nonatopic (Intrinsic) asthmatics. *J Immunol* 1999; **163**: 6321–9.

47. Djukanovic R. The role of co-stimulation in airway inflammation. *Clin Exp Allergy* 2000; **30**(Suppl 1): 46–50.

48. Rosenwasser LJ, Meng J. Anti-CD23. *Clin Rev Allergy Immunol* 2005; **29**: 61–72.

49. Linehan MF, Frank TL, Hazell ML, *et al.* Is the prevalence of wheeze in children altered by neonatal BCG vaccination? *J Allergy Clin Immunol* 2007; **119**(5): 1079–85. Epub 26 Mar 2007.

50. van Oosterhout AJM, Bloksma N. Regulatory T-lymphocytes in asthma. *Eur Respir J* 2005; **26**: 918–32.

What the future holds

ANGELA SIMPSON, JUDITH WOODFOLK, ADNAN CUSTOVIC,
THOMAS PLATTS-MILLS

KEY POINTS

1. The relationship between genotype and phenotype in asthma is not linear or unidirectional, but modulated by a number of environmental factors.

2. In asthma and other complex diseases, genetic predisposition needs to be taken into account when assessing the effect of environmental exposures; similarly, relevant environmental exposures need to be factored into the genetic association studies.

3. Only individuals with particular susceptibility will benefit from any specific intervention, whilst the same intervention amongst individuals with different susceptibility may cause harm.

4. There are major differences in dose response and immune response between mammalian and other allergens.

5. Although IgE antibodies to alphaGal are associated with anaphylaxis, IgE antibodies to carbohydrate epitopes have not been associated with asthma.

6. Management of allergic disease will have to recognize that different types of allergens require separate approaches.

What the future holds—on genes and environment

Asthma—an unstable phenotype

Asthma and allergies are the most common chronic diseases in childhood in the developed societies |1|. In contrast to most other common complex diseases (e.g. diabetes), asthma and allergic diseases start early in life and are unstable phenotypes which may progress or remit over time. Therefore, the optimum study design to investigate these disorders is the population-based prospective birth cohort, overcoming problems of recall bias (due to retrospective data collection) and permitting careful longitudinal phenotyping of subjects. Allergic status, lung function and bronchial hyper-responsiveness, physician diagnosis and medication usage can be accurately defined. In addition, environmental exposures can be contemporaneously measured (e.g. domestic endotoxin and allergen exposures, diet) to facilitate the study of gene–environment interactions.

Inconsistencies on the role of genetic factors in asthma

Although the evidence from twin studies suggests that there is a strong hereditary component of asthma |2|, genetic studies have produced heterogeneous results with little replication |3–5|. Several possible reasons for these inconsistencies in genetic association studies are common to many complex diseases (e.g. 'multiple disease-predisposing genes of modest individual effect, gene–gene interactions, gene–environment interactions, inter-population heterogeneity of genetic and environmental determinants of disease, the issues of multiple testing, laboratory and other measurement error, and positive publication and investigator-reporting biases' |6|). However, more specific to asthma is the fact that, although it is an unstable phenotype which starts in early life, most genetic studies have focused predominantly on adults, often with phenotypic heterogeneity or poor phenotype definition. In addition, little or no account has been taken of environmental exposures.

Inconsistencies on the role of environmental exposures in asthma

The fundamental role of the environment in the development of asthma and allergic diseases is emphasized by the rapid increase in prevalence which occurred in the last four to five decades |1|, a time-frame too short to be attributable to genetic factors alone. Various environmental exposures have been associated with the development of asthma and allergies. The environmental changes which have occurred in parallel include changes in diet and exercise, patterns of microbial exposure in early life with antibiotic usage and childhood immunizations, family size and childcare arrangements, and changes to housing design |7|. However, as with genetics, the data on the role of environment are often inconsistent, with the same environmental exposure. For example, cat ownership in different studies conferred an increase in risk |8|, protection |9| or no effect |10|. Similarly, published studies investigating the effect of day-care on the development of allergic disease are inconsistent, with some showing increased risk |11|, and others decreased risk |12–15| or no effect |16,17|. Furthermore, the timing of various environmental exposures adds an additional level of complexity. For example, antenatal and early life exposures to environmental factors are more likely to have a greater impact on the immature immune system and airways, and the subsequent development of disease, than those occurring in adulthood.

Interactions between genes and environment

The conflicting evidence on the effect of genetic variants and environmental exposures on allergic phenotypes may in part be consequent to the differences in study designs, definitions of exposures and outcomes or sample size. However, these inconsistencies may also reflect the fundamentally different nature of the relationship between genetic polymorphisms, environmental exposures and phenotype in complex diseases compared to diseases determined predominantly by genetic factors. The relationship between genotype and phenotype in complex diseases may not be linear or unidirectional [18], but modulated by a number of environmental factors. Thus, since the development of sensitization and/or asthma is likely a consequence of environmental factors acting upon genetically susceptible individuals through gene–environment interactions, to understand the role of either genes or environment it may be essential to study both.

Recent studies in mouse models of complex traits which included models of human disease such as asthma and immunological, biochemical and haematological phenotypes have strongly suggested that gene–environment interaction plays a crucial role in determining complex phenotypes [19]. Environmental covariates were involved in a large number of significant interactions with genetic background. Furthermore, the effects of gene–environment interactions were more frequent and larger than the main effects: half of the interactions explained more than 20% of the variance of the complex phenotypes studied.

We have recently demonstrated the existence of a gene–environment interaction in the development of allergy and eczema within the setting of a birth cohort study (the Manchester Asthma and Allergy Study [MAAS]) [20]. By taking objective measure of endotoxin exposure in the home and carefully phenotyping the children, we have shown that high endotoxin exposure is protective against the development of allergies and eczema, but only in children with a particular genotype group (C allele homozygotes of CD14/-159 rs2569190; Fig. 16.1). Furthermore, these results explain the disparities in association studies of this single nucleotide polymorphism (SNP) in different settings around the world. From our results, it is clear that when the gene is studied in isolation, in communities with naturally high exposure to endotoxin e.g. farming communities like the Hutterites, the T allele would appear to be the risk allele [21]. In contrast, in communities with naturally low exposure to endotoxin, the C allele would appear to be the risk allele [22]. In communities with a wide range of exposures there would be no apparent association between genotype and disease outcome [23], emphasizing the point that if the genotype were studied in isolation, irrespective of the size of the population studied, this effect would have been missed.

It has been suggested that in order to detect gene–environment interactions it is necessary to study tens of thousands of subjects [24]. However, we detected this interaction (and provided a plausible explanation for apparently irreconcilable differences in previously published data) with a modest sample size of 442 [20]. These results have been replicated by other groups with a comparable number of subjects [25,26]. In a marked contrast, the largest study of genetic determinants of immunoglobulin (Ig)E (which has not taken environmental exposures into account) was able to explain <1% of the variance [27], despite the fact that twin studies suggest heritability of ~60% [28] and the selected genes were appropriate. The accompanying editorial emphasized that the study of subjects from a broad geographic area with diverse unmeasured environmental exposures overlooked the fact that many associations between genes and phenotype may not be linear or

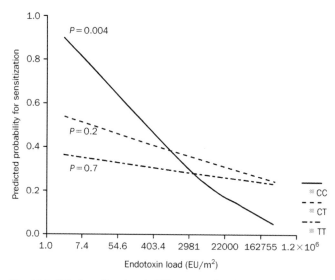

Fig. 16.1 Fitted predicted probability curves for allergic sensitization at age 5 years in relation to environmental endotoxin load in children with CC, CT and TT genotypes in the promoter region of the CD14 gene (CD14/-159 C to T), derived from the logistic regression analysis. There was no association between endotoxin load and sensitization for the TT and CT genotypes ($P = 0.7$ and $P = 0.16$, respectively). However, for the CC genotype group increasing endotoxin load was associated with a marked and significant decrease in the risk of sensitization (0.70, 0.55–0.89, $P = 0.004$)

unidirectional and that true associations may be lost in studies of this scale, concluding that 'hypothesis driven genetic epidemiology might be a more effective and interesting partner for disease-oriented biologic research' [18].

Conclusions on the role of genes and environment

Future studies will have to take into account the fact that the power to detect genetic associations clearly depends not only on size of population studied [29], but critically on accurate phenotyping and measurement of environmental exposures. Furthermore, to understand a disease that starts early in life, we will have to use birth cohorts with accurate prospective phenotyping at or around the onset of disease and contemporaneous measurement of relevant environmental exposures. This approach is not applicable to disease areas such as maturity onset diabetes.

In complex diseases such as asthma and allergies, genetic predisposition will need to be taken into account when assessing the effect of environmental exposures, and vice versa, relevant environmental exposures will need to be factored into the genetic association studies. Furthermore, epidemiological data are often used to identify potentially modifiable risk factors to help devise primary prevention strategies. However, it is important to emphasize that only individuals with particular genotypes will benefit from a specific intervention, whilst the same intervention amongst individuals with different susceptibility may cause harm.

What the future holds—the relevance of IgE antibody responses to different groups of allergens

The objective of an allergy evaluation is to identify specific sensitivities, both in order to educate the patient about the role of allergens in their disease, but also to help predict what approaches to treatment are most likely to be effective. The last few years have provided increasing evidence that 'all allergens are not created equal' [30,31]. In terms of management there are at least three major groups of allergens that have strongly different characteristics.

> **Group A:** Includes the pollens of grass, weeds and trees; the fungus alternaria; dust mites and cockroach.
> **Group B:** Animal dander allergens primarily those from cat and dog.
> **Group C:** The cross-reacting carbohydrate determinants on plant or mammalian proteins.

In addition, there are major differences between allergic diseases, which increasingly suggest that approaches to modifying T cell control with immunotherapy will have to be tailored.

The first two groups of allergens have different characteristics in terms of dose response and in particular in their ability to induce tolerance with high exposure. These differences may have major consequences in relation to predicting the effects of decreasing exposure [32]. We have already shown that decreasing exposure to cat allergens can lead to progressive decreases in IgG antibodies without a decrease in IgE production [33]. The result can be an increased level of sensitivity and symptoms. There are, of course, situations where decreasing food exposure has been reported to increase sensitivity [34].

While there are multiple 'causes' of the difference between animal dander and other allergens, a major factor may well be evolutionary difference, usually expressed in millions of years of (mya) [30,35]. Given that we have been separate from mites and insects for ~600 mya, while the comparable time for cats and dogs is only 65 mya [36], there are many ways in which this could influence the response (Fig. 16.2). It is also clear that we need to think not only about the proteins present in allergen particles but to consider all the constituents that could act as adjuvants. In addition to dust mite proteins, the mite faecal particles contain endotoxin; bacterial DNA; mite DNA; and chitin. Each of these could act on toll-like receptors (TLR). There are extensive data showing that sensitization to mite (or cockroach) allergens can occur at very low doses and it has been proposed that this response occurs with a direct switch to IgE outside germinal centres [37,38]. By contrast, many cat and dog proteins are less foreign and cat DNA is methylated comparable to human DNA. The argument would be that because sensitization to

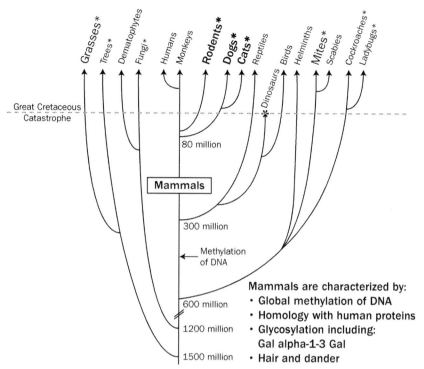

Fig. 16.2 Evolutionary distance and immune or allergic responses (with permission from *The Ancestor's Tale*: Richard Dawkins, 2005).

cat allergens requires higher doses, it occurs primarily in germinal centres where the response favours IgG and IgG4 antibodies because IgE B cells tend to undergo apoptosis in germinal centres (*see* Fig. 2.2) |38|.

If we consider T cell control as a primary target of immunotherapy; there are obvious lessons to be learned from the response to different allergens and from different diseases. High exposure to mite, cockroach, grass or ragweed consistently increases the prevalence and titre of IgE antibodies to these allergens. By contrast, for cat and dog, there is very little evidence that living in a house with an animal *increases* either the prevalence or titre of IgE antibodies |39–41|. Perhaps more importantly, many of the children and adults exposed to high levels of cat, dog or rodent allergens become 'tolerant' which includes an IgG4 antibody response to the major allergens *without* IgE antibodies |42–44|. Although the mechanisms of 'tolerance' to cats are not clear, there are good reasons for thinking that regulatory T cells play an important role |45|. In a climate where there are no mites or cockroaches, children who live in a home with a cat and have not become allergic as judged by skin tests, have a mean total IgE of ~20 IU/ml and no associated risk of asthma |46|. The challenge is to ask how we would go about inducing this 'tolerant' state. Estimates of exposure to cat allergen in a house with a cat are ~1μg Fel d 1/day |47|. What is interesting is that this does not appear to be far different from the dose recommended for sublingual immunotherapy |48|. Clearly, we need to answer whether local treatment, either sublingual or nasal, can induce a T cell milieu that is comparable to the effect of living with a cat.

In complete contrast to the tolerant state with high cat exposure, patients with atopic dermatitis (AD) have dramatically elevated total serum IgE (i.e. ~4000 IU/ml) |49|. Furthermore, this disease is characterized by active inflammation in the skin and persistent eosinophilia. Patients with AD have increased numbers of CD 25 high, Foxp3 positive, CD4 positive T cells. These cells would normally be classified as T regs. However recent evidence suggests that these cells may be activated T effector cells. More importantly, it appears that the inflammatory milieu in the skin can provide a site for changing T cells from a regulatory phenotype to activated effector cells |50,51|. The possible plasticity of regulatory T cells presents a challenge for immunotherapy and may help to explain why immunotherapy is so difficult in patients with AD. It is also possible that the plasticity of T regulator cells is relevant to understanding what happens in the lungs of patients with severe asthma. The challenge is to design new forms of immunotherapy that are designed both to induce tolerance but also to avoid activating T effector cells.

Cross-reacting carbohydrate determinants: alphaGal

In a recent study designed to understand the causes of anaphylaxis to cetuximab, it became clear that the patients who reacted had pre-existing IgE antibodies specific for the glycosylation of this monoclonal antibody |52|. In parallel with this, it has become clear that there are a large number of adults in this area of the United States (Virginia, Tennessee, North Carolina, Arkansas and Missouri) who have IgE antibodies to the oligosaccharide galactose alpha 1,3, galactose (alphaGal) |53|. Some of these patients present with a history of anaphylaxis or urticaria 2–4 h after eating beef, pork, or lamb |52,53|. There are several aspects of these results that could influence our understanding of the role of IgE antibodies not only in urticaria but also in other allergic diseases.

1. Although the IgE antibody to alphaGal is strongly associated with anaphylaxis and is often present in the serum in high titre (i.e. ≥ 30 IU/ml), the skin test responses to prick tests are generally modest (i.e. 2, 3 or 4 mm diameter). It is possible that the poor skin tests reflect the low affinity of IgE antibodies to carbohydrate epitopes which are relatively uncharged.
2. Synthesis of this sugar is dependent on the enzyme alpha 1–3 galactosyl transferase, which is expressed by all 'lower' mammals. As a result, the IgE antibodies cross-react fully, not only with beef, pork, and lamb, but also with cat and dog |52,53|.
3. Despite the fact that the patients have IgE antibodies that bind to cat proteins, there appears to be no association with asthma. Thus, among patients presenting to both the emergency department and the clinic, IgE antibodies to alphaGal are not associated with asthma.

Conclusion

The management of allergic disease is dependent on understanding the complex interactions between genetics, the environment, sensitization, inflammation and the resulting symptomatic disease. Rapid progress is being made in understanding different aspects of that complex process. This includes better ability to measure/analyse exposure, genetics and evidence for inflammation. We have focused here on gene–environment interactions, T cell control and the differences in immune responses to allergens of different types. There is major potential for improving treatment, but this will require a tailored approach. Most of us are well aware that immunotherapy, avoidance or pharmacotherapy can provide very successful treatment in some cases. The challenge is to harness current understanding of genetics, environment, lifestyle changes and their interactions to predict the correct approach. In addition, there will be important advances in techniques for immunotherapy, designed to act more directly on T cell control. It will be a pleasure to watch these developments over the coming years.

References

1. Asher MI, Montefort S, Bjorksten B, et al. Worldwide time trends in the prevalence of symptoms of asthma, allergic rhinoconjunctivitis, and eczema in childhood: ISAAC phases one and three repeat multicountry cross-sectional surveys. Lancet 2006; **368**: 733–43.

2. Duffy DL, Martin NG, Battistutta D, et al. Genetics of asthma and hay fever in Australian twins. Am Rev Respir Dis 1990; **142**: 1351–8.

3. Finkelman FD, Vercelli D. Advances in asthma, allergy mechanisms, and genetics in 2006. J Allergy Clin Immunol 2007; **120**: 544–50.

4. Ober C, Hoffjan S. Asthma genetics 2006: the long and winding road to gene discovery. Genes Immun 2006; **7**: 95–100.

5. Vercelli D. Discovering susceptibility genes for asthma and allergy. Nat Rev Immunol 2008; **8**: 169–82.

6. Palmer LJ, Cardon LR. Shaking the tree: mapping complex disease genes with linkage disequilibrium. Lancet 2005; **366**: 1223–34.

7. Schaub B, Lauener R, von Mutius E. The many faces of the hygiene hypothesis. J Allergy Clin Immunol 2006; **117**: 969–77; quiz 978.

8. Noertjojo K, Dimich-Ward H, Obata H, et al. Exposure and sensitization to cat dander: asthma and asthma-like symptoms among adults. J Allergy Clin Immunol 1999; **103**: 60–5.

9. Hesselmar B, Aberg N, Aberg B, et al. Does early exposure to cat or dog protect against later allergy development? Clin Exp Allergy 1999; **29**: 611–17.

10. Rhodes HL, Sporik R, Thomas P, et al. Early life risk factors for adult asthma: a birth cohort study of subjects at risk. J Allergy Clin Immunol 2001; **108**: 720–5.

11. Hagerhed-Engman L, Bornehag CG, Sundell J, Aberg N. Day-care attendance and increased risk for respiratory and allergic symptoms in preschool age. Allergy 2006; **61**: 447–53.

12. Ball TM, Castro-Rodriguez JA, Griffith KA, et al. Siblings, day-care attendance, and the risk of asthma and wheezing during childhood. N Engl J Med 2000; **343**: 538–43.

13. Celedon JC, Wright RJ, Litonjua AA, et al. Day care attendance in early life, maternal history of asthma, and asthma at the age of 6 years. Am J Respir Crit Care Med 2003; **167**: 1239–43.

14. Illi S, von Mutius E, Lau S, *et al.* Early childhood infectious diseases and the development of asthma up to school age: a birth cohort study. *Br Med J* 2001; **322**: 390–5.

15. Infante-Rivard C, Amre D, Gautrin D, Malo JL. Family size, day-care attendance, and breastfeeding in relation to the incidence of childhood asthma. *Am J Epidemiol* 2001; **153**: 653–8.

16. Nafstad P, Brunekreef B, Skrondal A, Nystad W. Early respiratory infections, asthma, and allergy: 10-year follow-up of the Oslo Birth Cohort. *Pediatrics* 2005; **116**: e255–62.

17. Salam MT, Li YF, Langholz B, Gilliland FD. Early-life environmental risk factors for asthma: findings from the Children's Health Study. *Environ Health Perspect* 2004; **112**: 760–5.

18. Vercelli D, Martinez FD. The Faustian bargain of genetic association studies: bigger might not be better, or at least it might not be good enough. *J Allergy Clin Immunol* 2006; **117**: 1303–5.

19. Valdar W, Solberg LC, Gauguier D, *et al.* Genetic and environmental effects on complex traits in mice. *Genetics* 2006; **174**: 959–84.

20. Simpson A, John SL, Jury F, *et al.* Endotoxin exposure, CD14, and allergic disease: an interaction between genes and the environment. *Am J Respir Crit Care Med* 2006; **174**: 386–92.

21. Ober C, Tsalenko A, Parry R, Cox NJ. A second-generation genomewide screen for asthma-susceptibility alleles in a founder population. *Am J Hum Genet* 2000; **67**: 1154–62.

22. Baldini M, Lohman IC, Halonen M, *et al.* A Polymorphism* in the 5' flanking region of the CD14 gene is associated with circulating soluble CD14 levels and with total serum immunoglobulin E. *Am J Respir Cell Mol Biol* 1999; **20**: 976–83.

23. Kabesch M, Hasemann K, Schickinger V, *et al.* A promoter polymorphism in the CD14 gene is associated with elevated levels of soluble CD14 but not with IgE or atopic diseases. *Allergy* 2004; **59**: 520–5.

24. Luan JA, Wong MY, Day NE, Wareham NJ. Sample size determination for studies of gene-environment interaction. *Int J Epidemiol* 2001; **30**: 1035–40.

25. Eder W, Klimecki W, Yu L, *et al.* Opposite effects of CD 14/-260 on serum IgE levels in children raised in different environments. *J Allergy Clin Immunol* 2005; **116**: 601–7.

26. Zambelli-Weiner A, Ehrlich E, Stockton ML, *et al.* Evaluation of the CD14/-260 polymorphism and house dust endotoxin exposure in the Barbados Asthma Genetics Study. *J Allergy Clin Immunol* 2005; **115**: 1203–9.

27. Maier LM, Howson JM, Walker N, *et al.* Association of IL13 with total IgE: evidence against an inverse association of atopy and diabetes. *J Allergy Clin Immunol* 2006; **117**: 1306–13.

28. Strachan DP, Wong HJ, Spector TD. Concordance and interrelationship of atopic diseases and markers of allergic sensitization among adult female twins. *J Allergy Clin Immunol* 2001; **108**: 901–7.

29. Chanock SJ, Manolio T, Boehnke M, *et al.* Replicating genotype-phenotype associations. *Nature* 2007; **447**: 655–60.

30. Platts-Mills TA. The role of indoor allergens in chronic allergic disease. *J Allergy Clin Immunol* 2007; **119**: 297–302.

31. Platts-Mills TA. Asthma severity and prevalence: an ongoing interaction between exposure, hygiene, and lifestyle. *PLoS Med* 2005; **2**:e34. Epub 22 Feb 2005.

32. Platts-Mills TA, Perzanowski M, Woodfolk JA, Lundback B. Relevance of early or current pet ownership to the prevalence of allergic disease. *Clin Exp Allergy* 2002; **32**: 335–8.

33. Erwin E, Satinover S, Hosen J, *et al.* Changes in antibody titers during prolonged decrease in exposure. Manuscript in preparation, 2008.

34. Flinterman AE, Knuist AC, Meijer Y, *et al.* Acute allergic reactions in children with AEDS after prolonged cow's milk elimination diets. *Allergy* 2006; **61**: 370–4.

35. Jenkins JA, Breiteneder H, Mills EN. Evolutionary distance from human homologs reflects allergenicity of animal food proteins. *J Allergy Clin Immunol* 2007; **120**: 1399–405. Epub 1 Nov 2007.

36. Dawkins R. *The Ancestor's Tale:* A Pilgrimage to the Dawn of Evolution. Houghton Mifflin Company, Boston, MA, 2004.

37. Sporik R, Squillace SP, Ingram JM, *et al.* Mite, cat, and cockroach exposure, allergen sensitisation, and asthma in children: a case-control study of three schools. *Thorax* 1999; **54**: 675–80.

38. Aalberse RC, Platts-Mills TA. How do we avoid developing allergy: modifications of the Th2 response from a B-cell perspective. *J Allergy Clin Immunol* 2004; **113**: 983–6.

39. Hesselmar B, Aberg N, Aberg B, *et al.* Does early exposure to cat or dog protect against later allergy development? *Clin Exp Allergy* 1999; **29**: 611–17.

40. Perzanowski MS, Ronmark E, Platts-Mills TA, Lundback B. Effect of cat and dog ownership on sensitization and development of asthma among preteenage children. *Am J Respir Crit Care Med* 2002; **166**: 696–702.

41. Erwin EA, Ronmark E, Wickens K, *et al.* Contribution of dust mite and cat specific IgE to total IgE: relevance to asthma prevalence. *J Allergy Clin Immunol* 2007; **119**: 359–65.

42. Platts-Mills T, Vaughan J, Squillace S, *et al.* Sensitisation, asthma, and a modified Th2 response in children exposed to cat allergen: a population-based cross-sectional study. *Lancet* 2001; **357**: 752–6.

43. Jeal H, Draper A, Harris J, *et al.* Modified Th2 responses at high-dose exposures to allergen: using an occupational model. *Am J Respir Crit Care Med* 2006; **174**: 21–5. Epub 7 Apr 2006.

44. Matsui EC, Diette GB, Krop EJ, *et al.* Mouse allergen-specific immunoglobulin G4 and risk of mouse skin test sensitivity. *Clin Exp Allergy* 2006; **36**: 21097–103.

45. Reefer AJ, Carneiro RM, Custis NJ, *et al.* A role for IL-10 mediated HLA-DR7 restricted T cell-dependent events in development of the modified Th2 response to cat allergen. *J Immunol* 2004; **172**: 2763–72.

46. Bjerg A, Hedman L, Perzanowski MS, *et al.* Family history of asthma and atopy: In-depth analyses of the impact on asthma and wheeze in 7- to 8-year-old children. *Pediatrics* 2007; **120**: 741–8.

47. Custis NJ, Woodfolk JA, Vaughan JW, Platts-Mills TA. Quantitative measurement of airborne allergens from dust mites, dogs and cats using an ion-charging device. *Clin Exp Allergy* 2003; **33**: 986–91.

48. Greenberger PA, Ballow M, Casale TB, *et al.* Sublingual immunotherapy and subcutaneous immunotherapy: Issues in the United States. *J Allergy Clin Immunol* 2007; **120**: 1466–8. Epub 22 Oct 2007.

49. Reefer AJ, Satinover SM, Wilson BB, Woodfolk JA. The relevance of microbial allergens to the IgE antibody repertoire in atopic and non-atopic eczema. *J Allergy Clin Immunol* 2007; **120**: 156–63. E pub 15 May 2007.

50. Reefer AJ, Satinover SM, Solga MD, *et al.* Analysis of CD25hiCD4+ "regulatory" T-cell subtypes in atopic dermatitis reveals a novel T(H)2-like population. *J Allergy Clin Immunol* 2008; **121**: 415–22. Epub 4 Jan 2008.

51. Li MO, Flavell RA. Contextual regulation of inflammation: a duet by transforming growth factor-beta and interleukin-10. *Immunity* 2008; **28**: 468–76.

52. Chung CH, Mirakhur B, Chan E, *et al.* Cetuximab-induced anaphylaxis and IgE specific for galactose-α-1,3-galactose. *N Engl J Med* 2008; **358**: 1109–17.

53. Commins S, Lucas S, Hosen J, *et al.* Anaphylaxis and IgE antibodies to galactose-alpha-1,3-galactose (alphaGal): Insight from the identification of novel IgE ab to carbohydrates on mammalian proteins. *Abstract JACI.* Feb 2008.

Acronyms/ Abbreviations

5-LO	5-lipoxygenase
5-oxo-ETE	5-oxo-eicosatetraenoic acid
A&E	accident and emergency
AAE	acquired angio-oedema
ABM	airway bronchial mucosa
ABPA	allergic bronchopulmonary aspergillosis
ABPM	allergic bronchopulmonary mycosis
ACE	angiotensin-converting enzyme
AD	atopic dermatitis
AEE	allergic eosinophilic oesophagitis
AEG	allergic eosinophilic gastroenteritis
AERD	aspirin-exacerbated respiratory disease
AFS	allergic fungal sinusitis
ALT	alanine aminotransferase
AMP	adenosine monophosphate
ANCA	antineutrophil cytoplasmic antibody
AP-1	activator protein 1
ARIA	Allergic Rhinitis and its Impact on Asthma
ASST	autologous serum skin test
AST	aspartate aminotransferase
ATP	adenosine triphosphate
BAL	bronchoalveolar lavage
BALF	bronchoalveolar lavage fluid
BBB	blood–brain barrier
BCG	Bacille Calmette Guerin
BHR	bronchial hyper-reactivity
BM	bone marrow
CAM	complementary-alternative medicine
cAMP	cyclic adenosine monophosphate
CAPS	Childhood Asthma Prevention Study
CCL	chemokines ligand
CCR	chemokines receptor
CCS	corticosteroids
CF	cystic fibrosis
cfu	colony-forming unit
cGMP	cyclic guanosine monophosphate
CHES	chronic hyperplastic eosinophilic sinusitis
CINCA	chronic infantile neurological cutaneous and articular syndrome
CLA	cutaneous lymphocyte-associated antigen
CNS	central nervous system
COPD	chronic obstructive pulmonary disease

COX	cyclo-oxygenase
CREB	cAMP response element-binding
CS	chronic sinusitis
CSF	cerebrospinal fluid
CT	computed tomography
CysLT	cysteinyl leukotriene
DBPCFC	double-blind, placebo-controlled food challenge
DHR	drug hypersensitivity reactions
DRESS	drug reaction with eosinophilia and systemic signs
EAA	extrinsic allergic alveolitis
EAACI	European Academy of Allergology and Clinical Immunology
EAR	early asthmatic response
ENDA	European Network of Drug Allergy
Eo/B	eosinophil/basophil
Eo/Bcfu	eosinophil/basophil colony-forming unit
EP2	PgE_2 receptor
ERK	extracellular signal-related kinase
ESB	European Standard Battery
ETFAD	European Task Force on Atopic Dermatitis
FACS	familial cold autoinflammatory syndrome
FasL	human gene encoding the ligand for Fas
FcR	Fc receptor (specific to IgG)
FDA	Food and Drug Administration
FESS	functional endoscopic sinus surgery
FEV_1	forced expiratory volume in one second
FLAP	5-LO-activating protein
FPIES	food protein-induced enterocolitis syndrome
GI	gastrointestinal
GM-CSF	granulocyte-macrophage colony-stimulating factor
GPCR	G protein-coupled receptor
GR	glucocorticoid receptor
GRE	glucocorticoid response element
GTP	guanosine triphosphate
HAE	hereditary angio-oedema
HCW	healthcare workers
HEPA	high efficiency particulate arrest
HETE	hydroxyeicosateraenoic acid
HLA	human leukocyte antigen
HPA	hypothalamo-pituitary-adrenal (axis)
HPETE	hydroperoxyeicosatetraenoic acid
HUVS	hypocomplementemic urticaria autoinflammatory syndrome
ICAM-1	intercellular adhesion molecule 1
ICDRG	International Contact Dermatitis Research Group
ICS	inhaled corticosteroids
IFNγ	interferon gamma

Ig	immunoglobulin
IκB	inhibitor κB
IKK2	IκB kinase-2
IL	interleukin
IL-4R	IL-4 receptor
i.m.	intramuscular
INH	inhibitor
iNOS	inducible nitric oxide synthase
INR	immediate nasal response (to allergen challenge)
IR	Index of Reactivity
IT	immunotherapy
i.v.	intravenous
IVIG	intravenous immunoglobulin
JNK	c-Jun N-terminal kinase
LABA	long-acting β-agonist
LAR	late asthmatic response
LT	leukotriene
LTA_4	leukotriene A_4
LTB_4	leukotriene B_4
LTC_4	leukotriene C_4
LTD_4	leukotriene D_4
LTE_4	leukotriene E_4
LTC_4S	LTC_4 synthase
LTRA	leukotriene receptor antagonist
LTT	lymphocyte transformation test
MAAS	Manchester Asthma and Allergy Study
MAP	mitogen activated protein
MHC	major histocompatibility complex
MUD	minimal urticarial dose
Mya	millions of years
NAAGA	N-acetylaspartylglutamic acid
NaCl	sodium chloride
NF-κB	nuclear factor-κB
NHLBI	National Heart, Lung, and Blood Institute
NO	nitric oxide
NP	nasal polyp
NSAID	non-steroidal anti-inflammatory drug
ODN	oligodeoxynucleotide
OR	odds ratio
PAF	platelet-activating factor
PCP	personalized care plan
PDE	phosphodiesterase
PEFR	peak expiratory flow rate
PET	positron emission tomography
PgD_2	prostaglandin D_2

PgE$_2$	prostaglandin E$_2$
Pgp	P-glycoprotein
PLA$_2$	phospholipase A$_2$
QOL	quality of life
RANTES	regulated upon activation, normal T cell expressed and secreted
RAST	radioallergosorbent test
REM	rapid eye movement
SAE	*Staphylococcus aureus*-derived enterotoxin
SAFS	severe asthma with fungal sensitization
SAM	sinobronchial allergic mycosis
SCIT	subcutaneous immunotherapy
sIgE	specific IgE
SIT	specific allergen immunotherapy
SLIT	sublingual immunotherapy
SNP	single nucleotide polymorphism
SPT	skin prick testing
TEN	toxic epidermal necrolysis
TGFβ	transforming growth factor beta
Th$_1$	T-helper-1 cell
Th$_2$	T-helper-2 cell
tIgE	total IgE
TLR	toll-like receptor
TM	trans-membrane
TNFα	tumour necrosis factor alpha
Tr 1	t-regulatory-1 cell
TSLP	thymic stromal lymphopoietin
UV-A	long wavelength ultraviolet
VCAM	vascular cell adhesion molecule
VCD	vocal cord dysfunction
VLA	very late antigen
WAO	World Allergy Organization
WHO	World Health Organization

Index